VINCENT PRICE
THE ART OF FEAR

I have perceiv'd that to be
with those I like is enough,
To stop in company with the rest
at evening is enough,
To be surrounded by beautiful, curious,
breathing, laughing flesh is enough,
To pass among them, or touch any one,
or rest my arm ever so lightly round
his or her neck for a moment –
what is this, then?
I do not ask any more delight –
I swim in it, as in a sea.

WALT WHITMAN,
I SING THE BODY ELECTRIC
(FROM LEAVES OF GRASS)

VINCENT PRICE
THE ART OF FEAR

Denis Meikle

ILLUSTRATIONS BY NEIL D VOKES

Reynolds & Hearn Ltd
London

To Jane,
who held the fort tenaciously while the battle raged outside its walls

FRONT COVER: THE CITY UNDER THE SEA *(1964)*
BACK COVER: *publicity shot from* THE BAT *(1959)*
FRONTISPIECE: *studio portrait circa 1970*
CONTENTS PAGE: THE ABOMINABLE DR PHIBES *(1970)*

First published in 2003 by
Reynolds & Hearn Ltd
61a Priory Road
Kew Gardens
Richmond
Surrey TW9 3DH

3022 4793 3/04

Reprinted 2004

© Denis Meikle 2003

A CIP catalogue record for this book is available from the British Library.

ISBN 1 903111 53 6

Designed by Peri Godbold.

Printed and bound in Great Britain by Biddles Ltd, Guildford, Surrey.

CONTENTS

ACKNOWLEDGMENTS

A book on the life and genre work of a man of as many accomplishments as Vincent Price was not a task which could have been achieved without the co-operation of a number of souls sympathetic to the cause. Those who assisted with research or the acquisition of materials were Richard Klemensen, Christopher Koetting, Wes Walker, Robert Fuest, Mark Miller, Adrian Rigelsford, Jonathan Rigby, Joel Finler, David Miller and Marcus Hearn. I thank them all.

I would also like to extend my thanks to three unique individuals – Richard Matheson, one of the foremost authors in the field of fantasy since his debut novel *I Am Legend* in 1954, who graciously consented to provide the Foreword for the book and whose contribution to some of Price's best-loved films was second only to that of legendary producer-director Roger Corman, who was kind enough to provide the Afterword, and comic-book artist Neil 'That's all'

Vokes, penciller without peer of *Superman Adventures* (DC) and *Parliament of Justice* (Image), who added the evocative sketches which I felt would be fitting for the opening of each chapter.

No project of this kind is possible without the input of those who have gone before. I have made much use of interviews conducted during four decades by journalists on both sides of the Atlantic, including Christopher Koetting, David Austen, Robin Bean, Lawrence French, David Del Valle, Ed Naha and others, most of whom have been credited in the text; to those whom I may have missed, I offer my apologies and my appreciation. I must also single out two works for especial praise – *The Complete Films of Vincent Price*, a careful and comprehensive career study by Lucy Chase Williams, and *Vincent Price: A Daughter's Biography*, a more personal appreciation of a public (father) figure by Victoria Price. Without these, this volume might not have been impossible, but it would have been made a damned sight more difficult.

Author Denis Meikle and Vincent Price on the Elstree Studios set of THE ABOMINABLE DR PHIBES *in 1970*

FOREWORD

Whenever people asked me what I thought of Vincent Price, my answer was immediate.

"He's the nicest man I ever met in the business." Or – later: "He *was* the nicest man I ever met in the business."

That he was.

How he became the utterly charming man he was would, doubtless, require a psychological life study. I can't imagine what that would entail but I can't say that, beyond a passing interest in such a study, I would really care, that it would truly matter to me.

For the years that I knew him, he was a kind, thoughtful and extremely amusing gentleman.

Not to mention what a superlative actor he was.

I met Vincent (he, immediately, asked me to call him by his first name) after I had written a film adaptation of Poe's *The Fall of the House of Usher*. The two heads of American International – Jim Nicholson and Sam Arkoff – had hired me to write the screenplay although, as I recall, my initial contact was with Roger Corman, who was going to produce and direct the film.

When I heard that the lead role was to be played by none other than Vincent Price, I was, of course, delighted. I had seen most of his films and always admired his acting skill and the impressive physical and mental persona he displayed in his varied portrayals both period and contemporary.

I met him on the set of *House of Usher* (which the title was now abbreviated to). At first, I was taken aback by his appearance. At that time, the image I had of him was, invariably, Van Dyke bearded. Yet his appearance (chosen, I am sure, by him) was exactly right for the role. Not even a moustache was visible on his face. Clean-shaven, white-haired (as I recall), he was the very image of what Roderick Usher *had* to look like – ascetic, pale and haunted by the curse on his house, subject to unending physical and mental affliction because of his hypersensitive senses of hearing and feeling – all of which Vincent conveyed with dignity, courage and acceptance.

I saw two other elements in Vincent's personality during the filming of *House of Usher*.

One was his charm and humour.

The other was his remarkable control of justified anger.

The first was delightfully apparent when people (no doubt relatives or friends of the cast or crew) came to observe the shooting of the film.

I have seen (not revealing any names) actors and actresses who gave no indication whatever of any attitude toward set visitors other than that they were intruders and unwanted distractions.

Vincent could not have been more different. He was, invariably, gracious to set visitors, not only answering their questions as though these questions were highly interesting to him but (always) concluding the brief encounter with a humorous remark that left them laughing and happy as he returned to the set – returned to the grim House of Usher and was, instantly, the agonised Roderick Usher once again.

As I recall, one of the visitors referred to the wall paintings of the past Usher family which (painted by talented artist Burt Shoenberg) were rather unnerving. "Oh, they're just plain folks," Vincent said, ambling back to the set.

As to the control of anger...

Co-starring with Vincent was a young actor named Mark Damon (now a highly successful distributor of European releases). When required to sound breathless, he was seen to run vigorously in place.

In one scene, he was to burst into Roderick Usher's room (appropriately breathless), carrying an axe which – fortunately for Vincent – had a blade made of hard rubber.

This he did, charging into the room, screaming "Usher!" and hurling aside the axe.

Unfortunately, Vincent was in the path of the hurled axe which struck him on the leg. Hard.

It was the only time I ever heard Vincent utter an epithet.

Immediately afterward, he strode rapidly from the set and walked around the interior of the sound stage, no doubt from room to room of the Usher mansion.

When he returned in a few minutes, he was Vincent again, charming, patient and forgiving. Mark Damon, of course, apologised profusely. Vincent accepted the apology with grace and shooting recommenced.

I have known actors who would not have reacted so maturely – and kindly.

But Vincent was unique; not only a wonderful actor but a wonderful human being as well.

When Vincent assumed the role of Robur (The Conqueror) in the Jules Verne twin novels, the second of which – *Master of the World* – became the title of the film, Vincent was, once again, the very essence of my image of him – Van Dyke bearded, wearing a white suit and Captain's cap, every inch (all 76 of them) the Master of the World.

It was during the filming of this picture that I had a brief contretemps with co-star Charles Bronson. I do not reveal it with any intention of criticising Mr Bronson but to reveal another reminder of Vincent's personality.

When I went in to watch them filming, I went over to Bronson and introduced myself as the writer of the film.

"Oh, don't talk to me," Bronson responded and walked away from me.

Later, obviously realising that he had gone too far, he came over to me and said, "I hear you're a very good writer."

Unfortunately, I am not and never have been blessed with Vincent's marvellous temperament.

"I *am*," I responded and walked away from Bronson.

Later, after lunch, having cooled down, I approached Mr Bronson and said, "Why don't we start all over again?"

That approach clearly worked and we chatted amiably for a few minutes, after which he said, "I hope you don't mind me saying your lines like a Polish coal miner."

I don't know why the admittedly florid, mid-Victorian dialogue disturbed him because he performed it with unerring skill.

The point of this anecdote is as follows:

The next morning, we approached each other and I smiled a greeting and said, "Good morning."

At which he walked past me without a word – and without a smile.

When I told Vincent what had happened, he surprised me by saying that Bronson was the only person

he had ever met who he could not "make friends with." Which, I have no doubt, was absolutely true.

Vincent's performance as Robur was perfect as far as I'm concerned. I regret the fact that the budget was so limited (though very high for American International) and that many of the action scenes were less than impressive. For I firmly believe that Vincent's performance was fully the equal of James Mason's in Disney's *Twenty Thousand Leagues Under the Sea*, which I hoped *Master of the World* would parallel in excellence.

Poe's *The Pit and the Pendulum* offered scarcely enough material for a full-length motion picture, providing no more than a climactic scene near the conclusion of the film. Fortunately, (or not) I had a plot for a shocker suspense film which I utilised for the script.

I think I must have cringed at Vincent's performance in *Pit*. Not because it was not completely professional and appropriate but because, at that point, I was beginning to feel a shade guilty for providing Vincent exclusively with dark, grim stories.

Which is why, in my next screenplay for American International – *Tales of Terror* – I inserted, in the middle of the film, a humorous approach to *The Black Cat* and *The Cask of Amontillado* (combined), knowing – but never before having written for – how Vincent was so funny – which he certainly could transfer to his screen roles.

Which, of course, he did with Peter Lorre and the delightful Joyce Jameson. A wine tasting contest during the story I still find extremely amusing.

And the commencement of Vincent's acting in tandem with Peter Lorre.

Now Peter had some difficulty in always remembering the exact wording of any particular speech he had to deliver. Ordinarily, this sort of acting irritates me considerably since I spend a lot of time shaping my dialogue as carefully as I can. In Peter's case, however, he was so totally engaging as an actor and a person that I could never summon up so much as an iota of irritation.

And – here's the point – Vincent always went along with this graciously and gracefully, altering his returned lines of dialogue as needed in order to accommodate Peter's altered lines. No fuss. No anger. He just did it. Peter, in a conversation we had once, told me that his usual dialogue approach used to drive Sidney Greenstreet bonkers since Greenstreet, being a meticulous stage actor, always read his lines word for word as written.

Not so Vincent. He went along with Peter's freeform dialogue without a tremor.

This flexibility was much in evidence during the shooting of *The Raven*, another Poe story which provided an opening scene and no more, being, in fact, a poem.

Added to the cast was the wonderful Boris Karloff, another stickler – so I was told – for exact transcriptions of dialogue. I hoped that watching Vincent's calm ability to cope with Peter's line readings gave Mr Karloff a little added measure of acceptance with the situation. As the writer, I certainly appreciated Mr Karloff's exact reading of the speeches I had created for him.

I was also pleased that I had written a full-length role for Vincent which was not, in any way, gloomy or dark but required great tongue-in-cheek humour from his character.

Which he provided effortlessly.

About this time, I took my wife and (then) two children, Richard and Tina, to see Vincent in his excellent stage performance as Mr Darling and the deliciously 'evil' Captain Hook in Barrie's *Peter Pan*.

At the conclusion of the play, I sent a note backstage, asking if we might stop by for a few moments to say hello. He, of course, unhesitatingly agreed and we went backstage where Vincent was, as always, perfectly charming to all of us – he had a special gift for charming young people – modestly thankful for our praise and the creator of an unhurried, pleasant conversation.

In brief, the same completely sociable Vincent he was at all times.

I remember with pleasure the lunch I had with the cast of my script for *The Comedy of Terrors* – Vincent, Peter Lorre, Boris Karloff and Basil Rathbone with the wonderful director Jacques Tourneur. All of them seemed pleased with my screenplay and the added pleasure of being directed by Tourneur. I'm not sure whether Joyce Jameson was there. I know Joe E Brown wasn't.

But what an honour for me to converse with these film icons, all of them completely friendly and light-hearted. I was especially pleased to have created a role for Vincent which would make use of another talent he had – the ability to deliver an acidulous line of dialogue with the best of them.

It was, indeed, a delight to watch this grand quintet of performers, helmed by Jacques Tourneur,

act the living hell out of my screenplay. It will always be a favourite of mine.

This was the last of my films with Vincent. I do not include *The Last Man on Earth* since I believe that Vincent was miscast in what turned out to be an inferior adaptation of my novel *I Am Legend*.

What to add?

An enormous admiration and respect for Vincent's extensive knowledge of fine art. As far as I know, only Edward G Robinson approached that knowledge.

An equally enormous appreciation of Vincent's performances in other films made for other production companies. I am especially fond of his skilled appearance as Cardinal Richelieu in M-G-M's *The Three Musketeers*.

A lasting memory of Vincent's warm personality.

When I learned that Vincent was terminally ill, I sent him a copy of a metaphysical book I had put together entitled *The Path*.

Unfortunately, Vincent misunderstood my motive. He thought I was looking for a written endorsement of the book. I wasn't. I had hoped that its subject matter might be of some comfort to him during his final days.

As ill as he was, he still wrote a note to me, thanking me for the book and apologising for not being well enough to provide me with the endorsement. As always, thoughtful to the end.

The last time I saw Vincent was on the backlot of Universal. My son Richard and I were walking there when we caught sight of Vincent standing in front of a sound stage.

We approached him and, though it had been a considerable number of years since our last meeting, he not only remembered me but, remarkably, Richard as well. He had last seen my son on a set for *Master of the World*.

We enjoyed a brief conversation, warmed by his charm and easygoing wit. Then we shook hands and parted, never to meet again.

What do I think of Vincent Price?

If there is indeed, a phenomenon known as Karma (as I believe there is), Vincent's is most definitely First Class.

RICHARD MATHESON
CALABASAS, CALIFORNIA
FEBRUARY 2003

What is Terror... ? Is it to awaken and hear the passing of time? Or is it the failing beat of your own heart? – Or the footsteps of someone who, just a moment before, was in your room... ? But let us not dwell on Terror... The knowledge of Terror is vouchsafed only to the precious few...

PRINCE PROSPERO (VINCENT PRICE),
THE MASQUE OF THE RED DEATH
(1963)

In the minds of fantasy fans, there are two kinds of screen actor: the movie star, and the star of horror movies.

In the beginning, there was Lon (born Alonso) Chaney, the so-called 'Man of a Thousand Faces' who, after an apprenticeship as a carpet-layer and paper-hanger, became internationally famous on the silent screen for playing monstrous grotesques in films such as *The Hunchback of Notre Dame* (1923), *The Phantom of the Opera* (1925) and *London After Midnight* (1927). Next up was Boris Karloff – 'the Uncanny' – aka William Henry Pratt of Camberwell, London, the itinerant and wayward eighth son of a British consular official who, after achieving belated stardom in *Frankenstein* (1931), eventually numbered 50 horror films among more than 150 screen appearances. In parallel with Karloff, and dragging the dead weight of *Dracula*'s cape behind him, was Hungarian-born Bela Blasko, alias Bela Lugosi – a one-time mine, factory and railroad worker who notched up three dozen horrors to his name in an acting career which came to span more than four decades.

Several minor players also carved out a niche for themselves in the Universal chillers of the war years: John Carradine, Lionel Atwill and Lon Chaney Jr among them. By the mid-fifties, there were some new kids on the block: the terrifying twosome of Peter Wilton Cushing and Christopher Frank Carandini Lee, both of whom, through their mutual association with Hammer Film Productions, became household names to horror fans the world over. Between the two of them, Cushing and Lee made 30 Hammer horrors, as well as numerous others for a host of copycat companies.

In tandem with Cushing and Lee, however, was an actor from St Louis in Missouri, whose screen career had actually begun in the late 1930s but whose rise to prominence in the halls of horror paralleled their own. His tally of fright-films rivalled that of his British counterparts, but his name became synonymous with the genre to a degree unmatched since the great days of Karloff and Lugosi.

Lon Chaney died in 1930, at the advent of sound. Lugosi was mainly a figure of the thirties and forties. Cushing and Lee, despite their regular outings for competitor companies, remained tied in the public mind to Hammer. And while Karloff and Lon Chaney Jr continued to appear in horror roles up to their deaths in 1969 and 1973 respectively, their screen profiles had long-since diminished. In terms of star-names in the field of horror for cinema audiences in the 1950s, 1960s and much of the 1970s, there was really only Hammer itself...

And there was Vincent Price.

Vincent Price made his first out-and-out horror movie, *House of Wax*, in 1953, 15 years after his Hollywood debut. Its tale of a crazed sculptor in wax, who casts his figures from plundered corpses, did not of itself launch Price on a career of fear. That honour fell to a film which he made in 1958 called *The Fly*, the success of which was partly due to its source as a short story accorded the accolade 'Best Science Fiction Story of the Year' by *Playboy* magazine.

The Fly set a precedent for Price which was consolidated in a long-running series of Gothic horror films for American International Pictures, based on the works of a pre-eminent figure in American letters, Edgar Allan Poe, and which began in 1960 with *House of Usher*.

Uniquely among his genre contemporaries, the majority of Price's excursions into cinematic fantasy were not written for the screen but for publication, in the first instance. More than half of the 40 films which eventually led commentators to christen him the 'Merchant of Menace' were drawn directly from literary sources – which is to say they were adapted from stories or novels and were not mere nods to literature, as were many entries in Hammer's Frankenstein or Dracula series. Great actors need great writers to support them, and Vincent Price had more than his share: Poe, Verne, Hawthorne, de Maupassant, Lovecraft, Shakespeare even – all were pressed into screen service on his behalf.

Price himself was an art collector and authority of no mean standing. A cultured and refined individual – well-bred, well-educated and, in theatrical terms, classically trained – his screen persona and mannered style of delivery demanded more from a script than the average Hollywood hack could provide. Whether he was characterising the fictional creations of Jules Verne (*Master of the World*) or Guy de Maupassant (*Diary of a Madman*), or paraphrasing the collected plays of the Bard (*Theatre of Blood*), Price brought a dimension of excellence to the horror film that, for a time during the 1960s and 70s, lifted it

free of the exploitation category and transformed it into a dark art.

With his many and varied personal interests, most of which occupied more of his time than his film appearances, Vincent Price was larger than life. He moulded the often dull clay of the movies in which he was obliged to appear by the sheer grace of his presence. Give him a half-decent line to say in addition, and he could transcend even the limitations which the genre itself imposed upon him. There was a time, long ago, when his very name sent shivers of fear down the spine. If fear is an art form, then Vincent Leonard Price was arguably its greatest exponent.

This book is a complete film-by-film account of Vincent Price's work in the field of horror: the triumphs, the tragedies and the turkeys. In more than three-dozen films over as many years, Price became a past master in the art of screen terror. He was one of the last of a breed of actor nurtured in the Hollywood studio system, and whose collective passing was brought about by changes in the industry which occurred in the 1960s. But Price crossed that divide by creating a new persona for himself in the horror genre, becoming a star twice over as well as a legend in his own lifetime.

Satin-tongued or satanic, Price oozed charm as much as he did menace in some of the most memorable movies of the macabre ever made. In the cinema of Terror, villains never came any bigger, or better, or more outrageously over-the-top than he did. From his genre debut in 1939 to his swan-song 50 years later, the fright-film career of Vincent Price is, in no small part, the history of the horror film itself.

Vincent Price: The Art of Fear is a chronicle of those years when cinemagoers all over the world trembled at the sight of his name and shuddered at the sound of his voice. The Price years were the high watermark of horror cinema in its first century. Vincent Price was the King, and this is the story of his reign.

ACT 1

A (HORROR) STAR IS BORN

We have found immortality, you and I. You must not be afraid...
IVAN IGOR (LIONEL ATWILL), *MYSTERY OF THE WAX MUSEUM* (1932)

On 10 April 1953, the first film from a major Hollywood studio to be photographed in the new novelty process of 3-D – or 'natural-vision', as its inventor Polaroid had christened it – opened at the Paramount Theatre in New York City. To take full advantage of the potential for screen thrills the new medium appeared to offer, the film in question was a horror story. Its maker was Warner Bros, and it was called *House of Wax*.

The previous 12 months had been a testing time for the Hollywood machine – literally as well as metaphorically. The impact of the new medium of television on the viewing habits of the average American citizen was becoming more pronounced than many industry pundits had envisaged, and it was a trend which rapidly was spreading beyond America's shores; in another few years, it would impact just as profoundly on Britain, then the second biggest market for Hollywood product.

In consequence, the studios were scrambling to develop new ideas or new technology. Film stories had already grown bigger – Mervyn LeRoy's *Quo Vadis*, the most lavish and expensive production in Hollywood history, at a cost of over $7 million and with a cast of 30,000 extras, had premiered in October 1951 – and the medium was looking to expand its own horizons and offer patrons an experience which could only be gained by giving up the living room and going out to the cinema again. September 1952 had seen the launch of Cinerama, an elaborate system comprising three projectors for the showing of films on a panoramic screen. By January 1953, Twentieth Century-Fox had begun to conduct its first tests of Cinemascope: "The world's new wonder that you see *without* special glasses!" (the one drawback of 3-D) and a technically simpler method of achieving the same result as Cinerama.

For the moment, however, all hopes were pinned on stereoscopy, or 3-D, especially when the first 3-D feature film to hit theatres, *Bwana Devil*, a low-budget action movie starring Robert Stack and Barbara

Britton, had cost producer Arch Oboler next-to-nothing and had taken $100,000 in its opening week of 26 November 1952.

In the race to cash in on what it perceived to be the 3-D 'boom', Warners had no time to develop an original screenplay. Instead, it dusted off an old warhorse from its back catalogue and rushed it into production. Warners' roster of fantasy subjects was by no means extensive but in 1932 the studio had shot a pair of horror films in another revolutionary process called 'two-strip' Technicolor: *Doctor X* and *Mystery of the Wax Museum*.

Both films featured Hollywood 'scream queen' Fay Wray and British stage actor Lionel Atwill in leading roles. *Doctor X* was a stodgy and stage-bound melodrama of the Old Dark House variety, set in a cliff-top sanatorium in which Preston Foster plastered his features in goo (or 'synthetic flesh', as his character preferred to call it) in order to turn himself into the so-called Moon Killer and wreak the requisite havoc. Both setting and structure of the film had barely outlasted the thirties, let alone suggested themselves capable of being updated for the fifties, and attention had switched instead to its companion-piece.

A black-cloaked figure, disproportionate and grotesque, the face a horrible formless mass of scarred tissue. He has practically no forehead. His face is a shrivelled bald pate of seared skin and bone, which recedes to a pointed cranium of unnatural contour. His eyes are alight with fanaticism and insanity. The face is a blot of drawn, unwholesomely coloured, hairless skin. He is lipless, noseless, and what traces of human features remain are frightfully distorted.
SCREENPLAY, *MYSTERY OF THE WAX MUSEUM* (1932)

Mystery of the Wax Museum had been adapted from a play by Charles S Belden called *Waxworks*. The film tells of Ivan Igor (Atwill), the proprietor of a London wax museum who suffers hideous disfigurement at the hands of an unscrupulous business partner when the latter torches their joint enterprise for the insurance money. Twelve years pass and Igor recreates his museum in New York, a city which has been subject to the clandestine attentions of a mystery Monster who steals corpses from mortuaries at dead of night. It transpires that Igor – deranged from having seen his life's work go up in flames and unable to mould the figures required of his tableaux due to his hands having been burned in the fire – has peopled his museum with bodies dipped in wax and chosen for their likeness to characters in the exhibits; this he has done in the guise of the Monster. The subterfuge goes undetected until the climax, because Igor's pièce de résistance is to have crafted a wax mask of his own face, which he wears to create the illusion that he survived the fire unscathed.

Blatantly borrowing from the classic unmasking sequence in Lon Chaney's *The Phantom of the Opera* of seven years before, this plot device nevertheless afforded *Mystery of the Wax Museum* the opportunity to deliver a coup de théâtre of similar power to that in the earlier film. Trapped amid the model-making machinery in the basement of the museum, Charlotte (Wray) is confronted by Igor, no longer a wheelchair-bound cripple but now walking unaided. He advances on her; terror-struck, she pounds at his face with her

CHAMPAGNE FOR CAESAR: *Vincent Price and a feathered friend*

fists and is amazed to see it crack, split open and fall away, revealing fire-ravaged features beneath. Atwill's climactic unmasking was one of the high points of 1930s horror cinema and it set him on course for a long career in monster movies, as it would do again for his successor in *House of Wax*.

The story was given a cursory update by screen-writer Crane Wilbur and elements of it were modified in line with the requirements of the Production Code – a cocaine addict who featured centrally in the first film became an alcoholic in the remake. As a result, the new version of *Mystery of the Wax Museum* may not have been a scene-by-scene retread of the original, but it was certainly a shot-by-shot one of what remained.

The 1932 production had provided much in the way of 'dimensional' effects to begin with: apart from the many shots of sinister-looking wax figures lit from below, a Monster sprang suddenly into view, corpses loomed up or toppled forward into frame, and there was the electrifying climax of an unmasking straight to camera. Warners added to this list only by incorporating what was to become an obligatory gimmick of the short-lived medium – that of throwing items towards the viewer; in the case of *House of Wax*, by appending to the museum's staff a barker with a paddling-bat, whose elasticated antics were ostensibly intended to encourage prospective patrons to enter but whose real purpose was to emphasise the 3-D.

For the Jekyll-and-Hyde role of the museum proprietor in what was originally slated as *The Wax Works*, director André de Toth required the talents of an actor who could be both benign and malevolent by turns, a suave and sinister figure in Atwill mould.

Such an actor had been making a minor name for himself in a series of smoothly villainous roles dating back to the forties, in films like *Shock* (1945), *Dragonwyck* (1945), *The Long Night* (1947), *The Three Musketeers* (1948) and most recently alongside Errol Flynn in *The Adventures of Captain Fabian* (1951), while 'madness' had been a characteristic of his high-camp portrayal of a soap-company president in the satirical *Champagne for Caesar* (1951). Vincent Price had taken time out from films for a return to the theatre, playing in a touring production of *Don Juan in Hell* with Agnes Moorehead, Sir Cedric Hardwicke and Charles Boyer, but de Toth tracked him down. "I met him a couple of times before and I liked him," he told Anthony Slide in 1995. "I always thought he was an edge man. You never knew which way he was going to go. He didn't have the big balls of Errol Flynn, but he was good

HOUSE OF WAX

looking, always. There was something there."

André de Toth was blind in one eye, an impairment which no self-respecting reviewer could allow to pass without remark when it came to the world's first stereoscopic horror film. Given what happened to Vincent Price's film career after *House of Wax*, however, it clearly had made de Toth twice as perceptive.

The end will come quickly, my love... There is a
pain beyond pain – an agony so intense it shocks
the mind into instant oblivion. We'll find
immortality together, and they will remember me
through you.

PROFESSOR JARROD (VINCENT PRICE),
HOUSE OF WAX (1953)

Vincent Price was born Vincent Leonard Price II on 27 May 1911 in a well-to-do suburb of St Louis, Missouri. He was the fourth child (and second son) of Vincent and Marguerite Price, his siblings being Harriet, James Mortimer and Laralouise, and his father was President of the National Candy Company. By the time he was 17, he had toured the capitals of Europe with the help of a bequest from his grand-mother and in pursuit of a maturing passion for art, and by age 18 he was enrolled at Yale University, like his father and elder brother before him.

The acting 'bug' had not then bitten any harder than the occasional appearance in a school play, but that was to change in 1934 after he had graduated from Yale. A teaching job in New York gave him the opportunity to tread the boards in a performance of Gilbert and Sullivan's *HMS Pinafore* and his fate was sealed. By the end of the year, Price was ensconced in London University's Courtauld Institute, studying Dürer for his MA by day but patronising theatres by night to watch Gielgud and Olivier on the West End stage.

When the chance came to join the company of the Gate Theatre, Price jumped at it and found himself cast as a gangster in a production called *Chicago*. This was followed by the role of the Prince Consort in Laurence Housman's *Victoria Regina*; by December 1935, he was playing the part on Broadway, his degree left to lapse in London. Vincent Price was 24.

Broadway success was his ticket to the West Coast and Hollywood and, within six months, Price was being screen-tested at Selznick Studios for feature roles in both *The Garden of Allah* (1936) and its planned production of *Gone With the Wind* (eventually released in 1939). He found the film

community utterly bedazzling, with one exception. "The only setbacks are the Jews and their power here," he wrote to his parents. "They are in command in all fields, and they, of course, are responsible for all the bad taste." (Price's anti-Semitic sympathies were far from unusual at this time and, in his case, were the product of a staunchly Protestant upbringing in ultra-conservative St Louis; they were to leave him as he embraced a circle of new, often Jewish, friends, but something of them would resurface when he came to be acquainted with American International.) Eighteen months later he was tested by M-G-M, this time for *Marie Antoinette* (1938). None of these films had his name on them, in the event – though he maintained that he was offered a role in the last but declined it. The same held true for *Juarez*, for which he was also tested by Warners only to lose the part to Brian Aherne.

An innately effeminate and over-theatrical manner might have had something to do with the stage-trained Price's run of bad luck, as the studios often went out of their way to portray their male stars as all-American and unambiguously heterosexual, both on screen and off. Whatever the reason, Price remained in New York, where he continued to hone his craft in repertory.

A brief interlude at Orson Welles' Mercury Theatre introduced him to his future wife, and in April 1938 Price married Edith Barrett Williams after a surprise courtship and long-time (and mostly long-distance) attachment to hometown girl Barbara O'Neill. The result was immediate: within three months of his marriage to Barrett (his co-star, along with Joseph Cotten, in a Mercury production of *The Shoemaker's Holiday*), the call came again. Price was placed under contract by Universal Studios and he made his long-overdue screen debut in *Service De Luxe*, with Constance Bennett, missing out on the chance to participate in the Mercury's Hallowe'en radio broadcast of H G Wells' *The War of the Worlds*.

Feeling uneasy in the role of leading man, Price persuaded Universal to try him out instead in character parts: "I talked them into letting me do a smaller part in which there was a chance of establishing myself as a character. I really didn't think I fit in the mould of a leading man in terms of Hollywood."

Price's film career may have begun in light comedy, but the production roster at Universal was becoming more and more dominated by horror product as the 1930s drew to a close. No surprise, then, that at only his third film out (after being loaned to Warners for

Boris Karloff in TOWER OF LONDON *(1939)*

The Private Lives of Elizabeth and Essex), he found himself in a pseudo-historical horror, foiling for Basil Rathbone and Boris Karloff inside the *Tower of London* (1939). Shot back-to-back with James Whale's jungle adventure *Green Hell* (in which Price also featured), *Tower of London* reduced history to a series of stateroom intrigues as Richard, Duke of Gloucester, and Mord, his faithful retainer and Constable of the Tower, plot between them to dispose of the heirs apparent to the throne of England in a Plantagenet version of Agatha Christie's *Ten Little Indians*.

Essentially a vehicle for the swaggering villainy of Rathbone after the success of his Sheriff of Nottingham in Warners' *The Adventures of Robin Hood*, the film turned out to be dishwater-dull under the lacklustre direction of Rowland V Lee, its battle-scenes conducted in rain and mist to disguise the paucity of their staging on the Universal backlot. Even Karloff in *Old Dark House* mode as the brutish Mord – idly unfastening an Iron Maiden to cleanse it of its human contents – could do little to lift a tedious trudge through

Shakespeare's uncredited Histories, devoid as it was of the wit or narrative concision of its original author.

> *I know you, Richard... Poison. You're trying to kill me!*
>
> **DUKE OF CLARENCE** (VINCENT PRICE),
> *TOWER OF LONDON* (1939)

To compensate for his relegation to fifth in the cast list after receiving co-starring credit in his first feature for Universal, Price was accorded a death scene which lasted almost as long as the cinematic Wars of the Roses themselves. A drinking bout between Gloucester and the Duke of Clarence (Price), organised as a pretext to Clarence's murder, allowed Price to take centre stage alongside the stars for a camp display of inebriety before his character ended up dunked in the mythical vat of Malmsey wine.

Robert N Lee's screenplay provided Price with little opportunity to sparkle; whimpering, simpering or twitching by turns, his Duke of Clarence was a

THE INVISIBLE MAN RETURNS

period clothes-peg for most of his time on screen. If his role in this film was insubstantial, however, his next for Universal was to remove him from the picture altogether.

As early as 1940, Universal's horrors were rapidly being downgraded from A features to B. *The Invisible Man Returns* was typical in that it employed little of the H G Wells novel which had inspired it (and which Universal itself had adapted in 1933) beyond its notional title character and the plot device of an invisibility serum.

Price played Geoffrey Radcliffe, wrongly framed for the murder of his brother, who stages his escape from Death Row at the eleventh hour thanks to a jab of invisibility-inducing Duocane courtesy of another 'brother', that of the first film's Invisible Man. The remainder of the story is taken up with Radcliffe's efforts to discover who framed him and why, before the volatile serum sends him insane. The film's equally transparent murder-mystery was not a patch on the bravura vision of the Wells original, and a slumming Sir Cedric Hardwicke turns out to be the fall-guy – literally in this instance, as he plummets to his death from a coal-skip at the climax.

> *You must realise that if the monster murders, the scientist hangs.*
>
> **INSPECTOR SAMPSON** (CECIL KELLAWAY), *THE INVISIBLE MAN RETURNS* (1940)

The Invisible Man Returns gave Price his first opportunity to play a 'monster', though only in terms of genre identification. His performance in the film was impeded by the artificiality of a stage accent which already had caused reviewers to mistake him for an Englishman. His *soto voce* delivery is also curiously muffled beneath the bandages at times, at least until the effects cut in and overdubbing takes over; even so, the Price voice at this stage was a poor substitute for the more incisive tones of Claude Rains, star of the 1933 original. It was to take several more appearances before Price was better able to relax with his natural Missouri twang – as well as a tonsillectomy in 1940. Price's Invisible Man would 'return' again in 1948, when he vocally reprised the role for the finale of *Abbott and Costello Meet Frankenstein*.

If nothing else, however, *The Invisible Man Returns* set Price on course for a lifetime's love affair with film wizardry and technical effects, which ultimately would lead him into *House of Wax*. "If the worst comes to the worst," Radcliffe remarks, when faced with the possibility that the antidote to his invisibility might never be found, "I can always get a job haunting a house." For the man who played him, it would and he did – but not for another 18 years.

Price made one last film for Universal before the studio allowed his contract to lapse and he moved to Twentieth Century-Fox, with whom he signed for another seven years. This was *The House of the Seven Gables*, based on the 1851 novel by Nathaniel Hawthorne. The story was steeped in Puritan virtue and capitalist vice, and its theme was the Gothic staple of past events intruding on the present – in the form of a family curse, in this case. Considering that the film originated at Universal, the home of horror, Harold Greene's script curiously omitted the (admittedly slight) supernatural overtones which are a feature of Hawthorne's original, contenting itself with the human drama of one New England cousin judicially wronged by the other for greed's sake, set against the backdrop of the famous seven-gabled manse.

The overly sentimental adaptation was made with one eye to the success of M-G-M's *Gone With the Wind* and focused on a family saga in which Price was required to age 30 years in the course of the narrative. The ageing process was less successful than the alterations which were made in the relationships between the various protagonists: Clifford (Price) and

Nan Grey and Vincent Price in **THE INVISIBLE MAN RETURNS**

Margaret Lindsay and Vincent Price in a publicity shot for
THE HOUSE OF THE SEVEN GABLES

Hepzibah (Margaret Lindsay) are brother and sister in the novel, lovers in the film.

Price had substituted at short notice for Robert Cummings, who became indisposed through illness, and his rhetorical style as Clifford Pyncheon somewhat overpowers that of his co-stars in the early scenes – though he still manages to out-act a typically detached George Sanders, no mean feat in itself. As a primer to Hawthorne's *The House of the Seven Gables*, Joe May's film was workmanlike and intense in the mild and inoffensive way of Hollywood at the time, but far from conscientious; as a chocolate-box romance of the war years, it provided a dutiful tug at the heart-strings.

> *You have the house... With it, you have inherited the Pyncheon tradition – all the tradition of your ancestors. You believe in those traditions, don't you? – You believe in your heritage. Then may you also inherit Maule's curse... God has given him blood to drink!*
>
> **CLIFFORD PYNCHEON** (VINCENT PRICE),
> *THE HOUSE OF THE SEVEN GABLES* (1940)

The roles allotted to Price at Fox were more eclectic. Even then, his first few appearances were inauspicious at best – *Brigham Young, Hudson's Bay* – and he continued to extend his range in the theatre, for the most part. A son, Vincent Barrett, was born to the Prices in 1940 and, by the time he turned 30 in 1941, Price's early matinée idol appeal had mellowed into an image which was not so easy for studio publicity machines to characterise. A knowing look, an instinctive arch of an eyebrow, a ready smirk at the corner of the mouth – all these had started to accord him a more sinister profile as an actor.

Price first essayed a line in smooth villainy on the Broadway stage, when he was cast as the duplicitous husband in an adaptation of Patrick Hamilton's *Gas Light* in 1941. Retitled *Angel Street* for American audiences (as was a British National film version of the year before, starring Anton Walbrook), Hamilton's perennial mood-piece enabled Price to spread his wings in a part which he described as "one of the meanest men ever written" but a "damned attractive one", as he tried to drive wife Judith Evelyn insane in order to facilitate a nightly quest for buried loot.

Despite the fact that *Angel Street* opened at the John Golden Theatre only two days before the bombing of Hawaii's Pearl Harbor on 7 December – President Roosevelt's 'day of infamy' and the harbinger of America's entry into World War II – it was an immediate success, running for nearly 1,300 performances (though Price left the cast after its first year).

His coquettish behaviour in response to rave reviews almost drove co-star Judith Evelyn insane for real, and her rebuke persuaded a contrite Price to disavow any notion of self-importance in the future. But in the suave and sinister role of Jack Manningham, he had, by his own admission, found his niche at last, although his contract with Fox and lack of a sufficient star name meant that he lost out to Charles Boyer when M-G-M mounted its own film version of the play in 1944 (with co-star Evelyn replaced by Ingrid Bergman).

Following *The Keys of the Kingdom* (1943), in which he played an itinerant Catholic priest, Price was issued his draft papers for the US Navy. He never saw active service, as it turned out: his own explanation was colour blindness, though his daughter has surmised that Fox interceded on his behalf due to the depletion of bankable stars in its ranks.

Another seven films of varying quality issued from Fox – of which *The Song of Bernadette* and *Laura* (both 1944) were the most distinguished – before the studio thought to star Price in *Shock*, a psychological thriller about a respected psychiatrist who allows an illicit affair to get in the way of his professional judgment. The role became his almost by default, thanks to the theatrical training which enabled him to master a wordy script for a speedy production in short order. As he explained to *Cinefantastique* in 1989: "When we did *Shock*, Howard Koch came to Lynn Bari and myself and said, 'We know the pictures are taking too long to make and we're going to have to cut down. You're the only two people I know in the whole studio who'll take the trouble to learn your lines and get on with it.' We did it in 18 days."

Price had earlier amplified on this aspect of his technique in *Films and Filming*: "I study the entire script every night, so that I have a feeling of where I am, where I have been, and where I am going. That way, they can switch the whole schedule for the following day, and I find that I am still in continuity with myself."

If a man wanted to – if he had courage, he could get rid of her and no one would ever know. A doctor has an advantage. I could give her insulin shock treatment...

DR RICHARD CROSS (VINCENT PRICE),
SHOCK (1944)

Studio portrait from **THE SONG OF BERNADETTE**

Shock was typical of the many cheap-and-cheerful noir thrillers which had begun to appear in the war years and which reflected the more cynical and disillusioned sensibility of those who made them and the characters who featured in them. Film noir as a genre concerned itself with moral equivocation, expressed by way of adultery, greed, persecution, revenge and, most often, murder – themes which were being played out on a global scale in the everyday news.

The films were contemporary in mood and dark in tone, and their anti-heroes and heroines were usually average 'Joes' who found themselves enmeshed in situations that were either out of their control or beyond their ken, resolution to which invariably meant resorting to violence. Film noir exemplified a world of chaos, in which society seemed perpetually to be on the edge of collapse and where law, order and moral prerogative had devolved into the hands, and guns, of its protagonists. They were a product of the intense social and psychological upheaval which was a consequence of conflict, and they would last right up to the mid-fifties, by which time the Truman

administration had been superseded by the more benign one of Eisenhower. Among the most memorable examples were *The Blue Dahlia* (1946) and *Dead Reckoning* (1947), but the cycle was to expire in a literal blaze of glory with Mickey Spillane and Robert Aldrich's *Kiss Me Deadly* (1955).

Shock was archetypal in that it revolved around an otherwise respectable psychiatrist named Richard Cross (Price), whose affair with his nurse leads him to murder his wife in a hotel room. The killing is witnessed by Janet Stewart (Anabel Shaw), who is holed up in the same hotel awaiting the return of her soldier-husband from a prisoner-of-war camp. Cross contrives to have the traumatised wife admitted to his sanatorium for observation, at which point moral dilemma comes into play: he first attempts to establish what she saw, but when this proves too incriminating to allow for her release, he tries to have her certified insane before deciding to kill her also.

Shock was a formula affair, with the opening scenes establishing the arena of conflict while the remainder explored how the various characters intended to extricate themselves from it. Cross is caught between loyalty to his profession and the supposedly siren-like charms of the devil in a white dress that is Nurse Elaine Jordan (Lynn Bari), but in Price's hands the character comes across as curiously passionless and disengaged.

Price had apparently read Richard von Krafft-Ebing's 1886 treatise *Psychopathia Sexualis* in preparation for his similarly devious role in *Angel Street*; if so, its case studies helped little with his performance in *Shock*. As Cross, he appears drawn and diffident, unable to play to the camera and seemingly unwilling to project either his personality or voice; the latter failing would continue to dog him into *The Three Musketeers*. It would be fair to say, in possible mitigation, that Price's marriage of only six years was already in serious trouble at this point.

The film's single indulgence in 'shock' treatment is occasioned by the escape of a pop-eyed John Davidson, a psychotic inmate who proceeds to threaten the hapless Mrs Stewart during a violent thunderstorm. Incorporated into the screenplay mainly for the benefit of the trailer, the sequence nevertheless engenders more suspense in two minutes than the rest of the cast can muster in the remaining 68.

However he may have been able to modify it for the stage, the Price persona on screen was more difficult to quantify. The camera is unflinching in its ability to capture the tiniest detail of physiognomy, the faintest trait of behaviour: with his hooded eyes, full mouth and slack jaw, his soft-spoken delivery and languidness of movement, Price seemed to be cast more to type when he essayed a simpering fop (*Tower of London*), a batty but benign scientist (*The Invisible Man Returns*), a fastidious Papal emissary (*The Song of Bernadette*), a shallow gigolo (*Laura*) or any number of Restoration dandies (*Hudson's Bay*, *A Royal Scandal*, a role which ended up on the cutting-room floor in *Forever Amber*).

Shock required of its protagonist that he harbour a ruthless streak beneath a placid exterior, an aspect of the role that Price clearly found difficult to convey. Consequently, his portrayal of Cross majors psychologically on the indecisiveness of an intrinsically weak man caught up in a spiral of events – not a characterisation predisposed to project its creator to stardom, though the film itself was elevated to feature status on release. His next film role typically capitalised on his last, but Price's transformation to screen super-villain would not be sudden, neither was it going to be particularly easy.

In February 1945, Fox cast Price as the Byronic anti-hero of *Dragonwyck*. The atmosphere of anxiety which breathed life into film noir had also brought about a revival in period thrillers of similar bent. With Universal having cornered the market in 'creature features', rival studios sought a more psychological base for their excursions into the genre, as well as declaring a preference for literary pedigree.

M-G-M was first in the field, putting Spencer Tracy and Ingrid Bergman into Stevenson's *Dr Jekyll and Mr Hyde* in 1941, followed by Fox in 1942 with Jesse Douglas Kerruish's *The Undying Monster*. Not to be outdone on its home turf, Universal fought back in 1943 with a lavish remake of *Phantom of the Opera*. Paramount entered the fray in 1944 with *The Man in Half Moon Street*. M-G-M replied that same year by recalling Bergman to play opposite Charles Boyer in *Gaslight* (the screen version of *Angel Street*) and then cast George Sanders and Hurd Hatfield in *The Picture of Dorian Gray*. RKO, lacking the resources which the big studios could bring to bear, nevertheless made its own contribution under the aegis of house producer Val Lewton with *The Body Snatcher* (1945). Fox returned to the running in 1945 with *Dragonwyck*, while Warners finished off the cycle in 1946 with *The Beast with Five Fingers*. Along the way, Fox had added *The Lodger* (1944) and *Hangover Square* (1945) to the roster, both of them starring Laird Cregar and both directed by John Brahm, whose evocation of Gothic landscape in *The Undying Monster* had been second to none.

The commonality of these films lay in a doom-laden scenario and the demise of the central character at the climax; *Dragonwyck* was no exception. Adapted from a novel by Anya Seton, *Dragonwyck* again paired Price with *Laura*'s Gene Tierney, on this occasion as a 'patroon' (landowner) of a Hudson River estate in the former Dutch colony of New York, circa 1844.

> *It was on an afternoon in May of 1844 that the letter came from Dragonwyck.*
> **ANYA SETON**, *DRAGONWYCK* (1945)

Dragonwyck was Seton's second novel after *My Theodosia*, and it was originally published in 1945; like its predecessor, it had become an instant best-seller. Seton opens her novel by quoting 'Alone', a poem written by Edgar Allan Poe in 1829, which is intended to allude to Price's character of Nicholas Van Ryn but could equally well have alluded to Price himself:

DRAGONWYCK

From childhood's hour I have not been
As others were – I have not seen
As others saw – I could not bring
My passions from a common spring.

Seton's detailed description of her patroon is as follows: "He was tall, over six feet, and of a slender build ... Here were the full flexible mouth, the aquiline nose with slightly flaring nostrils, the high and noble forehead accented by stern black brows ... Nicholas' eyes were not large and they were blue ... A peculiarly vivid light blue that was startling and somehow disconcerting in a face that might otherwise have belonged to a Spanish grandee." In 1945, Hollywood producers often took pains to cast actors in screen adaptations of well-known novels who most resembled their author's description, fearful of the backlash from a devoted readership were they not to do so. The 33-year-old Vincent Price fitted Seton's image to a tee; nevertheless, he had to wage an intense campaign within the studio to acquire it.

Dragonwyck is what used to be known as a woman's film, primarily because its protagonist is female but also because, at the time of its production, the bulk of the audience was similarly composed, their menfolk having gone off to war. Its dominant themes are therefore love, courtship, marriage, childbirth, domesticity and the problems of finding Mr Right; its dynamic that of a rite of passage, but from a feminine point of view. Ernst Lubitsch had been slated to direct but illness forced him to hand the actual shoot to the screenwriter of the piece, Joseph L Mankiewicz; Lubitsch died two years later. A clash of styles was the result, though little of the apparent conflict can be evidenced on screen. Nevertheless, it is Mankiewicz to whom the film owes a darker hue than his mentor might have intended.

Miranda Wells (Tierney) is courted by stately Dutch aristocrat Nicholas Van Ryn (Price) to serve as companion to his young daughter at Dragonwyck, his Gothic mansion in upstate New York. Van Ryn is a beguiling charmer and Miranda falls quickly under his spell, but, in shades of Brönte's Rochester, he already has a wife – not a mad woman in an attic, merely a biological impediment to his obsessive desire for an heir – and love soon turns to loathing when Van Ryn murders her, then marries and rejects

Miranda, all in the single-minded pursuit of a son.

Much of *Dragonwyck* is full-blooded Gothic Romance – *Jane Eyre* on the Hudson – as the virginal daughter of a God-fearing Puritan farmer is whisked off to the grand manor where she harbours dreams of marrying the handsome master of the house and becoming mistress of her very own fairy-tale castle. But whereas Charlotte Brönte's heroine thought that she had contracted to work for the Prince of Darkness before discovering to her delight that he was actually Prince Charming, Seton's has it the other way round: when Van Ryn loses first his lands and then the infant son for whom Miranda was baited from the start, darkness begins to descend and Gothic horror takes

hold. "He watches me all the time through those icy eyes of his," Tierney confides to suitor Glenn Langan – though another pair of eyes were watching Tierney for real: those of a young navy lieutenant named John Fitzgerald Kennedy, with whom the actress was to have an affair during the making of the film.

Like all good Gothic castles, Dragonwyck harbours a ghost in its 'Red Room' – that of Van Ryn's great-grandmother: "She prayed for disaster to come to the Van Ryns, and she swore that when it came, she'd always be here to sing and play ... She killed herself in this room," explains the sadistic senior maid. The curse that hangs over the household is downplayed in the film, as is the ghostly presence held to be responsible for it: "Do you hear it?" urges Van Ryn at the climax. "What?" "Nothing," he retorts. "The wind through the trees..."

All the elements of characterisation which were to feature in his Poe films of the 1960s are to be found germinating in Price's finely honed performance as Nicholas Van Ryn – proud, arrogant, drug-addicted, obsessed, afflicted by strange fancies and the keeper of a terrible secret from a haunted past. In Anya Seton's satanic patroon can be seen the genesis of Roderick Usher – not just a hint of what was to come but the whole man, fully formed and patiently awaiting his time upon the stage. There is more than a hint, too, of director Roger Corman's subsequent approach to Poe in Mankiewicz' way with the Gothic overtones of the tale, the alteration in Van Ryn's personality being prefigured by a spectacular thunderstorm, whose lightning illumines his brooding features as he stands before a gable window.

> There's no thunder in the world like the thunder of the Catskills. The lightning seems to set the mountains on fire, and they roar back at it.
> NICHOLAS VAN RYN (VINCENT PRICE),
> DRAGONWYCK (1945)

In Dragonwyck, Price began to come into his own at last. An imposing entrance in cutaway coat placed him firmly in the kind of period to which his looks, manner and natural grace were best suited. The similarity between the two characters was more than skin deep: Price himself, like Van Ryn in the novel, had taken the Grand Tour of Europe in his youth. "There had therefore been a succession of tutors, German and English, to prepare the boy for the cultural climax of the Grand Tour. He had spent two years travelling elegantly through England, France, Spain, Italy, and Germany, before returning to Dragonwyck," Seton had written of Van Ryn. Price, a voluminous diarist in his own right and avid culture-vulture whose love of the arts was unquestionable and quite possibly unparalleled among his contemporaries, noted of his own whirlwind tour through the capitals of Europe in 1928: "My first trip abroad will be, I hope, just a starter on a long life filled with voyages."

When Dragonwyck moves out to the snow-covered countryside or concerns itself with the grievances of the estate's tenant farmers, its power diminishes and it again reveals its origins in a pot-boiling Gothic romance set against a turbulent period of post-colonial social upheaval. It is Price who informs the film's dynamic, despite third-billing in the cast list below Tierney and Walter Huston (as Miranda's father). It is Price who dominates the proceedings with a literally commanding performance, as he falls inexorably from his hereditary state of grace to become a drug-addled murderer.

In a later narrative diversion omitted from the screenplay of the film, the novel's Van Ryn takes his new wife to meet a young author by name of Edgar Poe, and it is Poe who introduces the patroon to the sense-numbing properties of laudanum. Van Ryn is unimpressed with Poe's morbidity of spirit, and their relationship is short-lived. By a strange turn of fate, it was to be Price himself who came to make the poet's closer acquaintance.

Despite his imposing stature and boyish charm, Vincent Price was now destined to become a villain on screen. The patrician air of a pre-rebellion Southern gentleman, as exemplified by Nicholas Van Ryn in Dragonwyck, clung stubbornly to him. The intelligence that shone behind his luminous blue eyes could not be disguised, and intelligence in films was traditionally a mark of villainy. The Hollywood ethos of mass-market appeal decreed that the hero should be an 'everyman', capable of rising above adversity with nothing more than sound judgment, moral rectitude and two fists if needed. In the Hollywood world view, intellect was the prerogative of megalomaniacal psychopaths, education that of closet queens, and breeding a sign of hauteur and class prejudice. Everyman was not a graduate of Yale University; he was tutored by life itself. The cinema was not the theatre – dialogue-driven, and where the great roles are all clever men or women. To film producers and casting agents, Price's steely-eyed stare, aristocratic demeanour and silken tongue had the stamp of villainy about it, despite early studio attempts to promote him as a matinée idol in the time-honoured tradition.

But even Dragonwyck did not set Vincent Price on a path to screen villainy overnight; the time was not yet right. It did, however, supply him with a template upon which he would draw when the opportunity eventually presented itself.

> I entered into their ceremonies. I pretended I was possessed by their gods...
> MRS RAND (EDITH BARRETT),
> I WALKED WITH A ZOMBIE (1943)

The final years of Price's Fox contract coincided with the premature end of his marriage to Edith Barrett, young son notwithstanding. When he had decided to wed an actress, Price thought he was marrying into the theatre; Edith Barrett, on the other hand, thought she had been marrying *out* of it.

By the end of 1947, Vincent Price was divorced (after an earlier separation in 1944), as well as bereaved of both his beloved parents. A lifetime of experience had started to etch itself onto his features and darker, more complex roles followed suit. His gaze had assumed a more cynical caste; his jaw a firmer set. A foretaste of what was to come had been present in the actor in *Dragonwyck*, though neither its value nor the ambience in which it blossomed was recognised by Fox. After another smooth supporting role as a police inspector in *Moss Rose* opposite Peggy Cummins and Victor Mature, Price relinquished his contract and went on his way as a free agent, both personally and professionally.

A new Price was emerging, sanctified in 1948 by his role as the scheming Richelieu in an exotic M-G-M version of Alexandre Dumas' *The Three Musketeers* with Gene Kelly (as D'Artagnan), Lana Turner and Van Heflin, additionally graced with the writing of Robert Ardrey and the music of Tchaikovsky.

> *I am France, Louis; I am the state. These men have set themselves above me and it is I, Louis, and not you, who sit in judgment. I render that judgment now.*
>
> RICHELIEU (VINCENT PRICE),
> *THE THREE MUSKETEERS* (1948)

The rousing nature of the production – it had been mounted to showcase dance-king Kelly's acrobatic talents in the manner of Douglas Fairbanks – led a reviewer in *New Yorker* magazine in 1980 to liken Price's oily and strictly non-ecclesiastical portrayal of Dumas' famous Cardinal to that of 'an especially crooked used-car dealer.' Be that as it may in retrospect, the lavish film was high-profile and it led to other openings for the newest face in filmland's endlessly rotating roster of bad guys.

Less than a year after his acrimonious divorce from Edith Barrett, Price had whisked costume designer Eleanor Mary Grant off to Mexico to tie the knot at a private ceremony. Good screen roles continued into the new decade and, in 1951, he expanded his range

into madcap comedy with *Champagne for Caesar*, playing alongside his boyhood hero and the model for his famous pencil-thin moustache, Ronald Colman.

After a brief succession of memorable but hardly career-enhancing encounters with popular box-office attractions like Jane Russell and Robert Mitchum (*His Kind of Woman*), Errol Flynn (*The Adventures of Captain Fabian*) and Victor Mature (*The Las Vegas Story*, again with Jane Russell) between 1951 and 1952, another hiatus in his stop-start movie career saw Price cast in a revival of Christopher Fry's *The Lady's Not for Burning* opposite Marsha Hunt, as well as the touring production of George Bernard Shaw's *Don Juan in Hell*, before being offered a role on Broadway in *My Three Angels*, under the direction of José Ferrer.

The play conflicted with a new offer from Hollywood, however. Recalling the fun that he had in dealing with the trick effects in *The Invisible Man Returns*, Price declined the invitation from Ferrer and elected instead to play Professor Henry Jarrod in *House of Wax*. "I would love to have done the play," he told *Cinefantastique* in 1989, "but the people who did the play – it didn't mean anything to them at all. It was a great hit but it didn't help them in their careers, whereas *House of Wax* changed my life."

> *Come in – come in – come in, ladies and gentlemen. See the House of Wax! See the Chamber of Horrors!*
>
> THE BARKER (REGGIE RYMAL),
> *HOUSE OF WAX* (1953)

Very much an assembly-line production for its studio, *House of Wax* was allocated to house producer Bryan W Foy, who had started out in showbusiness as one of his father's (Vaudeville comedian Eddie Foy) 'Seven Little Foys' before going on to become an executive with Warner Bros. Responsibility for the screenplay fell to Warners staff writer (Erwin) Crane Wilbur, a one-time silent screen actor who, at 67, was also old enough to harbour a vivid recollection of the original film. Foy's previous feature was *Cattle Town*, with Dennis Morgan and Phil Carey, while Wilbur's was *The Lion and the Horse*, with Steve Cochran – both 1952, and both of them run-of-the-mill Western fare.

Wilbur confined the action of the new film to New York, a change which would have suited the hastily assembled cast – contract players all, most of whom,

A shot illustrating the huge 3-D camera at work on the set of House of Wax. *André De Toth (in jacket) directs Vincent Price and Phyllis Kirk*

Price excepted, were native to Manhattan and its environs. Paul Picerni was imported from *Cattle Town*, Frank Lovejoy (who was himself a product of noir sensibility and who specialised in playing rugged army sergeants or hard-bitten police captains) came from *Retreat, Hell!*, while ex-model Phyllis Kirk was last seen co-starring opposite Alan Ladd in *The Iron Mistress* (1952).

Wilbur also made some revisions in the composition of the *House of Wax*'s historical tableaux. The first film had featured an eclectic mix of notables from European history and literature: Marie Antoinette, Voltaire, Joan of Arc, Sir Walter Raleigh,

Jean-Paul Marat and so on. Joan of Arc and Marie Antoinette remained constant to both productions, but the staunchly European exhibits of the original film were shunted aside in favour of others more indigenously American. The centrepiece of Warners' new wax museum was now a predictable diorama of Lincoln's assassination at the hands of cracked actor John Wilkes Booth, supported by a Chamber of Horrors effigy of William Kemmler, the first man to die in the electric chair and herein made-up to look like museum assistant Charles Bronson, in his pre-superstar guise of Charles Buchinski. Anne Boleyn, Landru and a caveman were also present, the

Vincent Price, Charles Buchinski (Bronson) and Paul Cavanagh in HOUSE OF WAX

ragbag nature of the exhibits being due to Warners having had to collate what it could from a number of sources in something of a hurry.

The name 'Igor' smacked too much of humorous appellations which had since attached to dwarfed hunchbacks in Frankenstein films, so the innocent-sounding Professor Henry Jarrod was substituted in its stead. But of more detriment to the production was the removal or alteration of certain key scenes in the original, thus rendering the transcontinental 12-year time-lag between the two museums non-existent – *Mystery of the Wax Museum* had conscientiously deployed these constructs to explicate the insurance scam and to mask Igor's prior history. A non-essential subplot about a millionaire

playboy erroneously charged with murder was less damagingly disposed of.

The director's chair was assigned to André de Toth, a Hungarian émigré and war veteran who wore a piratical eye-patch and dined out on the story of how he had lost his eye in the trenches. Jack Warner was convinced that *House of Wax* would help save his studio and, by implication, Hollywood itself. He was also fully aware of the apparent contradiction in putting a one-eyed man in charge of a twin-lensed film. As de Toth recalled: "Jack Warner called me in and said, 'Listen, you want to make this film?' I said, 'Yes, sir.' He said, 'Take that goddam black patch off your fucking eye, because I don't want to be the butt of a joke. You understand? I don't want you on the lot

LEFT:
HOUSE OF
WAX

BELOW:
Vincent Price,
Philip Tonge
and Paul
Cavanagh in
HOUSE OF
WAX

with it until you finish shooting, and the picture is over.' So I put my black patch in my pocket – and I suffered because it hurt."

Minor amendments aside, Wilbur's script was the mix much as before:

> Wax sculptor Henry Jarrod (Price) is supposedly burned to death in a blaze at his museum, set by his ex-partner for $25,000-worth of insurance. Some time later, he reappears with a new museum and his partner is found hanged – the latest victim of a hideous Monster who seems also to be fond of stealing fresh corpses from local morgues. When Sue Allan (Kirk) discovers her room-mate, Cathy, murdered by the Monster, she is lucky to escape with her life as he pursues her through the city's streets. When Cathy's body vanishes from the morgue, Sue's suspicions are aroused by Cathy's resemblance to a figure of Joan of Arc in Jarrod's museum.
>
> Jarrod compliments Sue on her own resemblance to French queen Marie Antionette and in due course, she, too, becomes prey to the Monster. Finding herself in the museum's basement workshop, she is confronted by Jarrod and accuses him of stealing the bodies to supply himself with models for his tableaux. He grabs hold of her and she hits out – cracking his wax face and revealing him as the Monster. As Jarrod endeavours to mould Sue into his idealised image of Marie Antoinette, the police break into the museum and he is tumbled into his own vat of molten wax.

Publicity shot from HOUSE OF WAX

That look of horror spoils your lovely face – what
if it should show, even through the wax?
PROFESSOR JARROD (VINCENT PRICE),
HOUSE OF WAX (1953)

House of Wax is as handsomely mounted as
anything from a major Hollywood studio of the time,
but the rush to production (the film was shot in just
four weeks after only three months of preparation)
was in evidence both behind the scenes and in front
of the camera. The script had called for Jarrod to
attempt to flee the fire at the museum in the opening
scenes by clambering up a ladder towards a skylight
window, only to tumble back into the flames as the
ladder gives way beneath him. This set-up was
abandoned during shooting and replaced by the extant
one in which Price can be seen to duck through a
concealed exit while a breakaway set collapses at his
back. In other scenes, the actor races through lengthy
speeches with nary a pause for breath, as though a
single take was the order of the day. To climax a long
monologue on the provenance of his wax exhibits,
Price inserts a misquote from *Hamlet*: "Foul deeds will
rise, though all the world [earth] o'erwhelm them, to
men's eyes."

A stunt double does much of the fighting for Price,
a situation which the actor would regret not taking
more advantage of during his next outing. A certain
charnel grotesquerie attaches to the imagery of the
wax figures in flames – features molten and distorted;
eyeballs running from liquid sockets – but the real
horror of the film is supplied by Price's Monster, as he
pursues the fleeing Kirk with troglodytic gait through
the fogbound New York streets.

George Bau's make-up for the Monster is passable
in the half-light which de Toth allots to it all too rarely,
but it appears more waxen than the supposedly real
face of Jarrod when shown in close-up and garish
Warnercolor. Unlike the mask which Atwill wore in
the original, it adheres too closely to Price's own
angular features for the Monster to be anyone other
than Jarrod from the outset.

Lionel Atwill, aware that as Igor he was meant to be
clad in a wax mask, attempted to keep his features as
immobile as possible (to the extent of speaking some
of his lines through closed lips), reasoning that if this
effect jarred on the audience, all would be revealed by
his climactic unmasking. Atwill's realistic approach
was deemed too un-realistic in the final edit and
several of his close-ups were excised as a result, for

fear of giving the game away too soon. (A vestige of
Atwill's approach can be readily observed in the release
print; the effect is most noticeable in his climactic
scenes with Fay Wray, where he appears to stare past
her into the middle distance while imploring her to
submit to his scheme.) Vincent Price, on the other
hand, remains facially mobile throughout, rendering
his eventual 'unmasking' a con trick.

The sleight-of-hand is compounded when Jarrod
rises from his wheelchair and advances with military
bearing on Sue Allan, which completely negates his
hitherto spastic stance as the Monster. No such
anomaly featured in *Mystery of the Wax Museum* and
its inclusion in the remake can only be justified as an
attempt to further separate the characters in the
minds of the audience, and thus make the final
revelation that they are one and the same come as
more of a surprise. In the event, the effect is merely
ludicrous and it marks *House of Wax* down as horror
hokum, whereas the first film was more satisfyingly
cohesive in both these respects.

"He hobbled and swayed like a monkey," Glenda
Farrell's wisecracking reporter said in the original,
before adding as a gift to the publicity department:
"I don't know what he was, but he made Frankenstein
look like a lily!" The nearest that *House of Wax* can
come to engendering a similar frisson is when
Lieutenant Brennan (Lovejoy) gives Sue the benefit of
his professional judgment in respect of her phantom
pursuer: "You know that's the strangest description I
ever heard. No human being can look like that," he
professes sagely, having apparently never come across
a burns victim before.

The choreography of the action – less questionable
in 1932 – is palpably nonsensical even by the standards
of the early 1950s. Sue arrives at her lodgings to find
her friend murdered, yet the Monster remains in the
room until she enters and only flees by means of a
window *after* she has screamed, despite the fact that she
has telegraphed her presence in advance by knocking
on Cathy's door. And why go through the whole elaborate charade to begin with, when all that the Professor
had to do was entice Cathy back to the museum, as he
does latterly with Sue herself. When they come to
investigate the crime, the police quickly arrive at an
expedient solution: "It couldn't have been the same man
that took Miss Gray to dinner last night." "That's impossible," Sue concurs, as though the feeble exchange can
compensate for a plot structure that is at pains to direct
the viewer to exactly the opposite conclusion.

The film's standout sequence comes when Sue walks the halls of the empty museum at night in search of her beau, with an unseen Buchinski in tow – this not only provides a showcase for the eerie wax figures to be seen in their best (low) light, but for the depth effects as well. "It *is* Cathy; it's Cathy's body under the wax – I knew it all the time!" Sue exclaims when Jarrod's secret is uncovered. Phyllis Kirk had at first been reluctant to appear in the film as she had "no desire" to be the Fay Wray of her time, but contract players never argued with Jack Warner.

In the final minutes, Price goes from mildly unhinged to completely insane, whereas Lionel Atwill always looked to have booked his ticket to the funny farm, and the viewer is moved to wonder how Jarrod could have managed to come this far undetected to begin with. The transition did give Price an opportunity to grandstand the climax, however – "Everything I ever loved has been taken away from me, but not you, my Marie Antoinette, for I will give you eternal life!"

When it eventually opened in the UK, *House of Wax* was only the third film to receive the new 'X' rating (Price's next, *The Mad Magician*, would be the ninth), which had been instituted in 1951 to replace the old 'H' (for Horror) certificate and which restricted cinema entry to persons of 16 years and over. Notwithstanding, the British censor excised shots of a supposedly naked Kirk, manacled to a dais and clawing at the wooden sides of her proxy coffin.

In remake form, *House of Wax* was a B-movie in truth, but it was pole-vaulted to A-feature status by the timely attachment of colour and 3-D. *Mystery of the Wax Museum* had been a product of more undemanding times and the unreconstructed *House of Wax* just about managed to scrape by as a nostalgic slice of Grand Guignol. The film itself was as much of a spectacle as the eponymous emporium is supposed to be in the story, and it went on to take over $4 million during its initial release.

> *I'm going to give the people what they want – sensation, horror, shock. Send them out in the streets to tell their friends how wonderful it is to be scared to death!*
>
> **PROFESSOR JARROD** (VINCENT PRICE),
> *HOUSE OF WAX* (1953)

Vincent Price had again shown that he could play a sympathetic (if duplicitous) villain, but Hollywood, and the horror genre as a whole, was on the cusp of an irrevocable change. Even Warners' own 3-D sequel, *Phantom of the Rue Morgue* (1954, based on Poe's *The Murders in the Rue Morgue*), evinced more psychological depth and motivational insight than the old-style bogeyman horrors of *House of Wax*.

When it had finished with its mad sculptor, Warners was happy to rest on its laurels for the time being, but writer Crane Wilbur and producer Bryan Foy thought to make more hay from the components of their box-office smash while the projection lights were still shining.

Five months after the opening of *House of Wax*, the pair got together with Edward Small to mount a thinly disguised revision entitled *The Mad Magician*, again with Price. Brooklyn-born Small was a 61-year-old former talent agent turned independent film producer who had formed his first company, Reliance Pictures, in 1938. Price had been sold the project on the basis that production values, in terms of colour and 3-D, would be similar to its forerunner. In the event, *The Mad Magician* was indeed shot in 3-D but the only colour was to be found in the red and green lenses of the stereoscopic spectacles required to view it.

> *Gallico the Great presents his sensational new illusion – the Crematorium!*
>
> **DON GALLICO** (VINCENT PRICE),
> *THE MAD MAGICIAN* (1953)

This time script *and* story were provided by Crane Wilbur, and to assure his audience that they were in for a repeat of the treats they had enjoyed in *House of Wax*, *The Mad Magician* even overlaid its title-cards on a duplicate of the shot which had inaugurated its predecessor: a figure clad in hat and coat makes its way along a rain-sodden street towards the workshop of Professor Jarrod – or rather Don Gallico, 'the Great', a designer of elaborate tricks for stage magicians, who harbours ambitions to become one himself. He is subject to the same obsessions in relation to his craft as was Jarrod in relation to his 'people', and he proves just as gullible when it comes to those who would disabuse him of what he perceives to be his rightful place in the roll-call of the great.

Wilbur (who 30 years previously had written the original play on which the Lon Chaney vehicle *The Monster* had been based) concocts a more laborious scenario to account for Price's 'madness' on this occasion: Gallico is in hock to another business partner of bad character, who has already stolen his wife

Publicity shot fom THE MAD MAGICIAN

RIGHT:
**THE MAD
MAGICIAN**

BELOW:
*Vincent Price
and Mary
Murphy in*
**THE MAD
MAGICIAN**

and now plans to compound the injury by thwarting the magician's intention to showcase his tricks under his own name.

Contrivance rears its predictable head before the first reel is out, as Gallico lops off that of his grasping employer with a buzz-saw, and pops it into a Gladstone bag which promptly goes walkabout in New York when his female assistant accidentally exchanges it for another of the same type. In order to utilise all the tricks which were perceived to have made *House of Wax* such a success – the 'wronged' artist out for revenge; a swift descent into madness and murder; a series of extravagant deaths; a villain parading around in a mask (in this case, masks); a cauldron-like device around which to stage the climax – Wilbur concocts a scenario as inane and far-fetched as the mid-film notion that Gallico can dispose of a body simply by trundling it along to a local campus bonfire and depositing it on top to await the flames.

Already enfeebled by the weight of its internal inconsistencies, *The Mad Magician* borrows the plot of its director John Brahm's film of *The Lodger* (in which Jack the Ripper takes rooms in a lodging house to conduct clandestine 'experiments') in order to sustain itself for an entire reel, having already borrowed its 'bonfire' episode from Brahm's *Hangover Square*. But unlike Laird Cregar in *The Lodger*, Price finds himself in the house of the nosiest couple in the neighbourhood and, in no time at all, he is compelled to clamber out of the window to escape their prying, having managed to strangle only his former wife to death in the brief period of his stay. Gallico's landlady, a writer of mystery novels as things turn out, is played by Crane Wilbur's wife, Lenita Lane; both actress and character would crop up again in Wilbur's 1959 version of *The Bat*.

When Wilbur proceeds to purloin *The Lodger*'s use of fingerprint evidence to bring Gallico to book and provide tenuous connection to the various strands of a meandering plot, one could be forgiven for thinking that the film would have been called 'The Mad Lodger' were it not for the requirement of titular alliteration. Fingerprinting was "officially adopted by the French two years ago," announces the police lieutenant; it was *officially* adopted in France in 1916, but the first case to come to trial as a result of fingerprint evidence was in 1902 – which puts *The Mad Magician* in its correct period, two years on from *House of Wax*.

Wilbur even attempts to repeat the demented lyricism of the lines which had accompanied Price's grandstanding at the finale of *House of Wax*: "Actually, there'll be very little pain. Such a blast of heat brings instant oblivion. Can you hear it sing, lieutenant? – It has the voice of a mad bull!" Gallico exhorts as he primes his victim for a fiery demise in his Crematorium. The image of fire 'singing like a mad bull' is a little way short of the *Sonnets*, however. The nasal inflection which increasingly would come to distinguish the Price voice has its origins in *The Mad Magician*: a stunt fight between himself and newcomer Patrick O'Neal ended with more damage to the Price proboscis, which he first broke at college and which eventually required plastic surgery to correct.

The Crematorium, a steel-and-glass enclosure capable of roasting its occupant alive and of which much was made in the film's trailer, is yet another fake prop in terms of storyline. The opportunity for it to be used on stage, and thus provide a murder in full public view, is sadly neglected; it is merely demonstrated along the way before being fired up for a

climax in which it behaves in a wholly different fashion from that which the viewer has been asked to observe earlier in the film. Far from bringing the 'instant oblivion' that Gallico so luridly describes, the 3500° Fahrenheit blast of heat which is emitted from its open hatchway appears to have no impact whatever on the two combatants who end up laying into each other within toasting distance of it.

The depth-effects are staged more conscientiously by Brahm than they were by André de Toth, though they still amount to little more than hurling sundry objects towards the camera, but *The Mad Magician* was nevertheless a thoroughly cynical exercise in exploitation which its director virtually disowned in his later years.

Everything... Everything I ever had – my wife, my friends, my self-respect... Everything but the air I breathe!
> **DON GALLICO** (VINCENT PRICE),
> *THE MAD MAGICIAN* (1953)

The kernel of a good story lay buried inside *The Mad Magician*, but haste had ensured that whatever it may have been was allowed to disappear in a puff of smoke. What remained was a plot that lurched from one implausible circumstance to the next. The film devolves into a series of contrivances that echo the themes in *House of Wax*, but end up looking like one-reel prospectuses for any number of alternative versions.

Like those of his contemporaries who similarly were moulded by the studio system, Price's screen persona was larger than life, and he was best suited to roles which were larger than life also. The horror film, especially in its science fictional guise, was moving into a more realistic phase; the field of fantasy was becoming one of themes and ideas, and increasingly its concerns were reflecting the real world outside the narrow margins of the Hollywood machine.

Price was theatrically trained (and on the British stage, at that); he was not the kind of actor to whom naturalism came easily, and this ensured that he would remain sidelined by the horror cinema of the mid-fifties until a vehicle came his way for which he was better fitted. His grandiloquent style required to be subsumed into a Tale of Terror in the classic mould – one which was famous enough in its own right to remain untainted by the reputation of any who attempted to interpret it. At the birth of the

John Brahm and Vincent Price in a publicity shot from THE MAD MAGICIAN

atomic age, Hollywood was in no mood to revive any of the literary classics in the face of an onslaught of mutant monsters and alien invaders. Price's next role in the genre would see him seconded to a typical example of the former.

By the turn of 1954, however, it was not only a lack of suitable subjects that was to impede Vincent Price's rise to the ranks of horror star.

With no other offers on the table after *The Mad Magician* – despite the runaway box-office success of *House of Wax* – Price returned to the theatre in his hometown of St Louis, in another run of *The Lady's Not for Burning* and in *Death Takes a Holiday*. For an actor who had racked up two to three films a year on a regular basis since the 1940s, this seeming absence of suitable roles was unusual to say the least.

Since the 1940s, Price had also taken every opportunity that came his way to cash in on his image and perform in guest-spots on radio and television; he had been one of only a handful of celebrities to participate in the first coast-to-coast

broadcast in 1949. Of late, he had become a regular on CBS primetime's *Pantomime Quiz* (aka *Celebrity Charades*), a weekly game show sponsored by Camel cigarettes and hosted by Emmy Award-winning MC Mike Stokey. Early in 1954, Price was dropped from the show with no word of explanation.

Some months before, he and his wife had applied to have their passports renewed and had found themselves singled out by State Department officials, who requested them both to sign an 'oath of loyalty.' And while *The Mad Magician* was awaiting release through Columbia Pictures, the *Pantomime Quiz* setback took on a more sinister aspect when Price was informed by the studio that it required him to provide a written rebuttal of certain charges which had been made against him by anonymous informants in relation to alleged Communist activity.

Since 1947, Hollywood had been under siege from the Republican-led House Un-American Activities Committee (HUAC), chaired by John Parnell Thomas, which had been instructed to conduct Congressional hearings about the supposed infiltration of

Communist subversives into organised labour in the United States. The Committee's inaugural mandate had quickly come to embrace the film community as well, primarily to give it a higher profile but also from genuine concern that films were being used as left-wing propaganda by Communist sympathisers in the industry. These initial hearings had produced the unedifying spectacle of the 'Hollywood Ten', a group of industry dissidents, mainly writers, who had refused to testify before the Committee by standing on the Fifth Amendment and who briefly ended up behind bars as a consequence. A counter-attack on the workings of HUAC by the hastily convened 'Committee for the First Amendment', or CFA (which had been led by showbusiness luminaries like Humphrey Bogart, John Garfield and Edward G Robinson and instigated to advance the principle of free speech), had ended in disarray and a mass retraction of support for the 'Ten', but it was enough to bring the proceedings to a halt amid the welter of recriminations which resulted from its intervention. Congressman Thomas was subsequently indicted on bribery charges and imprisoned in 1949.

In 1951, after a self-imposed respite, the Committee had turned its inquisitorial gaze on the film capital with renewed vigour. Now chaired by Republican Senator Joseph 'Joe' Raymond McCarthy and under the direction of a Georgia Democrat named John Stephen Wood, HUAC had actively encouraged informants to contact law enforcement agencies with their suspicions regarding fellow actors, writers and directors. Those at whom such fingers pointed were called to appear before the House, where they either implicated other performers, pleaded their innocence or stood on the Fifth and declined to answer questions. Silence in court had already been taken as an admission of guilt, and careers had been lost among those who had adopted a less than temperate approach to the intimidatory tactics employed.

The 'Red Scare' paranoia which had come increasingly to the fore with the Cold War gave an air of legitimacy to the largely unsubstantiated accusations levied by McCarthy and Wood. And with the complicity of the studio heads, who collectively had issued an edict to the effect that they would not employ anyone known to be sympathetic to the Communist Party, an unofficial 'blacklist' had begun to operate within the industry. In Washington, the purging of behaviour deemed by the Committee to be Un-American went

further still – some 5,000 suspected homosexuals were eventually fired from Federal jobs.

In such a climate, no one was safe – and no one too big a star to stop the implied charge of 'traitor' from ending their lives in the limelight overnight. One of the many actors to have raised the eyebrows of officialdom was Canadian-born Raymond Burr, who had been making a name for himself as a heavy in films like *Horizons West* (1952) and *The Blue Gardenia* (1953), and with whom Price had been teamed in *His Kind of Woman* and, most recently, *Casanova's Big Night*. In 1948, Price had co-founded the Institute of Modern Art with, among others, Edward G Robinson and old friend Sam Jaffe; Jaffe and Robinson were also now under suspicion, as was Marsha Hunt, his leading lady in *The Lady's Not for Burning*. Actors who worked within the closed confines of the Hollywood studio system were often acquainted with one another, so this might have meant little by itself. But it went further than that.

Price had once belonged to the Hollywood Independent Citizens Committee of Arts, Sciences and Professions, at one of whose seminars he had voiced the opinion that art was altogether too important to be allowed to fall into the hands of government. At another function at which he had been called upon to speak, those who attended were entertained by Negro baritone Paul Robeson, a self-confessed Communist. During the war, Price had made speeches in support of America's allies – including the USSR; in 1947, he had appeared on behalf of the joint Anti-Fascist Refugee Committee. In that same year, he had put his name to an advertisement in the *Hollywood Reporter* on behalf of the CFA, which protested HUAC's interference in industry affairs. Last but not least, he had guested at a dinner arranged by the American-Russian Institute, at which he recited works by visiting Russian poet Konstantin Simonov. All these organisations were now considered by the FBI to have Communist connections.

If a shadow suddenly appeared to have fallen over Vincent Price's Hollywood career, it did not take him long to work out the direction from which it was cast. He was not even sure at this stage that he had actually been singled out for scrutiny by the FBI, acting on orders from HUAC ('grey-listed' as it was colloquially known). But the pervasive atmosphere of mistrust and suspicion which its activities had generated within the closed confines of the studio system was such that he decided to take matters into his own hands.

Through his attorney, and after seeking the advice of Mrs Mabel Hildebrandt, a former US assistant Attorney General, Price contacted the FBI direct. On 27 April 1954, in the company of his wife and with their attorney present, he was interviewed by two agents with the intention that he would make a statement on the record as well as answer any questions that they might wish to put to him in connection. He denied that he had ever had Communist sympathies, or that he had knowingly been a member of any organisation with Communist affiliations, and he refuted each and every allegation in relation to his dealings with the specific organisations which were listed in the charge, stating that all the invitations he had received to appear or speak at cultural forums had been accepted in good faith and in complete innocence. In shades of Oscar Wilde, who had been tried, but convicted, more than half a century before on another roster of false allegations, innuendo and rumour, Price even called his theories about art to his defence, declaring that it was his belief that art could not survive under Communist or Fascist influence, where no freedom of expression was allowed to exist, and he went on to defend contemporary art against the charge that it was Communist-inspired.

The one sour note came when Price suggested that he and the vast majority of those who had signed an advertisement in the *Hollywood Reporter* in 1947 in support of the CFA would not have done so had they been apprised of facts that had since come to light, and that all who stood on the Fifth Amendment as cover for treasonable activity should be considered subversive and dealt with accordingly.

If it was a performance, then it was the performance of Price's life. The FBI agents who questioned him were suitably impressed and stated that he appeared to be entirely co-operative and sincere throughout. When the lengthy interview came to a close, Price was informed with due gravitas that, notwithstanding the voluntary nature of his admissions, the FBI did not itself clear anyone for employment in the motion picture industry or anywhere else. In the climate of fear which was created by the 'witch-hunts', nothing could have been further from the truth.

Within months of Price's testimony to exonerate himself of the charges against him, Senator McCarthy had been thoroughly discredited and his Un-American Activities Committee disbanded. He died

three years later. John S Wood retired to his law practice and died in 1968. The taint of this 'purge' lingered in Hollywood for a long time, not so much because of the nature or purpose of the inquiry, but because of the methods used to achieve its ends. Both Sam Jaffe and Marsha Hunt found themselves blacklisted, along with 321 other actors, writers and directors. For Vincent Price, the episode represented a narrow escape from professional oblivion. He put copies of the documents which he had signed into brown envelopes and secreted them in the proverbial bottom drawer. Obsessed by a deep-seated fear of financial failure which had been instilled in him since childhood, he also vowed that, from this point on, he would accept everything that came his way – most particularly in the young medium of television – no matter what the role.

While his employment status within the industry remained uncertain, Price was deprived of his screen credit on a film which he already had completed for Paramount but which went into release in March 1954: *Casanova's Big Night*. (The same company was also to deny him credit for a voice-over in *The Vagabond King* a year later.) Additionally, he lost out to Karl Malden on another project which originally had been designed with him in mind: *Phantom of the Rue Morgue*, Warner Bros' 1954 follow-up to *House of Wax*, also shot in 3-D.

To make up for the shortfall in big-screen appearances, Price took whatever was offered. American television had kept its distance from the HUAC spotlight and the medium came to his rescue with roles in a number of one-off dramas for anthology series such as *Climax*, *TV Reader's Digest* and *Science Fiction Theatre*. Period-suited and heavily bearded, he played the lead in a documentary made on behalf of the American Petroleum Institute, which told the story of the oil strike pioneered by Edwin L Drake and Uncle Billy Smith at Titusville, Pennsylvania in 1859, which in turn inaugurated the American oil industry. The film is screened at the Titusville Oil Museum to this day, under the title of *Born in Freedom* – though the real Drake died in penury in 1880, having made not a dime out of his momentous discovery.

These and more kept the wolf from the door until 1956, when the Almighty himself – in his earthly form as safari-jacketed, bullwhip-equipped, autocratic Bible-belt director Cecil Blount DeMille – came down from the mountain-top, megaphone in hand, and returned Vincent Price to the Hollywood fold.

It may take time, but a way can – and will – be found.
COLONEL DRAKE (VINCENT PRICE),
THE STORY OF COLONEL DRAKE (1954)

Price returned 'officially' to the screen in March 1956, after Warners had made it up to him by offering him a co-starring role in *Serenade*, a vehicle for opera singer Mario Lanza, though that was actually beaten into release by *Son of Sinbad*, a frothy Arabian Nights confection that Price had made for RKO Radio and producer Howard Hughes more than two years before. A second RKO feature which the actor had shot in June 1954 – *While the City Sleeps* – was also held up in release for almost two years, due partly to his participation in the project.

The cloud which had obscured his film career for more than a year appeared finally to have lifted when Cecil B DeMille included Price among the all-star cast of a multi-million dollar remake of his own silent screen epic, *The Ten Commandments*, complete with relevant billing. The film went into production on a six-month schedule in the spring of 1955; its backer was Paramount, which hitherto had fought shy of advertising the Price name, but no one in the industry at that time would have argued with DeMille either.

In *The Ten Commandments*, Price was the architect of the Pharaoh Sethi's Golden City and Biblical recipient of Moses' murderous ire. The film's grasp of historical facts was a thousand years out but it eventually led Price to another of the same at the end of the following year. His next appearance on screen seemed more in keeping: he was hired by Twentieth Century-Fox to play the Devil in an ambitious adaptation of a best-selling exercise in pop anthropology which had been written by Hendrick Van Loon back in 1922, and which attempted to encompass the whole of human civilisation into its storyline, not just the Egyptian part of it.

Before embarking on *The Story of Mankind*, Price's acting skills had been relegated to the bargain-basement of television drama where he was called upon to appear in three episodes of *Crossroads*, an anthology series which depicted the work of the clergy! Playing Old Nick for producer Irwin Allen must have felt like a relief after all that

Vincent and Mary Price

sanctimonious sermonising, but it typified his television persona, which was at once benign, amiable and family-friendly – saint on the small screen, sinner on the large.

Price completed his role in *The Story of Mankind* early in 1957. Eighteen months later, his co-star and boyhood idol Ronald Colman – a movie icon of long standing – was dead. In 1959, the cinematically flamboyant Cecil B DeMille would also pass on to that great studio in the sky, and a school of film-making that dated back to *The Squaw Man* in 1913 would pass on with him. Since the early 1950s, more than 5,000 drive-in movie theatres had sprung up across America. On the other side of the Atlantic, meanwhile, a full 25 per cent of the British population was now under 18 years old. In terms of the emergence of a 'youth market' which trends like these appeared to point towards, Vincent Price's next outing on Hollywood stages was to be geared to a whole different audience from his last.

ACT 2

ROCK 'N' ROLL MONSTERS

Have you ever tried to explain to a sleepy police officer that your sister-in-law has just phoned to say that she has killed your brother with a steam-hammer?

GEORGE LANGELAAN, THE FLY (1957)

When it came to star-packed super-movies like *The Ten Commandments* (and Mike Todd's equally extravagant *Around the World in Eighty Days*), the concept of casting against type was an alien one. In consequence, Charlton Heston's Moses strode through an ancient civilisation whose demographic profile was striking in the extent to which it was composed of familiar faces, all of them in roles which played to audience expectation. John Derek was an action hero in Hebrew garb, Henry Wilcoxon a captain-at-arms, Edward G Robinson a devious schemer, Anne Baxter a seductress, Judith Anderson a matriarch, Sir Cedric Hardwicke a patriarch, and Vincent Price the villain who met his just desserts in the desert sands of Paramount's Culver City lot, in deference to his character in *House of Wax*.

The name of Vincent Price should have become synonymous not only with villainy but also with horror as far back as 1954, after *House of Wax*, *The Mad Magician*, and what was intended to have been his encore for Warners, *Phantom of the Rue Morgue* – and *would* have had, had not the trajectory of his career been impeded by the unwarranted attentions of the FBI. Nevertheless, he had been lucky; more than careers had been lost among others on whom the McCarthyite spotlight had fallen. Since then, he had been required to pull up his bootstraps and start over again on the Hollywood scene, his rising star as a leading man in *Laura* (for director Otto Preminger), *Dragonwyck* (Joseph L Mankiewicz), or *The Three Musketeers* (George Sidney) having been snuffed out forever by the over-zealous intrusion of authoritarianism.

Price had found himself relegated to essaying only minor roles in such disposable items as *Serenade*, and his future in films seemed suddenly to reside in the relative backwater of character parts in whatever

projects came his way. These were trying times, and he diverted his not inconsiderable energies into his beloved theatre and many artistic pursuits. Even his cameo appearance as the Devil in the star-studded Irwin Allen production of *The Story of Mankind* had ignited no flashes of inspiration among the creative brains of Hollywood as to how the Price talents could best be utilised.

1957 was another dead year. No feature films were offered him and Price had to content himself with a 'pilot' for a television series in which he and Peter Lorre played a pair of art dealers – *The Left Fist of David* was directed by Buzz Kulik, but it remained unsold. In the meantime, he bolstered the family coffers by volunteering himself as a candidate to answer CBS's *$64,000 Dollar Question*, which he won on his chosen subject of art history and then came back and won *again* (against Edward G Robinson) in a spin-off of the original called *$64,000 Dollar Challenge*.

Price's devotion to art and artists became a mainstay during the slack times, and he now threw himself into it with renewed vigour: gallery openings, lecture tours, after-dinner speeches – all of them contributed to his growing status as collector and expert on the culture circuit. As to his acting career, things were still looking bleak.

Vincent Price's early successes on the stage had not been matched by a similar rise in his stock on screen. Despite having appeared in more than 40 feature films since 1938, Price, at 46, remained a supporting act who seemed to fit into no particular mould as far as casting agents were concerned. His still-handsome but now bejowelled face deprived him of the romantic roles which might have been his after *Dragonwyck*, his 'grey-listing' had set him apart from the movers and shakers who could have shaped his career, and his insistence on returning to the theatre at regular intervals had removed him from a

Hollywood machine which might have nurtured him as a specific 'type.'

Price's enforced absence from the cinema screen had been coincident with the first term in elected office of the 34th President of the United States, Dwight D(avid) Eisenhower, the man who had brought an end to hostilities in the Korean War. The beginnings of a new era of peace and prosperity for the American people had been ushered in by a virtual revolution in popular music, spearheaded by a 20-year-old rockabilly singer from Tupelo, Mississippi, and a country and western outfit led by a 30-year-old ex-drinks-bottler with a beer belly and a 'kiss'-curl. Between them, Elvis Aaron Presley and William John Clifton ('Bill') Haley had introduced America, and the world, to what New York-based deejay Alan Freed christened 'rock 'n' roll' music. In their wake had followed a host of recording artists from both sides of the colour divide, many of whom were to become legends in their own lifetimes – Jerry Lee Lewis, Chuck Berry, Little Richard, Buddy Holly and Eddie Cochran, to name but the first of many. It had taken no time at all for the air of rebellion that was epitomised by rock 'n' roll to become integrated into the movies, as well.

The increasing affluence of youth was also changing the profile of the traditional cinema audience, and the demands of a younger demographic had forced Hollywood to make films with more youthful appeal. Noir thrillers had given way to tales of teen angst and juvenile delinquency, westerns were being replaced by monster movies, and musicals starring Doris Day and Howard Keel found themselves elbowed aside by those that showcased artists from the nation's 'Top Twenty', like Pat Boone, The Platters or Fats Domino.

Along with these changes, a new kind of actor had arrived. Stars such as Marlon Brando and James Dean had no classical training and even less regard for the declamatory approach of many of their peers, and in films like *The Wild One* (1954) and *East of Eden* (1955) they had at last wrenched Hollywood free of its long-standing ties to the stage. Price was a stage actor at heart, and already he was aware that few routes into film were likely to remain open to him as a result of such a seismic upheaval in popular taste. As he recalled for *Cinefantastique* in relation to his friend Basil Rathbone: "He had been a great Shakespearean actor, a great star in the theatre and in movies. And he suddenly found for himself – as we all did when Jimmy

Dean and Marlon Brando and those people came out, and there was a kind of speaking in the vernacular, and all of us spoke with trained accents and trained English and theatrically we were different in our approach to acting – that if you wanted to stay in the business, you bloody well went into costume pictures."

The fact that Price could also out-act most of his peers cut little ice with producers in an industry where actors were hired as a commodity and not for any innate talent they might possess. He could assume a villainous air with the best of them, but so could dozens of others and with a lot less subtlety. By the late 1950s, his suave charm was in danger of becoming a thing of the past. His meticulous approach to his profession seemed to be dated and stage-bound when set against the 'Method' acting advocated by Lee Strasberg at the New York Actor's Studio and adopted by a veritable tidal wave of new faces: Rod Steiger, Montgomery Clift, Paul Newman. "I really hate acting that is 'true to life'," Price informed *Films and Filming* in 1965. "Marlon Brando is a superb actor, but he is much more baroque than I will ever be – in *Sayonara*, he used an accent that was not Southern, it was coloured... a complete phoney from beginning to end."

One type of film which Price had not previously considered had now become hugely popular, however. Horror fantasy had always required a style of acting that was larger than life, to give credibility to what were otherwise incredible scenarios. It was also a genre which was much favoured by the young and which entirely avoided the attentions of so-called 'Method' actors, or anyone to whom an empathetic approach to characterisation was an essential of their technique. Price had never thought of adopting horror as his métier – he had enough trouble simply looking for work – but after years of wandering in the cinematic wilderness, he was about to find that it was intent on adopting him.

Working with DeMille was now followed by the next best thing in terms of Hollywood status – working with Alfred Hitchcock. Admittedly, the role Price was offered was no more than a character cameo in a single segment of the long-running MCA television series *Alfred Hitchcock Presents*, but it was another step in the right direction.

Since 1955, the half-hour format of *Alfred Hitchcock Presents* had provided a television showcase for short stories of mystery or the macabre, drawn primarily from magazines and the pulps. Each episode was introduced by Hitchcock himself, in typically lugubrious pose, though he personally directed less than two dozen of the 268 that eventually spanned seven years of prime-time. Among those that he graced with his presence was *The Perfect Crime*, a story by Ben Ray Redman which had first seen publication in *Harper's* in 1928, but which producer Joan Harrison had plucked from *Ellery Queen's Mystery Magazine* in 1951. Price and co-star James Gregory were initially thrilled to find themselves in the directorial hands of the maestro, until they became more familiar with his technique: "We looked over at him in one of the run-throughs and he was sound asleep, or else pretending to be sound asleep," Price recalled. "He did that all the time."

Just below that surface of studied courtesy, Mr Courtney, lies a cover. And the real Charles Courtney lives beneath that cover – impervious, untouched and unmoved.

JOHN GREGORY (JAMES GREGORY),
ALFRED HITCHCOCK PRESENTS:
THE PERFECT CRIME (1957)

In *The Perfect Crime*, Price plays Charles Courtney, a Sherlock Holmes-like consulting detective in 1912 New York, who prides himself on never having failed to deduce the malefactor in the numerous murders that required his involvement. To underline his unbroken record of successes, he maintains a trophy cabinet in which he keeps mementoes of the cases that he has solved. Defence attorney John Gregory (James Gregory) calls at his home to deconstruct his latest 'solution' and inform Courtney that he has just sent an innocent man to his death. Unable to tolerate the damage to his reputation that Gregory's revelation would cause, the bluff Courtney strangles his tormentor.

It becomes clear why Price was cast in the film when it ends with Courtney showing his trophies to a pair of reporters, one of whom catches sight of a small vase in a spot that previously had been left vacant for a token of the 'perfect crime.' Courtney's hobby is ceramics, and an adjacent room houses a kiln. He explains the vase away by declaring that it was just an experiment, for which he used "a rather special kind of clay."

In 1958, the boom in apocalyptic science-fiction films which Paramount had effectively set in motion with *When Worlds Collide* (1951) and *The War of the*

Worlds (1953) was still going strong, although it had been augmented with monster-fare of an increasingly disparate kind since Warner Bros unleashed *Them!* in 1954. In the face of the overwhelming popularity of a plethora of such films from a revitalised Universal-International, such as *This Island Earth*, *The Incredible Shrinking Man* and *Invasion of the Body Snatchers*, others opted to join the bandwagon. Of the remaining studios which comprised the Hollywood 'Big 5', M-G-M had taken the plunge with *Forbidden Planet* (1956) – only Twentieth Century-Fox, under then-president Spyros P Skouras, had so far managed to resist the trend, preferring to stick with its familiar diet of period costumers, musicals and lush romantic melodramas.

Fox's big hit of 1958 was to be the roadshow spectacular *South Pacific*. But the continuing threat from television, the expensive technical failure of Cinemascope 55 and a spate of slack financial returns from more conventional product had forced a rethink, and Fox therefore purchased the rights to a short story by George Langelaan which had been published in *Playboy* magazine in June 1957. The studio was not averse to farming an occasional exploitation programmer out to one of several 'shadow' companies, such as that run by B-movie producer and one-time theatre owner Robert L Lippert, where involvement was limited to distribution only. On this occasion, however, the wily Fox decided to put its corporate logo where its money was going.

The Fly was typical of the kind of horror stories which had come to dominate anthologies of weird tales since the 1930s. An emphasis on physical gruesomeness was the keynote of this new breed of fiction, and the proliferation of paperback publishing after the Second World War had seen the more traditional ghost story entirely supplanted by a more visceral stablemate in the 1950s, though the popularity of the latter was not so universal as that of the former.

Given its format, *The Fly* unfolds as a tale of mystery rather in the manner of Robert Louis Stevenson's *Strange Case of Dr Jekyll and Mr Hyde*, opening after the cessation of the events with which it is really concerned and travelling back in time to unravel the puzzle and supply a satisfactory solution to it.

The story is set in France, and it opens with Hélène Delambre informing her brother-in-law François that she has just slain her husband by

*Eugene Borden,
Herbert
Marshall,
Vincent Price
and Patricia
Owens in*
THE FLY

crushing his head in an industrial steam-press, a
crime for which she is immediately incarcerated in
an insane asylum. As a police investigation gets
underway, it transpires that André Delambre, who
worked for the French Air Ministry, had been
conducting experiments into matter-transference, and
that one such experiment had gone mysteriously, but
catastrophically, wrong. All is finally revealed in a
written statement penned by Hélène prior to her own
climactic suicide and read by François, who is also
the narrator of the tale. In an echo of Jekyll's
post-mortem confession in the Stevenson story,
Hélène reveals that André had experimented on
himself in his attempt to disintegrate/reintegrate
atoms and that, during the experiment, a fly had
inadvertently been allowed to enter the transmitter
and their atoms had intertwined, along with those of
an earlier failed attempt on the family cat.

André, as a result of this oversight, had ended up
with the fly's head (as well as the cat's ear and nose)
and, at his own request, Hélène had crushed the
offending article under the steam-hammer. Hélène's
confession is taken with a large pinch of salt by
Commissaire Charras of the Sûrété until François

stumbles upon a fly with a 'white head' which hitherto
has flitted in and out of the narrative. Finding it
trapped in a spider's web, he crushes it to death – as
Hélène had done to its human counterpart – and
buries it in a matchbox alongside his brother.

James Clavell's screenplay for the film stuck strictly
to the letter of Langelaan's short story, deviating from
it only in the matter of Hélène's suicide by cyanide
poisoning and the appending of a son to the Delambre
union, on the premise that a child might look less
foolish than an adult when it came to hunting down
an insect with a human head. Despite its American
leads and the domestic nature of the production, the
action was relocated to Canada rather than the States,
in an effort to accommodate the French names of
Langelaan's protagonists.

Whoever did this to André – they did it twice!
FRANÇOIS DELAMBRE (VINCENT PRICE),
THE FLY (1958)

Vincent Price was cast in the sympathetic but
essentially neutral role of François Delambre, his
name being employed for marquee value in the main,

Herbert Marshall and Vincent Price in THE FLY

while the role of the title-monster was allocated to Al Hedison, a Fox contract player who was required to spend much of his time on screen with his features hidden beneath a black silk towel. Another contract star, Michael Rennie (who had helped the company to success with *The Day the Earth Stood Still* in 1951) turned the film down and, despite objections from Fox Head of Production Buddy Adler, Price was brought in to replace him on the strength of the huge grosses that had greeted *House of Wax* five years earlier.

As a high-value studio production of what was essentially a pulp concept, *The Fly* has much to commend it. In line with the times, Langelaan's *The Fly* was a horror story in science fiction guise, but the film re-emphasised the sci-fi element and confined the horror to its two set-piece scenes: the discovery of

André's body under the steam-press – a genuinely horrendous image – and Hélène inadvertently stumbling upon the exact nature of the fate which has befallen her unfortunate husband.

The viewer has been primed throughout to suspect that André has absorbed the atoms of the fly that has entered his matter-transmitter at the inopportune moment; he *sucks* at his food under cover of a cloth, while his wife is out of sight but still within earshot, and starts to chalk increasingly desperate messages on the blackboard in his lab – "Brain says strange things now... feel my will going" – before the black pincer that was once his left hand can grab hold of his right to stop him, in scenes which would influence Terry Southern and Stanley Kubrick when they came to create *Dr Strangelove*.

The revelation, when it comes, is nonetheless one of the screen's greatest moments of shock: "I know it's worked!" Hélène exclaims, after André has again tried in vain to reverse the process, as she whips the towel away to reveal a giant fly-head, complete with shimmering eyes, a distended proboscis and twitching antennae, in an unmasking scene to rank alongside those of *The Phantom of the Opera* and *Mystery of the Wax Museum*.

George Langelaan had conceived it thus: "The horror was too much for me, too unexpected. As a matter of fact, I am sure that, even had I known, the horror-impact could hardly have been less powerful. Trying to push both hands into my mouth to stifle my screams and although my fingers were bleeding, I screamed again and again. I could not take my eyes off him, I could not even close them, and yet I knew that if I looked at the horror much longer, I would go on screaming for the rest of my life."

Hélène's screams are magnified by a shot of her face which is intended to emulate the view through the fly's compound-lensed eyes. It is this kaleidoscopic image, as much as the fly-head itself, which fully imparts the hammer-blow: '...her eyes seemed to be screaming with fear' was Langelaan's vision, and nowhere in the history of horror is the written word better translated to the screen. Ben Nye's superb mask for Al Hedison brings the monster to life in a way that bears striking relation to imagined reality (unlike that in the eventual sequel), and the moment of fright which the sequence engenders as André advances, his head jerking involuntarily from side to side, ranks as one of the most overwhelming ever committed to film.

The long and harrowing opening sequence of Hélène crushing André's head and arm in the press is starkly horrific in its clinical staging. At the other end of the scale, the climactic scene in which André the fly screams 'Help me!' from the confines of the spider web may be unintentionally risible, but it makes perfect sense in terms of the internal logic of Clavell's script – as the fly's brain has inexorably subsumed that of the man (a consequence which would be made more of in David Cronenberg's 1986 remake with Jeff Goldblum in the title role), so André's has taken control of the insect's.

Director Kurt Neumann, who died before the film went into release, makes good use of the Scope screen, though oft-repeated scenes of André's laboratory in full matter-transmitting flood ape those

in *Forbidden Planet* of only two years before, even to the inclusion of the 'electronic tonalities' which accompany the action. Despite its employment of De Luxe colour and Cinemascope surface sheen, *The Fly* was something of a throwback to mad-scientist movies of the 1930s and 40s; it was not the start of a new era in science fiction but the end of an old one. "There are things man should never experiment with," André remarks, harking back to the moral philosophies of the pre-atomic age.

Nevertheless, *The People* thought the film was "so skilfully built up, so well acted, and so taut with terror that the effect is harrowing," while the *Spectator* magazine conceded, somewhat reluctantly, that "plush horror has arrived; in other words, monstrosity has achieved a kind of respectability which is hardly a pretty thought..."

The film's most unsettling scene comes when André excitedly atomises the family cat, only to find that he cannot reintegrate it again. "A stream of cat atoms" emit a ghostly meow around the lab and hint metaphorically of the dangers ahead, both for André and for mankind itself. In such interludes did the science fiction films of the 1950s truly capture the essence of the 'brave new worlds' to which their protagonists were travelling with eyes wide shut.

> He was like an explorer in a wild country, where no one had ever been before... He was searching for the truth. He almost found a great truth but, for one instant, he was careless.
>
> **FRANÇOIS DELAMBRE** (VINCENT PRICE),
> THE FLY (1958)

After the first two reels, Price's contribution to the film is minimal and his name attaches to it only in retrospect. The real star of the show is Al Hedison, a Fox contract player for whom the studio had high hopes and who went from here to *The Lost World* (1960) before adopting his middle-name in place of his first and settling down as David Hedison to a long run in television's *Voyage to the Bottom of the Sea*.

However, the cumulative effect of having featured in two high-profile shockers now began to gravitate Price more assuredly towards a career in the macabre. With *The Fly*, sci-fi horror gained respectability; the conventional horror thriller was still to do so. Herbert Marshall's Inspector Charras struggled manfully with the prosthetic left leg the actor had worn in secret since losing his own in

Herbert Marshall, Charles Herbert and Vincent Price in THE FLY

World War II, but less manfully with a screenplay which required him to seek out a fly with a tiny human head. Marshall and Price almost died laughing when it came to shooting the climax of the film, in which the fly-torsoed André is discovered in a spider's web, headed for ingestion by the resident arachnid. They eventually managed to pull it off – just – but not without some cost to the credibility of what had gone before.

The Fly opened in the US in July 1958 and grossed $3 million for Fox from an investment of $350,000. The inevitable sequel followed it into production nine months later but, when it surfaced, it was audiences who were to find themselves dying of laughter.

> *Murder... You've seen guys beat a murder rap.*
> *Besides, who could frame a perfect murder better*
> *than you? – Crime is your business.*
> **PAUL HENDRICKS** (VINCENT PRICE),
> *KEY WITNESS*: TALL, DARK AND HANDSOME
> (1958)

In the meantime, the best that Vincent Price could manage to keep himself in the public eye was a job as host of a pilot for a dubious game show called *Key Witness*, in which a pre-filmed playlet was screened before an invited audience who could then win prize-money by answering questions of observation about the events they had just watched. Price doubled as a feature-player in the drama, a vignette of *Double Indemnity*, wherein he was allotted the role of a private detective with an eye for the ladies and a preference for a pencil-thin moustache. *Key Witness* also went unsold, despite Price's best efforts as smooth-talking emcee, but the moustachioed persona of 'Paul Hendricks' *did* find a slot for itself, independently of the vehicle which had brought it into being.

With the inevitable decline of the Hollywood studio system, new moguls were surfacing in place of the old – all of them entrepreneurs with their eyes to the main chance and their fingers firmly on the unpredictable pulse of public taste. A younger, more volatile audience required a faster, more flexible response from those who professed to cater for it. Rock 'n' roll music had been the vanguard of the change, but the cinema was catching up fast. The ability to sense and immediately reflect new trends had become the exclusive preserve of companies which were small and tight-knit. In place of the ailing 'Big 5', American International in the United States and Hammer and Anglo Amalgamated in Britain were the names that were now making all the running. Their common strategy was a simple one: find a subject with generic or contemporary appeal, buy it cheaply, and sell it *big*.

Alone with his thoughts in a coffee-bar outside M-G-M's studios one evening in July 1958, Price was accosted by a junior-league producer named William Castle. Castle was small-time; born William Schloss (of which 'Castle' was the literal translation), he had broken into the film business in 1939 as a trainee at Columbia under legendary studio boss Harry Cohn, after trying and failing to become an actor. By 1943, Castle was a contract director on second features for Columbia and he first made his mark with a thriller called *The Whistler* (1944), which went on to sire several sequels. In 1948, he acquired an associate producer credit on Orson Welles' *The Lady from Shanghai*.

Castle's speciality was thinking up gimmicks to aid ticket-sales, a penchant which had taken root during a brief period spent backstage with a touring production of Lugosi's *Dracula*, and a roster of reliable programme-fillers throughout the forties and fifties had secured him a position as a Hollywood journeyman of no great distinction. But in 1957, he had decided to put his flair for showmanship to better use by turning independent: the dividend had been immediate.

Castle was riding high on the biggest success of his career to date: a sub-Hitchcock thriller called *Macabre*, which revolved around the burial alive of a child and which had caught the attention of the trades through its ploy of offering to insure patrons against death by fright during screenings of the film. *Macabre* had gone on to recoup many times its production cost, and Castle was keen to capitalise on the aspects of it which he felt had helped to bring that about: a novel plot and an over-the-top advertising campaign. *Macabre* had bought William Castle a seat at Hollywood's top table and now he was seated opposite Price, pitching another grade Z horror film with an even more outlandish premise than his last:

"A millionaire invites six people to spend the night in a haunted house. He chooses the people carefully and offers to pay a great deal of money to each one if they agree to spend the entire night in the haunted house. During the night, many strange ghostly things happen... blood dripping from the ceiling... walls shaking... apparitions appearing. The millionaire – the part I want you to play – has plotted to kill his wife. She plots to kill you... It's a battle of wits."

As Castle tells it, Price's initial lack of interest was barely concealed by the obliging politeness of a tolerant ear, his only concern being the pressing one of typecasting. But Castle persisted. "She tries to throw you into a vat of boiling acid," he climaxed. "Suddenly you rise slowly from the vat... body eaten away. You're just bones, a living *skeleton*! Your skeleton scares the shit out of your wife and she loses her balance and falls into the vat of acid."

His audience was at a low ebb, however, having just lost out on another role of substance, and Castle had picked his moment well. "Charming," Price observed drily, and by the time the two of them left the table, he had agreed to the film in principle.

Price's own recollection of the deal with Castle was a little less whimsical: "My agent said, 'He won't pay you anything', so I said, 'Well, let's take a percentage'." And on that less fanciful basis, he and the Hendricks moustache signed up to star in *House on Haunted Hill*.

The ghosts are moving tonight – restless, hungry...
WATSON PRITCHARD (ELISHA COOK JR),
HOUSE ON HAUNTED HILL (1958)

William Castle's finest hour starts as it means to go on. *House on Haunted Hill* opens on a blank screen, but the soundtrack is soon filled with the noise of clanking chains, shrill screams and ghoulish laughter. A disembodied head appears in view: "In just a minute, I'll show you the only really haunted house in the world," advises Watson Pritchard (the creepy Elisha Cook). "Since it was built... seven people, including my brother, have been murdered in it. Since then, I've owned the house. I've only spent one night there and when they found me in the morning, I was almost dead." It is a brilliant entrée, precisely crafted to extract terrified squeals of delight from the bobby-soxers at whom Castle's film was primarily aimed.

Screenwriter Robb White was Filipino by birth, so the manifestations to come tended to be of the gnashing, wailing South East Asian variety, grisly and pantomimic. All of this makes for good, camp, Hallowe'en-style fun, though, and the tongue-in-cheek

Publicity shot from HOUSE ON HAUNTED HILL

tone is established from the off, when Price's head also appears in shot to intone the outline of the unlikely plot:

> *I'm Frederick Loren, and I've rented the House on Haunted Hill tonight so that my wife can give a party – a haunted house party... She's so amusing. There'll be food, and drink, and... ghosts. And perhaps even a few murders. You're all invited. If any of you will spend the next 12 hours in this house, I'll give you each $10,000 – or your next of kin, in case you don't survive. Ah, but here come our other guests...*
>
> **FREDERICK LOREN** (VINCENT PRICE),
> *HOUSE ON HAUNTED HILL* (1958)

Weird things befall the group of invited guests – most of them homing in on Nora Manning

(Carolyn Craig), a young employee of Loren's. By the time his wife Annabel (Carol Ohmart) is discovered hanging from a balcony, Nora is nearly out of her mind with fear. But all the occupants of the house have been armed with a pistol by their conscientious host, and when Nora is enticed into the cellar, she shoots at a figure that approaches in the dark. She has killed Loren himself. At this point, the real plot cuts in: it is all a conspiracy by Annabel and her psychiatrist lover David Trent (Alan Marshall), also one of the guests, to drive Nora mad enough to commit murder by proxy and dispose of Loren for them. Nora having flown the scene, Annabel and Trent arrive in the basement to confirm the dastardly deed – but the lights go out and Trent is tumbled into a vat of acid. A skeleton rises up out of the noxious liquid and Annabel follows her beau into the vat. Loren appears

Publicity shot from HOUSE ON HAUNTED HILL

unharmed, confesses to his five guests that he had known all along about the plot to kill him and had simply turned the tables on the murderous twosome, and places himself in the hands of the law.

The presence of a psychiatrist as the voice of sanity in the face of all the ghostly goings-on borrows from Ealing's *Dead of Night* (1945), but White gives the notion a twist by having him subvert his professional abilities to the furtherance of a murderous plan to dispose of Loren. Staying in a supposedly haunted house for a night was a staple of the literary ghost story – among of the best examples of the breed are H Russell Wakefield's *The Frontier Guards* and Michael Arlen's *A Gentleman from America* (which in 1958 was adapted for *Alfred Hitchcock Presents*).

Castle was unable to find a suitable venue for his haunted house-party, so he hired an art deco house in the Hollywood Hills designed by Frank Lloyd Wright;

consequently, the exterior shots of the supposed 'House on Haunted Hill' fail to gel with his pre-filmed Gothic interiors, but the anomaly passes by unnoticed in context. Some of the spectral occurences – in particular a scene in which the hanged Annabel looms into view on the other side of a window, complete with self-coiling rope – could never have been contrived by human agency, but such minor flaws are amply covered by artistic licence.

Carolyn Craig as the focus of the murderous prank is the weakest point of the film; neither very talented nor particularly attractive, she was a curious choice for the role and one can only assume that she was some-one's girlfriend. The weakness in Robb White's script is that it only allows suspicion to fall on Loren and/or his wife. But it gave Price more than his usual share of lip-smacking lines to relish, and he savours every one.

The Castle gimmick for promoting *House on Haunted Hill* topped that which the excitable showman had dreamed up for *Macabre*. In essence, it was comprised of a glowing 12-foot plastic skeleton, which was popped out of a box at the side of the screen and drawn along on a wire to dangle precariously over the heads of the audience. The complex mechanics of such a stunt confined its deployment to first-run houses only, but the word-of-mouth on 'Emergo', as Castle typically christened it, more than made up for its absence at other play-dates. Present or not, Emergo did the trick and *House on Haunted Hill* proved to be a box-office smash.

The film was advertised in addition as having the '13 Greatest Shocks of All Time!', which like everything which emanated from Castle was grossly exaggerated, but some of the 'greatest' shock-scenes in *House on Haunted Hill* do indeed deliver the goods, even without the prop of Emergo – particularly an encounter in a dark cellar with the blind wife of the creepy caretaker. Shocking or not, the iconography of the pulps is everywhere in evidence: blood drips from the ceiling, a severed head is found in a suitcase, a harpsichord plays of its own volition, a clawed hand reaches out from behind a curtain.

House on Haunted Hill is remembered for its iconic imagery in a number of sequences, the stills from which have supported numerous texts about horror films. But it is a murder mystery, in truth, modelled along the lines of Henri-Georges Clouzot's *Les Diaboliques*, and of a kind which Castle would repeat in *The Tingler* (1960), in *Homicidal* (1961) and again in *The Night Walker* (1964). The perambulating skeleton at the climax is just ridiculous, and it required all the help that Emergo could provide to pass muster even in story terms. Like all such plots (which Hammer's Jimmy Sangster later made into something of a spe-ciality), foreknowledge on the part of the protagonists is needed for events to go as planned, but if the end result is as entertaining as *House on Haunted Hill*, that is neither here nor there. "They're coming for me now, and then... they'll come for you," Pritchard exhorts to camera at the close, apparently oblivious of the rational explanation for all the spooky happenings which has just been imparted to him.

The crime you two planned was indeed perfect, but the victim is alive and the murderers are not. It's a pity you didn't know when you started your game of murder... that I was playing too.
FREDERICK LOREN (VINCENT PRICE), *HOUSE ON HAUNTED HILL* (1958)

Despite the fact that *The Fly* had performed a fiscal feat to rival that of *House of Wax* at the box-office and that *House on Haunted Hill* looked set to do likewise, Price's services were not called upon by casting agents for the remainder of 1958. A summons from *The Story of Mankind*'s Irwin Allen put him into *The Big Circus* at the start of 1959, as ringmaster Hans Hagenfeld; the part had all the makings of a scene-stealer from co-stars Victor Mature and Red Buttons, but it was underwritten and Price could do nothing with it in the event, save to parade around in a scarlet jacket and crack a bullwhip with DeMille-like panache. Nevertheless, he now had two consecutive hits on his hands with his forays into horror, and it was a new and more commanding Price who took to the stage for the expository opening of *Return of the Fly*.

In later years, Price was characteristically tolerant of one of the low-points of his entire acting career. "It was actually a better script than *The Fly*," he remarked of its sequel. "But the first one had taken the edge off it." Setting aside the vested interests of an actor when it comes to his own scenes in any specific film, *Return of the Fly* was in no way better than its predecessor. For one thing, it lacked the originality which was the first film's great strength. For another, Price had read only a rough draft of the script before signing to do the film and it was subsequently amended, reducing his role and the costs which would have accrued had it been shot as written.

Fox's lack of interest in pursuing a sequel to *The Fly* was exemplified by the fact that the studio farmed out the production to a subsidiary called Associated Producers in the form of 53-year-old Chicago-born quickie-merchant Edward L Bernds, merely retaining distribution rights in the final product. As a writer, Bernds had been responsible for *World Without End* (1954) and *Queen of Outer Space* (1956) and his previous directorial assignment was *High School Hellcats* (1958), so Frank Capra's one-time sound engineer was not a man whose name might have featured prominently on a short-list to stage a follow-up to the most successful science fiction film of its year had there been any real concern about the outcome. But like André Delambre's in *The Fly*, Fox's collective mind was currently elsewhere.

In light of the above, the plot of *Return of the Fly* was strictly grade Z material. André's son Philippe, now grown to manhood, takes up matter-transmission where his father left off, in the style of the Universal

Brett Halsey and Vincent Price in RETURN OF THE FLY

sequels of old. His unsavoury assistant is intent on stealing the secret for himself but when his scheming is exposed, a fight ensues. He knocks Philippe unconscious and attempts to dispose of him by placing him in the disintegrator along with a housefly: Hey Presto! – A man with a fly's head. The 'Fly' pursues the criminals to their lair and kills them both; back in the lab, nice Uncle François reverses the transmission process and returns Philippe to his normal self. No marks for originality there, then.

Bernds hired Brett Halsey – of *High School Hellcats* fame – to play the role of Philippe, but apart from Price and John Sutton (who previously had starred alongside Price in *Tower of London* and who was brought in to replace an ailing Herbert Marshall), the remainder of the cast were strictly from hunger. Even the limited participation of the two leads did not allow the film to be shot in colour, though Fox loaned its Scope lens to the production.

Price is accorded a strong opening scene, in which he recounts the events of the original to Philippe in what remains of the standing set from *The Fly* (and

after a night-watchman has warned them against entering the lab, as Universal's peasants were inclined to do whenever unwary travellers came within striking distance of Castle Dracula). The Price that filmgoers were coming to expect could now be seen fully formed as a result of his appearance in *House on Haunted Hill*. Alternately rolling both his eyes and his 'r's, he makes the most of the only good lines in the entire script:

> François: *It's just as he left it.*
> Philippe: *The equipment – all smashed.*
> François: *Yes, he did it... in a blind rage... to destroy the machine he created because it destroyed him. It destroyed him* and *your mother!*

Budget and ingenuity were all used up by this point, however. Philippe soon falls in with a pair of stock villains called Alan and Max – the latter of whom is a mortician and unlikely part-time 'fence.' Nevertheless, he enables the machine to work again with the minor irritant that the reintegration process causes 'giantism' in any non-human participants.

When Philippe is inevitably encumbered with the head of a fly, it is ten times the size of that in the original film (presumably to compensate for the lack of colour). With it comes a remarkable insight into the plot which has been hatched against him, and he dishes out a cursory revenge against the dastardly duo before returning to the lab to have the tear in his genes repaired.

Return of the Fly was the polar opposite of the film that had sired it: cheap, careless and crass. From its Universal-inspired opening of a doomy visit to a cobweb-encrusted 'mad lab' in the middle of a thunderstorm to its monster-rally finale, it is pure drive-in drivel.

According to writer-director Bernds, Price was disquieted by the quality of his script: "Some cuts were made to trim it down," he explained to Price's biographer Lucy Chase Williams. "Vincent liked some of the scenes we had cut, and he objected." Producer Bernard Glasser concurred – "He was not overly enthusiastic about the screenplay." Price's protestations were hardly surprising: he had been asked to reprise his character of François Delambre from *The Fly*, but François disappears from the action after the opening reel and only returns at the end to be shot, whereupon he spends the remainder of the story confined to a hospital bed.

In paring down the dialogue and the participation of the leads, half the film's meagre running time had consequently to be taken up by the activities of more cost-effective extras: in an interminable sequence, Max (Dan Seymour) paces nervously in his funeral parlour as though literally awaiting direction, two stunt men (who also alternated in playing the 'Fly'), twice the age of the actors whom they are meant to represent, enact the key fight scene, and sundry policemen mark time for John Sutton's absent Inspector Beecham, in order to spread his few appearances more evenly throughout the production. If budding directors required a lesson on how to hire actors for a few days' work and give the impression that they are in an entire film, *Return of the Fly* is the graduate paper.

No slice of fifties' shlock-horror was complete without its acid repartee, and even Bernds manages to come up with some: when François queries Philippe's whereabouts, the man who has just stuffed his body into the matter-transmitter replies: "That's an interesting question, Mr Delambre. Shall we say he's serving the cause of science."

As the Fly buzzes unconvincingly around the countryside, the stunt man occupying the monster-suit in place of Halsey can clearly be seen grappling with the unwieldy mask to stop it from toppling off his shoulders. The only scene that improves on the original is the brief, if risible, superimposition of Halsey's head on a fly's body. As an example of a no-budget B-movie, *Return of the Fly* makes *Plan 9 from Outer Space* look like classic sci-fi.

Price's appearance in *The Fly* had at least brought him other films in the same vein, though all had put him on the slippery slope to poverty-row perdition insofar as their production values were concerned, while the threat of typecasting loomed larger than ever. After *Return of the Fly*, he seemed to have nowhere to go but down, as had all those stars before him who had been forced to dip their toes in the murky waters of exploitation horror for the drive-in market. Basil Rathbone, whom Price played opposite in 1939's *Tower of London*, had recently been seen inducting soporific audiences into *The Black Sleep* (1956), Boris Karloff had tramped grudgingly round

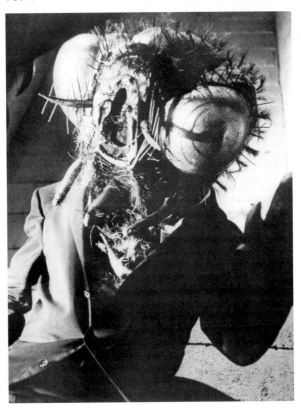

RETURN OF THE FLY

Voodoo Island (1957) before fashioning a monstrous mirror-image of himself for *Frankenstein 1970* (1958), and Glenn Langan, who had supported Price in *Dragonwyck*, had been stripped of his flesh and his dignity in *The Amazing Colossal Man* and *War of the Colossal Beast* (1958 and 1959 respectively).

Ignominy notwithstanding, typecasting was a way of life for those who worked in Hollywood: after *The Ten Commandments*, Charlton Heston's name had the sweep of history irrevocably attached to it. No longer was he able to feature in exotic melodramas like *The Naked Jungle* or *The Secret of the Incas* (both 1954); of late, he had been ensconced at the Cinecittà studios in Rome, clad in charioteer-leather and fielding questions from journalists who insisted on addressing him not as *Ben-Hur* but as 'Mr Epic.'

With Price, it was the scent of Gothic which now seemed to cling to him, like the cobweb which traps the unwary fly. The next offer to wing his way came in the form of *The Bat*; set in a suitably dark and dusty old house it may have been, but the only cobwebs in evidence were those to be found on the pages of Crane Wilbur's script.

> This is the story of how a middle-aged spinster lost her mind, deserted her domestic gods in the city, took a furnished house for the summer out of town, and found herself involved in one of those mysterious crimes that keep our newspapers and detective agencies happy and prosperous.
>
> **MARY ROBERTS RINEHART**,
> *THE CIRCULAR STAIRCASE* (1908)

Despite the catch-penny appearance of the 1959 remake, *The Bat* had a long and illustrious history. Pittsburgh-born Mary Roberts Rinehart wrote the original story on which the film was based as *The Circular Staircase*, which was serialised in *All-Story Magazine* in 1907 before its 31-year-old author revised it for book publication in 1908. Rinehart had intended the tale to be a parody of the 'pulp' mystery-thrillers which proliferated at the time, in which master criminals in weird guise vied for control of the New World, just as Jane Austen did before her in *Northanger Abbey*, in response to the absurdities of the Gothic horror novels which had preceded that.

Rinehart was more surprised than anyone when her 'semi-satire' of the strange comings and goings in an old mansion presided over by a murderous housekeeper not only was taken at face value but graced

with great popular success: "*The Circular Staircase* was intended to be a semi-satire on the pompous and self-important crime story," Rinehart recollected in her 1931 autobiography. "When later on as a book it was taken seriously and the reviews began to come in, I was almost overwhelmed ... The notices were excellent, laying great stress on the relief of humour in a crime story, and so I kept to myself the deadly secret that the book had been written as a semi-satire ... To my astonishment, I read that I had developed a new technique of the crime novel; that I had made the first advance in the technique of the crime story since Edgar Allan Poe!"

The novel was first adapted for the screen by Selig-Polyscope in 1915, in a version directed by Edward Le Saint and retitled *The Bat*. In 1920, Rinehart herself collaborated with celebrated playwright Avery Hopwood on a stage version of her tale, also retitled *The Bat*, which was produced on Broadway by Wagenhals and Kemper, ran for 867 performances and took in $9 million at the box-office. In 1926, she re-adapted the play as a novel and sold the rights to actor-turned-producer/director Roland West – after turning down an earlier offer from D W Griffith – who again filmed it as *The Bat,* complete with exotic art direction by William Cameron Menzies. Four years later, West remade his own film in sound, retitling it in the process as *The Bat Whispers*.

The differences between these last two were slight, and the basic plot devolves to a night in an old dark house, at present occupied by a mystery writer and her maid, wherein is hidden the proceeds of a nearby bank robbery. Sundry suspicious characters appear and disappear, most of whom, it eventually transpires, are in pursuit of said loot, and among them is the person who masquerades as 'The Bat', a murderous master-thief who originally had planned to rob the bank himself but was beaten to it by the local branch manager! West spiced up this creaky yarn with expressionistic trimmings and bravura camerawork, *The Bat Whispers* being further enhanced by a 65mm widescreen process called Magnifilm. Playing the role of The Bat (or Detective Anderson as he purports to be before his eventual unmasking) in *The Bat Whispers* was rubber-faced Chester Morris. "The Bat always flies at night," he cackles at the climax, a line which found echo in the advertising for the 1959 version: 'When The Bat Flies – Someone Dies!'

If Vincent Price thought that any of the innovations Roland West had brought to the property might be reprised in the 1950s remake, he was to be sorely disappointed. "I thought they would revive it and bring it up to date because, when I was a little kid, I had seen *The Bat* on the stage and it frightened me to death," he revealed in *Cinefantastique*. "I thought maybe it could have that same kind of hold on an audience, but it didn't because it wasn't a good script."

He's come back – back to the scene of his kills. Yes, that's who I mean – that's who did this: The Bat.
INSPECTOR ANDERSON (GAVIN GORDON),
THE BAT (1959)

In *The Bat*, Price plays Dr Wells (Walker in the novel), a character who had featured in the 1926 film but whose name had been changed to Venrees for *The Bat Whispers* (where he was played by the thickly accented Viennese actor Gustav von Seyffertitz). Dr Wells is a red herring in terms of the identity of The Bat, who turns out to be Detective Anderson as before, and Price's presence was employed as much for promotional gain (publicity stills from *The Bat* aped those from *House of Haunted Hill*) as it was for any particular quality the actor might have brought to the role. As *Variety* reported at the time: "As in nearly every other film he has made in the past two years, Vincent Price casts enough furtive glances to register as the ghoul, when, indeed, he isn't."

Neither is he a red herring in its purest sense, though: Wells murders the bank manager who has embezzled $1 million in securities and secreted them in a secret chamber in 'The Oaks', his country pile – his intention being to uncover the loot for himself. But Wells reckons without the intervention of The Bat, and he expires, shot to death, under a false confession which declares, in an attempt to throw the police off the real scent, "Here lies The Bat. Threatened by exposure he destroyed himself." Unlike previous versions of the story, Wells is given little opportunity to scour the mansion for ill-gotten gains under the pretext of house calls and he spends most of the film on the periphery of the action, looking no more as though he has just plugged a former friend full of holes than the live bats on which he conducts his unspecified experiments look to be relevant to the plot.

Very much secondary to this subplot is the actual narrative of the original, in which a writer of mystery stories named Cornelia van Gorder (Agnes Moorehead) has unknowingly rented the very

British reprint of the 1926 novelisation of THE BAT, *published by WDL in 1960*

mansion where the stash is hidden. Bumps in the night become the order of the day as The Bat prowls around the house in fedora, black face-mask and gloved hands – the left of which is clawed; it is a costume clearly modelled after publicity stills from *House of Wax*, where Price's monster-face was blacked-out. The real identity of The Bat, well concealed throughout, is further masked by the agility of the stunt-man who stands in for an aged Gavin Gordon (who in his younger days had played the millionaire playboy of *Mystery of the Wax Museum*, the role deleted in the Price remake).

House of Wax's Crane Wilbur, directing his own script, had again chosen to revive a creaky old melodrama which, on this occasion, remained every bit as creaky and melodramatic as the original. Thunder and lightning, slamming doors, creaking shutters, howling winds, an old dark house, secret panels and corny dialogue are the ingredients from which the screenplay is primarily composed. After seven reels of wearisome comings and goings, Wilbur disposes of more to-ings and fro-ings by a last-minute change in construction, switching from real time into flashback mode as Gorder 'dictates' the remainder of the events as though they had already occurred. It has

Lobby card from THE BAT

a jarring effect on the narrative, but it saved audiences another bout of gadding about in dark passageways.

Even when he is being used for the sake of expedience, Price gifts the film with its classiest moment when he injects what has now become the unofficial motto of the United States Postal Service (by way of Greek historian Herodotus and Persian messengers) into Crane's perfunctory script: "Neither snow nor rain [nor heat] nor gloom of night stays these couriers from the swift completion of their appointed rounds."

After four horror films in a row, Vincent Price was starring at last – but at what price to his reputation as a serious actor? Worse than that was the fact that his recent typecasting as villain-at-large seemed to be less in the minds of audiences in general than it was in those of producers and agents. Both *The Big Circus* and *The Bat* had cast him in the role of red herring, as though playing to the notion that the mere sight of his name in the credits would

predispose the viewer to assume it was he who would turn out to be the guilty party. Not so much a case of 'the butler did it' as of Price doing it. Consequently, he had no sooner finished with *The Bat* than he was required to do it again: William Castle came a-knocking at his door once more, pitching a new screenplay entitled *The Tingler*.

Castle had a genuine love for the movies and an infectious enthusiasm for the business as a whole; he was far removed from the average Hollywood suit – so much so that his antics were affectionately parodied by John Goodman in Joe Dante's *Matinée* in 1993. After *Macabre*, for which he had only been able to summon up the talents of William Prince and Jim Backus, Castle knew what he had in Price and fully intended to exploit it to the full.

"The character you play has a theory that the 'Tingler' is in everyone's spine," the producer advised Price. "Usually, people who are frightened scream, and screaming keeps their 'Tingler' from growing.

Judith Evelyn will play the part of a deaf-mute who runs a silent movie theatre. Experimenting, you scare the hell out of her. Because she can't utter a sound – is unable to scream – her 'Tingler' grows, crushing her to death. You operate, remove the 'Tingler' from her spine, and keep it in a glass jar in your laboratory. Then it escapes and gets into the silent movie theatre…" Despite Castle's autobiographical account, it was actually Price who suggested Evelyn for the role, to make up for the fact that the two had not got along when they played together on Broadway in *Angel Street* back in 1941.

"The 'Tingler' will attack the projectionist and then get onto the screen," Castle continued apace. "It'll be a movie within a movie. Audiences seeing it will think it's loose in the theatre they're in. We'll put your voice on the soundtrack and after the lights go out… you announce that the 'Tingler' is loose in the audience and ask them to scream for their lives… All hell will break loose."

No prizes for guessing how Castle's trick to promote *The Tingler* was intended to feature.

To aid the impression of 'all hell' breaking loose and bolster the hoped-for melée, Castle proposed to wire selected seats to a low-voltage charge, giving new meaning to the idea of electrifying an audience: 'Percepto' was the innocent-sounding name that he had concocted for his dangerous-sounding plan.

"D'you think it'll work?" Price asked meekly, and once more signed up for the party.

Buoyed by his success with *House on Haunted Hill*, Castle made a personal appearance at the beginning of *The Tingler* to warn his audience about the harmful effects of fear – especially those who were wired up to his personal generator. To emphasise the point, the film begins with a convicted killer being dragged off to the electric chair behind the credit titles.

Price is Warren Chapin, the pathologist in attendance, whose pet theory is that fear induces a living organism in the human body which eventually snaps the spinal cord. Chapin's problem is that he cannot prove the existence of the 'Tingler' without conducting an autopsy on someone who has literally been scared to death. Enter Oliver Higgins (Philip Coolidge), co-owner with his deaf-mute wife – who is conveniently traumatised by the sight of blood – of a small cinema that specialises in the screening of silent movies. Martha Higgins (Evelyn) is duly frightened to death by her scheming husband and Chapin, who has now procured evidence to back up

his theory by almost scaring his own tramp of a wife to death, extracts the elusive entity from Martha's corpse. The Tingler goes walk-about within the confines of the cinema and wreaks the predicted havoc, whereupon Chapin reinstates it in Martha's body and returns to general practice.

The convoluted scenario which Robb White concocts to advance the notion that primal fear has a physiological source has to be seen to be disbelieved. *The Tingler* is part monster movie, part psychological thriller and all schlock.

> *There's a force in all of us which science knows nothing about. That it's strong enough to shatter the spinal column we know, but what it is – what causes it to appear and disappear – that we don't know.*
>
> **WARREN CHAPIN** (VINCENT PRICE),
> *THE TINGLER* (1959)

Like the creature around which the tale revolves, *The Tingler* (which was originally drafted by Robb White as 'The Chiller') is a film which never would have seen the light of day but for the participation of Vincent Price or someone like him; its plot verges on the totally absurd. Nothing whatever happens in the first two reels, apart from the cast engaging in idle small-talk as Price establishes his character's interest in the mechanics of fear.

As before, Price is cuckolded by an unfaithful spouse and White's script supplies a nice line in sharp-tongued barbs between them, but the motivation is more transparent than it was in *House on Haunted Hill*. The domestic discord is there merely to provide Chapin with the opportunity to indulge in a cruel con-trick: he threatens to shoot his wife and, when she passes out as a result, he is able to x-ray her inert body and discover the Tingler. This follows on from an episode where Chapin has foolishly tried to experiment on himself in similar fashion: having read a book about the 'fright effects' which can be induced by LSD, he injects himself with the drug – though how he proposed to x-ray his own spine while in a state of abject terror remains unexplained. Castle flunked the opportunity to add some miscellaneous tricks to the mix at this point, leaving viewers to watch Price improvising an appropriate response. "Of course, I never really did LSD," he said, adding, "I wasn't much good at that because I didn't know what the effect was meant to be." Chapin's

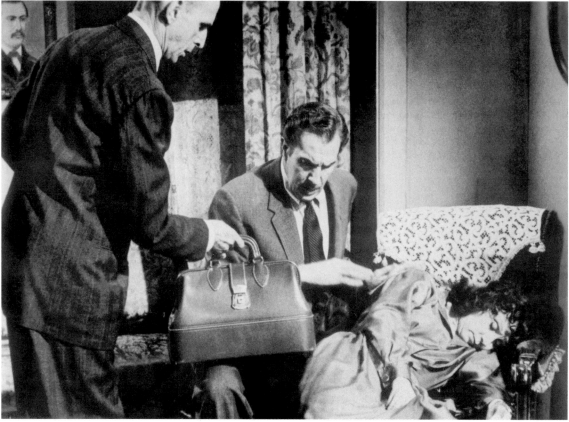

Philip Coolidge, Vincent Price and Judith Evelyn in THE TINGLER

employment of Timothy Leary's toxic tipple was something of a first; in a few short years, half the youth of America could have advised Price on how to go about the performance.

The film's fusillade of shock effects was reserved for the moment when Higgins scares *his* wife to death, which he does by rigging their apartment with a host of grisly apparitions. The imagery in this sequence was as much devised for the purposes of promotion as it was for the plot: a hairy arm wielding an axe; a scar-faced figure rising from the bed and advancing with a machete; a bath filling with blood, from which emerges a clutching hand (this last shot in colour in what was otherwise a monochrome film).

As movie monsters of the rubberised variety go, the Tingler itself is effective enough in its early scenes but is allowed to remain on screen too long, and by the time it attempts to strangle a sleeping Price at the instigation of his errant wife (an act for

which she goes unpunished), the wires controlling it become all too apparent. *House on Haunted Hill* had the benefit of working within a specific time-frame and a single location; but a similar plot situated in the suburbs somehow loses its edge. When the Tingler escapes from the container that Chapin has earmarked for it, whatever logic the story had tried to pursue finally eludes White and Castle at one and the same time.

Chapin reasons that in order to destroy the Tingler, he will have to return it from whence it came. Before he can do so, it proceeds to crawl amok in the cinema auditorium. "The Tingler is in the theatre," Price surmises, giving Castle his cue to unleash the film's secret weapon. At this point, the screen goes black and he exhorts the audience to scream:

Ladies and gentlemen, PLEASE do not panic. But scream – scream for your lives! The Tingler is loose in this theatre and if you don't scream, it may kill you. Scream! – Scream! Keep screaming... Scream for your lives! It's here – it's over here!

VINCENT PRICE ADDING 'PERCEPTO' TO THE TINGLER (1959)

'Percepto' was the name which Castle had coined for his electrifying seats but, according to Price, the idea "didn't work." To provide himself with some additional security and to heighten its effectiveness, Castle had also filmed the scene where Martha finds herself in a 'bathroom of blood' in colour. Even that was confined to domestic play-dates, though; when *The Tingler* was screened in the UK, the whole film was in black-and-white.

Once the lobster-like genie is put back in the bottle, the film has no obvious ending in play. Castle tricks one up by having Martha's revivified corpse sit bolt upright in bed (where she has expeditiously remained since expiring earlier on) and glower at her husband, frightening him to death. This was the stuff of 'ghost train' rides; as narrative, it is pure piffle.

Although all ten of the horrors that William Castle produced between 1958 and 1965 might look the same in retrospect, the fact is that only the first five of them were accorded A-feature status at the time of their original release. In the UK at least, only the first three – two of which featured Vincent Price – received a circuit booking. Both *13 Ghosts* and *Mr Sardonicus*, while positioned as the top half of double-bills, nonetheless were relegated to playing in independent houses and 'flea-pits.' All Castle's films thereafter were returned to the second-feature status with which he had been all too familiar prior to *House on Haunted Hill*.

When he and Price parted company, Castle lost the best asset to have come his way in three years as an independent producer. Castle tried to replace his absent star with others of a similar mould, Donald Woods and Joan Crawford among them. But Price was irreplaceable; he had brought a sobering presence to the kind of horror fare in which Castle had begun to specialise, and with him gone, the films that followed increasingly took on the appearance of cheap clones of whatever their producer considered to have currency at the time.

Price's new-found celebrity as an authority on art following the ratings success of *$64,000 Dollar Challenge* was marred by a Congressional investigation into the 'rigging' of quiz shows, similar to that over the payola scandal which had rocked the record

industry and ended deejay Alan Freed's career. The source of the complaint was a show called *Twenty-One*, but inquiries were soon extended to embrace the genre as a whole. As a winning contestant in a high-profile show, Price became embroiled in the controversy. Through legal representation, he admitted to having been surreptitiously 'coached' before instalments of the *$64,000 Dollar Challenge* and to have been afforded advance knowledge of some of the questions, if not the answers. He was further provided with the wherewithal to make a 'draw' of the final round against fellow-actor Edward G Robinson, which, after some soul-searching, he did – splitting the prize-money down the middle and using his half to donate art works to UCLA.

Price disavowed the workings of the committee, declaring quiz shows in general to be one of the truly educational benefits of television, before adding, somewhat naïvely, "regardless of how they were phonied up." Press interest pursued him more relentlessly than had *The Tingler*, but once *Twenty-One* had been taken off the air, the affair was quickly forgotten.

Though Castle had been upping the promotional ante with *The Tingler*, another black-and-white film was soon pulling in ten times the crowds by the simple but effective ploy of denying admission to anyone who arrived at a theatre after the show had commenced. 'Phoenix, Arizona – Friday, December the eleventh – Two forty-three p.m.' was the less hysterical onscreen announcement that heralded the arrival of Alfred Hitchcock's *Psycho*, a low-budget shocker which effectively ended the fad for outrageous gimmicks and changed the face of the horror film into the bargain. As luck would have it, Vincent Price underwent a similar change of face at the same time.

Castle followed up *The Tingler* with *13 Ghosts*, another breezily original confection which foisted 'Illusion-O' on an unsuspecting public ('3-D' glasses without the 3-D!), although it was somewhat diminished by leaden pacing and a lack of star presence in its line-up. The following year, *Homicidal* also got along without star names by cashing in on the success of *Psycho* and upping the gore quotient – but even with a 'Fright Break', the film was relegated to co-feature status alongside Hammer's *The Terror of the Tongs*. It took Castle several more years of undistinguished programme-fillers like *Zotz* and

I Saw What You Did (as well as an ill-starred attempt at Gothic horror in *Mr Sardonicus*) before he finally relinquished the gimmick-ridden and increasingly imitative monochrome fare for which he had become renowned, scoring his biggest success when he restricted himself to the producer's chair and allowed Roman Polanski to hold the bridle of *Rosemary's Baby* (1967).

William Castle's own directorial skills were perfunctory, his work in the field on a par with the crude sales tactics which he employed to promote it. The less engaging and jaw-droppingly brazen were the gimmicks, the more transparently flat and functional did the films which they supported appear to be. "He wasn't a great movie director, but he knew how to put this kind of film together," Price said of him. There were some clever Hitchcockian riffs in *Macabre*, most notably when a gun is discharged from beneath a camouflage of umbrellas in echo of a similar scene in *Foreign Correspondent* (1941), but such occasional stylistic flourishes were inflexions at best.

Castle's reputation as a shockmeister rests as much on the contributions of writers like Robb White (*House on Haunted Hill*, *The Tingler*, *13 Ghosts*) as it does on the brash inanity of his stunts. Few theatres, in reality, actually experienced Emergo – fewer still Percepto – though the novelty value of both processes ran ahead of them. *13 Ghosts* fared better, as the mechanics of distribution to theatres, even third-run houses, of thousands of pairs of Polaroid glasses had been in place for some half-dozen years prior to the film's release. *Homicide*'s 'Fright Break' could be enacted without any third-party software, and so was suffered by all who saw the film. *Mr Sardonicus*'s 'Punishment Poll' (in which viewers had to cast a vote for the climax of their choice) was straining after effect, however, as even the most sympathetic audience was by then aware that no alternative ending to the film could possibly have been standing by awaiting their decision, and that the requisite comeuppance for Baron Sardonicus would therefore ape that in the Ray Russell novella from which the film was adapted.

After *Mr Sardonicus*, the gimmicks effectively ended and Castle was more reliant than ever on the wit of his writers. Consequently, his best film was *The Night Walker*, made in 1964 from a script by Robert Bloch and executed with a great deal of wit and savvy, in addition to its functioning as a swan-song for Hollywood greats Robert Taylor and Barbara Stanwyck.

Emergo and Percepto notwithstanding, there is nothing to suggest that *House on Haunted Hill* and, in particular, *The Tingler* would have been any better received than similar films of the time had it not been for the participation of Vincent Price – the fate of Castle's subsequent offerings, *sans* Price, makes that all too plain. Impressing himself on the actor in a Hollywood coffee-shop after the success of *The Fly* was a stroke of great good fortune for William Castle; were it not for that lucky circumstance, his claim to fame in the horror stakes might have been no more substantial than that of a glorified Edward D Wood. An outrageous concept combined with the stabilising and self-mocking presence of Price were the factors which elevated *House on Haunted Hill* and *The Tingler* to cult status. After the latter, it was another director whose career was to benefit from a liaison with filmland's newest horror star.

Throughout 1958-9, horror films had been emanating from all quarters. In Britain, the vast majority of them had been awarded the ubiquitous 'X' certificate which, in terms of box-office appeal, was more alluring to the public at large than the alternative benefits of colour, Scope or 3-D put together. Only the staid Rank Organisation, which controlled the Odeon and Gaumont chains under chairman John Davis, had refused to pander to what it considered to be the base instincts of its prospective audience. No such inhibitions were allowed to cloud the commercial judgments of its main rival in the marketplace, Associated British Cinemas (ABC), which was happy to take product from all-comers, no matter how contentious.

Since 1958, Rank had made an exception to this rule with regard to the product coming out of Bray Studios under the banner of Hammer Films, due in part to that company's recent tie-up with Universal International and Rank's existing agreement with the latter. In a few short years, Hammer had become a world leader in the field of the horror film, and ABC had sought a similar product-base with which to compete with Rank on this front.

At the same time, the pre-eminent purveyor of exploitable low-cost, high-return horrors in the United States was American International Pictures. AIP – as it came to be known – had been set up in 1954 by Realart sales manager James H (Hartford) Nicholson and showbusiness attorney Samuel Z (Zachary) Arkoff as the American Releasing Corporation, but it had changed its name in 1956 after moving into low-budget production through its alliance with a 30-year-old independent producer-director named Roger Corman.

In filmmaking terms, Corman was a human dynamo. Detroit-born, his upbringing had been conventionally Midwestern until his parents moved to California when he was 14. After a schooling at Beverly Hills High and a term at Oxford University (where he wrote film scripts in his spare time), the young Corman had decided to set himself up as a movie producer. To do so in the most economical way had meant doubling up as director, as well. Speed, saleability, and shoestring budgets became the watchwords of Corman's approach. After cutting his producer's teeth on *The Monster from the Ocean Floor* for Lippert Releasing (1954), swiftly followed by two Westerns and a motor-racing drama called *The Fast and the Furious* (1955; remade in 2001 with Vin Diesel), he had persuaded Nicholson and Arkoff to step into the breech vacated by Robert Lippert and arrange front-money for a three-picture deal which commenced with his first directorial effort – *Five Guns West* (1955).

Corman's debut as a genre director came with the science-fiction opus *The Day the World Ended* in 1956 (after he had financed *The Beast with 1,000,000 Eyes*), which James Nicholson had the foresight to pair with his own *The Phantom from 10,000 Leagues*. Such double-billing of similarly themed subjects started a trend and, with Corman's help, ARC was turned into AIP and embarked on a path of supplying cheap, populist fare to the drive-in market.

From 1956 on, Nicholson, Arkoff, Corman, and other independent producers such as Bert I Gordon and Herman Cohen (Nicholson's former boss at Realart), collectively were responsible for a whole glut of exotic cult classics with titles like *It Conquered the World* (1956), *Invasion of the Saucer-Men*, *I Was a Teenage Werewolf* (both 1957), *How to Make a Monster* (1958), *A Bucket of Blood* (1959) and more – many more. With new legislation impacting on traditional distribution monopolies, continuing theatre closures and the major studios in disarray over the changing nature of their audience profile, the time had been right for the likes of Hammer and AIP to grab a share of the market. By 1959, however, the sci-fi boom of preceding years was almost over, AIP no longer was the only outfit churning out exploitation quickies for the teen trade, and the appeal of *War of the Colossal Beast* playing

alongside *Night of the Blood-Beast* had passed the point of exhaustion.

While Vincent Price was still promoting *The Tingler* for William Castle, Corman met with Nicholson and Arkoff to discuss their next joint project. The three decided to pool the budgets which habitually had been set aside for two black-and-white films and make a single feature in both colour and Scope. AIP had its very own William Castle in producer Herman Cohen, who had lighted the way by reversing Hammer's policy of American co-production and arranging a similar deal with a British distributor – Anglo Amalgamated, who distributed AIP's films in the UK – for his *Horrors of the Black Museum* (1959), which had enabled him to shoot the film in colour and Scope. Corman thought to follow suit with a story that he had read as a child and never forgotten: Edgar Allan Poe's *The Fall of the House of Usher*.

And he knew exactly whom he wanted for the leading role:

"Vincent also adored Edgar Allan Poe, so in my negotiations with him, it really didn't take much arm twisting to convince him to star in *House of Usher*. We had already hired Richard Matheson, a well-known science fiction novelist who had also written several scripts for *The Twilight Zone*, to pen the screenplay for *Usher*."

The prospect of a return to period horror after five films in a row which had clad him in lounge suits or the white coat of a lab technician was one which filled Price with glee: "I'm really kind of a baroque actor in a way, in that I believe in the gesture and in drama. I like it. I hate acting that is true-to-life because it never is."

Castle had planned to put Vincent Price into *13 Ghosts* (1960), his next feature along the same gimmick-driven lines as *The Tingler*, but before the opportunity could present itself, AIP offered Price the film which more than any other was to consolidate his image as a horror icon and place him alongside Chaney, Karloff and Lugosi as one of the all-time greats of the genre. It was an unlikely choice for a company which had made its name from bug-eyed monsters and bathing-suited damsels in distress, given that it was an adaptation of a short story by one of the fathers of American literature. But Poe's *The Fall of the House of Usher* did feature a damsel in distress (albeit crinoline-clad); more than that, the House *itself* was a monster.

ACT 3

TALES
OF TERROR

During the whole of a dull, dark, and soundless day in the autumn of the year, when the clouds hung oppressively low in the heavens, I had been passing alone, on horseback, through a singularly dreary tract of country; and at length found myself, as the shades of evening drew on, within view of the melancholy House of Usher.

EDGAR ALLAN POE, *THE FALL OF THE HOUSE OF USHER* (1839)

Edgar Allan Poe was born in Boston, Massachusetts on 19 January 1809; his mother was an actress. In a turbulent, poverty-stricken but artistically driven life of a mere 40 years, Poe became what Vincent Price adjudged to be *"the* great American writer and one of the great writers of the world." The short stories Poe collected into two volumes of *Tales of the Grotesque and Arabesque* in 1840 (later popularised as *Tales of Mystery and Imagination*) are among the best known in the literature of Terror, and the root of their power lay not in the spooks and goblins of Gothic but self-confessedly 'of the soul.' Poe's mother Elizabeth died when he was a little under three years old, of pneumonia brought on by 'consumption', or tuberculosis, and Poe biographer Wolf Mankowitz eloquently summarised the lasting impact that this tragedy was to have on the sensibilities of the boy: 'The small fairy-like figure of his mother, wearing her best gown, her face white as wax after the hectic colour of her last days, illuminated by candles, an ultimate dream-lady deep in her mysterious sleep, remained one of the most haunting images of Poe's childhood.'

The most famous of Poe's many famous tales, *The Fall of the House of Usher* was originally published in William E Burton's *Gentleman's Magazine* in 1839, before its author included it in his own collection of *Tales of the Grotesque and Arabesque* in 1840. The story was written four years after Poe's marriage by secret ceremony to his 13-year-old cousin Virginia Clemm (he married her again, 'officially' on this occasion, in the spring of the following year), whom he referred to as 'Sis' and who even then was suffering the pangs of the disease which had killed his mother.

The Fall of the House of Usher is concerned with the morbid obsessions of Roderick of that name, who believes that his sister Madeline is subject to an hereditary but unspecified disease. When Madeline appears eventually to succumb to the mysterious malady, Roderick has her entombed in the family vault – prematurely as it turns out, for she breaks free of the confines of her casket and returns, 'blood upon her white robes', to claim her brother for the grave.

There is much that is autobiographical in *The Fall of the House of Usher*, not least of which was Poe's preoccupation with death and the dying, with the wan and wasted females who littered his family history (he had seen his mother cough her life's blood onto her pale gown as she was breathing her last), with the taint of incest which attached to his marriage and with the curse which the writer, in the deeps of self-pity coloured by depression, became ever more convinced hung over his own House.

Poe's *The Fall of the House of Usher* had been filmed several times before – in 1928 in France by Jean Epstein, assisted by Luis Buñuel (a concurrent American version was made by James Sibley White and Melville Webber), in 1942 (also in the US and 8mm format) by Curtis Harrington, featuring a young Anthony Perkins (but with Harrington himself playing the roles of Roderick *and* his sister), and in 1947 in Great Britain by Ivan Barnett, complete with an 'H' (for Horror) certificate. None of these had done more than cursory justice to the story, all of them being too concerned with film as experimental art: Epstein's was an empty exercise in style in which the Ushers were a married couple, the wife's return from the grave serving only to save her husband from the imminent collapse of the house, while the British version, starring Kay Tendeter and Gwen Watford as the Usher twins, was notable only for the totality of the tedium by which viewers were engulfed throughout its 70 minutes. "Acting, direction, photography and other technical aspects seem almost amateurish," *Variety* said at the time.

Nicholson and Arkoff had been convinced by Roger Corman to follow Herman Cohen's lead, abandon their lucrative line of black-and-white double-bills and take the plunge into colour. With Cohen over in England preparing to shoot *Konga* in colour, Vincent Price was approached and offered a three-picture deal, the first of which was to be Corman's proposed production of *House of Usher*.

"Vincent was the consummate professional," Arkoff remarked in later years. "[He] was always prepared, and he had his own fans – a built-in audience he brought to AIP with him. That was the kind of actor we liked. Earlier in his career, Vincent had enjoyed substantial success as a character actor on the New York stage and in motion pictures, but got much more attention as the star of horror movies. The horror picture buffs loved him, thanks to films like *House of Wax* and *House on Haunted Hill*. We gave him one more house as a co-star..."

As Corman remembered it, Price's services did not come cheap: "I got the go-ahead for a 15-day schedule and a production budget of around $270,000, a large proportion of which went to the actor I wanted for the part of Roderick Usher... It was the most money AIP had ever gambled on a film." According to Lucy Chase Williams, Price's actual salary was more conservative, in keeping with what had been extracted from producer William Castle for *House on Haunted Hill*: "In fact, his fee for at least the first two American International movies was $35,000, paid in instalments of $3,000 per month over the subsequent year."

Either way, Corman was delighted: "In Vincent, I found a man of cultural refinement for Usher. He was a first-rate actor and handsome leading man who had a distinguished career. I felt audiences had to fear the leading man but not on a conscious, physical level, based on strength. I wanted a man whose intelligent but tormented mind works beyond the minds of others and who thus inspires a deeper fear."

Corman's inflated recollection of his budget shortfall may have been coloured by some creative accounting on Sam Arkoff's part, as were Arkoff's own anecdotes: "We paid Vincent Price $50,000 for *House of Usher*," he expanded in his autobiography. "And by his last Poe movie, he was making $80,000. That was a lot of money for AIP, and I wasn't sure that we could afford Vincent. But I sat down with him,

and we negotiated an agreement that we both could live with. I guaranteed him a series of pictures and we deferred his payments. That made him affordable to us – and we clearly got our money's worth."

With his profits from *House on Haunted Hill*, Price could afford to take the chance. But of equal importance was the artistic satisfaction he still craved. "It was a gamble," Price concurred. "I think there comes a time in everybody's career when you suddenly say, money isn't everything; I want to take a gamble on something I believe in."

With Price signed on for the pivotal role of Roderick Usher, the remaining pieces of the planned production fell swiftly into place.

Novelist Richard Matheson had already been brought on board to furnish the screenplay and, whereas Poe's Usher had been a mirror-image of his creator – '...a finely moulded chin, speaking, in its want of prominence, of a want of moral energy; hair of a more than weblike softness and tenuity; these features, with an inordinate expansion above the region of the temple, made up altogether a countenance not easily to be forgotten' – Matheson's version had sported a 'Van Dyke' beard and dark hair, like Vincent Price in *The Song of Bernadette* or *The Baron of Arizona*. In the event, Price decided to go his own way and in a moment of inspiration, he opted to have his own locks bleached and to wear no facial hair whatever. "In *Usher*, I bleached my hair white and wore pure white make-up with black eyebrows," he told David Austen in *Films and Filming*. "I don't think anybody had done that since Conrad Veidt – there was this whole extraordinary thing that he was ultra-sensitive to light and sound, so I tried to give the impression that he'd never been exposed to the light, someone who had just bleached away."

Price's wan appearance effectively literalised the ascetic nature of Usher as written, and added a dimension of tangible physicality to the 'morbid acuteness of the senses' with which the Poe character was oppressed: "I can hear the scratch of rat-claws within the stone wall," Roderick intimates in the film.

Amending Poe's title to 'The Mysterious House of Usher', AIP set Corman to work with colour, Scope and his regulation crew to aid the enterprise.

The history of the Ushers is a history of savage degradations, first in England and then in New England – and always in this house. Always in this house. The pall of evil which fills it is no

Vincent Price and Mark Damon in **HOUSE OF USHER**

*illusion: for hundreds of years, foul thoughts and
foul deeds have been committed within its walls...
The house itself is evil now!*

> RODERICK USHER (VINCENT PRICE),
> *HOUSE OF USHER* (1960)

There is some debate in literary circles as to
precisely where the tale is set, some critics considering
it to be in England, where Poe found himself in
melancholy exile for a number of years from the age
of seven onwards (in the village of Stoke Newington,
now a suburb of London). Despite its author's non-
specificity, there are clues in the narrative which point
to that conclusion: Roderick's sister is the *Lady
Madeline* as was Poe's Ligeia, whose abode is
unequivocally on the British mainland. The house
itself dates from 'feudal' times; the very name – Usher
– smacks of the Royal Court, as alluded to in *The
Haunted Palace*, the poem which Roderick recites to

the narrator of the tale during his sojourn there. It is
not a 'house' at all, but a stately home – a veritable
castle, complete with turrets, suits of armour on show
and a natural drawbridge or 'causeway', as Poe has it.
The rooms are immense, with vaulted ceilings and
arched doorways, and hung with tapestries; it has a
mausoleum in the grounds, and a dungeon-crypt set
deep in the bowels of the earth beneath.

Nevertheless, Matheson went the conventional
route and set his version in the expected locale of its
author's own New England. The house in the film is
therefore a colonial manse of Puritan vintage, like
Hawthorne's *The House of the Seven Gables* – though
Matheson hedged his bets by allowing Roderick to
indulge in some exposition: "This house is centuries
old. It was brought here from England, and with it
every evil rooted in its stones." Poe's House of
Usher was of European origin; AIP's is on the
outskirts of Boston.

Vincent Price, Mark Damon and Harry Ellerbe in HOUSE OF USHER

Then something crept across the land and blighted it... A plague of evil.

RODERICK USHER (VINCENT PRICE),
HOUSE OF USHER (1960)

In *Son of Frankenstein* (1939), the Baron's young wife spies a fog-shrouded diorama of blighted tree and blasted heath as she journeys to the ancestral home; "What strange-looking country," she notions. The scene that met her gaze was Universal Gothic, not Transylvanian travelogue, and it finds echo in the prologue to *House of Usher*: opportunely filmed on the site of a recent blaze in the Hollywood hills, the film's establishing shot of horse and rider approaching the forbidding mansion is not an exterior landscape but an interior one – that of the subconscious mind. Corman was unambiguous about his intent: "There

are no eyes in the unconscious and so I thought the films should be all interiors or, if exteriors were necessary, they should be set at night."

By steeping himself in the psychology of fear, Corman gave *House of Usher* a depth and dimension far beyond anything which had gone before. "The house is the monster," he was said to have told Sam Arkoff, but it was more than a good story: in conceiving of the house and its barren grounds as an interior landscape – festooned with cobwebs, infested by rats, and permanently afflicted by storms – Corman was free to utilise the trappings of the Gothic to full effect, and the Usher manse, with its labyrinthine corridors, ivy-strewn battlements, uneasy foundations, terror-haunted crypt and buried secrets, became the literal extension of its morbid master's tormented subconscious.

But if the house was the monster, then it was also *female*. Corman again: "The house can be seen as a woman's body with its openings – windows, doors, arches... The corridor becomes a woman's vagina. The deeper you go into the dark hallways, then, the deeper you are delving into, say, an adolescent boy's first sexual stirrings. These are contradictory urges – an irresistible attraction and desire for sex and the fear of the unknown and illicit." This overtly Freudian approach to the Terror film may say more about a puritanical streak in Roger Corman than it does about the psychological preoccupations of Edgar Allan Poe, but it works for the film and it would continue to work in at least the next two of AIP's Poe adaptations.

Matheson and Corman's House of Usher is Dragonwyck Manor 15 years on, where Nicholas Van Ryn has survived the bullet in white-haired dotage, preternaturally offended by the continuing intrusion of modernity into his hermetically sealed world and obsessed by the prospect of another defective heir to further tarnish his family's once-proud name, and where death and dissolution are all that now remain to be organised. The affinity of the two films in style and content is remarkable, not least for the casting of Vincent Price in the key roles. Just as Seton borrowed the setting of her novel from Poe – acknowledging the debt by incorporating him as a character in her own fiction – so Matheson did likewise with Seton's allegory of tainted lineage. Poe's *The Fall of the House of Usher* is a fixation on incest and 'bad blood'; AIP's film is a Gothic allegory about 'inherited' evil. If Roger Corman had not seen *Dragonwyck*, then Richard Matheson certainly had. "I got to know Richard Matheson, and I thought he had captured the essence of Poe," Price reflected.

*Two pale drops of fire guttering in the vast,
consuming darkness – my sister and myself.
Shortly, they will burn no more.*
           RODERICK USHER (VINCENT PRICE),
           HOUSE OF USHER (1960)

Towering over the film, like the spectral giant in *Metzengerstein* or even Walpole's *The Castle of Otranto*, is the gaunt and ghostly presence of Price's Roderick Usher. "*Usher* was a projection of Roderick's fevered and deranged mind," Corman expanded further. "More precisely, it was an emanation of the unconscious mind of Poe himself. I felt that Poe and

Freud had been working in different ways toward a concept of the unconscious mind, so I tried to use Freud's theories to interpret the works of Poe. We created a story about the last insane days of Roderick and Madeline Usher, living in seclusion in the family home, with its deeply fissured creaking walls." Albino-haired and draped in scarlet frock-coat, Vincent Price epitomised Corman's vision of a romantic recluse with a 'fevered and deranged mind'. The casting was impeccable, and Price would forever remain the archetypal Poe-tagonist.

Psychoanalytical sound-bites apart, Corman's evaluation of Poe went no deeper than the madness, sin and horror that the writer himself, in his studiedly clinical manner, outlined as being the soul of his plots. *House of Usher* distilled the essence of the New England master by aping his method of paring a story to its essentials. Poe wrote much of his short fiction to various formulae which he had devised to prove his contention that it could be wrought to a 'distinct pattern to achieve certain effects.' Matheson's interest in Poe was self-confessedly negligible, and he and Corman followed the same approach, constructing their scenarios to precise peaks of horror and terror, laughter and suspense. The technique worked as well for the filmmakers as it had for Poe himself, until the speed at which succeeding films began to surface ultimately betrayed the process. When the mechanics of their construction extended to the repetition of stock-shots and re-use of familiar props (to save on cost), the rigidity of the approach became obvious to all.

The filming of *House of Usher* was one of those rare occasions where necessity proved to be the mother of invention. Saddled from source with a small ensemble cast of only four players, Corman was forced to extract his palette of effects from the brooding atmosphere of malignancy which hangs over the narrative. The bulk of the film's production budget of $270,000 had gone on Cinemascope, colour, and AIP's acquisition of Vincent Price, so its director was heavily reliant on technical ingenuity to garnish his first major feature with the scares that the audience would naturally expect of it. In this, he did not disappoint. Many of the modest yet cumulatively terrifying tricks which Corman achieved through simple but effective staging soon became clichéd by their indiscriminate use in subsequent Poes, but in *House of Usher* they were both new and compelling.

A long and elaborate discourse detailing the Usher family history (and entirely invented by Matheson, for no such scene exists in Poe) gives credence to the evil nature of the house. Roderick's monologue is illustrated by some magnificent oils of the Usher dynasty, painted by Burt Schoenberg, which in themselves were striking examples of 'pop' art, reminiscent of the work of William Blake. (Schoenberg's abstracts have precedent in the tale, in which Poe literalises the 'Nightmare' of Henry Fuseli in the passage: 'at length, there sat upon my very heart an incubus of utterly causeless alarm.')

> *Anthony Usher – thief, usurer, merchant of flesh... Bernard Usher – swindler, forger, jewel-thief, drug-addict... Francis Usher – professional assassin... Vivienne Usher – blackmailer, harlot, murderess; she died in the madhouse. Captain David Usher – smuggler, slave-trader, mass-murderer...*
> **RODERICK USHER** (VINCENT PRICE),
> *HOUSE OF USHER* (1960)

The protagonist of the story is Poe himself, but Matheson's script substitutes a beau of Madeline's named Philip Winthrop (Mark Damon), who sets the drama in motion by calling on the Usher mansion to inquire after her welfare. His stay is unexpectedly prolonged by a sudden deterioration in Madeline's health, which ultimately leads to her demise. Roderick Usher hurriedly has his sister interred in the family crypt, but Winthrop soon discovers that Madeline (Myrna Fahey) is not dead after all: a sufferer from 'catalepsy' – a condition that apes the appearance of death – she has been buried alive to bring an end to the Usher line! Now quite mad as a result of her ordeal, Madeline breaks free from her funereal constraints and strangles her brother as the house goes up in flames.

In Poe's tale, Roderick betrays his original intent, which is to keep watch over Madeline in the knowledge that her demise *may* have been premature; the film darkens this by having Roderick plot her demise from the start, albeit for allegedly altruistic reasons.

> Usher: *Yes, even now, I hear her.*
> Winthrop: *No...*
> Usher: *Yes... alive! Deranged, infuriate... Can you not hear her voice?*
> Winthrop: *Where? – In the name of God... Where?*
> Usher: *Below... Twisting, turning; scratching at*

> *the lid with bloody fingernails... Staring, screaming; wild with fury – the strength of madness in her. Can you not hear her voice? She calls my name: Roderick... Roderick...*
> **VINCENT PRICE AND MARK DAMON**,
> *HOUSE OF USHER* (1960)

From its doom-laden opening to its despair-filled close, *House of Usher* is full-blooded Gothic horror of the old school. Corman creates a tangible air of expectancy and foreboding throughout, aided by some restrained scoring from the versatile Les Baxter with variations on a recurring motif. Baxter became to AIP what Bernard Herrman had been to Hitchcock, a consistently inventive and under-appreciated talent, without whose sweeping symphonies of horror many of its films would have been much diminished; if Price was Master of the Macabre, then Baxter was the maestro.

The Usher line is unequivocally inbred, and Roderick's unspoken fear about embarking on a similar relationship with his twin-sister is at the heart of Poe's story; it is to the credit of Price's performance that the sub-textual taint of incest is allowed to linger on in the film, even if it is notionally offset by Madeline's love for Philip Winthrop.

Matheson enlarged the finale of Madeline's return from the tomb by investing her with a preternatural strength, inherited from her ancestors for the occasion. "Three-quarters of my family have fallen into madness, and in their madness have acquired a superhuman strength, so that it took the power of many to subdue them," Roderick conveniently forewarns, while Corman conveys this Usher 'madness' in action through the simple but effective deployment of close-ups of the otherwise diminutive Fahey's mascara-ringed and wildly staring eyes.

Poe's narrator is overcome by hyper-sensitivity to the viscous vibes of the Usher house – referred to as 'a pestilent and mystic vapor' – in the same manner as its master, but Matheson discarded this in favour of a more natural anxiety on Winthrop's part concerning the safety of the structure. Art director Daniel Haller had constructed a brilliant set, aided and abetted by superb glass-shots of the exterior of the house, and Corman utilised both to the full; the action is constantly punctuated by cut-aways to the Usher mansion viewed from afar, which fix the narrative in its time and place, a grammatical flourish noticeable by its absence in Hammer's films. "Danny

Vincent Price and one of Burt Schoenberg's canvases in **HOUSE OF USHER**

Haller was an invaluable team player," Corman acknowledged. "Working around the clock, sketching out sets on paper napkins and then building them through the night, sometimes finishing them just minutes before the cameras began rolling."

Corman notwithstanding, Matheson elaborated on the *sentience* of the house to a lesser degree than Poe, whose protagonists are assailed by a storm of supernatural potency which effloresces the house and its firmament with an unnatural glow, as did St Elmo's Fire to the masts of the Pequod in Melville's *Moby Dick*. In the screenplay, physical manifestations were confined to a loose banister, a precariously balanced cauldron of gruel and an ever-widening fissure in the wall, which opened climactically as the house caught fire (a tad too quickly for realism, but effective all the same).

The deep and dank tarn closed sullenly and silently over the fragments of the 'House of Usher'.
SCREEN CAPTION, *HOUSE OF USHER* (1960)

In the UK, *The Fall of the House of Usher* – its full title having been reinstated for more literary-minded British patrons – was the recipient of full and half-page ads in the national press, at a time when Fleet Street titles still sold in their millions. The success of the film in America was repeated on the ABC circuit, where it became the latest in a line of high-class (if not always high-budget) horror chillers which had begun to receive critical as well as public acclaim for not having to rely on shock tactics or gratuitous gore to foster their chills.

Time and succeeding films in the resulting series have inevitably diluted the impact that *House of Usher*

FAMOUS MONSTERS OF FILMLAND *Issue 9*

taken the idea from Poe to begin with), *House of Usher* should have turned out like *Dragonwyck*, at best – essentially a potboiler. Instead of that, it became the high-point of horror for a generation of genre fans.

Instrumental in the film's success was the characterisation of Roderick Usher, which had seen Vincent Price cast in the role that he had been born to play. With his white hair, gaunt features and luminous blue eyes, and clad, for the most part, in scarlet frock-coat and cuffs, the Price of *House of Usher* was almost unrecognisable as the Price of old, a far remove from the homely, cherubic and faintly comedic figure of *The Tingler*. "A lot depends on the effects," he said. "Laurence Olivier goes the whole gamut of his profession; he always has white hair, a nose, or something... which is the fun of acting really!" Price had taken off the pounds to play the part and it had benefited his performance no end. Ascetic, effete, fragile, morose and melancholic – Vincent Price was Poe's Roderick Usher to the life.

Winthrop: *Is there no end to your horrors?*
Usher: *No. None whatever.*
      MARK DAMON AND **VINCENT PRICE**,
      HOUSE OF USHER (1960)

Corman's *House of Usher* added a new weapon to the arsenal of effects in horror cinema – catalepsy: a trance-like state that aped the appearance of death and was invariably a prelude to burial alive. The word itself tapped into a universal fear. For a time, catalepsy became the king of cinematic terrors, replacing all manner of traditional tricks in the quest to frighten audiences out of the price of admission tickets. Catalepsy provided screenwriter Matheson and AIP not only with the plot of *House of Usher*, but of several of the films that were to follow in the now inevitable series:

In *Usher*, Roderick Usher had knowingly buried his cataleptic sister alive; in the second Poe – *Pit and the Pendulum* – Nicholas Medina fears that his wife has been buried alive. In *The Premature Burial* (scripted by Charles Beaumont and Ray Russell, but adherent to the formula at Corman's diktat), Guy Carrell fears that he will be buried alive, his father having suffered that very fate. Back with Matheson, Fortunato was to find himself walled up in the 'Black Cat' segment of *Tales of Terror*, while 'M. Valdemar', in another episode from the same film, is kept in a state of living death, true to the original story. In *The*

had on its initial release. There had been nothing quite like it before. Unlike many of the Hammer 'horrors' with which it competed head-on, it was genuinely frightening. It was also innovative; besides its vivid deployment of widescreen and colour, the array of cinematic tricks which its director had been forced to adopt to speed along his monochrome quickies of only a few years before looked fresh and inventive when applied to a film which gave every appearance of being a large-scale production from a major studio. Through sheer technical virtuosity, Corman revealed himself to be a great visual stylist and he rewrote the rules of the genre with the first of the AIP Poes.

House of Usher was Gothic horror for the modern age: fluid tracking-shots, whip-pans, zooms, shock-cuts – all the technical flamboyance in the inventive director's repertoire had been brought into play to enhance the drama. Given the paucity of its plot (a mad woman is released from confinement in a coffin to attack the man who precipitously put her there – a construct which had formed the climax to Val Lewton's *Isle of the Dead* in 1945, which had also

Raven, a broad pastiche of all that had gone before, Erasmus Craven's father lies buried in a permanent state of consciousness, while another of the same, *The Comedy of Terrors* (not a Poe, but plotted in the Poe idiom), relies for its climax on a return from the grave of its cataleptic occupant, as *House of Usher* had.

The Masque of the Red Death, also penned by Beaumont, could find no way of including premature burial in its story (although Prospero spends the night-hours asleep in a coffin), but *The Tomb of Ligeia* (written by Robert Towne) could. The lady may have been buried but she is not dead – her will ensuring her eventual release from the bonds of a mortal grave, as does Morella's in the episode of the same name in *Tales of Terror*. *The Oblong Box* has burial alive in abundance, and it was central (along with other Poe themes) to the convoluted plot of *Murders in the Rue Morgue*. By that time, the whole paraphernalia of catalepsy and premature burial had run its course in effectiveness.

In a 1970 essay on Roger Corman entitled 'Descent into the Maelstrom', critic David Pirie wrote of Price's contribution: 'In *Usher*, he is indisputably superb. More overtly incestuous and evil than the Poe hero, he nevertheless retains all the characteristics of temperament that Poe so carefully delineated, from the moment when, in a spell-binding facial close-up, he pulls open the door of his room.'

'Poe's classic horror tale has been fixed on film in fine style,' wrote Paul Beckley, critic of the *New York Herald Tribune*. 'It concentrates on atmosphere, makes no bones about its necessary artifices and, most crucial, walks conscientiously in Poe's stylistic steps.' He also went on to single out the acting of Price, 'whose intellectual grasp of this bizarrerie is fine to see.' The paper gave Price the accolade of an award for best performance of the year as Roderick Usher. The trade magazine *Variety* was prophetic in addition: 'Corman has turned out a go at Poe that is certain to inspire several more cinematic excursions into this author's extremely commercial literary realm.'

Having availed itself of a star in Vincent Price, AIP sought to put him into a film which would consolidate his status as an above-title performer as well as add a new string to both of their bows. Rather than rush him straight into another Poe adaptation (thoughts of which were not uppermost until the unexpectedly high grosses began to come in), the company cast him in what was intended to be a spectacular aeronautical adventure entitled *Master of the World*, in which he would play Robur the Conqueror, a maniacal aviator whom author Jules Verne had cloned from his own character of Captain Nemo, the satanic submariner of his 1870 novel *20,000 Leagues Under the Sea* (which had itself been filmed by Walt Disney only six years before).

If AIP had similarly availed itself of the funds that were really required of its grandiose scheme to launch Robur's giant airship, the 'Albatross' might have opened up new horizons for all who flew in her. The film showed itself to be more than capable in every department save one, that of its cheese-paring budget. Responsibility for the special effects was handed over to the cut-price 'Projects Unlimited' team of Tim Barr, Wah Chang and Gene Warren, who would become better-known for their work in television's *The Outer Limits*; they rose to the challenge, and model-maker Jim Danforth constructed a wonderfully eccentric airborne battleship for Price's Robur to command. Once the miniature Albatross was in the can, however, the film simply ran out of money.

I am master of the seventh part of the world, larger than Africa, Oceania, Asia, America, and Europe, this aerial Icarian sea, which millions of Icarians will one day people.
JULES VERNE, *ROBUR THE CONQUEROR* (1886)

Master of the World was an amalgam of two novels by French science-fantasy author Jules Verne: *Robur the Conqueror* and *The Master of the World* (also known in translation as *The Clipper of the Clouds*). Verne wrote *Robur the Conqueror* at the pinnacle of his fame as a popular novelist and it was published in August 1886, when he was 58. It quickly followed *Journey to the Centre of the Earth* (1864), *20,000 Leagues Under the Sea* (1870) and *Around the World in Eighty Days* (1873) onto the best-seller lists, another in the unofficial collective of *voyages extraordinaires* under the expert guidance of Verne's long-time publisher Jules Hetzel. *The Master of the World*, on the other hand, was published in November 1904, a mere four months before Verne's death in March 1905, at the age of 78. Both novels feature the same protagonist and are structured in a similar manner, but the difference between them, and between their individual characterisations of the pioneering aviator around whom the stories revolve, is marked. It was a difference which the film was required to take on board, along with its motley crew of abducted passengers.

In *Robur the Conqueror*, a mysterious stranger gatecrashes the Weldon Institute, a club for ballooning enthusiasts, and advances the idea of heavier-than-air flight. When he is summarily ejected from the building, he has his crew kidnap the President and Secretary of the club, along with the President's valet, whereupon he takes them on a high-altitude voyage around the globe in a turbine-powered airship called Albatross. As unwilling guests of the enigmatic aviator who has announced himself only as Robur, the three experience many (largely unmemorable) adventures along the way before they finally ditch onto a small island, cut the Albatross and its crew adrift, and inexplicably detonate an explosion on board which causes it to fall into the sea. Some time later, the President is inaugurating his latest balloon when the Albatross appears on the horizon, scuppers the flight, but saves the balloon and its occupants. Robur takes his leave of the assembly by promising to share his amazing invention with mankind when it is ready to receive it more generously.

If the plot of *Robur the Conqueror* sounds like that of *Twenty Thousand Leagues Under the Sea*, it was no coincidence. The price of fame for Jules Verne was prodigious output, and he often reworked themes and ideas in other contexts. There is a hurried tone to the novel, and a severe lack of dynamic during a long middle section in which the airborne travellers are on little more than a map-reading exercise aboard the Albatross, but its author's infectious enthusiasm for the wonders which he goes to great technical pains to create survives untarnished. *Robur the Conqueror* was an optimistic vision of the future, which ends with the technologist informing the citizens of the United States that he will return to share his secrets with them when the time is right – like Klaatu in *The Day the Earth Stood Still* (1951).

Such an eventuality was never to come about, however, and the deep pessimism displayed by *The Master of the World* painted a quite different picture of man's future in the air, more akin to the dystopian fantasies of H G Wells. The two books are as philosophically opposed to each other in their treatment of their common theme as are the theories which are debated in *Robur the Conqueror*'s fictitious Weldon Institute about the comparative merits of airships and balloons.

In *The Master of the World*, Robur is now insane – "a dangerous madman, blasphemous and uncontrollable," according to science fiction author John Clute, and nowhere is this polarisation more apparent than in Verne's renaming of Robur's mighty airship from Albatross in the first to Terror in the second.

Within a few years of *Robur the Conqueror*'s American publication, reports of strange sights and mysterious lights in the sky began to appear in the newspapers. The 'mystery airship' scare, as it came to be known in UFO circles, started in November 1896 and continued through to May 1897. Witnesses reportedly saw cigar-shaped flying machines hovering above their farms or decamped in the countryside, from which humanoid creatures alighted to ask for water or, in one instance, "four dozen egg sandwiches and a flask of coffee." A commonality to many of these reports was the presence of a Robur-like figure who referred to himself simply as 'Wilson', as well as a ship's crew of about seven or eight. One farmer even described a machine which had "wings and fins," just like Verne's Albatross.

Airship technology was relatively unknown in the United States before 1901, though it was well advanced in Europe, but that in itself does not preclude a band of enterprising individuals with financial backing from having experimented in the field. Either that, or Jules Verne's fable of a colossal sky-ship had reached parts of the country which were susceptible to fictitious tales of invasion from the clouds 40 years before anyone heard of Orson Welles.

You are being carried through space, by a ship of several tonnes weight, at a speed of some 150 miles per hour...

ROBUR (VINCENT PRICE),
MASTER OF THE WORLD (1960)

Master of the World opens with an amusing but overlong and essentially incidental montage of early attempts at flight, which could as easily have been encompassed within its credit titles. In *Robur the Conqueror*, Robur's base, like Nemo's, was on an island in the Pacific Ocean, somewhere 'between the Equator and the Tropic of Cancer' and staffed by a contingent of 50 souls; *Master of the World* transferred it to a symbolically dormant volcano in the Appalachian mountains. A studio-bound prologue dispenses with the preliminaries, and the story proper gets underway when Robur's flying machine

Charles Bronson, Henry Hull, David Frankham, Mary Webster and Vincent Price in **MASTER OF THE WORLD**

finally takes to the skies, its hold stuffed with bombs.

In according Robur a 'mission' to exterminate war, screenwriter Richard Matheson enlarges on the motivation of Captain Nemo in *Twenty Thousand Leagues Under the Sea*. No such premise exists in Verne's novels, but just as Verne had broken *Robur the Conqueror* into its constituent parts to furnish his aeronaut with a second adventure, so Matheson recombined them in turn, ending up with a more obvious clone of *Twenty Thousand Leagues Under the Sea* than had their author in either instance. "The future belongs to the flying machine," Robur announces – and how right he and his far-sighted creator were proved to be.

The film's Albatross is twice as large as that in the novel and clearly designed with Disney's Nautilus in mind, but it is a splendid creation, even if a little less practical than Verne intended from his own painstaking descriptions; for one thing, Verne's sky-ship had *wings*. "It would take ten years for a balloon to circuit the earth," Robur informs his guests. "The Albatross can do it in ten days." Price cuts an imposing figure as the white-suited Conqueror, bushy eyebrows and a full beard giving the character a more saturnine look.

He was also offered more conventional support in the form of rising star Charles Bronson as federal agent John Strock and Henry Hull as Prudent, President of the Weldon.

Henry Hull, after an eclectic career which had included an appearance as the *Werewolf of London* (1935), had recently specialised in playing grizzled frontier types and came to the film after biting the dust of *The Oregon Trail* with an arrow in his belly. His bellicose performance as the Voice of Unreason grates on the intellect but offers Robur the opportunity to advance his philosophy of first-strike response in the face of belligerence. In 1960, such a position was still viewed as ethically indefensible; 40 years on, and it is Robur who appears to be in tune with the times while those who oppose him look like a bunch of namby-pamby pacifists. Robur wins the moral argument in the film as well, but not the practical one. "Can you believe his ambition is an evil one?" Bronson is asked. "His ambition, no – but his method, yes," replies the Wise One, who then suggests that the captives employ the same kind of pre-emptive strike in which Robur excels to destroy him also. Modern warfare is upon the

Vincent Price, Mary Webster and Henry Hull in **MASTER OF THE WORLD**

world with the advent of the flight, and neither side appears to be immune to its inconsistencies.

Les Baxter again provides a stirring score and, while it eventually intrudes through overuse, he cleverly contrives to accompany the scenes of battle with a chord sequence based on 'Mars, Bringer of War' from Holst's *The Planets*.

> *Officers and crew of the American war-vessel, this is Robur speaking. You have exactly 20 minutes to evacuate your ship. At the end of that time, it will be destroyed!*
>
> ROBUR (VINCENT PRICE),
> *MASTER OF THE WORLD* (1960)

Robur's aerial attacks are waged against mismatched stock-footage from *Fair Wind to Java* (1952), *Lady Hamilton* (aka *That Hamilton Woman*; 1941) and *Henry V* (1944), while some of the process shots of the Albatross are better than others, depending on the quality and trajectory of back-projection footage. "Is that London?" Bronson asks, his enquiry explained by the fact that he is shown observing a

16th-century version of same, complete with extant Globe Theatre. In another anachronism, cannon fire is returned from below at the bombarding airship, but those on the depicted square-riggers would not have possessed the elevation to do so, since they were never predicated on having to shoot things out of the sky.

"We happen to be prisoners on the ship of a man who would willingly destroy the world in order to save it, Mr Evans," Bronson explains to his fellow captive in a speech which taxes the actor's abilities in period vernacular to the limit, and Matheson adds Biblical quotations to the apocalyptic scenario for good measure, though he misses the chance of Bible *readings* to bond the loyal crew of the Albatross to its master.

In attempting to match the Disney epic of 1954, the film becomes over-ambitious: Albatross soars across continents with Robur announcing his aims on the 'voice magnifier' and backing up his words with a salvo of shells. In no time at all, the governments of the world are in apparent disarray and ready to submit to the Conqueror's demands. It is at this point that Strock chooses to undo all of the good work and destroy the Albatross. While gainsaying the fact that formula must triumph no matter what, the evident success of Robur's stratagem does tend to undermine the philosophical debate in which the protagonists partake between comedic interludes.

Matheson's over-larding of Verne's original results in Robur subduing the collective will of world governments by means of a hold full of bombs in an airship made from paper-pulp. It all seemed more feasible in Nautilus, which was at least constructed of iron and proved impossible to detect when submerged. The objective of Projects Unlimited was to make the Albatross look appropriately archaic if not downright Heath-Robinson, but its concept worked against the film in the end, which had required a machine as invulnerable as Nemo's to give its extravagant plot a convincing air of credibility.

William Whitney's direction is uninvolving, keeping the participants at one remove from the viewer throughout, and the effects footage rarely matches the requirements of the scripted action. Vitto Scotti provided predictable comedy relief as a ship's cook forever gathering up pots and pans after aerial manoeuvres. The end credits even revealed the presence of a song – entitled 'Master of the World' and sung by Darryl Stevens – but it was deemed unworthy in the final analysis and excised from the mid-section of the film before it went into release.

The 40-year-old Bronson – the former Charles Buchinski of House of Wax, and another Method performer who had since essayed a number of rugged action roles in films like Roger Corman's Machine Gun Kelly (1957) and John Sturges' The Magnificent Seven (1960) – felt himself to be a 'fish out of water' in Master of the World. According to Matheson, he and Price did not get along during the shooting, despite frequent attempts by the latter to break the ice. Bronson was something of a macho man in real life also; consequently, there may have been more than professional antipathy between the two.

Even the climax echoes Disney as Robur, mortally wounded and surrounded by his loyal crew, quotes from Isaiah when fate overwhelms his ship in the form of the onrushing sea:

> Our flight is almost over now... 'And he shall judge among the nations, and shall rebuke many people: and they shall beat their swords into plowshares and their spears into pruning hooks:

> nation shall not lift up sword against nation, neither shall they learn war any more.'
>
> ROBUR (VINCENT PRICE),
> MASTER OF THE WORLD (1960)

In the style of House of Usher, the film ends with a screen caption containing a quote from Jules Verne, erroneously credited to The Master of the World: 'I take my dream with me, but it will not be lost to humanity. It will belong to you the day the world is educated enough to profit by it and wise enough not to abuse it.' It was actually a paraphrase of Robur's parting speech in Robur the Conqueror but befitting of the piece as a whole – though details like that would come to matter less as AIP's association with classic works of literature went on.

In Britain, Master of the World was released as co-feature to a comedy about army life called On the Fiddle, which was notable for containing the last screen appearance of rising star Sean Connery before James Bond rocketed him to super-stardom. On the Fiddle carried an 'A' certificate, which restricted entry to those under 14 unless accompanied by an adult and further reduced the target audience for its running-mate's 'U'.

Despite his explosive demise in Master of the World, the way remained open for the character of Robur to reappear in some unauthorised AIP sequel, should popular success have dictated it. Any such plan came to earth with a bump once the box-office take was counted, and Price was back with Poe less than four months later.

Price later pronounced upon the film for Shriek magazine: "I loved Master of the World, because I thought it had a marvellous moralising philosophy... a man who sees evil and says 'Destroy it!' It is the great Jules Verne concept." Verne himself, like others of his countrymen on the recommendation of Baudelaire, coincidentally admired and was influenced by the works of Edgar Allan Poe, whose short story Three Sundays in a Week had been the inspiration for Around the World in Eighty Days; the connection was insufficient to offer its star the same opportunity to shine as had House of Usher, however.

The notion of waging war in order to promote peace is as timely – and idiosyncratic – in an age when terror can authentically rain from the sky as it was when Verne wrote his novel. Had Master of the World been made by Disney, or another of the majors, it might have represented Vincent Price's finest hour on the fantasy screen. Matheson's script was up to it, as was Price's commanding performance as Robur. The good ship Albatross also did Verne proud. But it was too ambitious a project for American International and has ultimately to be considered a failure in consequence.

Down – still unceasingly – still inevitably down!
I gasped and struggled at each vibration.
I shrunk convulsively at its every sweep.
  EDGAR ALLAN POE,
  PIT AND THE PENDULUM (1843)

To convince Sam Arkoff to put *House of Usher* – a film devoid of atomic mutants, bug-eyed saucermen, werewolves, vampires and other poster-friendly manifestations of the fifties' sci-fi boom – into production, Roger Corman had famously informed the joint head of American International that the *house* was the monster. The 'house' was also the monster in *Pit and the Pendulum*, the next Poe vehicle for Vincent Price, but in a more subtle and better integrated way, though a reference similar to that in *Usher* was still inserted into the script for insurance' sake, along the same lines as before: "The malignant atmosphere of this castle – it destroyed her," Price says vaguely of the circumstances which have led to his young wife's recent death.

Price critiqued the Poe original for *Shriek*: "The Pit and the Pendulum is an almost foolproof horror story. Every element of horror is in it – walls closing in, the heat, height, the rats ... and the menace of a great razor-sharp blade." Foolproof or not, Nicholson and Arkoff had their own views on the merit of the master's work: "Poe writes the first reel or the last reel. Roger does the rest," AIP's president told the trades.

Pit and the Pendulum was unique in the annals of Hollywood horror films for choosing to set its story in 15th century Spain. Prior to this one, few had dared to venture further back than 19th century *mittel*-Europe and most were set contemporaneously – Universal's own *Tower of London* in 1939 having been one of the rare exceptions. Richard Matheson may have been forced by the relative brevity of the original Poe stories to invent entire plots in support of them (a fact for which he was often criticised), but his faithfulness to the spirit and *settings* of Poe cannot go unremarked. Consequently, *Pit and the Pendulum* takes place at the time of the Inquisition, an extravagance which Universal had evaded when it

included the Poe scenario in its version of *The Raven* in 1935.

The Spanish Inquisition was legally inaugurated in September 1480, ostensibly to tackle the problem of 'heresy' in general but effectively to ferret out recidivists among the Jewish communities of Spain which were being required by law to convert to Christianity. In 1482, the prior of a Dominican friary in Segovia named Tomás de Torquemada was appointed as an 'inquisitor' and, by October the following year, he had been promoted to inquisitor general by Papal bull, the power of his office being extended to cover the whole of Spain. Between 1480 and 1530, some 2,000 heretics are recorded as being condemned by the Inquisition to be burned at the stake, many after having suffered torture to induce a confession. This was the institution's bloodiest period; the Spanish Inquisition survived for more than 350 years, but its power and influence slowly diminished after the middle of the 15th century.

Do you know where you are, Bartolome... ?
I'll tell you where you are. You are about to enter
Hell, Bartolome – Hell! ... The nether world,
the infernal region, the abode of the damned...
The place of torment. Pandemonium, Abbadon,
Tophet, Gehenna, Narraka... the Pit! ... And the
Pendulum. The razor-edge of destiny. Thus, the
condition of man: bound on an island from
which he can never hope to escape; surrounded
by the waiting pit of Hell; subject to the
inexorable pendulum of fate – which must
destroy him, finally.
  NICHOLAS/SEBASTIAN MEDINA (**VINCENT**
  PRICE), *PIT AND THE PENDULUM* (1961)

Pit and the Pendulum opens unforgettably on a miasma of swirling oils, overlaid with a reverberating percussive score by Les Baxter that again echoes the 'electronic tonalities' employed in *Forbidden Planet* (1956). Poe's story is set in 1808, at the time of Spain's occupation by the armies of Napoleon, but Matheson chose to set the period back some 250 years to the last days of the Inquisition's inaugural term of office. In a very Poe-esque take on things, Nicholas is implicitly impotent from having seen his father torture and murder his mother as a small boy, and it this which lies at the root of Elizabeth's adulterous affair with Dr Leon. The casting of Luana Anders as Catherine Medina gave Nicholas a younger

Filming PIT AND THE PENDULUM

sister than is possible in Matheson's script, given that her mother was murdered while Nicholas was still a boy – a fact which did not go unnoticed by Price himself: "In *Pit and the Pendulum*, we had Luana Anders, who has an extremely contemporary presence, and she just didn't fit into this period horror film." The support is nonetheless uniformly competent, despite its predictable importation from other Corman vehicles.

Nicholas Medina (Price) and his sister Catherine (Anders) reside in a castle which is permeated by the memory of their sadistic father

Sebastian, who had been a regional 'inquisitor.' Nicholas is still in mourning for his newly deceased wife Elizabeth (Barbara Steele) when her brother arrives to investigate the tragedy for himself. Nicholas explains that Elizabeth's death was due to a "peculiarity of temperament" but Barnard (John Kerr) refuses to believe him. A series of inexplicable events appear to indicate that Elizabeth's ghost is walking abroad and Nicholas agrees to disinter her corpse, fearing that she may have been buried alive. It transpires that she was, and Nicholas suffers a breakdown. The same night, a voice calls him from the crypt; he makes his way there, and

Elizabeth rises from her tomb. Fleeing before the apparition, Nicholas collapses in the torture chamber, his mind gone. Elizabeth is not dead, however, and the whole was a plot concocted by Elizabeth and her lover, Dr Leon (Anthony Carbone), to drive Nicholas mad. But Nicholas recovers in the persona of his father, killing Leon and throwing Elizabeth into an iron maiden. Barnard enters and is strapped beneath a pendulum blade. As the blade descends, Catherine and a manservant break into the chamber and free Barnard, while Nicholas is tumbled to his death in the pit. The torture chamber is sealed shut, but Elizabeth is unknowingly left alive in the maiden.

In its story of a wife who might have been buried alive, Matheson followed the formula of the first film a little too closely for comfort, though he was forced to ring the changes on the reason *why* Elizabeth Medina, in this instance, had suffered such a fate. Discarding the idea of catalepsy (which Beaumont and Russell would promptly revive for the third film in the series, *The Premature Burial*), he found a suitable alternative in Price's back-catalogue. "*Pit and the Pendulum* was ridiculous because we took a little short story about a guy lying on a table with that razor-sharp blade swinging over him, and had to make a story out of it," Matheson said. "I just imposed a plot from an old suspense mystery on that basic premise." The 'old suspense mystery' in question was *House on Haunted Hill*, whose plot had devolved into a conspiracy between the protagonist's wife and her doctor-lover to jointly murder her husband. Matheson affixed this to the Poe story, with the modification that the motivation would be to drive Price mad, not murder him, and thus send him reeling in the direction of pit and pendulum. It has to be said that the ploy worked a treat: the Poe ambience masked the fact that the basic plot of *Pit and the Pendulum* was of relatively recent vintage and owed its contrivance to Robb White.

In its tale of murder, adultery, plotting and revenge, Matheson's makeover of Poe has all the ingredients of Jacobean tragedy and, once again, resonances of *Dragonwyck* crop up in the screenplay: Price is accorded the very un-Spanish Christian name of Nicholas, while the alleged ghost of his wife is given to playing the harpsichord during the hours of darkness, in shades of Van Ryn's grandmother, Azilde, in Anya Seton's novel.

When Barnard hears the sound of the pendulum in action after entering the crypt and is moved to investigate, Nicholas deflects his enquiry with the explanation, "It is an apparatus, sir, that must be kept in constant repair." According to Lucy Chase Williams, it was Price who amended Matheson's dialogue at this point to make it more specific. If so, it serves to indicate that actors do not always have a handle on the bigger picture: why would Nicholas keep his father's instruments of torture – which are anathema to him – in 'constant repair'? Moreover, what was he doing in the torture chamber to begin with? The scene was contrived to introduce the pendulum at an early stage and to hint towards the climax, but it would appear that neither Matheson nor Price really thought that one through.

In those far-off days of 1961, disfigured corpses were rarely seen on screen and *Pit and the Pendulum* made much of its central set-piece, wherein the occupants of the castle open Elizabeth's vaulted tomb so that Nicholas can discover the post-interment condition of its tenant. Corman extracts maximum suspense along the way, his camera lingering on every pick-axed brick in the wall, every creak of the coffin lid, until Nicholas' 'loud, long scream of despair' reveals as fact what he has feared as fancy all along. From this point on, Corman cranks up the suspense in steadily increasing degrees.

In a sequence of extraordinary power, Nicholas is enticed to the crypt by the siren-sound of someone calling his name. As he reaches the tomb, the coffin lid opens, a figure rises out of the darkness, and the real stuff of nightmares comes joltingly to the fore: Nicholas flees before the approaching apparition, fumbling over each successive door as he tries in vain to find a key which will fit the lock. If Corman had studied the psychology of fear before embarking on his Poe films, what he learned was never better realised than here.

Deep in the bowels of the castle, the long-awaited climax is played out to the strains of *House on Haunted Hill*: "It's taking too long," Annabel Loren tells her lover in Castle's film as she contemplates her husband's demise; "Why couldn't you wait one more day?" Dr Leon asks Elizabeth after she has broken *her* husband's spirit with her spectral charade in *Pit and the Pendulum*. Nicholas is not Frederick Loren, however, and shorn of a skeleton to aid him in plunging his wife into an acid vat, he kisses Elizabeth lasciviously on the lips and thrusts her bodily into a waiting iron maiden:

THE PIT AND THE PENDULUM
in TECHNICOLOR and Panavision   (x)
Starring
VINCENT PRICE
JOHN KERR · BARBARA STEELE
Anglo Amalgamated Film Distributors Ltd.

A British front-of-house still from PIT AND THE PENDULUM

I'm going to torture you, Isabella. I'm going to make you suffer for your faithlessness to me. Before this day is out, you will be begging me to kill you – to relieve you from the agony of Hell into which your husband is about to plunge you..
NICHOLAS/SEBASTIAN MEDINA (VINCENT PRICE), PIT AND THE PENDULUM (1961)

The pendulum set was worth all the trouble that Daniel Haller went to in order to create it, for it not only provided the film with a dazzling climax but the genre as a whole with the most bravura finale in the first half-century of its history. Haller's ability to make a little go a long way paralleled that of Bernard Robinson, who performed the same creative function for Hammer. "The Pit was there and the Pendulum went right up to the roof. It was one of the most exciting sets I've ever seen," Price told David Austen. "And there was this maze of passages I had to sneak through. I said to Roger, 'This is fine ... the dark

passages are very claustrophobic, but nothing happens. Now there's one thing that men are really afraid of, something they absolutely hate, and that's cobwebs. Let's rig some up.' The props man spun a really glorious creation. And then as I walked into the camera a whole cobweb plastered my face ... you could literally hear the men go 'Ugh!'"

A scything pendulum similar to that in the film had featured at the climax of Universal's *The Raven* (1935) and another would crop up in *Die Schlangengrube und das Pendel* (*Blood Demon*; 1967), though they too were significantly larger than their creator's "crescent of glittering steel, about a foot in length." A more faithful rendition of Poe's story appeared on French television two years after Corman's film as a half-hour short, starring Maurice Ronet. *Le Puits et le pendule* was directed by Alexandre Astruc and it reinstated the original's climax of the oubliette, where the walls of the prison bore down on the helpless inhabitant; Matheson had

Filming **Pit and the Pendulum**

preferred that his 'walls' be metaphorical, closing in on Nicholas' mind. Such torture as was occasionally used against the faithless by the Inquisition took several forms, though none of them as elaborate as those dreamed up by Poe and depicted in *Pit and the Pendulum*.

And now for you, Bartolome, my beloved brother, while you are still alive... my ultimate device of torture.

Nicholas/Sebastian Medina (Vincent Price), *Pit and the Pendulum* (1961)

Once again, Corman waxed interpretationally lyrical: "Put together correctly, the classic horror sequence is the equivalent of the sexual act. The sharp, shocking event at the end that releases the tension is the equivalent of the orgasmic climax ... There is growing tension and release – all analogous to the rhythms of a sexual act." Singling out this scene in particular, he said, "On the unconscious level, the pendulum and the pit are male and female symbols." While Freudian parallels can be drawn about the rhythmic descent of Haller's pendulum, a more precise analogy might have required that Francis Barnard be climactically cut in half, to encourage an appropriate ejaculation of bodily fluid. As he happens to escape this fate at the end of *Pit and the Pendulum*, one should perhaps see it, in Corman's terms, as a case of *coitus interruptus*.

After Barnard has been rescued, the camera zooms in to Nicholas lying at the bottom of the pit, alongside Dr Leon. He is mortally injured but clearly still alive, and in the scene as shot, he raised his head and said, "Elizabeth – what have I done to you? ... What have I done to you?" in echo of Roderick Usher's parting line, "There was no other way... No other way." Corman decided that last words were an unnecessary appendage and edited them out.

Cult icon Barbara Steele, ex-Rank starlet and star of Mario Bava's *La maschera del demonio* (released as *Black Sunday* in the US; 1960), took exception to the fact that she was dubbed throughout; Corman thought that her British accent had failed to 'blend' with those of the other actors. She promptly resumed her career in her adoptive country of Italy when shooting on her first and last Hollywood film came to an end. "I find that it's very difficult, when one is a young actress, to make this type of film," she said of the experience. "When one is no longer young, one calls oneself Vincent Price."

After two films where he had indulged in more extravagant make-up, Price had reverted to his usual self as Nicholas Medina, with only a few curls and an Elizabethan ruff to offset his familiar features. As his father Sebastian Medina, however, both in flashback and in his Hyde-like take-over of Nicholas' personality in the film's penultimate scenes, he adopted a crooked gait, a croak in his voice and a lop-sided smile.

Pit and the Pendulum is the only horror film of Price's, other than *House of Wax*, where the climax depends for its effect on the revelation of its star as Monster; in that, it improved immeasurably on its forerunner. The 'transformation' came as a complete surprise to all who saw the film at the time of its release, no one knowing what the outcome of his descent into madness was likely to be, other than the fact that it was guaranteed to involve a pendulum. Sebastian had cleverly been depicted only in an expository flashback, where his voice was unheard under his daughter's narration but his black deeds were paraded in full view. When he finally surfaced in Nicholas' skin, the effect was as startling as the mask that cracked on Jarrod's face to reveal the hideous creature beneath. A parallel is to be found in Matheson's 1969 novel (and subsequent film) *Hell House*, where the presence of Emeric Belasco hangs with similar malevolence over the narrative.

Regional 'inquisitor' Sebastian Medina was the greatest monster that Vincent Price ever played – a sadistic cripple, wild-eyed and wicked, and quite, quite mad. Whether snarling in rage at his intended victim or swaying in rhythm to the humdrum of his hellish device, like Hugo's famous bell-ringer atop the Paris cathedral, he plies his torturous trade with a gleam in the eye and only the sound of a scream to soothe his savage breast. If proof were needed that Price was indeed the Master of Fright, then it was to be found at the climax of *Pit and the Pendulum*.

Pit and the Pendulum is one of the eight or so horror films – *House of Wax*, *House on Haunted Hill*, *House of Usher*, *The Masque of the Red Death*, *Witchfinder General*, *The Abominable Dr Phibes*, *Theatre of Blood* – out of more than 40 in total, on which Vincent Price's reputation for hair-raising truly rests. It is a cleverly contrived trip into cinematic nightmare, for which no one was better equipped than he to act as tour-guide. As Nicholas Medina, he is vulnerable and venal, benign and bedevilled by turns, and while his performance in the film may not have possessed the subtle qualities of that in *House of Usher*, it is every bit as memorable.

Like *Usher*, *Pit and the Pendulum* had been shot at Producer's Studio – a small complex on Melrose Avenue in Hollywood, hitherto known as Raleigh Studios, which had passed through several managements since its inauguration in 1915. In its early days, it had been home to Douglas Fairbanks and Mary Pickford's United Artists Corporation, and silent swashbucklers *The Mark of Zorro* and *The Three Musketeers* had both been produced there (in 1920 and 1921 respectively). The 1950s had seen its confined stages turned over to television for use in series like *Perry Mason* and *Have Gun Will Travel*, but it had remained a low-rent proposition to all-comers.

Pendulum apart, the exteriors of the Castillo Medina, like House of Usher, were entirely a construct of exquisite glass paintings, so the film was accomplished within the regulation AIP budget. Nevertheless, it was a daring move, and its success was predicated on ballyhoo and the impact of the awesome torture device of the title. *Pit and the Pendulum* was treated to an ad campaign which was every bit as far-reaching as that of its predecessor. The bullish approach of promoters like William Castle had left its mark on the genre and AIP pushed its film with the tag-line '$10,000 Dollars if You Die of Fright!' adding, in small print, 'during the opening of the coffin.' It was less subtle than the prefixing of the simple '...The Ungodly ...The Evil' to the title of *House* of *Usher* for that film's theatrical outing ('Edgar Allan Poe's overwhelming tale of Evil & Torment' in its British incarnation), but it paid dividends: *Pit and the Pendulum* became a top box-office draw on its release in the US, taking more than $2 million in rentals against a production budget of $300,000.

Acknowledging the part that Price had played in the film's success, the *Financial Times* called it 'a Tod Slaughter spectacle for those who are willing temporarily to set aside their finer judgment,' though the *Hollywood Reporter* spotted the sudden sprint of an outsider in what until then had been a one-horse race: 'a class suspense-horror film of the calibre of the excellent ones done by Hammer.'

An idiosyncrasy of AIP's Poe series was the extent to which supporting players appeared to confine their screen activities to these films alone, never to be heard from again once they had strutted and fretted their hour upon the self-contained stage of Poe, AIP and the early 1960s. In one or two cases, it is almost true: Myrna Fahey, for instance (Madeline Usher in *House of Usher*) died of cancer at the age of only 40, and although Luana Anders (Catherine Medina in *Pit and the Pendulum*) notched up a number of other screen credits, none were as notable and she also died of cancer, aged 53.

> *... the agony of my soul found vent in one loud, long, and final scream of despair.*
>
> **SCREEN CAPTION**,
> *PIT AND THE PENDULUM* (1961)

With shooting over on *Pit and the Pendulum*, Vincent Price had honoured his three-film contract with AIP and, in April 1961, he left the US with his wife for a lengthy excursion to Europe. The trip was intended to take in sight-seeing tours of Great Britain, Greece and Egypt, but with the continuing downturn in the motion picture industry in general, Price had also planned to go where the work was. In 1961, the work was in Italy.

The on-going popularity of Italian 'sword-and-sandal' epics – several of which had been bought for US distribution by AIP itself, including *Goliath and the Barbarians* (1959) and *Goliath and the Dragon* (1961) – ensured a steady stream of migrant actors to Cinecittà in Rome; the most successful of them, Steve Reeves and Gordon Scott, were already in permanent residence in the Eternal City. Price was no exception and, during the summer of that year, he starred in

two *peplum* of his own: *Queen of the Nile* (*Nefertite, regina del Nilo*) and *The Black Buccaneer* (*Gordon, il pirata nero*). When they were released in the UK two years later, *Films and Filming*'s Ian Johnson concluded that Price was "still his cunning old evil self" in the former, while the same magazine's David Rider felt that he had given "a richly amusing performance" in the latter.

In the meanwhile, Roger Corman thought to use the commercial success of his first two Poe films as a bargaining chip with AIP, to bolster his cut of the action. When negotiations stalled, he decided to make another Poe with the newly formed Pathé distribution company (sired from Pathé Film Laboratories) instead; with Price unavailable, Corman hired Ray Milland and Hazel Court to star in *The Premature Burial*. Word soon reached the canny Arkoff and AIP bought the film back from Pathé while it was still in production, using its lab-work with the company as leverage in the deal.

When Nicholson and Arkoff walked onto the set, Corman was taken aback. "I thought: They have *never* shown up like this before. And why are they smiling?" "Welcome back to AIP," Arkoff announced triumphantly, explaining the position to the director and later noting in his autobiography that Corman 'seemed delighted with the news.' *The Premature Burial* thus became the unofficial third of the AIP Poes, but without Vincent Price, and the episode represented one of the few occasions in his colourful career where Corman found himself ruthlessly outflanked.

The Premature Burial became the most exquisitely photographed of the early Poes, but it somehow lacked the vibrancy of its predecessors, as though Corman, thwarted in his plans to produce independently of AIP, had carried on mechanically and merely reprised his box of tricks in the expected manner. The British Film Institute's *Monthly Film Bulletin* considered that the production as a whole relied "rather too heavily and uninventively on the vocabulary of gloomy graveyards, Gothic mansions, swirling ground-fogs, bats, candelabra, and opulent spider-webs."

Former golden boy at AIP, Herman Cohen, producer of a string of hits for the company from *I Was a Teenage Werewolf* to his newest, *Konga*, also chose the wrong moment to try to re-negotiate his percentage deal with Arkoff; he, too, was given short shrift and promptly departed the scene for sound-stages new, though he was never again to create anything like the stir that he had with American International.

> *This incident I have digressed to mention, because this Malay ... fastened afterwards upon my dreams, and brought other Malays with him, worse than himself, that ran "a-muck" at me, and led me into a world of troubles.*
>
> THOMAS DE QUINCEY, *CONFESSIONS OF AN ENGLISH OPIUM EATER* (1821)

On his return from an idyllic six-month sojourn on the continent of Europe (during which time his wife had unknowingly conceived), Vincent Price found himself hoist into *Confessions of an Opium Eater* for another producer of dubious credentials by name of Albert Zugsmith. Zugsmith's crowning achievement had been to produce the cult classic *Touch of Evil* (1958) for Orson Welles, Charlton Heston and Marlene Dietrich, but since then his ventures in the movie business had nose-dived into erotic exploitation.

Confessions of an English Opium Eater was an 1821 monograph by Mancunian essayist Thomas de Quincey, which did what it said on the label by describing the author's addiction to opium in the decade before he decided to commit it to print. The concept behind any film adaptation was therefore uncertain at best, but the de Quincey novel had first been proposed for production by William Castle in 1959, in the wake of a sudden interest in all things Far Eastern. By the time it had passed down the line to Zugsmith, what had become a noir plot about an undercover narcotics cop in period costume had been padded out with the concrete overcoat of obtuse narrative and supposed philosophical profundities whose connection to de Quincey came only in the use of his title, *sans* nationality, as well as that of his surname for its leading character.

House of Usher and *Pit and the Pendulum* had been runaway successes for AIP but did not yet portend a series as such, although Nicholson and Arkoff had woken up to what they had in Vincent Price and were keen to re-open negotiations. In the meantime, Price was still going from job to job, his name on the marquee being employed to prop up otherwise ailing projects of increasingly independent means; *Confessions of an Opium Eater* fell into this second-string bracket of bread-and-butter commissions which had begun with *Return of the Fly*.

CONFESSIONS OF AN OPIUM EATER

The part of 'Gilbert' de Quincey was Price as working actor, turning up on set, speaking his lines, and generally going through the motions of an inexplicable scenario which primarily had been mounted for the exploitation market. Had the film been made a decade later, ample nudity alone would have justified its existence; as it was, it attempted to get by on the appeal of exposé and an occasional shock-shot of a mouldering corpse. Despite excellent technical credits (Joseph Biroc, photography; Eugene Lourié, art direction), all it really evinced was the old Hollywood system continuing to flounder in the face of television, while its main assets – actors such as Vincent Price – remained all at sea in the ever-changing tides of early sixties cinema.

> *I am de Quincey... I dream, and I create dreams... Out of the opium pipe, I see sailing into our vision a junk; its cargo, women – women bought or stolen from all over the mysterious Orient. Their destination, and mine, the human auctions in Chinatown.*
>
> OPENING NARRATION (VINCENT PRICE), *CONFESSIONS OF AN OPIUM EATER* (1961)

Gilbert de Quincey (Price) is a one-time gunrunner turned government agent, who is acting undercover to destroy the white slave trade in San Francisco's Chinatown. The plot, such as it is, can only occasionally be glimpsed through chinks in a narrative construction which presents the viewer with the double whammy of a pretentious concept and amateurish handling, coupled to portentous dialogue riddled with such Confucius-he-say homilies as "There is no poison in the green snake's mouth as in a woman's heart" or "The superior man blames himself; the inferior man blames others."

Price plods through this leaden affair uncomfortably attired in serge jacket and sailor's cap, the latter lifted from him only by the rushing waters of the sewer into which he climactically plunges and by which he is swept to his death, or at least out of the clutches of the zany Mister Zugsmith. The actor is completely miscast in the proactive role of de Quincey; he can muster up neither the bearing nor the brutish balletics required of the typical two-fisted action hero. Assaulted by the obligatory motley of yellow-peril assassins wielding a variety of knives and hatchets, he is bemused or petrified by turns.

True to its source, a central episode in the film finds Price in an opium den, and a couple of reluctant puffs on the pipe of dreams brings on the requisite lap-dissolve nightmare, a repeat of recent experiences, among which, it would seem, were trips to a drive-in movie theatre to see AIP's own *Invasion of the Saucer Men* and *Voodoo Woman*. This dream sequence having been deemed insufficient by Zugsmith to convey the horrors of opium sleep, Price's subsequent escape from the den and flight across the San Francisco rooftops is filmed in slow motion, which only amplifies the gangling actor's lack of natural athleticism and makes it all too clear that his ability to outwit his pursuers owes more to camera tricks than it does to any innate quick-wittedness on the part of his character.

Like many tall men weighed down by their own stature, Price was not a very physical actor and the more strenuous were the requirements of a specific script, the more incapable he became of fulfilling them. He was at his best moving stealthily around a stylish set, relying on gesture and facial expression, and the measured pace of Corman's Poe series suited him admirably.

Confessions of an Opium Eater played in the UK as *Evils of Chinatown* after an interval of more than two years. Following brief outings on a variety of double-bills in third-run houses, its fate was the same as that of Price's character in the film: it went straight down the drain.

That Price's agent had managed to involve him in such a ridiculous farrago is indicative of the fate which was befalling many Hollywood players of similar stature at the time. The studio system had

been on the point of collapse since the late 1950s, and Price and others like him had woken up to find themselves recast as roving guns for hire, never too sure where the next tepid screenplay was going to come from. In the face of such terminal insecurity, his next move was a foregone conclusion.

> *Was it a dream of the poppy or was it at last reality as, once again, I put out to sea? Were these the widening waters of Death – or the gates of Paradise?*
>
> CLOSING NARRATION (VINCENT PRICE),
> *CONFESSIONS OF AN OPIUM EATER* (1961)

It was one thing for competitor companies to express an interest in AIP's dish of the day, but some of them seemed to be eyeing the family silver as well. Among the Poe titles which had been up for consideration as a follow-on to *House of Usher* was *The Masque of the Red Death*, but independent producer Alex Gordon (whose younger brother Richard had recently co-produced *Grip of the Strangler* and *Corridors of Blood*, both with Boris Karloff) had already announced it for production.

Gordon's main claim to fame came from having plied his trade on the bottom rung of the Hollywood ladder alongside Ed Wood, the writer-director of *Plan 9 From Outer Space*, but the one-time publicity agent for singing cowboy Gene Autry had made a number of drive-in titles for AIP, including *The She Creature* and *Voodoo Woman*.

Gordon had not produced for AIP since 1958, when friction between himself and Arkoff had led to a parting of the ways. On leaving the company that he had helped to establish, he had announced a slew of productions in the horror category, among which were two written by his new wife Ruth Alexander, his erstwhile assistant on *The Atomic Submarine* (1959) – *The Hound of Hell* and *The Mask* [sic] *of the Red Death*. Nothing had come of the Gordons' proposed productions in 1959-60 (which had also included a version of Robert Louis Stevenson's *The Suicide Club*), but the existence of an extant script based on the story and emanating from a quarter where antagonism was in play was enough to convince Arkoff that AIP should hold fire on *The Masque of the Red Death* for the time being. Gordon continued to announce his version at intervals right up to September 1962, by which time 'Fantascope' had been added to its brief list of attributes; needless to say, it was never produced.

With the success of their first three films together, Nicholson and Arkoff moved quickly to offer Price a long-term contract with American International Pictures – his first since that with Fox in 1940. The industry standard was seven years and at this stage in their formative relationship with the actor, the two proposed that it be non-exclusive. The deal promised the kind of security that regular plane-trips between Hollywood and Rome could never provide, and Price signed on the dotted line. From AIP's point of view, it bought a Hollywood name and rubber-stamped its move away from drive-ins and towards legitimacy.

"I particularly enjoyed being around Vincent," Sam Arkoff enthused in later years. "He was much more intelligent, sophisticated, and cultured than some people might expect from a *horror* movie star." Without further ado, Price was cast in his third, but Corman's fourth, Poe film.

Very suddenly there came back to my soul motion and sound – the tumultuous motion of the heart, and, in my ears, the sound of its beating.
EDGAR ALLAN POE,
THE PIT AND THE PENDULUM (1843)

In the meanwhile, Richard Matheson was running out of both ideas and enthusiasm with regard to Poe. Rather than expand another relatively plotless and less well-known story into a cocktail of typically Poe-esque ingredients, he decided instead to employ three – or more accurately, four – minor tales in an anthology piece. These were *Morella*, a combination of *The Black Cat* and *The Cask of Amontillado*, and *The Facts in the Case of M. Valdemar*.

Morella – the weakest of the four – concerns a wife who comes back from the grave by taking possession of the body of her daughter. In *The Black Cat*, a man inters the corpse of his murdered wife behind a wall, only to find his deed undone by the wailing of a black cat which he inadvertently bricked in with her. *The Cask of Amontillado* is similar in theme, though the motive, in this instance, is revenge for unspecified wrongs. *The Facts in the Case of M. Valdemar* deals with a man who is kept in a state of living death by hypnotic trance, and who promptly decomposes when the spell is eventually lifted. These four stories were compressed by Matheson into three *Tales of Terror*.

This is the beat of a human heart... Sit very still and listen. Is your heart beating in this same

Studio portrait from TALES OF TERROR

rhythm? You are experiencing the heartbeat of a dying man, and it is with death and dying that we concern ourselves. What happens at the point of death? – What happens afterwards?
OPENING NARRATION (VINCENT PRICE),
TALES OF TERROR (1961)

After the more conventional melodramatics of *The Premature Burial*, *Tales of Terror* opened on a blank screen, intersected by drips of blood; these dissolved into a trick-shot of a beating human heart as Price narrated in melancholy refrain. It was an impressive prologue which harked back to the baroque pre-title sequence of *Pit and the Pendulum* and intimated that Corman had lost none of his talent for evoking atmosphere, nor yet his appreciation of Poe, in the interval between the two films.

Corman's contretemps over *The Premature Burial* had left its mark, however. Shackled once more to the yoke of AIP, his director's spirit could be seen to flag

within the first reel, where all his previous theories were summarily abandoned and Gothic mood dropped away from the film as quickly as would the tissue on M. Valdemar's putrefying face at the climax of the final episode.

> *And, hourly, grew darker these shadows of similitude, and more full, and more definite, and more perplexing, and more hideously terrible in their aspect. For that her smile was like her mother's I could bear; but then I shuddered at its too perfect identity – that her eyes were like Morella's I could endure; but then they too often looked down into the depths of my soul with Morella's own intense and bewildering meaning.*
> **EDGAR ALLAN POE**, *MORELLA* (1835)

Poe's *Morella* is an allegorical muse about death and rebirth through the mechanism of one's own off-spring which, unusually for its author in introspective mood, actually goes out of its way to give its ubiquitous narrator a name – Locke – thus saving Matheson the trouble of having to invent a moniker for Vincent Price in the opening segment of *Tales of Terror*.

Corman's *Morella* is almost a digest of the ideas and effects which those involved had crafted for the previous films in the series – a 'beginner's guide' to Poe, AIP-style. Lenora returns to her father's manse; there she finds Locke in mourning for his long-dead wife, whose mummified corpse resides in an upstairs room; "Morella, my beloved wife, your murderer has returned," he announces to the predictable portrait on the wall.

By now, the Gothic paraphernalia of the Poes was becoming as outlandish as their plots: Locke's derelict and decrepit mansion is so thickly festooned with cobwebs that a chainsaw would be required to cut through them. He appears to have survived on nothing but whiskey for 26 years, his only companions a rat and a pet tarantula. Lenora (Maggie Pierce) finds all of this only mildly eccentric, however, and adopts a conciliatory approach. But her presence incites the ghost of Morella (Leona Gage) to go a-wandering, and a tussle for Lenora's soul ensues. Morella's spirit takes possession of her body and uses it to wreak an unlikely revenge on the husband who has foolishly remained faithful to her for more than two decades. "All these years, I've waited to return ... All these years, I've waited to avenge myself!" cries the wrathful wraith before strangling the poor sap. The drapes are set alight, and stock footage from *House of Usher* burns to the ground as the three perish in the flames.

Corman tried to vary the mood by post-production processing, bleaching out the colours of the episode to leave black, white and green predominant. It was an act of desperation, for *Morella* was already muted by repetition in all other respects. Its plot was familiar, its sets were second-hand, and its conclusion was cloned from *House of Usher*. In less than two years, the scenarios – as well as the scenery – which AIP had contrived for its Poes had become so over-used as to appear farcical rather than frightening. Price turns in one of his more intense performances for a pasta of pre-digested ingredients and a storyline into which even Matheson could barely be bothered to breathe life or logic. Its function in *Tales of Terror* was merely to prime the viewer for the better episodes which presumably lay ahead of it, however, though on the evidence of *Morella*, followers of Price and Poe were given no reason to feel optimistic.

The thousand injuries of Fortunato I had borne as best I could, but when he ventured upon insult I vowed revenge. You, who so well know the nature of my soul, will not suppose, however, that I gave utterance to a threat. At length, I would be avenged...

EDGAR ALLAN POE,
THE CASK OF AMONTILLADO (1846)

Everyone had more fun with *The Black Cat*, which brought a bloated Peter Lorre out of semi-retirement to play a drunken waster who is cuckolded by the pompous wine connoisseur Fortunato. Montresor murders his wife and walls her body up in his cellar in company with the protesting wine-taster. His subsequent free spending arouses the suspicion of the police, who investigate; they are about to give him a clean bill of health when a hideous screech incites them to tear down the wall – Montresor has inadvertently encased his wife's pet cat in the makeshift tomb, as well.

Lorre was a 57-year-old Hungarian émigré of singular visage, who had made a career for himself in Hollywood after rising to prominence with a chilling portrayal of a child-killer in Fritz Lang's *M* (1931). His best-remembered roles had come in the forties, among them *The Maltese Falcon* (1941) and *The Beast with Five Fingers* (1946), but he had continued to play in a more minor key throughout the fifties and sixties, notably in Disney's *20,000 Leagues Under the Sea*. Weight problems had impeded his progress as time went on, but the roly-poly role of the inebriate husband in *The Black Cat* was one to which he was ideally suited. Price played Fortunato, the preening poseur whose adulterous escapades fall foul of Montresor's pickled sense of poetic justice.

The story itself had been filmed numerous times before, most famously by Universal and Edgar Ulmer in 1934, with Karloff and Lugosi playing the leads, though the plot of Ulmer's version had been further removed from Poe than anything Richard Matheson had so far thought to devise for AIP. Like many authors, Poe re-used themes and ideas, and it was *The Cask of Amontillado* which produced the character of Fortunato, walled up in a wine-cellar for his obnoxious behaviour by the scheming Montresor during a carnival in medieval Italy. *The Black Cat* is actually a reprise of *The Tell-Tale Heart* (both were written in 1843), in which insane protagonists commit random acts of violence in response to perceived wrongs.

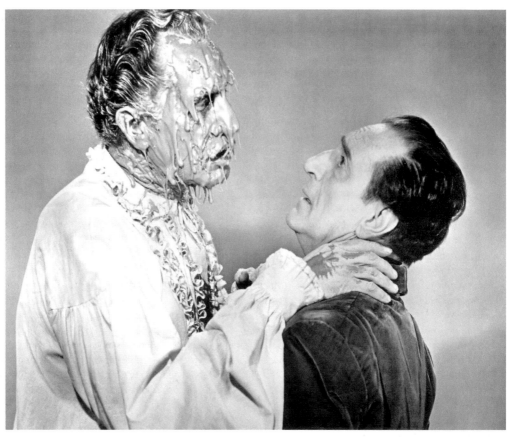

Vincent Price and Basil Rathbone in a publicity shot from TALES OF TERROR

Matheson elaborated the two into one, and wrought a satisfyingly comedic episode wherein Price was afforded an opportunity to prove that he had lost none of his talent for mugging to camera since the great days of *Champagne for Caesar*.

The amalgamation of the two tales produced some anomalies: no explanation is offered as to why a pair of New Englanders should have been christened with Florentine names, nor whither comes their expertise in the grape. And despite having a brace of stories to serve as his base, Matheson still could not extend them sufficiently to avoid the extraneous inclusion of another now-obligatory feature of the AIP Poes: a dream sequence (in which Lorre's head is bounced back and forth between the lovers like a medicine ball). Corman tried to enliven the show by adding a new brush to his palette in the form of freeze-frame transitions, but a lethargy was creeping over the proceedings, not just in Montresor after another night on the town.

The very fact that *The Black Cat* was played as farce showed the way that the wind was blowing,

however, and that the series was nearing its natural end. Even the title-cards which habitually signed off the films were becoming a cursory and carelessly worded addendum to be taken simply as read, rather than forming part of a cohesive whole: 'I had walled the [black] monster up within the tomb – Poe.'

I have been sleeping – and now – now – I am dead.

EDGAR ALLAN POE, *THE FACTS IN THE CASE OF M. VALDEMAR* (1845)

"What exactly is it that occurs at the moment of death – especially to a man who, in that moment, is not permitted to die?" Price interjects in voice-over as *Tales of Terror* moves to a climax with *The Facts in the Case of M. Valdemar*.

For the final episode of the trio, Lorre was replaced by Basil Rathbone, a notable screen villain in his own right in the 1930s, and the face and voice of Sherlock Holmes for several generations of Conan Doyle enthusiasts. Rathbone plays Carmichael, an oily schemer intent on performing a 'momentous experiment' on the dying Mr Valdemar (Price). "Mr Valdemar has consented to be mesmerised *in articulo mortis*," he explains to Valdemar's wife (Debra Paget), "which is to say – " "At the point of death," clarifies Dr James (David Frankham). "I fear it sounds more dreadful than it really is," Carmichael assures her, his plan having been devised to include an experiment of sorts on the body of Mme Valdemar, as well. Valdemar dutifully expires, and his soul is held in stasis by Carmichael's hypnotic chicanery. The purpose of Poe's story was to ponder the imponderable location of the 'limbo' into which the captive Valdemar is now plunged, but this aspect is glossed over as the hypnotist's thoughts turn to the second part of his plan. A fumbled advance at the foot of Valdemar's bed inspires the living corpse to rise from his months-long sleep and take the errant Carmichael to task, his tormentor dying of fright as Valdemar decomposes messily on top of him.

...before that whole company, there lay a nearly liquid mass of loathsome – of detestable putridity.
SCREEN CAPTION, *TALES OF TERROR* (1961)

Rathbone gives a commanding performance as Carmichael – if a little too literally so, as the script runs out of ideas towards its climax and the mesmerist is reduced to screaming "I command you!" to the unco-operative corpse at ever-increasing intervals. Nevertheless, *The Facts in the Case of M. Valdemar* is a taut and efficient slice of storytelling, made the more effective by the technical restraint which Corman exhibits throughout. Debra Paget stood in for Patricia Medina, who was originally cast to play Valdemar's wife and who had last been seen as the Wicked Stepmother in *Snow White and the Three Stooges* (*Snow White and the Three Clowns* in the UK). Medina may have felt that working with Price, Lorre and Rathbone would have been too much like a repeat performance.

The British censor retained the long (and quite horrifying) lap-dissolve disintegration of Valdemar as he bore down on Carmichael but removed the pay-off to the sequence, in which the camera panned to the floor of the room to settle on what remained of Valdemar's corpse, lying prostrate across its prey. Minor trims had been required in all of the Poes, ostensibly to reduce the impact of some of the shock scenes, but this was the first time that an entire shot had been excised and

substituted by a fade to black. Future films in the series were to fare a great deal worse.

Tales of Terror was a curate's egg of a film, switching between the Gothic hyperbole of *Morella* to the broad farce of *The Black Cat* and back again to the conventional dramatics of *The Facts in the Case of M. Valdemar* – a patchwork piece, in truth, the whole of which could barely amount to the sum of its disparate parts. Price is excellent in all three episodes, responding in kind to the novel incursion and casual professionalism of a pair of co-stars of equal esteem, but a deep sense of déjà vu is pervasive throughout. "All three tales are told with Corman's customary skill (and most of his customary trappings, as well – including all the silverware, carpetings and furniture one has come to know so well from *The Pit and the Pendulum*, *The Premature Burial*, and *The Fall of the House of Usher*)," wrote John Cutts in *Films and Filming*. But he added: "Price remains, as ever, the elegant barnstormer he is, and how good it is to see that suave swine Basil Rathbone back in business again."

Matheson's haste in scripting *Tales of Terror* is evidenced by the fact that he constructed no 'wrap-around' narrative in which to contain the stories, in the way that Amicus would later do in their own series of portmanteau productions – nor did he provide them with much in terms of connectivity on their own account. The Price narration supplied a tenuous link, but even that merely spoke of inquiring into what happened at the point of death. It is this lack of internal cohesion which ultimately does *Tales of Terror* down. Matheson had written numerous half-hours for *The Twilight Zone*, episodes of which would be played back-to-back in syndicated re-runs. *Tales of Terror* fares no better: not so much a feature film as a collection of cutting-room cast-offs, all of which failed to make eight reels. It served up a triple helping of Price, to be sure, but one can sometimes have too much of a good thing.

The rate at which AIP was beginning to move through the remaining tales in the writer's oeuvre suggested that, after four films, its Poe shows were running out of steam. For all their flair and garishness, the *Tales of Terror* were nothing more than twists-in-the-tale, a format which television had increasingly begun to make its own. Something other than cobweb and crypt would be required if the series was to continue. At the box-office, however, the film did only marginally less well than its predecessors, so continue it would. Preview audiences in the US had singled out *The Black Cat* episode for special

Boris Karloff, Peter Lorre and Vincent Price in a publicity shot from THE RAVEN

mention. AIP took note and decided that the next film in line would be a comedy from start to finish.

Afraid, my dear... ? There's nothing to be afraid of...

DR SCARABUS (BORIS KARLOFF),
THE RAVEN (1962)

Edgar Allan Poe's immortal poem *The Raven* was published in the *New York Mirror* in January 1845. It earned for its author the meagre sum of $14 in total, but much more in terms of universal acclaim. It also brought him a degree of popular fame, as children would clutch at the raven-like tails of his black frock-coat and address him by the title of the work, at which Poe would turn to them and reply, "Nevermore!"

The diminished returns from *Tales of Terror* demanded at least the same level of added attraction in terms of star-presence for *The Raven*. Consequently, Boris Karloff's illustrious name was added to the cast list along with those of Price and

Lorre, while Hammer scream queen Hazel Court, who had moved to the US after marrying film director Don Taylor, was brought in to fill out the low-cut gowns. "I don't think the picture was really meant to be a comedy," Court said afterwards. "It evolved into one on the set." Matheson and Corman had intended otherwise, but the remark said much about how funny *The Raven* actually turned out to be.

Once upon a midnight dreary, while I pondered,
* weak and weary,*
Over many a quaint and curious volume of
* forgotten lore –*
While I nodded, nearly napping, suddenly there
* came a tapping,*
As of someone gently rapping, rapping at my
* chamber door.*
''Tis some visitor,' I muttered, 'tapping at my
* chamber door –*
Only this and nothing more.'

EDGAR ALLAN POE, *THE RAVEN* (1845)

While Price recites Poe's verse in the regulation way, *The Raven* opens over a montage of stock shots from *House of Usher* and *Pit and the Pendulum* intercut with Monterey seascapes, all of it looking as if it was composited of off-cuts from previous films, spliced together, which indeed it was. Invariably advanced as the most expensive Poe production to date at $350,000, *The Raven* somehow managed to look like the cheapest, with a plasticene corpse, an appalling castle matte, hastily constructed interiors, a woeful lack of 'special' effects and shoddy editing. Either inflation was taking its toll on the series, its three stars were collectively more expensive than anyone had imagined, or the Pathé lab had at last taken revenge for *The Premature Burial* by charging up the optical work.

A raven duly alights on the literary bust of Pallas in the study of medieval wizard Erasmus Craven (Price) and turns into Peter Lorre, who has been sent by wicked Dr Scarabus (Karloff) to entice Craven to his castle, from where he intends to extract the secrets of Craven's magical dexterity by fair means or foul (no pun intended).

According to the Lancer paperback by Eunice Sudak, which was released to tie in with the opening of film, *The Raven* was set in 'England at the end of the Middle Ages – a time of fear and superstition, a time when Magic was not just a word but an absolute reality, a time when strange things went Bump in the night.' The sleeve-blurb went on to add: 'Who was the raven?/Could anyone ignore the warning from beyond the grave?/Do you dare spend one night in Dr Scarabus' sinister castle?/Will your heart stand the suspense?/Is your stomach strong enough to bear the brutal torture of an innocent young girl?/And what of the wanton, lustful beauty whose name was Lenore?'

Front-of-house still from THE RAVEN

RIGHT:
*Peter Lorre and
Vincent Price in*
THE RAVEN

BELOW:
THE RAVEN

The first two reels move at a pace so leaden they could appeal only to those who are likely to be amused by a talking bird or the ingredients in a magician's laboratory, such as jars labelled 'entrails of troubled horse.' Lorre plays the same drunken sot that he essayed in *Tales of Terror* and his improvisational style works against Price's more formal approach, the effect of which was to throw off the latter's timing as he waited for his cues, some of which never came. Karloff was said to have been similarly fazed by Lorre's ad-libbing approach.

The idea of a magic duel by means of hand gestures alone was a novel one, even though its source can be traced to Conrad Veidt's wicked Jaffar in Korda's *The Thief of Baghdad* (1940), or hokum of more recent vintage such as *The Seventh Voyage of Sinbad* (1957). If the film is notable for anything, it is that it represented one of Jack Nicholson's first screen appearances of note. Miscast here, he looks like any one of a dozen other AIP contract players. The passage of time has since told a different story.

The film's funniest scene has Price and Lorre neatly fold a coverlet off a coffin, which Lorre

What indeed? In terms of synopsis, this would serve as well as any, save to append the fact that whatever intrigue was contrived ends with a duel between rival magicians (Price and Karloff) which brings the house down, literally not metaphorically.

promptly throws over his shoulder when Price looks the other way. Corman's direction is half-hearted – nowhere more so than in a fight scene which sees Price's lumbering manservant subdued by a screaming girl and his own inability to aim an axe straight. Oblivious to such defects, *Time* magazine thought the film "a snappy little parody of a horror picture cutely calculated to make the children scream with terror while their parents scream with glee."

Daniel Haller again makes clever use of available stage-space to create a castle interior with vast, vaulted halls, an illusion only betrayed by the stilted pace at which the cast have to run along its forced-perspective corridors. "One cannot fight evil by hiding from it," Price's magician says sagely, as though expounding a statement of foreign policy. The duel itself was primitive, even by the standards of 1963: the majority of the effects are achieved by cutting in camera or cartoon animation, and a scripted sequence which required four stone gargoyles to come temporarily to life had to be conveyed by a zoom-lens and coloured lights. The cast put their collective heart and soul into the affair, especially Karloff in an arduous role, but haste is apparent in shots where they can clearly be seen to be bracing themselves against falling debris. The castle ultimately collapses, the *Usher* roof caves in again and *The Raven*'s sets were struck in readiness for the next opus – or not quite, on this occasion.

Matheson was at a loss for an appropriate feed-line for the inevitable rejoinder which Price was destined to deliver at the fade-out – "quoth the Raven, 'Nevermore'" – but he felt obliged to employ it regardless.

I'm afraid I just don't have it any more.
Dr Scarabus (Boris Karloff),
The Raven (1962)

The slapstick approach to *The Raven* may have been in keeping with the American taste for such laboured antics, but it was less attuned to the British, for whom it held limited appeal. Even Anglo Amalgamated, home of the Carry Ons, opted to sell the film as straight horror, and to leave it up to audiences to decide whether it was funny or not. The censor's predictable 'X' certificate aided it to that end, and it was paired with a second 'X' in the form of *Dr Crippen*, a monochrome reconstruction of the life and crimes of Hawley Harvey Crippen (played by Donald Pleasence), the Edwardian wife-poisoner who was hanged in 1910. Broad comedy was a road down which AIP trod at the expense of ticket sales and theatrical play-dates in the UK, a situation which was to become more pronounced when it cast Price in the role of Dr Goldfoot.

Having carefully formulated the rules by which his Poe films were to be made, Corman had found himself unable to vary them by other than the most direct means – one which he had inaugurated in *A Bucket of Blood* (1959) and *The Little Shoppe of Horrors* (1960): he had introduced comedy into them. There were aspects of the four films which had come close to self-parody in any event, so it was in many ways a logical move. But it was a dangerous and self-destructive game to play (possibly intentionally), because it had threatened to make the whole concept of Gothic horror thematically irretrievable should AIP decide to soldier on regardless. It is to his credit that after sending up the fifth film in the series, Corman was able to return to first base and ensure that the last two Poes which he personally directed were to be among the finest of all.

The Raven may have been the fifth Poe adaptation, but it was made after Vincent Price had returned from a break away from AIP to pursue other projects.

When shooting was finished on *The Raven*, Corman famously utilised the final two days of Boris Karloff's contract (as well as the extant sets) to throw together another film on the back of a bankable name, which he wrote on the run with actor Leo Gordon. The end result was *The Terror*, a piece of Gothic froth inspired by the Poe cycle and sired by opportunism. Anecdotes about the production of *The Terror* have featured time and again in books about the director, invariably accompanied by squeals of admiration for Corman's derring-do, which basically involved encouraging an aged and arthritic Boris Karloff into a swirling studio tank for the sake of a quick buck.

Before *The Terror*, however, Corman had mounted *Tower of London* to utilise a star who happened to be available at a convenient moment – and on that occasion, it had been Price who had been enticed to hock his talent to a tawdry affair which seemed to signify that denied the luxuries of Panavision and Pathecolor, Corman's heart was still very much in the bargain basement.

INTERMISSION

The Tower of London – a monument to the corruption of the soul, where, in the shadowed past, a man gained the throne of England despite the insane ambition that drove him to evil and murder... He escaped the headsman's block, but he could never escape the ghosts of his conscience...

OPENING NARRATION (PAUL FREES),
TOWER OF LONDON (1962)

While Vincent Price fidgeted nervously over news of a happy event in his domestic affairs that looked likely to reach its conclusion in the early part of 1962, Roger Corman had been left to twiddle his thumbs as AIP concentrated on gathering in the revenues from its first four Poes. "My brother knew an independent producer named Eddie Small," he told Ed Naha. "Eddie liked the Poe films and wanted to bankroll a similar picture; he figured the *Tower of London* story would be fine. I said sure – I wasn't doing anything at the time."

'Eddie' Small was the same Edward Small of *The Mad Magician* fame, who had set up and subsequently closed down a number of convenience companies over the years. With his current partner Robert Kent, he had formed Vogue in 1958, under whose banner they had co-produced *It! – The Terror from Beyond Space*, while his own Edward Small Productions recently hosted *Jack the Giant Killer* (1961). Their latest incarnation was Admiral Pictures, or 'AP', initiated to feed off the back of Price and company, if not actually Poe himself.

With Corman on board, his regular crew at AIP followed suit. Script duties for a film which had been announced to the US trades under the more grandiose title of 'A Dream of Kings' fell to Leo Gordon and Amos Powell, both buddies of *Tower of London*'s director. Gordon was an habitual heavy in B-movie fare due to a psychopathic demeanour and stone-killer eyes, but his pretensions to literacy also saw him co-script *The Terror*. Powell's credentials went back only as far as *T-Bird Gang* (1959), which Corman had produced for Filmgroup, the outfit he operated with his producer brother Gene. As 'James B Gordon', Kent also contributed to the screenplay to make it a three-hander in final draft, in a side of the business to which the adage 'more is less' is especially relevant. "I found myself working on a movie with a script that was weak, to say the least," Corman later confessed. "The film just didn't have the impact it could have had."

Part of the reason for *Tower of London*'s 'lack of impact' was the fact that Corman had been sold the film by Small on the basis that it would be shot in colour, only to find when he arrived on set that his camera was loaded with monochrome stock.

94

*Do I laugh to myself because I am ambitious
and would be a king? Or do I laugh at myself,
a misshapen thing that traffics with evil to gain
a throne?*

RICHARD OF GLOUCESTER (VINCENT PRICE),
TOWER OF LONDON (1962)

Like the Universal film which preceded it, *Tower of London* supposedly depicts the rise to power of Richard III of England through the murder of all who stood in his way, including the young 'princes in the tower', Edward V and his brother. On this occasion, Price was elevated to the role of Richard, orchestrating the murder of Clarence instead of being on the receiving end of it. Shot in black-and-white at Producer's Studio on sets left over from *Pit and the Pendulum*, Corman's hysterical epic was a sad return to the bad old days of shoot-and-run: "It is the night of April 9th, in the year 1483 – the night that Edward IV, King of England, will die," the portentous narration intones, after which all veracity is rigorously excluded from a film whose concept of English history makes *Prince Valiant* look like a newsreel.

Tower of London was Shakespeare's Richard Crookback without the Shakespeare, though writers Amos Powell and the two Gordons had tried to mimic the Bard with blunt verse like "Is this defeat, that I stand alone here?" ("Is this a dagger which I see before me?" – *Macbeth*) and the inexplicable "Is it what men do that darkens the skies, or do the skies blacken the souls of men?" ("The evil that men do lives after them,/The good is oft interréd with their bones" – *Julius Caesar*). To put critics off the scent, however, there are a few lines which can claim descent from *Richard III*, to which this film, unlike Universal's, owed most of its plot. The excruciating "And you, sun – you were born this morning, but you are dying now" as Richard looks for any trace of extras on Bosworth Field is the closest the screenplay comes to acknowledging its source. ("Now is the winter of our discontent/Made glorious summer by this sun of York.")

In *Tower of London*, Price delivers a performance of such unseemly high camp that it could only have been fuelled by vaingloriousness or lack of sleep; not so much Richard of Gloucester as Quasimodo of Notre Dame. This is a Richard who *lives* in the Tower of London, reigns for barely a day (he reigned for two years, from 1843-5) before being summoned to Bosworth, a mere afternoon's march away, and wages war by flailing his broadsword against a backdrop of

clips from the 1939 version of the tale, whose own battle scenes were already depleted by studio economics. He is plagued by *Hamlet*'s ghosts, plotted against by *Othello*'s Moor, brought low by a pair of *Romeo and Juliet* lovers, and is cursed to die like *Macbeth*. He presides over a cardboard castle where intrigue is served before breakfast, assassination comes after dinner and evenings are passed in convivial conversation with numerous spectres, of whom there appear to be more in residence than there are palace courtiers. In Shakespeare's *Richard III*, the ghosts appear in the last act only.

If Universal's film had been little more than an historical excuse for Boris Karloff to parade around a torture chamber in club-foot and scowl, Admiral's remake was one for Vincent Price to trot out his already familiar repertoire of grins, grimaces and lop-sided leers. Price starts the proceedings in conventional mode but, within two reels, has descended to cartoon antics as he lopes and lisps from one victim to the next, trampling credibility and his own integrity under velvet-soled feet. No one could expect history to be better served by a ham-fisted Hollywood hack-job than it was by the Bard himself, but a film that displays a map of middle England that looks more like

TOWER OF LONDON

Middle Earth deserves to be consigned to the mire into which Richard plunges appropriately at its climax. "What could he have seen that drove him to his death?" Sir Justin inquires. "Justice," opines the knight. Early reviews were much more likely.

Price showboats his way through this medieval miscellany, cackling and conniving by turns, erect despite a hunched back the size of the White Tower, as though he had decided to give up acting altogether and bow out by revealing its mummery for the farce it often is. He spends much of the film communing with said ghosts, though on this evidence he might have thought them the shades of his performances in *Laura, While the City Sleeps* and *Dragonwyck*. Morris Ankrum, veteran of better days in fright films (often as a military bigwig, as in *Invaders from Mars* in 1953) appears in outsized Archbishop's robes to kiss his career farewell as he arranges for Price to be crowned. (Ankrum died two year later.) TV sitcoms have laughter-tracks; *Tower of London* had a 'crowd' track to mask the solitude of its king's coronation.

Corman had trod the ground of Middle-Age make-believe once before, in *The Undead* (1957), and his *Tower of London* was untimely ripp'd from the same page of history as it never was nor ever could have been. But despite the occasional crib from his own roster of effects (Richard's dead wife rises from her tomb as did Nicholas Medina's in *Pit and the Pendulum*), even dross on this scale could not suppress the natural talent of one of the most influential directors of his generation, and the film proved to be but a blot on the landscape of a unique career.

To Vincent Price, however, *Tower of London* became more of a landmark. It helped to turn him from character actor into caricature; from heavyweight to lightweight. His three Poe films may have been burdened with economies of scale, but they had still been perceived as prestige productions for all that, and they had rescued Price from another blip in his career which had seen him descend to the likes of *Return of the Fly* and *The Bat*. He appeared now to be in danger of exercising that same fatal lack of discretion again; the film was a turkey and he was the ham. It entrenched in the minds of those for whom his performances had always teetered on the edge of farce that camp was the name of his game. The *Tower of London* stood in a place to which Price should never have ventured; his character had been crowned King of England but he had crowned himself the king of hokum. And this time around, there was no road back.

The film was released by the fledgling Tigon Film Distributors in the UK. Unbowed by his experience and some of the worst reviews of his career, Price moved straight into a second for Admiral Pictures, the inspiration for which came from a writer who genuinely went insane, not three who only went money-mad.

For Vincent Price, compensation for the iniquities of *Tower of London* came in the form of a baby daughter – Mary Victoria by name – who was born on 27 April 1962 after shooting was over. He could therefore be forgiven for having had his mind on other matters while playing Richard on auto-pilot, as he could for wishing to enhance the domestic purse. Now blessed with both a son and a daughter (despite a 22-year age-gap between the two), the Prices had no more children. For the sake of their father's professional standing, it was just as well.

> "I'd give anything to be there," said Isbister, "just to hear what he would say to it all."
>
> "So would I," said Warming. "Aye! So would I," with an old man's turn to self pity. "But I shall never see him wake."
>
> He stood looking thoughtfully at the waxen figure. "He will never wake," he said at last. He sighed. "He will never wake again."
>
> But Warming was wrong in that.
>
> An Awakening came.
>
> H G WELLS, WHEN THE SLEEPER WAKES
> (1899)

By March 1962, AIP had announced its intention to follow-up the success of *Master of the World* by casting Vincent Price in a lavish adaptation of the futuristic H G Wells novel, *When the Sleeper Wakes* (alternatively, *When the Sleeper Awakes*) from a screenplay by Ray Russell. (AIP's title was variously an amalgam of the 1899 original and Wells' 1910 revision of his own novel, which he retitled *The Sleeper Awakes*.) It was further announced that the proposed film would go before the cameras in December. Two years later, the 'sleeper' had still not awakened and company president James Nicholson felt obliged to explain the delay to *Famous Monsters of Filmland* editor Forrest Ackerman: "We've had five scripts done on that film and we haven't had the right one yet," he soothed. After another year, Martha Hyer's name was added to the cast list of Wells' 'fantasia of possibility', but still the project slumbered on.

Woody Allen's *Sleeper* finally put paid to the idea in 1973.

Vincent Price could not afford to wait around in the manner of Wells' somnolent hero for a matter of months, let alone years. AIP, in consideration of his plight, had allowed him to sally forth of his own accord while it wrestled with its elusive screenplay. By the time Price returned from his wanderings, Sam Arkoff had moved to ensure that he was never to be allowed out on his own again.

What is the matter with me? It is he, the Horla, who haunts me, and who makes me think of these foolish things! He is within me; he is becoming my soul. I shall kill him!
GUY DE MAUPASSANT, *THE HORLA* (1887)

AIP had mined such a rich seam of box-office gold with its adaptations of Poe that competitors soon thought to unearth other authors in a similar vein from whom they might extract an equally lucrative series. It had already occurred to Roger Corman, while filming *The Premature Burial*, that the weird tales of H P Lovecraft might offer such an opportunity, but some were looking further afield than the literary history of the United States for inspiration.

The weird tradition in the British Isles seemed to belong to Hammer Films in adaptive form, though, truth to tell, Hammer never ventured much further than the works of Mary Shelley or Bram Stoker. Continental Europe had sired few writers who had ploughed the field sufficiently to create oeuvres on which enterprising producers might draw, but one such was Guy de Maupassant.

Independent producer Robert E Kent, veteran of a host of genre offerings like *Curse of the Faceless Man* (1958) and *The Four Skulls of Jonathan Drake* (1959) and co-writer of *Tower of London* under his pseudonym of James B Gordon, was the first outside of AIP to try to capitalise on the combination of Vincent Price and the pen of an author dipped in the literature of Terror. Kent also sought to hedge his bets by hiring the same clutch of Corman regulars to function behind the scenes, including ubiquitous set designer Daniel Haller. There had been more to the success of the five Poe films than Price and a few technicians, however, as *Diary of a Madman* – which went before the cameras in July 1962 as 'The Horla' – was quick to exhibit.

Kent entrusted the direction of 'The Horla' to Viennese émigré Reginald Le Borg, who had learned

FAMOUS MONSTERS OF FILMLAND *Issue 14*

his trade with Universal on second-feature fare like *The Mummy's Ghost* (1944). In the fifties, the cultured Le Borg had been forced to slum it for a summer at Hammer, where, in the manner of one who had studied at the Sorbonne in his youth, he directed *The Flanagan Boy* in his dinner-suit prior to supping every evening at the Savoy. The remainder of his recent career had done little to support his evident taste for the finer things of life: he had directed *The Black Sleep* in 1956 and *Voodoo Island* the following year. The only things that realistically could be said about either of them was that they had starred Rathbone, Chaney Jr and Karloff.

All my life, I have sought knowledge; now, I was granted knowledge rarely granted other men. No more hideous fact could have been conceived to terrify my mind: the Horla really live. They cannot be seen; still they are tangible, composed of solid matter. Only the Lord knows if they are flesh and blood as we are. Why are they here? – Why has their evil been turned loose upon the earth?
SIMON CORDIER (VINCENT PRICE),
DIARY OF A MADMAN (1963)

RIGHT:
DIARY OF A MADMAN

BELOW:
Vincent Price and Harvey Stephens in **DIARY OF A MADMAN**

French magistrate Simon Cordier (Price) finds himself subject to the unwanted attentions of an invisible entity, the Horla, after visiting a murderer in the condemned cell. Possessed by the evil spirit, Cordier embarks upon random acts of violence, starting with the crushing of his pet

goldfinch and ending with the killing and decapitation of a young woman whom he has hired as a sculptor's model (Nancy Kovack). When he discovers that the Horla, though invisible, is not impervious to fire, Cordier traps it in his study and sets the room ablaze. He succeeds in destroying the Horla, but is himself engulfed in flames and burned to death.

Following the example set by the dual source for *Master of the World*, *Diary of a Madman* was based on two stories by the French writer Guy de Maupassant: *The Horla* and *Diary of a Madman*. The invisible Horla comes from the first, the character of the magistrate, the incident of the goldfinch and the impulse to murder are from the second, while the actual 'diary' format features in both. Maupassant was a novelist and prolific short story writer, and these two were among the last in a long and illustrious career. *The Horla* shared its theme with a story by the American writer Fitz-James O'Brien called *What Was It?* (1859), which was the first to introduce the idea of a malign invisible entity. But it is to de Maupassant that the film

Vincent Price and Nancy Kovack in DIARY OF A MADMAN

owes the concept of a race of such beings, and while he was content merely to depict the mental turmoil of one who suddenly finds himself on the receiving end of things in *The Horla*, de Maupassant's delusional (and very modern) take on random slaughter in its companion piece provides the real narrative drive for the film which opted to combine the two.

Injudiciously advertised on release as 'The Most Terrifying Motion Picture Ever Created', *Diary of a Madman* was a hostage to fortune from the off. There was little in it to warrant such a claim. The 'Horla' effects are unsubtle at best: a green light plays over the eyes of those about to succumb to the creature's malign influence, reminding one of the spots which were unsteadily directed at Lugosi's pupils in *Dracula* (1931). The murder of Odette (Kovack) is influenced by the shower scene in *Psycho*, but only in the way that a pavement artist might be influenced by Pissarro.

Le Borg's direction is uninvolving, his means of suggesting the presence of the Horla being to pan slowly around the sets while a disembodied voice booms out the expected threats. Price acts much of the film to thin air, in the way that contemporary stars play to digital effects added later. While he manoeuvres smoothly through his predictable repertoire of emotions, he is clearly uncomfortable in a role which not only requires him to converse with an intangible enemy but to become corrupted to the cause of mayhem at its behest. Cordier romances Odette by alluding to the work of Heinrich Heine, a German poet of Jewish origin who was popular in France in the 19th century and died in exile in Paris in 1856. The nod bears all the hallmarks of Price having appended a cultural tid-bit of his own into an otherwise tepid script to give it a bit of a lift – which is not to discredit the journeyman scribblings of Robert E Kent, but had such a reference been integral to the original, more might have been made of the relationship between the pair were it to have been underscored by verse from the author of 'The Lorelei.'

The Horla is glimpsed briefly at the climax when it is consumed by the conflagration which Cordier has set for it, while a lucky trick shot sees Price meet with a more convincing fiery end than Roger Corman had been able to provide. These few seconds apart, the Horla's impact on the cinema of Terror was muted indeed. "Wherever evil exists in the heart of man, the Horla lives," Father Raymonde (Lewis Martin) declares at the finish, reminding viewers that the last time they saw this particular priest intone a dire warning, he was immediately fried by a Martian death-ray – in George Pal's *The War of the Worlds* (1953).

"The terror one feels in the belief of approaching madness is...", writes Cordier in his titular diary. When de Maupassant wrote his tales in 1897, he was himself experiencing the first symptoms of the madness which was to cost him his life five years later. Seen in that light, *Diary of a Madman* is a more convincing account of one man's struggle with an invisible force than it might otherwise appear to be.

In addition to de Maupassant, Kent had alighted on the tales of indigenous author Nathaniel Hawthorne, a contemporary of Poe's. In their whimsical approach, Hawthorne's short stories were more akin to the rural fancies of Washington Irving, who had been influenced by a lengthy exposure to European Gothic after moving to England in 1815. The difference between the two was in their background: Irving was a New Yorker, while Hawthorne came from a Puritan stock which had been active in the infamous Salem witch-trials of 1692. The part which one of his ancestors had played in condemning 19 innocents to death haunted Hawthorne throughout his life and came to feature time and again in his fiction. His best-known novels, *The Scarlet Letter* and *The House of the Seven Gables*, were both born in the God-fearing flames of judicial retribution, the latter concerning a blood-feud between the Salem families of Pyncheon and Maule.

Armed with the material of another writer whose work fortuitously resided in the public domain, Admiral lost no time in shunting the amenable Price from de Maupassant to Hawthorne. The next in its proposed pair of films was put onto the floor in August, virtually back-to-back with the first, but as a compendium piece on this occasion, featuring three separate stories.

For its second outing, Admiral devised a formula that more obviously derived from AIP. The film went into production as 'The Corpse-Makers', but this was soon changed to cash in on the success of *Tales of Terror*, the film reverting to Hawthorne's title for the

collection of short stories from which one of its three episodes was drawn: *Twice Told Tales*.

Hawthorne's *Twice-Told Tales* was first published in 1837, then revised and expanded in 1842; of the 20 stories in the original text, Kent chose only *Dr Heidegger's Experiment*, to which he added *Rappaccini's Daughter* (1844) and a heavily abridged draft of the author's 1851 novel *The House of the Seven Gables* as a climacteric. None of these overly simplistic and decidedly old-fashioned moral allegories were natural candidates for a film which chose to project itself on screen via a title-card that proclaimed 'A Trio of Terror'. But in 1962, the incorporation of Vincent Price's name in a cast-roller could have financed an adaptation of the fables of Aesop.

Within its portmanteau structure, the film was much influenced by the techniques which currently were being employed in similar anthologies on television, like *The Twilight Zone* and *The Outer Limits*, even to the extent of adding moralising homilies to the close of each episode. Price naturally featured in all three of the tales, but none of them added up to more than the sum of his parts.

"My dear old friends," said Dr Heidegger, motioning them to be seated. "I am desirous of your assistance with one of those little experiments with which I amuse myself in my study."
Nathaniel Hawthorne, *Twice-Told Tales: Dr Heidegger's Experiment* (1837)

Dr Heidegger's Experiment was a short commentary on human nature which might better have suited one of Warner Bros' 'Merrie Melodies.' The doctor in question is a cartoon alchemist who has formulated an elixir of youth, from which he invites four friends to partake while he observes the results. The quartet consists of a widow and three rival suitors from days gone by; as they quaff the liquid and shed their years, old enmities return and a renewed outbreak of ancient hostilities is only prevented when the rejuvenating effect of the potion wears off. The moral of the tale is that age or experience do not of themselves bring wisdom, only the appearance of it.

The film elaborated this notion into a three-hander featuring Price, Sebastian Cabot and Mari Blanchard. Cabot plays Heidegger, who in true Poe tradition unaccountably keeps the body of his long-dead fiancée in a crypt at the bottom of his garden. He and his friend Alex (Price) find that the cadaver has been

Vincent Price
and Beverly
Garland in
**TWICE TOLD
TALES**

saved from putrefaction by exposure to a strange salt
which has filtered into the crypt in rainwater.
Heidegger collects a phial of the solution and the two
imbibe – within minutes, they are their youthful
selves again. He then thinks to feed the liquid to the
corpse of his beloved. She too revives, but old passions
are aroused and a 38-year-old secret is revealed: Alex
had also loved Sylvia and had poisoned her on the very
night of her wedding to Heidegger out of jealousy. A
tussle ensues and Heidegger is killed, but the effects
of the solution wear off and Sylvia crumbles to dust.
An old man once more, Alex has killed his one true
friend for the sake of a memory.

> *Man's dream of eternal youth – an illusion that
> begins with the first awakening of his mind and
> lasts until the moment when he goes to his final
> rest. Only a dream, perhaps, but what would life
> be without our dreams?*
>
> **NARRATION** (VINCENT PRICE), TWICE TOLD
> TALES: DR HEIDEGGER'S EXPERIMENT (1962)

Dr Heidegger's Experiment belongs to Sebastian
Cabot, a portly character actor who in later years was
to earn more from his talent for voice-over than from
his appearances on the screen. Cabot puts heart into
the unlikely part of the geriatric doctor who has pined
for lost love for almost four decades. As Alex
Medbourne, Price has little to do but watch and wait
while Heidegger embarks on his precipitous
experiment, but the array of expressions he employs to
intimate to the audience the real nature of the relationship between himself and Sylvia (before the plot
intercedes to do the job for him) are craft itself. Given
that he is afforded few close-ups by Sidney Salkow's
half-hearted direction, Price's playing in these crucial
scenes is the more remarkable. *Dr Heidegger's
Experiment* is an interesting short, let down by crude
special effects, a fatal lack of pace and an ending as
lukewarm as that of the story on which it was based.
And nothing in the episode quite approaches the *frisson* which is to be found in Hawthorne, when the
recipients of the elixir prance around the laboratory in

Vincent Price
and Brett
Halsey in
**TWICE TOLD
TALES**

the bloom of illusory youth in front of a mirror which insists on reflecting their real selves.

The next tale was equally unusual, but the film's overall tendency towards melodrama and signal absence of any real horror was even more pronounced in *Rappaccini's Daughter* than it had been in its predecessor.

> *When, in his walk through the garden, he came to the magnificent plant that hung its purple gems beside the marble fountain, he placed a kind of mask over his mouth and nostrils, as if all this beauty did but conceal a deadlier malice.*
>
> NATHANIEL HAWTHORNE,
> *RAPPACCINI'S DAUGHTER* (1841)

A young man comes upon a beautiful girl in an apothecary's garden. Attracted to her, he makes advances, but finds to his horror that her blood has been artificially reconstituted by an over-protective father and that she is the literal possessor of a kiss of death. Discovering himself infected through his own proximity to her, he demands that she swallow an antidote; she dies as a result, and Rappaccini's misguided attempt to chemically protect his daughter is undone.

Kent's screen treatment adhered more closely to Hawthorne's story on this occasion, and thus it depicted his quaint Gothic romance (with its fairy-tale trappings of wicked guardian, virginal princess,

handsome young prince, strange brew and secret garden) anachronistically intact. Again, any potential for horror is minimised, as might have been expected of a fable whose sole purpose was to make a laboured point about the misappliance of science and the road to Hell being paved with good intentions.

Story and film are both set in Renaissance Italy and Brett Halsey, who had been teamed with Price in *Return of the Fly* and was shortly to depart his native shores to pursue a more lucrative career in modern Italy, cuts an attractive figure as the ill-starred suitor of Beatrice, Rappaccini's poisoned daughter (Joyce Taylor). Fearing himself infected by the same serum, he reaches out to a spider that is spinning its web, whereupon the unfortunate arachnid turns a pretty purple and expires; the scene might have been seen as an in-joke about revenge for what befell his screen father at the climax of *The Fly* were it not for the fact that it exists in Hawthorne's original.

As the alchemist Rappaccini, Price hovers on the edge of the narrative, elegantly clad in a smoking jacket – though most of the smoking, in this episode, emanates from objects which inadvertently come into contact with the botanical results of his chemical engineering. This includes their creator, who climactically immolates himself on his own poisoned plant.

> *Where does evil begin? Where does it end? Can the eye of Man really discern the fine line that*

separates sanity from... madness? If not, can there be a judge so wise that he can measure a man's reasons for the sins he commits?
NARRATION (VINCENT PRICE), *TWICE TOLD TALES: RAPPACCINI'S DAUGHTER* (1962)

On this showing, *Rappaccini's Daughter* was the kind of mad scientist movie that might have been made by the Brothers Grimm had they had access to Technicolor cameras rather than quill pens – it was not so much old-fashioned as belonging to another era entirely. The last episode of the trio was *The House of the Seven Gables*, which even in abridged form at least offered the opportunity for its director to indulge in some of the supernatural mayhem which Universal had seen fit to exclude from its own version. But here too, *puppenspielen* effects intruded to destroy the illusions before they had time to begin.

Now, Sir, whenever my thoughts recur to this seven-gabled mansion – (the fact is so very curious that I must needs mention it) – immediately, I have a vision or image of an elderly man, of remarkably stern countenance, sitting in an oaken elbow-chair, dead, stone dead, with an ugly flow of blood upon his shirt-bosom. Dead, but with open eyes!
NATHANIEL HAWTHORNE,
THE HOUSE OF THE SEVEN GABLES (1851)

Hawthorne wrote *The House of the Seven Gables* in 1850, constructing it from incidents in Massachusetts' Puritan past (including a real murder similar to the one in the story), and a visit to a cousin's house in Turner Street in Salem, which was reputed to have at one time possessed seven gables. The theme of the novel is best summed up in a phrase that Hawthorne committed to his notebook the year before he started work on the tale: "To inherit a great fortune; to inherit a great misfortune." Universal had adapted the basic narrative in 1940, but the episode in *Twice Told Tales* concerned itself solely with the back story, which involved a 'secret of incalculable wealth' that was supposed to be hidden in the ancient manse, as well as a curse that warned the males of the Pyncheon line that they would be given 'blood to drink' at their moment of death.

Gerald Pyncheon (Price) therefore arrives at the House when the bulk of Hawthorne's story has already unfolded, intent on conducting a search for the hidden treasure. To explicate things, the screenplay drags in a précis of the book which laboriously delineates the feud between the Pyncheons and the Maules – minus Hawthorne's main player – and literalises what was intended to be symbolic in the original: namely, that the Pyncheon manse was built over a grave-site.

To cut to the chase, various ghostly visitants reveal the aforementioned grave to be that of Matthew Maule, the originator of the curse. When Pyncheon disinters the corpse, he discovers a plan of the House and thus the location of the loot. But Maule's skeleton is missing a forearm; on the unlocking of the hidden chamber, a skeletal hand reaches out of the darkness to strangle Gerald. The curse having been fulfilled, the House implodes and is no more.

Thus did the House of the Seven Gables come to its end... Destroyed by the decay and greed that corroded its very foundations. It was a time now for Matthew Maule to find... peace.
CLOSING NARRATION (VINCENT PRICE),
TWICE TOLD TALES: THE HOUSE OF THE SEVEN GABLES (1962)

Cluttered as this episode is by its constant need to sustain itself through references to a plot which it had chosen to discard at the outset, it nevertheless enjoys some effective moments of Grand Guignol: as the curse begins to tighten its grip, the walls of the House run with blood; when the key to the alleged fortune is finally unearthed, Pyncheon turns on his grasping sister and buries a pickaxe in her skull ("It's a night for celebration... but I intend to celebrate *alone*"). But none of this has anything to do with Hawthorne, while the climactic collapse of the old manse owes more to Poe's House of Usher than it does to *The House of the Seven Gables*. AIP regulars from sci-fi films gone by, Richard Denning (*The Day the World Ended*) and Beverly Garland (*It Conquered the World*), are imported to bolster the numbers of the warring clans, but terror is largely absent and the last tale of the trio is driven to its tame conclusion by some old-fashioned interplay between a pair of spectral lovers.

A happy ending is appended to the destruction, whereby Pyncheon's wife falls into the arms of a descendant of Maule's. A similar situation applied to the novel itself, however, where after a brilliant chapter intimating the death of Pyncheon, Hawthorne effectively decried all that had gone before it and contrived a climax which better suited the predominantly female readership for whom he felt the book eventually destined.

To a degree, *The House of the Seven Gables* can be seen as a literary puzzle in the manner of Charles Dickens' *The Mystery of Edwin Drood* (1870), in that the author's original intention will never be known. On the other hand, Admiral's intentions for Vincent Price had become all too clear, especially to Sam Arkoff. In the meanwhile, Price had signed with Robert Lippert to shoot a Richard Matheson script in Rome. But the next time he returned from the Via Veneto, he was to find himself back at AIP for good.

Neither *Diary of a Madman* nor *Twice Told Tales*, despite being shot by different directors, could manage any of the mobility of camerawork or fluidity of style which Corman had brought to the Poes. Le Borg and Salkow were studio functionaries, more in tune with churning out TV fare of an undemanding nature than they were with the intricacies of engendering terror. For all his faults, Corman was a stylist – an *auteur*, in the modish parlance of a new breed of cinéastes reared on *Cahiers du Cinéma* – and he had stamped his style on the whole Poe series as surely as Price had now created a niche for himself as the archetypal Poe-tagonist.

Vincent Price was an actor who rarely broke sweat; he was much too *louche* and svelte and silky-smooth as a performer to stoop to anything so low as real emotion, and he would grumble in interviews that Corman never provided him with much in the way of direction. But there had been a chemistry between the two and, however it had been achieved, Price came closer to giving of himself for Roger Corman than he did for any other director that he worked for throughout the remainder of the sixties and seventies. Actors are rarely best-placed to judge such matters, and Price is on record as considering Sidney Salkow (with whom he was to work again when he afforded union back-up on *The Last Man on Earth*) in a favourable light. Salkow may have been capable of supplying a suitably *simpatico* attitude towards his actors on set, but as a filmmaker he was adequate at best.

If Price simply 'walked through' the films that he made away from AIP in 1962-3, as though their various scenarios were but fleeting shadows on a backdrop against which he could deliver his stock performance of antagonism alternated with anguish, none would more literally depict the actor as commodity alone on a sea of schlock than *The Last Man on Earth*, which he

went into after touching base with AIP for *The Raven*. Fortunately for Price, his return from wandering in the wasteland of an Italian sci-fi thriller was to reunite him with Roger Corman once more.

> *Before they could get at him again, he slammed the door in their faces, locked it, bolted it, and dropped the heavy bar into its slots. Robert Neville stood in the cold blackness of his house, listening to the vampires scream.*
>
> **RICHARD MATHESON**, I AM LEGEND (1954)

The history of *The Last Man on Earth* dates back to the early days of Hammer Horror. The film was based on *I Am Legend*, the debut novel of author and screenwriter Richard Matheson, which was originally published in 1954 to considerable acclaim. While Hammer was in production with *Dracula* in November of 1957, house producer Anthony Hinds bought the rights to Matheson's story of a vampire plague which had swept across the earth, and flew the author to the UK to write the script. This Matheson did under a new title (*The Night Creatures*), but both his screenplay and the idea in general were given a definitive thumbs-down by an anxious British Board of Film Censors and its then-Secretary, John Nicholls.

The equivalent body in America, the MPAA (Motion Picture Association of America), was just as concerned. It pointed out in a letter to Hinds that the proposed script contained brutality, profanity, bad language and immorality, as well as an "over-emphasis on gruesomeness," all of which would have denied the proposed film a Code Seal of Approval in the US. Val Guest had already been signed to direct, but Hammer was left with little choice; the company retained the title (which it utilised for the US release of *Captain Clegg* in 1962), but it sold Matheson's script to Robert Lippert, an 'indie' with ties to Fox shadow company Associated Producers.

Unlike most of its peers, Associated had continued to produce second-feature sci-fi fare for its parent to distribute long after the boom days of the 1950s had reached their end. Associated had independently been responsible for *The Hand of Death* and *The Day Mars Invaded Earth* (both 1962), while Lippert would fly across the Atlantic to oversee *The Earth Dies Screaming* (1964), which was soon followed by *Curse of the Fly* (also 1964). Never ones to waste an idea, let alone a purchased screenplay, Lippert and Associated teamed up in January 1963 to mount an Italian co-production

based on a redraft of the Matheson script by William F Leicester, a staff writer on the likes of *Gunsmoke* and, later, *Bonanza*.

Having lost its original title, the revised version had been retitled *The Last Man on Earth*, but to remove it even further from its source, Matheson chose to employ the pseudonym of 'Logan Swanson' for his screen credit. Sicilian-born Ubaldo Ragona was hired to direct the film, while Sidney Salkow was charged with overseeing an 'Americanised' version.

In brief, *I Am Legend* concerned the attempts of Robert Neville (Robert Morgan in the film) to both survive and find a cure for said plague. Holed up alone in his house, he is nightly assailed by the vampire horde until eventually he stumbles upon another survivor, Ruth. But Ruth is a hybrid, whose body has evolved to accommodate the plague bacilli – and she is not alone. Ultimately it is Neville, with his stakes and his garlic, who poses a threat to the new order and

who therefore has to be disposed of. He opts to take his own life, bemused by the thought that, in the new tomorrow, it is *he* who will become 'Legend.'

Matheson had contrived a less downbeat ending for his original draft, but the problem which remained unresolved in the reworked version was that any film derived from it should really have been made years before. In Ragona's hands, *The Last Man on Earth* looked as though it had been.

> Another day to live through; better get started. December, 1965 – is that all it has been since I inherited the world, only three years? Seems like a hundred million...
>
> **ROBERT MORGAN** (VINCENT PRICE),
> *THE LAST MAN ON EARTH* (1963)

Due to the international nature of the co-production, most of Matheson's dialogue had been stripped from

THE LAST MAN
ON EARTH

the script and replaced with narration, so individual territories could more easily dub the film into their respective languages. This had a major impact on the narrative structure. In the original, Neville's predicament was presented in prologue before a flashback formed the bulk of the story and brought things up to speed; in *The Last Man on Earth*, the same flashback is delayed until the tale is well underway, which brings the mid-section of the film to a grinding halt. The most significant change comes at the climax, however, which jettisons both script and story in favour of a prolonged night-time chase, which ends with Morgan cornered in a church and symbolically speared to death by the 'new' humans.

Shot in Rome but ostensibly located in some unspecified Europolis, the bleak cityscapes of *The Last Man on Earth* effectively encapsulated the prevalent mood of Cold War paranoia and the ever-present threat of global conflict which had influenced Hammer's *The Damned* (1961), and which had become more acute after the Cuban Missile Crisis, four months before the film went into production. The plague-pit into which Morgan hurls the bodies of those he has killed is an enduring

image, all the more so because of its spare staging on an extant landfill site.

In Matheson's story, Robert Neville becomes the problem instead of the cure; so it was with Vincent Price. No one who had read the novel would have cast Price in the role of Neville had he *been* the last man on earth. In Robert Lippert's eyes, it seems he was.

Price neither wields a stake with the conviction of Peter Cushing, nor looks as though he is cruising the deserted streets to any purpose more life-threatening than the procurement of art treasures. His performance lacks energy and drive, both of which might be adjudged to be in character but neither of which are. Given that he represents the focus of the film for the whole of its 86-minute running-time, his limp-wristed approach to the role is nothing short of a dereliction of duty. *The Last Man on Earth* required a powerhouse performance from whoever played Morgan, and Price left it to Charlton Heston to deliver one in a 1971 remake called *The Omega Man* (which was less faithful to its source but much better at depicting its protagonist's struggle against solitude, despair and the encroachment of inevitable fate).

The most effective scene in the film comes at the midway point, and features in both novel and original script: Morgan refuses to have his wife cast into the plague-pit and himself buries her at dead of night. He returns home to ponder his isolation when he hears a noise outside and sees the door-handle turn. He throws open the door, and a figure emerges from the darkness: it is his wife. "Robert..." she pleads. A genuine sense of terror is engendered by this brief interlude, which owes something to the W W Jacobs story *The Monkey's Paw*, but Ragona fails to sustain the mood in the other vampire attacks, where Morgan's undead assailants are even more lethargic and ineffectual than he is.

The film was universally dismissed at the time of its somewhat sporadic initial release due to its cheapskate production values, disjointed script, weak performances, murky photography and determinedly downbeat storyline. If ever a horror subject required a tour-de-force from an actor in order to carry an audience along, *The Last Man on Earth* was the one. Price failed it in every respect. Years of walking through such roles now seemed to be taking their toll; even a montage of scenes which purport to show Morgan stalking and staking the vampires – inserted in post-production to pep up proceedings in the early stages of the tale – fails to inspire anything but tedium. Price's evident lack of interest in the role is almost as infectious as the plague which his character is ostensibly determined to defeat, and the *longeurs* he is forced to endure while waiting out the nightly attacks are every bit as interminable for the viewer as they are for Morgan himself. "Another day..." he says again halfway through the proceedings. He might as well have added "...another dollar."

The Last Man on Earth went unreleased in the UK until 1966, more than three years after it was made. Even then, it found few venues willing to entertain it. It may have had Price's name on the posters, but that was still required to be attached to items of quality, and not just any old tat from the suitcases of travelling producers.

In a little under 12 months during 1962-3, Vincent Price had starred in six horror films, only two of which were produced by AIP.

Price's three for Admiral Pictures may have originated with authors other than Poe, but to the lay audience, there appeared to be little difference – they were all period horrors, and all of them featured similarly eccentric central characters, haunted by fear and plagued by inner demons; *Twice Told Tales*, in particular, had adhered to the same anthology structure as *Tales of Terror*. Prior to these and *The Last Man on Earth*, Price had participated in one other which was equally dire (*Confessions of an Opium Eater*), and AIP's involvement in the five was no more than tangential. None of this was doing the company or its primary asset any long-term good. Price's credibility as a performer was being undermined by repetition and over-exposure, and AIP's investment in him was starting to look a little shaky. Arkoff knew that AIP alone had to provide Price with the working security he so consistently sought, and Arkoff therefore re-negotiated the actor's contract to ensure a continuous flow of roles in which he could utilise his talents in return for a new exclusivity clause. "After a time, according to his contract, he could only do horror or sci-fi pictures exclusively for us," Arkoff told Lucy Chase Williams. "He could do other pictures, but *not* horror pictures."

From this point on, Vincent Price would only make the kind of film for which he is now renowned in association with AIP, and Arkoff's definition of 'horror' was wide-ranging – "If he slapped someone's face, that was a horror picture. It was a very complete definition!"

With Price back in the fold, Arkoff announced a slew of new productions over the next five years, 11 of which were ostensibly to originate in the writings of Edgar Allan Poe. Among the more conventional propositions, like *The Haunted Palace*, were esoterica such as *The Angel of the Odd*, *The Four Beasts in One* (which in its literary form is obscurely subtitled *The Homo-Cameleopard*), *The Thousand-and-Second Tale of Scheherezade* and *The Gold Bug*.

Most of this was standard industry hype, though it was also designed to show willing to the actor who had now become the exclusive property of AIP. Of the more exotic titles in the list, only *The Gold Bug* was actively considered for production, and it would be so for the next seven years. "It was something we thought of making simply because it was a Poe," Arkoff told Christopher Koetting in 1996. "It was really Poe's most complete story, but it would have been hard for us to do because it's not horror." In that single statement of principle, and in practice as the 1960s got into their stride, was the fate of Vincent Price finally decreed.

No sooner was the ink dry on their redrafted compact than Arkoff hustled his charge into a waiting coach and sent him packing towards *The Haunted Palace*.

ACT 4

TALES
OF TERROR
(REPRISE)

I advise you, Mr Ward, to leave this village... I advise you to flee it as you would from a madman with a knife, who feels compelled to destroy you before you can destroy him.

DR WILLETT (FRANK MAXWELL), THE HAUNTED PALACE (1963)

riginally slated as 'The Haunted Village', *The Haunted Palace* went into production in April 1963, immediately after Price returned from filming *The Last Man on Earth* in Rome. His last film for AIP and Roger Corman had been *The Raven*, which Corman now privately considered to have been the last gasp of the Poe franchise in its existing form.

The Haunted Palace was a departure for both of them, and while Richard Matheson had set to work on a strictly non-Poe comedy in the same macabre vein, Corman had called upon Charles Beaumont, co-scripter of *The Premature Burial*, to pen a screenplay based on a novel written in 1927 by H P Lovecraft and called *The Case of Charles Dexter Ward*. The stumbling block was that the film had to be set in 'Poe' period, to utilise the costumes and standing sets of the erstwhile series.

Corman had wanted to film *The Case of Charles Dexter Ward* with Pathé, after making *The Premature Burial*; he further intended that it should feature the same cast, namely Ray Milland and Hazel Court, with the addition of Boris Karloff. But his reinstatement at AIP put paid to that idea and Vincent Price had automatically been allotted the role of Ward in Milland's place, along with the requisite nod to Poe. "I fought against calling it a Poe film," Corman told Ed Naha, "but AIP had made so much money with Poe films that they just stuck his name on it for box-office appeal." Roger Corman has had little else to say about *The Haunted Palace* over the years; Sam Arkoff may have found the Pathé affair amusing, but the joke did not appear to have been universally shared.

Charles Ward, as we have seen, first learned in 1918 of his descent from Joseph Curwen. That he at once took an intense interest in everything pertaining to the bygone mystery is not to be wondered at; for every vague rumour that he heard of Curwen now became something vital to himself, in whom flowed Curwen's blood.

H P LOVECRAFT,
THE CASE OF CHARLES DEXTER WARD (1927)

Howard Phillips Lovecraft is considered by many to be a spiritual successor to Poe. Both were New Englanders (Poe from Boston; Lovecraft from Providence, Rhode Island); both wrote for magazines primarily (the 'pulps' in Lovecraft's case); both died young and passed their lives in relative seclusion, and both were creatively concerned with Terror. There the similarities end, though, for while Poe's stories were psychological in approach, Lovecraft's were invariably part of a self-invented collective known as the 'Cthulhu Mythos', a science-fictional cosmology which reworked the Christian myth of Satan in favour of a pantheon of demonic entities known as the 'Old Ones.'

Lovecraft's novel is set in 1928, roughly contemporaneous to the period in which it was written. The protagonist in the novel is Dr Willett, who is investigating the curious case of Charles Dexter Ward by virtue of his position as the family physician; Ward is incarcerated in an insane asylum at Providence, Rhode Island, accused of necromancy. As Willett probes deeper into the circumstances which led Ward to his present predicament, he discovers that the young man had developed an unhealthy obsession with a 'lost' ancestor who bore him a remarkable resemblance – Joseph Curwen, who in times past was rumoured to be a warlock. Employing techniques gleaned from Curwen's private papers, Ward had tried to raise Curwen from the dead, and the unholy consequences of his alchemical experiments had brought about his confinement. Willett explores Ward's home and finds a maze of underground tunnels which lead to chambers containing the abhuman results of occult dabblings...

...he discerned only the brick-faced top of a cylindrical well perhaps a yard and a half in diameter and devoid of any ladder or other means of descent. As the light shone down, the wailing changed suddenly to a series of horrible yelps; in conjunction with which there came again that sound of blind, futile scrambling and slippery thumping. The explorer trembled, unwilling even to imagine what noxious thing might be lurking in that abyss; but in a moment he mustered up the courage to peer over the rough-hewn brink, lying at full length and holding the torch downward at arm's length to see what might lie below.

H P LOVECRAFT,
THE CASE OF CHARLES DEXTER WARD (1927)

Realising the truth at last, Willett confronts Ward. He knows now that the man in the cell is not Charles Dexter Ward at all; he is Joseph Curwen, conjured by black magic, who has killed Ward and taken his place on the earthly plane. A more powerful spell on Willett's part brings an end to Curwen's temporary tenancy.

While held by common consent to be a 'Mythos' tale, *The Case of Charles Dexter Ward* is not strictly part of the cycle in that it does not feature any of Lovecraft's fabled gallery of Old Ones, while the grimoire, Necronomicon, warrants only a passing mention. Rather, it is a pure tale of black magic (like *The Thing on the Doorstep*, to which it bears striking affinity), and a prospective adapter might have side-stepped the more overt elements and treated it as such. Charles Beaumont chose the opposite route and concocted a digest of iconic data that cluttered and conflated his script, as well as making no sense whatever to anyone not steeped, anorak-style, in the minutiae of Mythos lore. The result was a patchwork of Lovecraftiana, subverted into a stereotypical tale of possession and set in a Gothic castle which inexplicably has been transplanted to New England "stone by stone" from "Europe, somewhere – no one knows... No one wants to know," as one of the locals all too candidly explains.

In the meantime, James Nicholson had turned up a poem by Edgar Allan Poe which had been incorporated into *The Fall of the House of Usher* but which was actually written (and first published) some months earlier: *The Haunted Palace*. This was considered sufficient to provide the appropriate association, as well as an early voice-over verse for Price and the regulation

caption at the close. *The Case of Charles Dexter Ward* now became Poe's *The Haunted Palace*, and everything else was down to Charles Beaumont.

Poe's contribution to *The Haunted Palace* lay only with its titular abode (which replaced Ward's 'modest two-and-a-half storey wooden town house' in Olney Court, Providence); the story of a protagonist possessed by the evil spirit of a demonic ancestor springs entirely from *The Case of Charles Dexter Ward*. But anything more obviously Lovecraftian than the bare bones of his plot is confined to an expositional exchange concerning Joseph Curwen:

Dr Willet: *He was a strange man; there were terrible rumours about him.*
Ward: *Such as?*
Dr Willet: *It was thought, Mr Ward, that he had gained possession of a book called the... Necronomicon. Have you heard of it?*
Ward: *No.*
Dr Willet: *Well, it obviously never existed except in the minds of the superstitious, but they claimed it held enough secrets to give a man absolute power. Of course, every mythology has such a book, but the Necronomicon supposedly contained formulas through which one could communicate with, or even summon, the Elder Gods – the Dark Ones from beyond who had once ruled the world, now are merely waiting for an opportunity to regain that control. Cthulhu... Yog-Sothoth... Dreadful rubbish, I know; still, the people of Arkham believe it. They claim that Joseph Curwen, and two other warlocks, were trying to open the gates to these Dark Gods...*
Ward: *Open the gates... How?*
Dr Willet: *They claim that Joseph Curwen was trying to mate those beings with humans... to create a new race, through which the gods could regain the control. That's how they explain the mutated births – unsuccessful experiments passed on from generation to generation, carried in the blood.*

FRANK MAXWELL AND VINCENT PRICE,
THE HAUNTED PALACE (1963)

Beaumont's reading of Lovecraft's universe was strictly biological in tone, if not founded on the Nazi-inspired science of eugenics. In essence, it all comes down to mutants locked up in attic rooms, the

Debra Paget and Vincent Price in **THE HAUNTED PALACE**

by-products of necromantic breeding programmes between human females and inexplicable life-forms from beyond the stars. *The Haunted Palace* set the concept in train, but it would be continued (albeit obliquely) in *Monster of Terror* (1965) and made unequivocal in the more explicit *The Dunwich Horror* (1969). The 'Mythos' stories on which these films were based were more complex than that, and grounded as much in philosophy as physiology, but *The Haunted Palace* dispensed with the esoterica of ritual to concentrate effort on the creation of a new race of beings by purely conventional means.

Charles Ward (Price) and his wife Ann (Debra Paget) have inherited a 'palace' in the New England village of Arkham that was owned by Ward's great-grandfather, Joseph Curwen, a warlock who was burned at the stake 110 years before. Ward soon falls under the influence of Curwen, whose spirit emanates from a portrait in the hall; together with two companions, he resurrects the body of a former mistress, Hester Tillinghast. After avenging

themselves on the villagers for the sins of their forefathers, the four continue with Curwen's diabolical scheme, which involves interbreeding local girls with an entity confined in the castle crypt. As Ward/Curwen prepares to offer up his wife as a sacrifice, the villagers storm the castle as did their ancestors a century before. Ward and wife are rescued in the nick of time by Dr Willett, but Curwen remains in possession of Ward's soul.

I don't know how I can ever repay you for what you've done, Dr Willet, but I intend to try...
    CHARLES DEXTER WARD (VINCENT PRICE),
        THE HAUNTED PALACE (1963)

With *The Haunted Palace*, AIP appeared intent on descending to the depths Hammer would plumb in *The Evil of Frankenstein* after a similar period of retrenchment (the two were made only six months apart). Gone was the care and crafting which had marked out the earlier Poes and in their stead had come unseemly haste, a perplexing sense of time and place, and an over-reliance on formula to counter the effects of the usually competent Corman being disorientated by the unfamiliar terrain.

The blame for some of it could be laid at the feet of the novel on which the film was based: a difficult book at best, and one which no self-respecting scribe would have attempted lightly, let alone try to graft onto a poem by Edgar Allan Poe at his masters' behest. Components from *The Case of Charles Dexter Ward* are scattered across the screenplay like confetti: the portrait of Curwen; the ancient altar in the crypt; the team of fellow-wizards, Orne and Hutchinson; the theme of necromancy. Deprived of a cohesive narrative in which to dwell, however, they merely conjoin to become a bluffer's guide to Lovecraft, to which the concept of human sacrifice in the palace basement is entirely incidental.

Price strides above it all, as usual, and makes the most of another opportunity to essay good and evil alternating in the same character, as he had in both *Pit and the Pendulum* and *Diary of a Madman*. 'Joseph Curwen' stands as his coldest and most clinical characterisation, but behind Price is a backdrop of utter

Vincent Price and Debra Paget in THE HAUNTED PALACE

confusion as a colonial diabolist conjures an extra-dimensional demon from the pulp age of the 1930s.

The holes in the plot are manifest and yawn wider than the pit in which Curwen has kept his personal entity for more than a century. When the tale gets underway, three subplots come into play, and all of them in the second half. The first is the continuation of the mating ritual with the Thing in the crypt, which had been teased in the extended prologue and for which Curwen has notionally been summoned from beyond the grave. The second is the attempted revivification of Hester Tillinghast (Cathie Merchant), and the last is the notional revenge which Curwen insists on extracting from the descendants of those who put him to the torch. All vie for supremacy in Beaumont's script and none attain it, and the cracks which open up are pasted over by Curwen acolytes Lon Chaney Jr and Milton Parsons (speaking dialogue by Francis Ford Coppola), who have increasingly to rebuke their master for his tendency to become distracted from their mutual aim. At the climax, Curwen tells a captive Willet that the task upon which they are engaged is beyond the doctor's ken, adding, "As a matter of fact, we don't fully understand ourselves." One is tempted to wonder if this was the actor speaking, as well as the character.

Curwen's 'revenge' is itself a half-cocked affair: he has a list with five names inscribed upon it yet manages to despatch only two of them. Nor is it revealed how his servants have managed to survive in the castle in the intervening years, yet his young mistress apparently perished (and so has to be revivified). If these were not enough, the ending is baffling in its inconclusiveness: as the demon is about to lay two pairs of flippers on Ann, Ward's spirit triumphs over Curwen's and he frees her from her bonds. Willet hastens her out of the burning building and returns for Ward; he finds him on the altar steps but Orne, Hutchinson and Tillinghast are now nowhere to be seen. As Willet helps Ward to flee the scene, he leaves the trapdoor to the pit wide open for any self-respecting monster with a modicum of curiosity to follow on behind.

Responsibility for much of the mess rests with screenwriter Charles Beaumont, and therein hangs a tale. When Beaumont was hired to write the film, he had already overstretched himself in trying to keep pace with existing commitments, not least of which were pressing episodes for *The Twilight Zone* and *Alfred Hitchcock Presents*. To get around such problems, Beaumont had been in the habit of farming

THE HAUNTED PALACE (note stagehand at left, lost in studio mist)

his projects out to any number of ghost writers who shared the fee but not the credit, foremost among whom was Jerry Sohl.

Who, other than Beaumont, tried to make sense of *The Haunted Palace* is open to question, but the aimless wanderings through labyrinthine corridors, the endless repetition of key scenes, the loss of narrative direction halfway through and the botched ending make it plain that there were more toilers behind the scenes than were given credit on screen. If Charles Dexter Ward found it difficult to keep his feet on the ground during his stay in *The Haunted Palace*, he was clearly not alone.

Price switches effortlessly between the personae of Ward and Curwen with only a minimum of eye-shadow to assist the transformation. Ward is enacted as the dulcet-toned Price of benign bemusement while Curwen is the Price of the shrill nasal whine, particularly when berating his wife for spying on him. (As a piece of titillation, the script throws in the scabrous undertow of the ever-present threat of rape, when Curwen wakes to the fact that he has a physical body at his disposal and a convenient partner over whom he can exercise his "husbandly rights.") Like all good villains, he also acquires a nice line in sarcastic witticisms: "Torquemada spent many a happy hour here a few centuries ago; it was old then," he says of his abode (and as though to justify the insertion of stock-footage from *Pit and the Pendulum*.) Either the Curwen 'palace' is actually Castillo Medina imported wholesale from Spain, or the Grand Inquisitor discovered America before Columbus did.

*Debra Paget
and Vincent
Price in* THE
HAUNTED
PALACE

*A slight noise attracted my notice, and looking to
the floor, I saw several enormous rats traversing it.*
EDGAR ALLAN POE,
THE PIT AND THE PENDULUM (1843)

All the tried-and-tested tricks of the previous Poes
are applied to *The Haunted Palace* with equal fervour
as characters glide down endless cobwebbed corridors,

avoiding rats and fighting shy of the incumbent
tarantula (which had become such an habitual
member of Corman's casts that one critic was moved
to observe of American International that it was the
only company in Hollywood to have a spider under
long-term contract), but they lack for resonance. The
Gothic trappings of Poe formed no part of Lovecraft's
universe, whose mainstay was cosmic terror and

visceral shock, and the mismatch merely results in a hybrid which is transparent in purpose and depressingly sombre in tone. Corman could avail himself of no formula to deal with Lovecraft as he had with Poe, so he turned instead to Universal for inspiration; thus Ward/Curwen skulks in his castle like a vampire of old before his nefarious activities are brought to a precipitate end by a motley of rhubarbing villagers brandishing flaming torches.

The finale of the film, in which the characters descend a stairway of Piranesian proportions to reach an eldritch altar, wherein a Kong-like being lurks beneath a huge trapdoor raised on a chain-link pulley, is one of considerable latent power. For a moment, the rancid spiritual terror of Lovecraft's fiction is admirably captured in a first, brief and imprecise glimpse of the Thing through the crosshatching of its prison. But as Price begins to chant an untypical incantation in cod-Latin, the effect is cut short by the expeditious arrival of the Arkham cavalry.

Art director Daniel Haller used the entire sound stage for this cellar-crypt, as he had in *Pit and the Pendulum* – turning it into what the locals describe as "the home of Satan himself," though a notional reference in Poe's poem to the demon that dwells within was too subtle by far for the lay audience to grasp: "...vast forms that move fantastically to a discordant melody."

Were *The Haunted Palace* to have been made as Lovecraft and not had a false structure of Poe imposed upon it by AIP, it could have become a minor cult classic in its own right, with its awesome set-piece climax and majestic musical score by Ronald Stein. But obscure references to a pantheon of devil-gods left the casual viewer bemused, while aficionados were appalled to find that the work of one of the greatest exponents of the Tale of Terror in 20th century fiction had been denuded of its narrative, buried beneath a little-known poem by a different writer altogether and set in a period which belonged neither to one nor the other. The *town* of Arkham was a village with but a single street down which came mutants at dusk, and H P Lovecraft's vision of a foetid monster from beyond the stars looked like an Aurora kit of the Creature from the Black Lagoon with a couple of extra arms stuck onto its sides.

And travellers now, within that valley,
Through the red-litten windows see
Vast forms, that move fantastically

To a discordant melody,
While, like a ghastly rapid river,
Through the pale door
A hideous throng rush out forever
And laugh – but smile no more.

EDGAR ALLAN POE,
THE HAUNTED PALACE (1839)

In the UK, *The Haunted Palace* was held up in release for more than two years. When it did eventually open in late 1965, the censor-cuts which had previously been prescribed by the BBFC remained intact (the film was originally submitted for classification in August 1963); among them were the removal of a shot of Hester Tillinghast's mummified corpse sitting up in its coffin after Curwen's first (failed) attempt at revivification, and a close-up of a fire-scorched head. This left little in the film for anyone to scream about.

AIP's so-called 'sixth' Poe played on the lower half of a double-bill with *Monster of Terror* (aka *Die, Monster, Die!*), a second and more sincere attempt to adapt Lovecraft for the screen. Based on the story *The Colour Out of Space*, *Monster of Terror* was again set in the fictional village of Arkham – though in keeping with its source, the action took place in the present day. Ever on the look-out for humorous traps into which unwary filmmakers might inadvertently fall, cinemagoers erupted in gales of laughter when 'Arkham' appeared on screen for a second time in *Monster of Terror* after it had just featured so centrally in *The Haunted Palace*. By the time a trench-coated Nick Adams blustered his way through familiar swathes of English countryside masquerading as Lovecraft's 'fear-haunted' New England, it was too late to redeem things.

Both films suffered by comparison to one another, though the studio mists of *The Haunted Palace* were marginally more convincing than the efforts of the fog-machine to enshroud the overused battlements of Oakley Court in *Monster of Terror*. Californians may have felt similarly defrauded in 1969, when AIP substituted Monterey for the coastline of Dunwich in its third Lovecraft adaptation, *The Dunwich Horror*. However, the source of the mountainous swells from many a Poe film was at least masked off by a glass-shot on that occasion.

Matheson had now completed his comedy, another pastiche of elements which had featured in his Poes, and which he had titled 'The Graveyard Story.' With

Roger Corman in Yugoslavia (shooting a World War II adventure for United Artists called *The Secret Invasion*), Matheson also took on the role of associate producer for the occasion, alongside Anthony Carras. Finding his new script in less experienced hands, Matheson suggested 59-year-old noir veteran Jacques Tourneur for the director's chair in the absent Corman's stead, to helm a film that was designed to team Price with Lorre and Karloff again, as well as reunite them all with Basil Rathbone.

To genre enthusiasts, Tourneur's star will forever shine for the trio of evocative low-budget thrillers which he made for RKO and producer Val Lewton in the forties: *Cat People* (1942), *I Walked With a Zombie* and *The Leopard Man* (1943) – as well as a revisionist masterpiece shot in 1957 in similar style, *Night of the Demon*.

Tourneur had his own theories about trends in the market and the way in which things seemed to be going: "There are now in the States three horror half-hour television shows every week, and they've taken the edge off the horror films because they've made them so ridiculous that it's very difficult to frighten anyone now." As a pointer to the future for AIP and others in the Gothic horror business, he added, "For the next five or six years, horror films will be dead and from now on, it'll be adventure stories."

Hammer had begun to sense the same sea-change in audience tastes and, under the aegis of executive producer Michael Carreras, was already planning to produce a large-scale adaptation of H Rider Haggard's novel *She*. Nicholson and Arkoff, however, had settled on comedy as the best means of maintaining AIP's contract with Vincent Price, as well as its increasingly tenuous contact with the New England world of Edgar Allan Poe.

Filming of 'The Graveyard Story' began in the first week of September 1963, five months after *The Haunted Palace*. Vincent Price had spent the intervening summer overseeing the purchase of thousands of original works of art as part of the newly inaugurated 'Vincent Price Collection,' to which he was now contracted for retail and mail-order giant Sears, Roebuck & Company, while his wife turned their Benedict Canyon home into a repository for the hundreds of paintings she had volunteered to frame ready for sale. Price had also been asked to sit on the White House Art Committee under the chairmanship of First Lady Jacqueline Kennedy, a post which further boosted his standing in the world of art expertise.

In such a climate of undiluted optimism about his personal affairs, Vincent Price was happy to exchange the dour atmosphere of the Corman Poes for a little light relief, and the role of the self-seeking Waldo Trumbull in 'The Graveyard Story' harked back to the satirical serendipity of soap magnate Burnbridge Waters in *Champagne for Caesar*.

Jacques Tourneur may have been right in principle about the waning appeal of horror films, but he was to be proved wrong in practice, for he had reckoned without an industry that would show itself determined to squeeze the last drop of blood from the genre before abandoning it to its cyclic fate, throwing his calculations out by as many years again. He made a second mistake with regard to 'The Graveyard Story', which was now retitled *The Comedy of Terrors*, seeing it as a film for "mature, thinking people who appreciate satire – who appreciate cynical humour." In that particular, however, he was not the only one.

The miscalculation for all concerned was that, unlike Corman's *The Raven*, Tourneur's *The Comedy of Terrors* did not seem to audiences to be laughing with them but *at* them.

> *Is there no morality left in the world?*
> **WALDO TRUMBULL** (VINCENT PRICE),
> *THE COMEDY OF TERRORS* (1963)

Trumbull (Price) and Gillie (Lorre) are a pair of bumbling undertakers. A whole year's rent arrears finds them threatened with eviction by their landlord, Mr Black (Rathbone). "Has it been a year?" Trumbull enquires. "Each and every unpaid day of it," Black retorts. The two have been in the habit of rustling up trade for themselves by suffocating prospective customers, and they decide that Black should join the growing list. A bungled attempt at murder leaves Black the victim of a seizure; he is pronounced dead but is subject to cataleptic trances and subsequently awakens. The pair have him entombed regardless, but he escapes and pursues them with an axe. In the ensuing melée, Trumbull falls victim to his own nefarious schemes and Black ends up dead again (or does he?).

The Comedy of Terrors is the *Some Like It Hot* of the horror genre, and its nod to that Billy Wilder classic of 1959 was underlined by a cameo from lugubrious silent screen comedian Joe E Brown as a gravedigger. In a film filled from beginning to end with banter and

Boris Karloff, Basil Rathbone, Peter Lorre and Vincent Price in a publicity shot from THE COMEDY OF TERRORS

repartee from all of the cast, the bulk of the work falls to Price. But with Tourneur confining Lorre to his lines as scripted, Price gives a beautifully timed comic performance, ably supported by Karloff, and Basil Rathbone in particular.

Tourneur had wanted the piece to be played straight, preferring the humour of dialogue and situation to speak for itself, as in *Arsenic and Old Lace*, but he was outnumbered in his view by a cast who collectively had been reared on a broader style of comedy routine. (He nevertheless lit the film in deep shadow, against which their overtly slapstick antics are sometimes at odds.) But so sharp are the verbal exchanges that *The Comedy of Terrors* can stand comparison with a typical Neil Simon vehicle and looks to have been sourced from the stage to begin with, rather than written directly for the screen. Joyce Jameson, also making a return from *Tales of Terror*,

sings 'He is not dead but sleepeth' at Black's funeral in prelude to the unexpected revival of the deceased and there is the sublime absurdity of a running gag which has Black declaiming, "What place is this?" each and every time he awakes from his catatonic trance.

The Comedy of Terrors was an altogether more sophisticated affair than *The Raven* – the production enjoyed the benefits of a different eye behind the lens, a refreshing range of new sets (as well as location shooting), a fast pace and witty dialogue.

Here are a few examples:

Trumbull (to Amaryllis, in respect of her father's collection of objets d'art): *He did more than collect curious objects, madam, he also fathered one.*

Trumbull (threatened with exposure by Gillie): *Mr Gillie... Felix... friend... I put it to you: who in*

your discerning estimation do you think they're most likely to believe, eh? – Mr W Trumbull, respected citizen and entrepreneur of death, or Mr Felix Gillie, wanted fugitive and confessed bank robber?
Gillie: *I've never confessed! ... They just* proved *it.*

Trumbull: *I'm afraid, madam, that he has made his final crossing to that Stygian shore.*
Mr Phipps: *What?*
Trumbull: *He's dead.*

Gillie (attempting to pick a door-lock): *Hey, I have an idea – maybe there's a bolt on the inside.*
Trumbull: *There's a bolt on the inside of your head, Mr Gillie, and it's loose.*
Gillie: *But that has nothing to do with doors.*

Karloff had been the first choice to play Mr Black, but Rathbone was substituted due to the physical requirements of the role. It was a switch which undoubtedly improved the prospective film. Rathbone camps up his early stage career as a Shakespearean actor by quoting copiously from *Macbeth* as he pursues his tormentors with an axe, while Karloff was left free to indulge in some delicious verbal by-play as Price's doddery old father-in-law, at his best when delivering a potted history of ancient burial-methods: "Egyptians used to hollow 'em out and pour 'em full of resin... yank their brains out with a hook."

In the original script, all the characters died at the finale; thinking that too much of a bad thing, AIP had Matheson devise a happier ending in which Lorre and Jameson only seem to be dead before they recover from the injuries which have been inflicted upon them and walk hand-in-hand into the proverbial sunset to begin a new life together. In fact, Peter Lorre died for real – three months after *The Comedy of Terrors* opened – on 24 March 1964.

The poor reception which the film was accorded on release may have had to do with its opening on Christmas Day 1963, just a month after the assassination of United States' President John F Kennedy, whose name was unfortunately alluded to in the character of John F Black. At that particular moment in time, no one felt much like laughing about death.

Tourneur was philosophical: "Cycles of horror films are between six and seven years, then they go out in popularity," he informed *Films and Filming* in 1965. "*The Comedy of Terrors* was the transition film ... It was

a parody on Shakespeare, a comedy on horror films [which was] not, I believe, understood very well." AIP re-released the film in 1965 under its working title of *The Graveside Story*, pairing it with a similarly retitled *Panic in Year Zero* (*The End of the World*), a sci-fi thriller which Ray Milland had both directed and starred in and which originally played alongside *Tales of Terror*; there was no great improvement in the receipts for either.

Americans had neither understood the Shakespearean allusion in the title nor the acid wit in the screenplay. *The Comedy of Terrors* was not the simple knockabout of *The Raven*, any more than it was the chill buffoonery of *The Black Cat* episode in *Tales of Terror*. But its director remained optimistic about its reception in the UK: "I'm sure that in Britain it'll be much more understood because it was cynical comedy, a bit in the old René Clair tradition, and no one knew what it was all about in the States."

Tourneur's hopes went unfulfilled. *The Comedy of Terrors* was released by Anglo as usual, but after the confusion of squawks which had been emitted by *The Raven*, no suitable play-date could be found. The film eventually gained an art-house opening in London's West End, where it was screened for a week before disappearing entirely from view.

Literally a Black farce of a kind which was more attuned to European tastes than American, *The Comedy of Terrors* was ahead of its time. Eight years later, three films in a row would mine the same vein of sardonic humour and provide Vincent Price with some of the biggest hits of his long career on screen.

Since the late fifties, escalating costs within the American film industry had forced many of the major studios to shoot productions abroad, where labour was cheaper. By 1963, the need to engage in such 'runaway' production had trickled down to the likes of American International, which, after almost a decade in the business, was now a major player itself.

Lower returns from AIP's recent Poe films had prompted the accountant in Arkoff to invoke the mantra of lower costs, and lower costs meant shooting outside Hollywood. Foremost among the locations on offer away from America's shores was England, which had always nurtured an indigenous and long-established studio set-up similar to that in Los Angeles, shared a common language, and was once more in the middle of one of its habitual economic crises. British film technicians were regarded as

The Masque of the Red Death

Vincent Price and Hazel Court in THE MASQUE OF THE RED DEATH

wilfully slower and more rigidly unionised than their Californian counterparts, but their skills gave more bangs for the buck and the soon-to-be-devalued pound sterling of new Labour Prime Minister Harold Wilson's first government made facilities in the UK too good an opportunity for a budget-conscious Hollywood film company to miss. Arkoff therefore decreed that the next Poe would be shot in Britain.

Offered the chance to trade the Hollywood hothouse for the cooler air of the British capital, Price grabbed it with both hands, little realising at the time where it would eventually lead. With his Sears chequebook at the ready and his new contract in his back pocket, Price

set off for London in the third week of November 1963, finally to star in *The Masque of the Red Death*.

Awakened from his long sleep by the news, Alex Gordon tried to file an injunction against the film and its makers upon its completion; it was summarily thrown out of court. Minor legal technicalities notwithstanding, Price's powerhouse performance in the seventh instalment in the series stood testament to the fact that, after 25 years of trying, Vincent Price at last felt that he had arrived.

The 'Red Death' had long devastated the country. No pestilence had ever been so fatal, or so

Harvey Hall, Doreen Dawne, Brian Hewlett, Vincent Price and Patrick Magee in **The Masque of the Red Death**

hideous. Blood was its Avatar and its seal – the redness and the horror of blood...

Edgar Allan Poe,
The Masque of the Red Death (1842)

Roger Corman had originally wanted to film *The Masque of the Red Death* after *House of Usher*, but AIP's legal wrangle with Alex Gordon prohibited it. Whatever were Corman's reasons for this choice – which he professed in retrospect to have been admiration for Ingmar Bergman's *The Seventh Seal* (1957) – the clue is in the story itself: unlike all the other Poes which Matheson was asked to adapt after the first, *The Masque of the Red Death* has a breadth of narrative ideally suited to a feature film. Despite its paltry length in literary form, it has a plot, a setting, a dynamic and a climax: all the elements required of drama. It is also palpably cinematic, with a vivid description of the gaudy decor of the bizarre palace in which the bloody revel takes place.

Whereas a screenwriter of Matheson's calibre might have been thought of as essential in order to craft something out of the nothingness of *Pit and the*

Pendulum and *The Raven*, the structure of *The Masque of the Red Death* had already been put in place by Poe:

It is medieval Italy, and the Prince Prospero has sealed himself inside his castle to await the passing of the Red Death, a pestilential plague that is ravaging the countryside. The prince has given similar succour to a thousand of his fellow nobles, and a bal-masque is arranged to while away the long hours. As the festivities get underway, Prospero spies a figure in grave-robes and sets out in pursuit. When he challenges it, the figure turns and reveals the truth – the Red Death has entered the castle, and all its occupants succumb.

And now was acknowledged the presence of the Red Death. He had come like a thief in the night. And one by one dropped the revellers in the blood-bedewed halls of their revel, and died each in the despairing posture of his fall.

Edgar Allan Poe,
The Masque of the Red Death (1842)

Richard Matheson had already passed on the chance to write more Poes, so the script of the film was again offered to Charles Beaumont – who now not only had taken to drink but had begun to experience the first throes of the degenerative brain disease which was to kill him less than four years later at the age of 38. To show why he had been in such demand as a writer of weird fiction, Beaumont came up with a masterstroke: he turned Prospero into a devil-worshipper and his castle into a shrine to Satan. Whether or not the jaundiced view of the world which came to be expressed in the prince's philosophical musing was a product of Beaumont's condition can only be a matter for conjecture, but it invested *The Masque of the Red Death* with a gravitas which was not lost on critical opinion and sanctioned the seventh Poe as one of the finest macabre fantasies ever committed to film.

Beaumont's screenplay was clever, literate, but not a little ponderous, and Corman turned to R(obert) Wright Campbell, who had written a number of his early productions, including *Teenage Caveman* (1958) and his first film as a director, *Five Guns West*, to pep things up. For the sake of speed, Campbell simply sewed another Poe tale into the mix.

Hop-Frog is an allegorical fable about a pair of dwarf lovers, Hop-Frog and Trippetta, and the cruel revenge that the one takes on those who have insulted the other (hoisting them on the end of a rope and putting them to the torch). The tale had been penned by Poe in 1849, the year of his death, and its advantage in this context was that it took the form of a single episode, and so could be stitched into the extant script of *The Masque of the Red Death* with a minimum of disruption. The only difference between Poe's original and its counterpart on screen (aside from the renaming of the vengeful dwarf) was in the number of victims trussed and burned; in Poe's story, there are *eight*.

> *Can you look around this world and believe in the goodness of a God who rules it? Famine, pestilence, war, disease, and death – they rule this world. If a God of love and life ever did exist, he is long-since dead. Someone – some... thing – rules in his place.*
>
> PRINCE PROSPERO (VINCENT PRICE),
> THE MASQUE OF THE RED DEATH (1963)

Before 1963, films about black magic had been few and far between. The silent cinema had flirted with the black arts on occasion, while Mark Robson's *The*

Seventh Victim (1943) had all but obscured its satanic theme under a blanket of obliquities. Because of censorship restrictions and blasphemy laws, any cinematic dabblings in the occult had been conducted under the more inoffensive guise of 'witchcraft' and restricted to the comedic antics of eccentric house-wives (*I Married a Witch*, 1941; *Bell, Book and Candle*, 1958). Jacques Tourneur had crafted a genuine black magic thriller, and without the female of the species, in *Night of the Demon*, only to find her 'pricking her thumbs' again in *Night of the Eagle* (1961) in the crone-like form of Margaret Johnston. *The Masque of the Red Death* would venture closer to the thorny theological issue of devil-worship than anything which had preceded it, even though cinemagoers in its country of origin were ultimately to be deprived of the (fabricated) details of ritual.

Corman brought his eye to the main chance along with him for the filming of *The Masque of the Red Death*, purloining sets and furnishings which previously had been paid for out of the budgets of more expansive features. But AIP also pushed the boat out a little and paid for a handsome supporting cast, both in quantity and quality, as well as assigning Nicolas Roeg as Director of Photography. Roeg's credits prior to this had included photographing *Death Drums Along the River* for rogue producer Harry Alan Towers, but his confident way with the camera invested *The Masque of the Red Death* with a sumptuous look which would remain unrivalled by any other film in the Poe series.

Price's arrival in London was feted by much press attention, not least because his co-star as Francesca in the upcoming film was 17-year-old Jane Asher, who was currently dating Paul McCartney, one of the four members of a band that was about to become the most famous in the history of pop: The Beatles.

> *Why should you be afraid to die? – Your soul has been dead for a long time.*
>
> MAN IN RED (JOHN WESTBROOK),
> THE MASQUE OF THE RED DEATH (1963)

The Masque of the Red Death follows Poe's tale to the letter, to the extent of incorporating in Prospero's castle its author's psychedelic imagery of multi-coloured rooms with windows "of stained glass whose colour varied in accordance with the prevailing hue of the decorations of the chamber into which it opened." The tenants of the castle are, of course, given flesh to

Jane Asher and Vincent Price in THE MASQUE OF THE RED DEATH

falcon, and Alfredo (Patrick Magee) provides amusement for Hop-Toad (Skip Martin) when the vengeful dwarf torches Alfredo's gorilla-suit while he hangs suspended from a chandelier. But while revellers come and gorily go, all effort is directed towards the climax of the film, when the Red Death glides through the castle's apartments sowing dew-drops of blood on Prospero's guests wherever he passes.

The necessary opposition to Prospero's self-serving satanic creed is supplied by Francesca, a young Christian girl whom the prince has rescued from the plague-infested village. While she provides the obligatory sweetness and light, it is Prospero, like the Devil, who is given the best tunes to play. "A hundred years ago, an ancestor of mine was a Christian monk; he was made Examiner of an early inquisition," he tells her. "He tortured over 600 men, women and children in order to save their souls for your God of love." Francesca stares in bewilderment: "I cannot answer; I have no learning," is all that she can say in response.

In subtextual terms, *The Masque of the Red Death* gives the appearance of being a diatribe against 'evil'

wear in addition to their medieval robes – Francesca and Gino (David Weston) are a pair of young lovers caught up in Prospero's plans, Juliana (Hazel Court) is the prince's mistress, whose marriage to Satan ends with her bloody despatch at the talons of his favourite when, in fact, it is an allegory about fundamentalism in any form. Francesca is left to doubt her faith at the finale every bit as much as Prospero, and the film's philosophical heart is more succinctly summarised in an exchange between Gino and the Man in Red than in its feeble attempts to combat the extravagant certainties of Prospero's dark ideology with spiritual truths. "Who is *your* God?" Death asks. "The true one," Gino unhesitatingly replies. "Yes..." the figure nods, wearily. Poe's 'Red Death' was tubercular, but Corman's is a hymn to the poetry of horror. The final dance of death is as daring and original a sequence as any in the history of the genre, helped in no small measure by the superbly sonorous score of David Lee, reminiscent of the 'Bacchanale' from Saint-Saens' *Samson and Delilah*.

> Prospero: *There is no other God – Satan killed him.*
> Man in Red: *Each man creates his own God for himself – his own heaven, his own hell. Your hell, Prince Prospero, and the moment of your death...*
> Prospero: *Let me see your face... !*
> **VINCENT PRICE** AND **JOHN WESTBROOK**, *THE MASQUE OF THE RED DEATH* (1963)

Price himself has less time on screen than in the recent past but he makes the most of every moment and his performance is the better for not being allowed to dominate the film. "Your master?" Francesca queries, when he lets slip the appellation. "Satan," Prospero replies. "The Lord of Flies, the Fallen Angel... The Devil." "Garotte them!" he barks in his opening scene, to discourage indiscipline in the ranks; "Burn the village to the ground," he commands, to rid his serfs of the virulence in their midst. "I will take you by the hand and lead you through the cruel light to the velvet darkness," he urges, when persuading Francesca to join him in the "glories of Hell". Prospero is Price at his most coldly sadistic, yet he still manages to evoke sympathy for a man whose quest is less to torture and tame than it is to seek a willing partner to share equally in his passion for living.

Price's familiar mannerisms and easy accessibility as a star performer could never wholly be submerged by any role; he was, after all, Vincent Price first and foremost. But the rapport with the viewer on which such films depend nevertheless belies superb acting technique. When one thinks of *Pit and the Pendulum*, one thinks of Nicholas Medina, not Price – when one thinks of *The Masque of the Red Death*, one thinks of the doomed defiance of Prospero. So appealing does he seem to make the prince's unholy pursuits that Francesca can be forgiven for yielding ultimately to temptation and deciding to join him on the left-hand path; Price invests Prospero with a majesty which is outdone only by the supreme authority of Death itself.

The support, in the main, are a match for their man, especially Jane Asher who, despite her lack of stature in comparison and tender years, underplays her role in perfect contrast to Price's grandiloquence. Before the masque begins, Prospero taunts his charge by devising a contest to the death between Gino and her father (Nigel Greene), where each has to pierce his arm in turn with a choice of five daggers, one of which is coated with a deadly poison. In a superb display of theatrical precision, Price outlines the rules as he spears the daggers into the foreground of a low-angle shot, where they come shudderingly to rest like an array of golden crucifixes at the foot of the screen – a miniature Golgotha of Prospero's own omnipotent making.

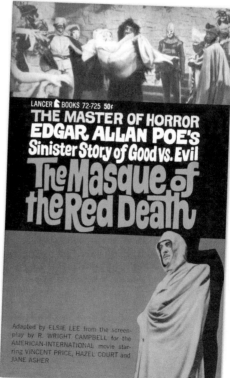

The tie-in novel of **THE MASQUE OF THE RED DEATH**, *published by Lancer*

Jane Asher and Vincent Price spent time shopping in London when not filming THE MASQUE OF THE RED DEATH

The Masque of the Red Death was a real comeback, for Poe and for Price. Writing in *Sight & Sound* in 1964, and after noting that he had once been referred to as a 'sissified Bela Lugosi', Peter John Dyer had much to say about Price's performance in the film. 'Price here presents evil intellectually, the relish tempered with cool disquisitions on the nature of fear, the domination over others effortless and indisputable, the moments of frenzy stylised and arresting.' He went on to rhapsodise in similarly glowing terms about his contribution to the climax: 'It is Price alone who makes the weakest scene, the Masque itself, work. As the Red Death stalks through the crowded ballroom, condemning the guests to nothing more alarming than a spraygun of letterbox paint, one is held by the sight of Price in his sheikhish fancy dress, pursuing and then fleeing the intruder. While the rev-

ellers contort themselves in balletic poses, Price relies upon hieratic gestures, arms cumbrously upraised and features pained.'

> *And Darkness and Decay and the Red Death*
> *held illimitable dominion over all.*
>
> SCREEN CAPTION,
> *THE MASQUE OF THE RED DEATH* (1963)

While Vincent Price had been languishing in the B-movie worlds of William Castle, *Return of the Fly* and *The Bat*, the lush Technicolor productions of Britain's Hammer Films had dominated the horror market. From 1958 to 1960, the name of Hammer had become synonymous with horror, so much so that the phrase 'Hammer Horror' had become a colloquialism for genre films as a whole. *House of Usher* – and a series of tactical misjudgments on Hammer's part which had brought box-office disaster on its head in respect of *The Two Faces of Dr Jekyll* (1960), *The Phantom of the Opera* (1961) and several others – changed all that. AIP's addition of widescreen to an already sensuous use of Pathécolor not only grabbed the lion's share of the declining market but the horror crown itself. While Hammer had retreated into black-and-white for a raft of features from *The Damned* (1961) to *The Nanny* (1965), AIP had set about consolidating its position as the world's foremost exponent of the terror film with *Pit and the Pendulum*.

In the UK, all American International's Poe films up to *Tales of Terror* had premiered at the imposing venue of the London Pavilion in Piccadilly Circus, as had Hammer's before them, and the long-standing rivalry between the respective firms of Hammer's Carreras & Hinds and Anglo Amalgamated's (Nat) Cohen & (Stuart) Levy, had swung in favour of Anglo. But the move into comedy with *The Raven*, the indecisive double-billing of *The Haunted Palace* and *Monster of Terror*, and a switch of emphasis to 'Beach Party' movies (none of which were released in Britain) toppled AIP from the top spot within two years of its having attained it. By 1963, the high-points of horror were coming from unpredictable sources – Alfred Hitchcock's *The Birds*, Robert Aldrich's *Whatever Happened to Baby Jane*. The move towards realism in the cinema in general, which had been set in train by the kitchen-sink dramas of the British 'new wave', and a lack of continuity of product from both Hammer and American International, had sent the market for horror films into a temporary downturn.

In another year, Hammer would reclaim some of the ground it had lost with the help of a newly formed Warner-Pathé and a nationwide campaign for the double-helping of *Dracula Prince of Darkness* and *The Plague of the Zombies*; saturation advertising would again show itself as the difference between success or failure at the box-office. By then, it was AIP who were raising the white flag and churning out ham-fisted spoofs like *Dr Goldfoot and the Bikini Machine*, which theatre managers also passed on in UK distribution. For now, however, AIP still maintained its increasingly shaky position – though under the prevailing conditions, it had to content itself with an off-West End venue for *The Masque of the Red Death*, at the New Victoria Theatre in London's Victoria Street – which from here on would also be the new home for horror

in general, in line with its reducing status as a commercial proposition.

The Masque of the Red Death received good critical notices, partly because it was seen as a domestic production and partly because at this juncture serious film reviewers were all weaned on *Cahiers du Cinéma* and thus were able to spot the allusions to Ingmar Bergman's *The Seventh Seal*. The film was successfully paired in release with another Corman thriller, *The Man with the X-Ray Eyes* – a prize-winning entry in 1963's Trieste Festival of Science Fiction Films – but its box-office reception in Britain was somewhat impeded by its having had to suffer the most injurious case of censorship cuts since William Castle's *Mr Sardonicus* in 1961.

The film had featured two examples of satanic black mass, both of them fictional and both conducted with a considerable amount of cinematic restraint by Corman. In the first and more incidental of the two, Hazel Court's Juliana brands her ample bosom with the mark of Satan before a devil's altar, while in the second, she is subjected to one of the Poe films' trademark dream sequences and, during an hallucinogenic 'marriage' to the Prince of Darkness, endures the death of a thousand cuts at the hands of a trio of costumed demons who dance around her writhing torso like escapees from the Ballet Rambert. Both these sequences, which together totalled six minutes of screen time, were excised in their entirety by the British Board of Film Censors.

Juliana's bloody demise for real at the claws of Prospero's falcon was allowed to remain in the film, so it was not deprived of all its horror in the name of public propriety, but the impact of its devil-worshipping theme was much reduced. In the British cinema of the time, cuts required by the censor that were not actively participated in by the production company concerned were simply removed from a film at source and the loose ends spliced together; it was therefore obvious to the viewer when excisions were made because of the 'jump-cuts' which invariably accompanied the loss of footage. In the case of *The Masque of the Red Death*, the situation was compounded when the front-of-house stills which were distributed to theatres featured shots from both the missing scenes.

Six months later, Price was at Shepperton for another in the series. In the meantime, James Nicholson, the 48-year-old President of American International, had been conducting an affair with a

Vincent Price and Elizabeth Shepherd in THE TOMB OF LIGEIA

23-year-old actress from Wenatchee in Washington State whom he had first spotted in a film called *Ride the Wild Surf*, directed by Hazel Court's husband Don Taylor. Sylvia Nicholson had consequently filed for divorce and, in settlement, she was awarded 50 per cent of her husband's shares in AIP. This diminution of Nicholson's half of the company left Sam Arkoff in sole charge and he was quickly promoted to Chairman of the Board over his erstwhile co-owner, with his name superseding that of Nicholson on film credits from this point on. The name of the actress at the centre of the storm was Susan Hart, who would now become a regular at AIP, starting with the film *Pyjama Party* (1964). After shooting was complete on *The Tomb of Ligeia*, Hart was to become something of a regular in the films which Vincent Price would make over the next two years as well.

> *I cannot, for my soul, remember how, when, or even where, I first became acquainted with the Lady Ligeia. Long years have since elapsed and my memory is feeble through much suffering.*
> **EDGAR ALLAN POE**, *LIGEIA* (1838)

AIP had once again found itself in uncharted waters insofar as audience familiarity with the Poe original was concerned; as a result, the new film commenced production early in the summer of 1964 not as *Ligeia*, but as 'The House at the End of the World', an acceptable alternative given that Poe's abbey is situated "in one of the wildest and least frequented portions of fair England." Be that as it may, that was also dispensed with in favour of 'The Last Tomb of Ligeia' before its makers eventually settled on a more concise derivative.

As Price remembered it, *"The Tomb of Ligeia* was vaguely based on an idea that Roger and I had once. I had said I had always wanted to do a picture in a ruin, but actually using the ruin as an actual place, with real furniture in it and the ruin around it, which I thought would be very effective. This is sort of what he adapted to *The Tomb of Ligeia*, which I think was the best one we ever did."

Ligeia is another of Poe's laments to lost love, as represented by the Lady Ligeia. The story is one of his early essays in pure Gothic, penned during a particularly productive period in New York after years of indulging in opiates. The Germanic influence is strong, and exemplified by the fact that its eponymous narrator lives in a castle on the banks of the Rhine with Ligeia, the wife of his 'bosom' and a lady of oddly Egyptian ancestry. After her predictable death (all Poe's women at this stage died young and consumptive), he typically takes solace in opium and moves to England, where he buys a vast, decaying, castelled abbey. Having now remarried, events reach their inevitable conclusion as his new young bride first comes to resemble Ligeia, then finally comes to *be* her.

Throughout the tale, Poe makes much of a quote from the writings of 17th century Christian scientist Joseph Glanvill: "Man doth not yield himself to the angels, nor unto death utterly, save only through the weakness of his feeble will" (which is given a slightly more colloquial reading in the film). Glanvill was an apologist for a spirit-world whose existence he felt to be provable by experimental means, so his enlistment by Poe was an attempt to add veracity to his theme of a restless ghost.

The story's narrator goes as unnamed as ever, though Ligeia's replacement in his affections (and the person on whom her occult attentions eventually focus) is given the Cornish-sounding appellation of Rowena Trevanion. Screenwriter Robert Towne filled in the blank by coming up with the name of Verden Fell for Price's character, which the actor insisted on pronouncing as 'Verdenfell' during filming. The role was reportedly written for Richard Chamberlain who, not long before, had set female pulses racing as television's *Dr Kildare*, though why Towne should have thought that AIP would put a Poe story into production without Vincent Price in the lead has remained unrecorded. The fact that Towne, a protégé of Corman's, was hired by the same man who had wanted both Lovecraft and Ray Milland for *The Haunted Palace* might have had something to do with it.

That the part of Verden Fell was written for a younger man is unarguable, however, and the 53-year-old Price was required to have his locks dyed black in order to more convincingly play the romantic interest of Elizabeth Shepherd – still a slip of a girl at 27 in 1964. There was a viable dramatic reason for Price's 'Grecian 2000' look though: it formed a symbolic connection between Fell and Ligeia, who is also raven-headed in the film, to distinguish her character from that of the fair-haired Rowena. Nevertheless, the amorous attachment between the two appears forced, which conveniently suited the strictures of the plot: Fell keeps the mummified body of his first wife in another marriage-bed sited in the tower-room of his abbey home, so his drawn features

RIGHT:
Vincent Price,
John Westbrook,
Elizabeth
Shepherd and
Oliver Johnston
in THE TOMB
OF LIGEIA

BELOW:
Oliver Johnston,
Vincent Price
and Elizabeth
Shepherd in
THE TOMB OF
LIGEIA

tombstone. Yet it was there yesterday when we
came upon the Lady Rowena.

> VERDEN FELL (VINCENT PRICE),
> THE TOMB OF LIGEIA (1964)

With *The Tomb of Ligeia*, a sense of realism finally
intruded upon the Poe series – not only because the
tale was staged in natural surroundings, but because
the script constantly questions the Gothic precepts
which previous films had taken for granted. What
Robert Towne attempted was a genuine ghost story,
not the spooky operatics of the *Morella* sequence in
Tales of Terror or the magical jiggery-pokery of *The
Haunted Palace*, but a real tale of the supernatural
along the more suggestive lines of the Val Lewton
thrillers of the 1940s.

Verden Fell is haunted by the spirit of his first wife,
but does her spirit reside for real in the malevolent cat
that roams the abbey or is it all a figment of his fevered
imagination? Corman's style is too in-your-face to make
much of the ambiguity, but he does what he can.
Returning to the abbey after her honeymoon, Fell's
new bride Rowena finds dark strands in her hairbrush;
she is subsequently hypnotised by Fell and speaks in
Ligeia's voice; the black cat menaces her at every turn,

and haunted demeanour are not altogether out of
place in scenes where he courts his new bride amid
the ruins of Swaffham Priory in the county of Norfolk.

> *Early this day, I have found myself standing once
> again before Ligeia's grave, allowing me to
> observe a rather singular circumstance: the date
> of her death has disappeared from Ligeia's*

appearing to grow in stature and strength as it claws at the door of her room.

The honeymoon period is correspondingly brief, as Fell retreats to his own apartments in a mysterious tower-room. "I sleep alone, I eat alone, and that's as it should be. After all... I'm not his wife, am I?" a frustrated Rowena confides to a handy standby who has loved her from afar. The conclusion is much as expected: Fell is a necrophile, who shares a bed with the corpse of the dead Ligeia each night.

"The world of Poe was the world of the unconscious," Corman had said of *House of Usher*. "Being the world of the unconscious, I thought it could be recreated better within the artificial confines of a stage than it could be in broad daylight. I didn't want to use location shots. I didn't want the film to be shot realistically." When it came to *Pit and the Pendulum*, he deliberately altered a scripted interlude of Nicholas and his wife in the early days of their marriage *outside* the castle walls, so that it fitted in better with this notion. But in *The Tomb of Ligeia*, Corman cast aside his psychoanalytical theories and approached things from a fresh perspective: Fell and Rowena are shown wandering on a beach after their marriage, as well as paying a (second-unit) visit to Stonehenge. In this film, Corman lets the drama speak for itself, imposing little by way of Gothic ambience. It was left to Robert Towne to provide the allusions to Poe, which he does with a nod to *Pit and the Pendulum* in particular as Fell recounts his days

with Ligeia by his side and, in her absence, fears for his sanity as he finds himself increasingly unable to account for his night-time movements.

Price plays the brooding Fell remarkably po-faced, his features partially obscured by a pair of contoured dark glasses which he dons to materially signify Ligeia's hypnotic control over his 'feeble' will. In a film already chock-full of symbolism, the glasses are a prop too far: put them on, and Fell is under Ligeia's spell; take them off, and he is his own man again.

"He is a man who, had he not married an absolutely monstrous woman who would not leave life – even in death, would have been a perfectly normal man and married the other girl," Price said of Fell, simplifying things for readers of *Shriek*. "And of course things like this do happen; there are men who are obsessed with their dead wives." Maybe so, but the clash of styles which soon becomes apparent between the supernatural element of the tale and the more material approach to horror which Corman had correctly adopted for his previous adaptations of Poe – mouldering corpses lying in state, inherited madness, climactic collapse – remain at odds with each other in the film.

It's not his doing, ma'am. It's hers – hers! – The Lady Ligeia's. Her eyes... Before she died, she held him with her eyes, the way he did with you that night. She told him: she was not dying, would never die, but would remain here waiting for him. And that every night, he must come and

THE TOMB OF LIGEIA

*care for her. Be with her. And that during the
day, he must forget the night. And he would
forget, yes. Sometimes, I've seen him struggle to
remember; struggle against her madness. But the
night always fell, and with it, her madness
always fell upon him...*

KENDRICK (OLIVER JOHNSTON),
THE TOMB OF LIGEIA (1964)

For all its attempt to try something new and
travel the road of the psychological ghost story in the
wake of Robert Wise's *The Haunting* (1963), the
climax falls back on the Poe clichés of *Morella* –
Rowena becomes Ligeia, Ligeia becomes Rowena,
and the matter is resolved in the predictable
conflagration for which Corman has a ready-made
furnace standing by in the centre of the tower-shrine.

Elizabeth Shepherd and Vincent Price in THE TOMB OF LIGEIA

"Think me mad; think whatever you will – but leave this abbey now!" Fell yells, as Corman yields to the inevitable and falls back on familiar motifs: Fell is blinded (by the cat) in the way that Dr Xavier was at the climax of *The Man with the X-Ray Eyes*, the room is set on fire and the *Usher* roof comes crashing down for the last time.

Ghost stories require a chill ambience to be effective, not the noonday sun or the purifying flames of melodrama. "He's a firebug," Price noted of Corman. "He lit the whole bloody stage. Terrible. The poor cat..." It might have been apt to have said of *The Tomb of Ligeia* that Roger Corman bowed out of the Poe films in a blaze of glory; instead, they bowed out of him.

The boundaries which divide Life from Death, are at best shadowy and vague. Who shall say where the one ends, and where the other begins?
      SCREEN CAPTION, THE TOMB OF LIGEIA
(1964; FROM POE'S THE PREMATURE BURIAL)

Many critics have lauded *The Tomb of Ligeia* as the best of the AIP Poes, due, in part, to its lack of artificiality. But it is the very absence of theatrical contrivance which puts it on a par with its director's lesser works of Gothic pretension. Stripped of the grandiose studio designs which in Corman's view had been integral to the creation of psychological landscapes, the film is often little more than a travelogue, with a troupe of wandering players parading in the foreground. Corman was never so assured in the field as he was on the stages of Producer's Studio, and while genuinely more unsettling than many previous Poes, *The Tomb of Ligeia* lost out in popular appeal to the baroque splendours of its gaudier companion-piece, Mario Bava's three-parter, *Black Sabbath* (*I tre volti della paura*), in which an equally bewigged Boris Karloff featured prominently as an aged *wurdulak*.

At the time, however, and coming in the wake of the well-received *The Masque of the Red Death*, reviews remained uniformly positive. "If you just love being scared, this is the one that will do it," advised the *New York Daily News*. "Fluid camerawork, first-rate colour, sumptuous period sets and an impassioned performance from Vincent Price blend perfectly to bring a great Gothic tale of terror to the screen," enthused the *Los Angeles Times*; while its British namesake struck a particularly highbrow note,

considering the subject: "At last Mr Corman has done what it always seemed he might be able sometime to do: make a film which could without absurdity be spoken of in the same breath as Cocteau's *Orphée*," the *Times* pronounced.

Despite all the belated praise, Corman had decided that the time had come to move on from Poe. "I was repeating myself, taking ideas, images, themes, and techniques from my own earlier work," he wrote in 1990. "I just stopped, because I just didn't want to do any more."

The Poe films, like the poet himself before his untimely death on 7 October 1849, could no longer stand on their own two feet. Corman's notion of filming *The Tomb of Ligeia* on location was to be his last attempt to ring the changes in a formula within which he felt himself to be trapped. He could see no way forward and only one way back: another injection of humour into the flagging proceedings. Before *The Tomb of Ligeia*, *The Gold Bug* had again been rewritten, this time as a comedy, but even that proposition had not been enough to encourage him to stay the Gothic course.

In 1960, *House of Usher* had reminded the world that the blood of the Gothic still ran red and warm. In his lavish excursions into the landscapes of madness, death and decay that lay at the heart of Poe's *Tales of Mystery and Imagination*, Roger Corman had shown that Gothic Horror had required nothing more than a dust-down and a shake-up to be as pertinent as it was during the height of its popularity at the beginning of the preceding century. Corman's Poe films had exemplified the Gothic for the new age. They captured the essence of a form which was long since thought to have been sidelined by modernity – familial insanity and the harbouring of dark secrets; coffins and crypts; cobwebbed passageways and a festering aura of physical and moral corruption; vengeful ghosts and scabrous sexual impulses; obsession; lingering death-in-life. In Vincent Price, aesthete and Renaissance man, Corman had found the perfect instrument through which to connect the present with the past.

"I think the Poe films really suffered when Roger left," Price told Ed Naha. "We were going to do *The Gold Bug* when he decided that he had had enough. I could understand his reasoning, but his absence was certainly felt. Roger had a feel for the subject-matter, a point of view that subsequent directors seemed to lack."

The last script for *The Gold Bug* had been supplied by Charles Beaumont. "It was set in the South, after the Civil War," Corman explained. "Vincent Price was a plantation owner who had convinced his one remaining slave – to be played by Sammy Davis Jr – that the South had won the Civil War. Basil Rathbone was a visiting English carpetbagger who comes upon this deserted plantation. It was really very funny, but it was becoming outrageously distanced from Poe so we decided not to make it." "They wanted to turn it into a horror film," Price said, with respect to AIP. "You can't do that without completely perverting the story, because it's a story of detection."

...the beetle, which he had suffered to descend, was now visible at the end of the string, and glistened, like a globe of burnished gold, in the last rays of the setting sun...

EDGAR ALLAN POE, THE GOLD-BUG (1843)

The Gold Bug may have been able to uncover the treasure of Captain Kidd, but without the likes of Corman to guide it, it remained singularly unable to furnish itself with a suitable script. Accordingly, it was now to go the way of all flesh (as over a similar period of time would *When the Sleeper Wakes*). The *Gold Bug* had failed to transmute into box-office gold, either for AIP or for Vincent Price, and the best of the Poes were now behind them both.

Price paid his own tribute to Corman: "My greatest respect for him was for his wisdom in choosing the best people in various fields of the art to launch his career. We all worked together on all those Poe films and Roger achieved, through his appreciation and use of all their talents (and, I might add, the talents of the actors young and old who believed in him), something very similar to the unity and dedication that once existed under the old studio system."

The Masque of the Red Death and *The Tomb of Ligeia* had been such consummate and confident examples of the filmmaker's art that Corman had at last found himself courted by the big boys. In 1966, he directed *The St Valentine's Day Massacre* for an approving Twentieth Century-Fox at an estimated budget of $1.5 million – the most money that he had ever been allocated on a film. AIP put its Poe series on ice for a year and then asked him if he would direct one more film. He declined. The company decided to carry on regardless, but as it found out to its cost, there was only one Roger Corman.

Vincent Price's acquisition of works of art to enhance the domestic furnishing departments of the 755 Sears stores spread throughout the United States carried on undisturbed by his regulation appearances for AIP. So much so, that it soon became the subject of one of Sam Arkoff's most familiar anecdotes: "During the filming of the later Poe movies, many of which we made in England, I visited Vincent at the London hotel where he was staying in what struck me as the worst section of the city," he related in his autobiography (and in reality the Cadogan, in Chelsea's Sloane Street!). "And I was shocked at how simple both the hotel itself and Vincent's own room were. No elaborate suite with comfortable sofas. No room service. Instead, it was a small, bare single room – just large enough for Vincent's lanky six-foot-four frame – that didn't even have a toilet of its own. When he had to use the bathroom, he went down the hall. 'I don't get it,' I told Vincent. 'We're paying you $80,000 for 15 days' work, and we've increased your expense money to $1,000 a week. With that kind of money, can't you afford something better than this room?' 'Sam, if you loved art as much as I do, maybe you *would* get it,' he explained. 'I'm buying art with that $1,000 a week. Who needs a toilet?' Van Gogh and Rembrandt would have loved this man!"

No one loved Vincent Price more than Arkoff himself, however, as American International had made no attempt to acquire a 'stable' of stars (having relinquished its ties with Ray Milland when his three-film contract expired after *The Man with the X-Ray Eyes*) and thus was reliant on him alone. But of equal importance was the fact that Price's work on behalf of good causes and his well-publicised areas of expertise also meant that he was his own best ambassador, and thus he saved the company time and effort in promoting him.

Bolstered by the success of *The Masque of the Red Death* and *The Tomb of Ligeia*, AIP announced to the British trade press that it would make 12 films in the coming year, at an overall cost of £15 million, six of which were to be shot in England. James H Nicholson clarified the position thus: "It will consist of terror, suspense and science-fiction thrillers on the one hand and musicals and comedies keyed to the world's teenage market, on the other. The terror and science fiction pictures will be made in Britain. The light entertainment will be produced in Hollywood." Britain's teenage market was not so enamoured of

Vincent Price, Tab Hunter and David Tomlinson in THE CITY UNDER THE SEA

Frankie Avalon, Annette Funicello or Tommy Kirk, however, and none of AIP's 'light entertainment'' offerings – like *Beach Blanket Bingo, How to Stuff a Wild Bikini* (both 1965) or *Ghost in the Invisible Bikini* (1966) – would see release in the UK, any more than had *Beach Party* (1963) or *Muscle Beach Party* (1964) before them, or many of the ultra-violent 'biker' movies which were to come after them.

With Roger Corman's voluntary absence having imposed a hiatus on the Poe series, attention at AIP switched to other sectors of the market. The next workout for Vincent Price now had to be plucked out of the air, but if *The City Under the Sea* looked to have more in common with *Master of the World* than with *The Tomb of Ligeia*, it was wholly intentional: by 1964, colourful and undemanding adventures were making a return to the big screen after years of being side-lined in the wake of the British new wave of realist dramas. Many of these could loosely be categorised under the heading of science fiction, so another in similar vein would adhere to AIP's stated policy. But an indicator of the audience at which the new film

was really aimed could be discerned in its choice of screenwriter: Charles Bennett.

Sussex-born Bennett had enjoyed long writing associations with both Alfred Hitchcock and Cecil B DeMille. In 1957, he had turned his talents to horror for the first and only time and had given the screen a classic of the macabre in *Night of the Demon*. Latterly, however, he had been responsible for a number of highly coloured extravaganzas from the Fox stable and producer Irwin Allen (for whom he had also penned *The Story of Mankind* and *The Big Circus*, both of which had featured Price): *The Lost World* (1960), *Voyage to the Bottom of the Sea* (1961) and an adaptation of Jules Verne's *Five Weeks in a Balloon* (1962).

When it came to 'terror', Arkoff and Nicholson were quite unable to see past the success of their Poe series and correspondingly felt duty-bound to append some lines of Poe to any film which featured Vincent Price, no matter what the subject or source. The transparency of this approach had been made obvious to all by *The Haunted Palace*, whose provenance was too well known to be disguised by the facile attachment of an unconnected title and a discordant snatch of verse over its freeze-frame finale. But *The City Under the Sea* was marginally more suitable as a candidate for such easy-going exploitational conceits.

Despite an original screenplay by Bennett, an appropriate allusion was to be found in a Poe poem from 1845 entitled *The City in the Sea*:

> *Lo! Death has reared himself a throne*
> *In a strange city lying alone*
> *Far down within the dim West*
> *Where the good and the bad and the worst*
> * and the best*
> *Have gone to their eternal rest...*

AIP had now acquired the services of Louis M 'Deke' Heyward, a prolific writer of radio comedy and ex-MCA executive who had taken his nickname from a show which he fronted in the 1940s called *Deacon Speakin'*, and whose other speciality was the teen scene. 'Deke' Heyward soon found himself responsible for *Sergeant Deadhead the Astronaut* (1965; with Frankie Avalon) and *Ghost in the Invisible Bikini* among other disposable items, but at this stage in his dealings with AIP, he was cast as roving trouble-shooter. Nicholson sent him to England to 'doctor' the script and he ended up taking co-credit after revising much of it as shooting progressed. According to Price, Heyward's rewrites included the Poe verses which he had been asked to incorporate into the piece:

> *But lo, a stir is in the air!*
> *The wave – there is a movement there!*
> *As if their tops have given Death his undivided*
> * time...*

The concluding line is not from Poe, which might explain why it fails to rhyme. Heyward's tampering with the poet's work might also explain why the actual title of the poem failed to make it as the title of the film, which went before the cameras at Pinewood in November 1964. It did, however, furnish Price's character with an opportunity to deliver its remaining verses as exposition over a mid-film montage, even if all but the last few lines still ended up in the wrong order: "While from a proud tower in the town/Death looks gigantically down."

Supporting Price were light-comedy lead David Tomlinson, who had become familiar to American audiences through his appearance in *Mary Poppins*

(1964), the ubiquitous Susan Hart (or Mrs James H Nicholson as she was soon to become known) and Tab Hunter.

Art Gelein, or Tab Hunter (as he was re-christened after his discovery by Rock Hudson), had been 'outed' as gay by the scandal magazine *Confidential* in 1955; he had survived that episode with his reputation intact through publicity tricks like the judicious employment of 'beards' (arranged girlfriends). While they were shooting *The City Under the Sea*, Price seemed to some of his colleagues to take a more than professional interest in his young co-star and his next film, by coincidence, would find him playing opposite another 'macho' male lead with a similar bent. Price had never made an issue of his sexuality – nor had he ever needed to – but before the end of his career it seemed destined to make an issue of him.

> *Cornwall, 1903. Ben (Hunter) and Harold (Tomlinson) set off from their hotel in search of Jill (Hart), whom they believe has been kidnapped. The trail leads them to Lyonesse, a lost city in the sea off Land's End ruled over by an 18th century squire known as The Captain (Price); he and his band of smugglers have themselves been stranded in the city for more than a century. Lyonesse is imperilled by a volcano, however, and its demise is now imminent. After a series of adventures, the companions manage to escape – closely followed by The Captain. But the immortality which was his within the walls of the city does not extend to the outside world; on reaching land, he reverts to his true age.*

The film had been assigned to Jacques Tourneur to direct, who now was not only the next best thing to Corman but had helmed an equally water-logged adventure in Italy, when he ploddingly put Steve Reeves through his muscular paces in *The Giant of Marathon* (1960). In terms of the shooting, Tourneur's placement represented a straight swap, but so capable was Corman on the executive side of things that it took *three* suits to replace him in that area.

Because of his standing within AIP and the way their joint histories had intertwined, Roger Corman had both directed and produced the films he made for the company, including the previous Poes. (George Willoughby and Pat Green had served as associates on *The Masque of the Red Death* and *The Tomb of Ligeia* respectively, to satisfy union stipulations regarding

The City Under the Sea

their status as British productions.) But with Corman gone, the rot set in immediately. Set designer Daniel Haller had been assigned to the role of producer on *The City Under the Sea*, with hired hand Willoughby acting as executive on the British side of things and Heyward mediating between them.

All three were intent on stamping their own personalities onto the production, rather than let veteran craftsman Jacques Tourneur do the job for them. Friction between the various factions surfaced in short order; Haller was professed to be unhappy with Tourneur's vision while Willoughby dithered, and Heyward had eventually to make his presence felt to calm things down. Too many cooks predictably spoiled the broth, and the result ended up swilling around on screen for all to see.

> *This is my world. I am their king. No – more than their king... They believe that I am Death – Death, looking gigantically down from my tower. And they're right; I am Death, because the means of death is in my hands. But I'm also Life, for the same reason...*
>
> **THE CAPTAIN/SIR HUGH TREGATHION** (VINCENT PRICE), *THE CITY UNDER THE SEA* (1964)

The hand of Tourneur is evident from the outset, as a body is washed ashore on a storm-swept Cornish beach and locals mutter ominously about Lyonesse – "the lost city in the sea" whose phantom bell rings out a death-knell. "There are things no man should have to see – or hear," a fisherman warns, "and there were red in the sea, like blood-colour." Wind and rain batter at the façade of the cliff-top hotel wherein are ensconced the protagonists, in a piece of scene-setting which calls to mind the sequence in *Night of the Demon* when Dana Andrews discovers that he is intended to be the next victim of Karswell's mystic runes. The shadow-play is sustained up to the first incursion of one of The Captain's army of 'gill-men', caught in the reflection from a sliver of glass which Ben hurls at his night visitor. But from the moment that our intrepid heroes descend through the passageways of an ancient tin-mine towards the fabled city in question, another film comes garishly into play and juvenilia soon carries all before it.

Anyone looking to *The City Under the Sea* for evidence that Tourneur's return to filmmaking in Britain might have produced something on a par with

the director's previous excursion to the UK for *Night of the Demon* was to be bitterly disappointed. Even Price has a hard time making himself heard above the anodyne banter of Disney émigré Tomlinson, the patter of one-time Western lead Hunter, the heavy-breathing of a horde of second-rate gill-men and the clucking of a 'comedy' chicken. The end result has the appearance of two different films having been edited together and quite failing to mesh, a common practice of AIP's over the purchase of foreign films for domestic distribution.

The City Under the Sea was an attempt to capitalise on the kind of adventure fantasy made popular by Columbia producer Charles H Schneer and his 'Dynamation' collaborator Ray Harryhausen – whose most recent release, *Jason and the Argonauts* (1963) had produced the requisite box-office bonanza – but it fails on all counts bar one, which is the presence of Price to lend some gravitas to the otherwise puerile proceedings. His contribution apart, the film is neither funny nor frightening, its spectacular set-pieces too obviously studio-bound and financially impoverished.

Price's oratorical style is subverted at every turn by a script which has him searching for verbal nuggets among a dross of endless repetition and requires that he address a speech to a mere 'Dan', as opposed to a Mr Winthrop, a Mr Barnard or even an Alfredo. "Dear Deke, you're screwing my career into the ground," he reportedly said to Heyward only half in jest on reading the latter's rewrites. An interminable underwater chase (shot in standard ratio by the second unit and stretched to fill the Panavision screen) sees the participants back where they began in time for the volcano to erupt and the fibreglass set to collapse around them, but between times, all else is tedium.

As The Captain's features are terminally aged in lap-dissolve animation – "We tried to do this last scene with make-up, but it didn't work," Price said – he bows out in voice-over with a last quote from Poe, and the line that Heyward had cut-and-pasted into the intro was finally given its correct reading. It is from the 1831 version of the poem, originally entitled *The Doomed City*:

> *And Death to some more happy clime*
> *Shall give his undivided time.*
>
> **CLOSING NARRATION** (VINCENT PRICE), *THE CITY UNDER THE SEA* (1964)

Jack Mullaney and Vincent Price in **Dr Goldfoot and the Bikini Machine**

The film was retitled *War Gods of the Deep* for US release, presumably to distinguish it from 1953's *City Beneath the Sea* starring Robert Ryan and Anthony Quinn, though its new title turned out to be every bit as phonetically similar to an Italian sword-and-sandal epic of only four years before, *Warlord of Crete* (*Teseo contro il minotauro*; 1961). It was also the recipient of some anachronistic effects footage, spliced in from imported Toho monster-fest *Atragon* (1964) and intended to depict the underwater pumps which the gill-men were supposed to have built – and which its British set designer had decided it could do without.

When Price finished *The City Under the Sea*, he packed his bags with £25,000 worth of paintings which he had purchased on behalf of Sears and returned to Los Angeles to play Captain Hook in a theatrical production of *Peter Pan*, followed by

another round of television appearances on both the Danny Kaye and Red Skelton Shows.

The City Under the Sea had been below par in every respect, and not for the last time would Heyward's 'contribution' to a script turn out to be the literary equivalent of turning gold into brass. Price now wanted a break from straight horror, and AIP came up with an idea which would settle him back in LA for a time while an ailing Boris Karloff stepped into his shoes to keep the British end of its 'terror and science fiction' franchise afloat. Saddled with the same title of 'The House at the End of the World' during production as was *The Tomb of Ligeia*, *Monster of Terror* began shooting at Shepperton Studios in February 1965, with art director-turned-producer Daniel Haller in the director's chair for this one, and promising a film which would contain "a monster to end all monsters." For Vincent Price, *The City Under the Sea* had represented an end to all monsters for the time being.

> *My aim is diabolically simple: I'm going to control the world. I have invented the ultimate in ultimate weapons – the one weapon that can positively destroy man: woman!*
>
> DR GOLDFOOT (VINCENT PRICE),
> *SHINDIG!: THE WILD WEIRD WORLD OF*
> *DR GOLDFOOT* (1965)

Following *The City Under the Sea*, AIP put Price into a pair of fatuous comedies in order to fulfil Arkoff's promise to him to keep him plentifully supplied with work. The films in question had drawn inspiration from the line of muscle-bound beach movies which AIP had always seen as a second string to its corporate bow and from the numerous James Bond spin-offs which had been doing the rounds, like Dean Martin's 'Matt Helm' series or that featuring James Coburn's 'Derek Flint.' The Bond films had started a trend in megalomaniacal super-villains, and no self-respecting secret-agent thriller had been complete without its resident madman desirous of taking over the world. The fad had moved swiftly into weekly TV series of all shades of seriousness, descending just as swiftly into parody, and thus Price's name had begun to top the list of guest stars who queued up to don the mantle of super-villain-of-the-week.

AIP's idea had been to marry its beach bimboes to a musical satire on Bond-style mayhem. The third and latest Bond feature had been *Goldfinger*, named after its Midas-like protagonist, and James Nicholson (credited pseudonymously) came up with the wheeze of calling the film *Dr Goldfoot and the Bikini Machine*, in deference to Dr G's diabolical device for ensnaring unwary governments as part of his plan to – you guessed it.

The plot hardly warrants consideration, save to say that Price's Goldfoot creates an army of bikini-clad female robots who entice various bigwigs to participate unwittingly in his nefarious scheme. A 25-minute television special shot for ABC's networked *Shindig!* show and titled 'The Wild Weird World of Dr Goldfoot' gained it a deal of publicity and *Dr Goldfoot and the Bikini Machine* became a substantial hit in the US, though it passed relatively unnoticed in the UK, where it received a 'U' certificate and few plays, despite its satirical nods to (and use of clips from) *Pit and the Pendulum*.

Dr Goldfoot and the Bikini Machine was directed by Norman Taurog, veteran of a number of Elvis Presley vehicles, and it had started out interspersed with songs. The musical interludes were dropped in production, however; three months before the film's US release in November 1965, the Beatles' explosion was to reach New York's Shea Stadium and the pop ditties which had been written for *Dr Goldfoot* already sounded a decade out of date. Nevertheless, the film took close to $2 million on its domestic outing and ensured itself of a sequel.

Dr Goldfoot and the Girl Bombs adhered to the same formula, except that some of the 'girls' now exploded on contact (hence the title). To recoup some of the extraordinary expense of the original, the sequel was farmed out as a US-Italian-Spanish co-production to Fulvio Lucisano, who nominated a befuddled Mario Bava to direct. Bava was the stylish hand behind *Black Sunday* and most recently *Black Sabbath*, but he was currently bedevilled by problems with a wife, a starlet and grief over the death of his father and, according to Price, made up much of the action as shooting progressed. Pop idol Fabian made an even poorer substitute for the first film's Frankie Avalon, and the proceedings were dominated by an Italian 'comedy' duo named Ciccio and Franco. "We had one person speaking Portuguese, several of them speaking Italian," said Deke Heyward. "Vincent would shake his head in disbelief and say, 'What is happening to me?' Not only did he not understand the Italians or the Portuguese or the Spanish – he didn't understand Fabian!"

Price coasted through the *Goldfoot* films with a style of camp comedy every bit as robotic as the girls whom his character feigned to create, and which ultimately moved *Variety* to comment that it made one doubt "this could be the same actor who once played Albert to Helen Hayes' Victoria on Broadway." "The most dreadful movie I've ever been in," Price said later of *Dr Goldfoot and the Girl Bombs* – a reflection not entirely out of sympathy with Arkoff's own. "We fed several pictures to Vincent that if times had been different, if horror pictures had been doing well, we probably wouldn't have made. Since we had him under contract, we had to use him." Use him AIP did, and next he was hoist into *House of a Thousand Dolls*.

For Sam Arkoff, the words 'terror and science fiction' now came to mean an exploitation piece about

George Nader and Vincent Price in HOUSE OF A THOUSAND DOLLS

RIGHT:
*Vincent Price
and Ann
Smyrner in*
**HOUSE OF A
THOUSAND
DOLLS**

BELOW:
*Vincent Price
and Martha
Hyer in* **HOUSE
OF A
THOUSAND
DOLLS**

the white slave traffic in Tangiers. Arkoff had struck a deal to loan Price out to globetrotting producer Harry Alan Towers, a buccaneering independent among whose more legitimate ventures was a series of Fu Manchu films starring Christopher Lee. "Arkoff always had a penchant for falling in love and getting in bed with rogues and scoundrels," Heyward remarked. "He was totally fascinated by Harry Alan Towers." The planned venture became a Spanish-German co-production, which brought George Nader into the picture. Nader had spent much of the 1960s carving out a career for himself in West German *krimi* after being 'outed' in Hollywood and sacrificed to the tabloids to save the reputation of ex-lover Rock Hudson. Towers produced *House of a Thousand Dolls* under Heyward's all-seeing eye (penning it under his usual pseudonym of Peter Welbeck) and AIP secured for itself the US distribution rights.

*I flatter myself that I have cultivated good taste
in almost everything, especially living.*
    FELIX MANDERVILLE (VINCENT PRICE),
    HOUSE OF A THOUSAND DOLLS (1967)

A title-card succinctly delineated the premise: "The film you are about to see is based on White Slavery as it exists in certain parts of the world even today – Each year thousands of young girls fall victim to these highly organised rings and are sold into lives of prostitution. They are held in bondage with narcotics, and in most cases, sent to far corners of the world never to be heard from again." In the event, the same could have been said of the film which set out to explore the phenomenon.

Price played Felix Manderville, a stage illusionist whose act was a cover for the kidnap of young girls forced into prostitution at the House of the title. The slave trade is organised by a mysterious figure known only as the 'King of Hearts', but when he and his female assistant try to spirit away the wife of two-fisted Stephen Armstrong (Nader), they get more than they bargained for. The subterfuge is uncovered, Manderville is killed in the resultant fraças, and his assistant is exposed as a 'Queen' rather than King of Hearts.

The film was a turgid affair, the purpose of which was occasional glimpses of half-naked female flesh which proved insufficient to satisfy even the raincoat brigade. "One day after filming I walked back to the set to see what was going on," Price recalled. "They were re-filming exactly the same sequence we had shot earlier, only the ladies in it were stark bare-ass naked. They weren't even the same women." Price's naïveté, if authentic, is witness to the fact that he had only one eye on the ball during such foreign excursions, preferring to tread the tourist trail than concentrate on the business in hand; he sleepwalks his way through the role of Manderville, with no thought for anything as arduous as an actual performance.

As the improbable slave-traffickers, Price and Hollywood diva Martha Hyer were about as menacing as current pop duo Sonny and Cher – though *House of a Thousand Dolls* used the lesser-known British band of Cliff Bennett and the Rebel Rousers to provide its title song. Hyer had married powerful Paramount producer Hal B Wallis the previous year and most of the film's meagre budget was expended on a wardrobe befitting her new-found regal status. "I'm not really a bad person," she pleads on her unmasking as the Queen of Hearts. "I just have a very highly developed sense of survival." (AIP was still intending to star her opposite Price in its much-delayed adaptation of *When the Sleeper Wakes*, which might explain her inclusion in the cast list in the first place.)

House of a Thousand Dolls may have been a holiday in the sun for Vincent Price, but it was another spell at Cold Comfort Farm for his film career. Manderville falls to his death during a climactic police raid on the house, but it was the actor's reputation which landed with a thud at the bottom of the stairwell. In the UK, the film was picked up by Gala Film Distributors and played only sporadically in flea-pits after a brief West End opening on the sexploitation circuit.

For all of their ups and downs, Price's first seven years with AIP had nevertheless been beneficial for both parties, while his concurrent arrangement with Sears, Roebuck had been the icing on the cake. Since 1964 and the aesthetic (though not actual) departure of Roger Corman, as well as the corporate emasculation of James Nicholson, Arkoff's AIP had been less accommodating than that of old. The Goldfoot franchise had fallen flat on its face and Arkoff himself consistently displayed a distressing penchant for doing expedient deals with rogue traders; thus Price had found himself sold into *House of a Thousand Dolls*. *The Gold Bug* may have gone to the wall in the process, but there was still the promise of *When the Sleeper Wakes* to maintain his interest and, ever the optimist, he remained convinced that better things awaited him in the wings.

AIP's experience with *Dr Goldfoot and the Girl Bombs* had convinced Arkoff that such runaway productions could no longer be organised by a scouting party. In June 1967, at the start of the 'summer of love', AIP set up a more permanent London office in Upper Grosvenor Street, Mayfair, and Louis 'Deke' Heyward was nominated as Head of European production, the idea being for the company to embark on a new programme of A-features initiated in Britain. Along the way, AIP managed to secure the services of one-time Hammer publicity agent Dennison Thornton – or 'Scoop', as he was more affectionately known. "We could produce more cheaply there," Heyward said of his relocation from Beverly Hills to the UK. "I was glad to get out of the US; I was unhappy with what was going on socially and politically at the time."

Now that the time had come for Vincent Price to consider the renewal of his contract, he was inclined to adopt the attitude of 'better the devil you know.' Over the next few years, he was to be plagued by a number of different devils.

ACT 5

THE
MERCHANT
OF MENACE

They took her an hour before dawn – Hopkins, Stearne, and Martin Lacey, gaoler of Manningtree and gravedigger of St Mary's on the Heath. If they had hoped to interrupt her during some sacrilegious activity they were disappointed, for when they pushed open the unlocked door of her cottage the old beldam was snoring contentedly on her bed with a blanket drawn up to her chin.

RONALD BASSETT, WITCHFINDER GENERAL (1966)

By 1965, Vincent Price had variously been christened the Merchant of Menace, the Sovereign of the Sinister or the Master of the Macabre. His name had become as synonymous with horror as Karloff's and Lugosi's before him, or Cushing's and Lee's in tandem with him. The accolades were both a blessing and a curse. For Price himself, they meant constant work in the one genre which defied box-office trends and continued to command a devoted audience throughout the 1960s, but they also meant that unscrupulous producers would seek to cast him in second-rate fare solely for the sake of his name.

Price's obsessive desire to keep working inhibited his critical faculties when it came to the reading of scripts, a blind spot he shared with Christopher Lee. As a consequence, many otherwise mediocre productions had begun to find themselves graced with the Price presence, for no better reason than the promise of a contractual cheque and the occasional trip to Europe. Price's screen career was already finding itself seconded to his interest in art, none of which was helped by studio publicity machines which tended to concentrate on the latter at the expense of the former.

After years of featuring in films which had required little more of him than that he fit snugly into period costume and look malevolent or horrified by turns, Price had fallen back on a stock repertoire of florid gestures, eyeball-rolls and knowing smirks. The money had poured in, not only from his film roles but from his commercial pursuits, as well. It had all become just a little too easy. No longer was he a mere actor; he was Vincent Price – media personality, and he was constantly being called on to guest-star in *Batman* (as 'Egghead'), *F Troop* (in 'V for Vampire'), *Get Smart* or *The Man from U.N.C.L.E.* to name a few, in all of which he camped up his image to the point of self-destruction. In the sequel to *Dr Goldfoot*, he had created 'girl bombs', while as Professor Multiple in an episode of *Voyage to the Bottom of the Sea* (which reunited him with Al – now David – Hedison), he had manufactured 'The Deadly Dolls.'

His time having been occupied with the creation of pneumatic weaponry, Vincent Price did not appear in another new horror film until 1968. These 'gap' years were less evident to British audiences because Anglo's release of AIP's Poe films in the UK had lagged a long way behind their American screenings due to the monopoly position of the two main cinema chains, Odeon and ABC, and more limited opportunities for distribution as a consequence. Even so, there was a vacuum, which was filled by *House of a Thousand Dolls* and, after a three-year delay, *The Last Man on Earth* – both of which received only limited play in third-run houses.

Price's contract with AIP was due for renewal. After more than a decade spent scaring the pants off audiences, he was faced with a stark choice: he could remain a star in his own right, albeit in the field of horror, or he could play supporting roles in other people's films. Trapped between a rock and a hard place, Price signed with American International for a further seven years on the promise of more money and bigger and better roles. The exclusivity clause was to remain in place, though; he was still prohibited from making horror films for any company other than AIP. "Sam was a genius at being a lawyer," Deke Heyward said. "He knew how to make contracts. He tied up Vincent Price."

THE MAN FROM U.N.C.L.E. *('The Fox and Hounds Affair')*

With the changing climate in terms of audience taste, Vincent Price little realised at the time that the days of *Master of the World*, *The Comedy of Terrors* or even *Dr Goldfoot* were finally gone, and that horror was the only thing for which AIP would now want him.

By the time Price reappeared on screen in a new horror production – *Witchfinder General* – Lorre and Rathbone were dead and Boris Karloff was seriously ill (he would die in 1969). Roger Corman had switched his attention to gangs, gangsters and acid (*The Wild Angels*, *The St Valentine's Day Massacre* and *The Trip*), and a 'summer of love' had epitomised a world which seemed to anyone over 30 to be changing out of all recognition. It was a more sober and reflective Price who resurfaced in East Anglia to play in a costume piece about witch-hunting in Puritan England.

Having set up a more permanent shop in the UK, AIP had entered into an arrangement with the newly enfranchised Tigon Films and its chief executive Tony Tenser – a man with a "dodgy reputation," according to Heyward – to co-produce a film from a novel to which Tenser owned the rights and whose background was the English Civil War. "It became part of my edict to find things for Vincent to do," Heyward

explained. "We were coming to the end of Vincent's contract and I was able to make a deal for less than $150,000 ... The attractive thing about the picture was the price."

The attractive thing to Sam Arkoff was the Price, and the actor had been assigned to the fledgling production as part of the deal, to play opposite a cast of relative unknowns, including Ian Ogilvy and Hilary Dwyer.

The values of the old Hollywood had passed away in the fifties, but something of them had managed to survive in British studios until well into the sixties. When Price returned to the UK in 1967 for the first time since playing in *The City Under the Sea*, even that crumb of comfort could no longer be guaranteed. In every aspect of the business, the old guard had taken a back seat to a new generation of young Turks full of bright ideas and with a feel for the mood of the moment. In place of the venerated (and venerable) Jacques Tourneur came the vagaries of a volatile director to whom an actor of Price's calibre and expertise was of no particular concern. The culture clash which resulted was an experience from which the respected star did not quickly recover, and it had the effect of colouring black his performance in the one of most sombre and Manichean roles of his career.

Much has been written about *Witchfinder General* over the years, and a cult of personality has sprung up around its young director – Michael Reeves – who died in 1969 at the age of 25. Combined with the myths which tend to be generated in the wake of such tragic circumstances, mostly relating to the animosity between Reeves and his star during shooting, the true worth of this low-budget exercise in historical horror has since been exaggerated out of all proportion.

There is a tale in film circles to the effect that one day during shooting, Price is supposed to have inquired of his director, somewhat testily: "I've made 90 films; what have you made?" To which Reeves is reputed to have replied: "Two good ones." If this caustic exchange did indeed take place, then Reeves was exaggerating, as anyone who has seen *Revenge of the Blood-Beast* can testify. Price, on the other hand, was not, and Reeves might have had some difficulty in disputing the artistic integrity of *The Eve of St Mark*, *The Baron of Arizona* or *While the City Sleeps* if pushed to do so. Vincent Price, however, was never one for pushing.

WITCHFINDER GENERAL

Now, with all the country's energies directed towards the prosecution of the war, with Anglican Catholics fighting for their king and Puritans for their beliefs, religious fervour with all its pagan undershadows was becoming intense. It was a situation that Matthew Hopkins intended to exploit to the full. He had already tasted blood, gained respect, and lined his pockets. He was hungry for more.

RONALD BASSETT,
WITCHFINDER GENERAL (1966)

Witchfinder General was adapted from a novel of the same name by Ronald Bassett, which in turn was extrapolated from episodes in the comparatively brief but singularly violent career of Matthew Hopkins, the lawyer son of a Suffolk minister. In March 1645, at the height of the Civil War, Hopkins capitalised on religious tension in the Protestant strongholds of the Eastern counties of England by 'fingering' an old crone named Elizabeth Clarke as a witch. Clarke was duly 'swum' and the confession thus extracted resulted in 32 suspects being arraigned at Chelmsford Assizes. Spurred by this success, the self-appointed Witchfinder General offered a similar service to the gullible burghers of other towns and villages. From Essex, he travelled to Suffolk with his assistant John Stearne, where among those detained

Louis Heyward visits Vincent Price during a break in filming **WITCHFINDER GENERAL**

and subsequently hanged was a 70-year-old parson from the village of Brandeston, John Lowes. Around this incident does *Witchfinder General* revolve.

Bassett supplied Lowes with a niece, and she with a beau in the form of a cavalry officer in Cromwell's New Model Army. This gave the story its dynamic, as the motif of revenge is put in play for what trooper Ralph Margery (renamed Marshall in the film) considers to be injudicial murder. He pursues Hopkins relentlessly, until the Witchfinder falls into his hands in a country inn from whence he is despatched by hanging. Reeves' version has Hopkins try to turn the tables on Marshall by having him arrested for witchcraft and whisked off to a nearby dungeon, but he is climactically hacked to death for his pains.

Ronald Bassett was as much a historian as he was a novelist, and *Witchfinder General* is thorough in its eye for period detail and convincing in its portrait of the social conditions which prevailed in England

during the Civil War. Several of those involved in the making of the film dismissed its source novel out of hand; patently they had never read it, for it stands as a brisk and thoroughgoing piece of work, engagingly written. Loyal to a fault, Price was also inclined to defend the film's bloodthirsty climax as historically accurate, protesting that the real Hopkins had in fact received worse treatment at the hands of the mob than had been meted out to him by Michael Reeves.

The real Matthew Hopkins died in bed at his home in Manningtree, Essex, of tuberculosis, in 1647. Bassett appreciated that the needs of drama required him to die 'by the sword', and he justified his decision to hang Hopkins at the climax of his novel by quoting a passage from the vicar of Bury St Edmonds in Suffolk, who asserted that Hopkins had himself been 'swum' (and presumably hanged as a result), while accepting that the tale was probably apocryphal.

Indeed it was, and there were many more where it came from as folklorists rushed in to mete out natural justice to a sorry story where none such had existed in life. 'As no judicial entry of his trial and execution is to be found in any register, it appears most probable that he expired by the hands of the mob,' wrote Charles Mackay in *Extraordinary Popular Delusions* (1841).

As Tom Baker's screenplay had sought to follow Bassett's novel rather than historical fact, its first draft had Hopkins die in a typically Poe-esque conflagration. When it was realised that the film crew would not be permitted to torch the National Trust property of Orford Castle in Norfolk, the scene was amended by Reeves to have trooper Marshall chop the Witchfinder into pieces with an axe.

> *I am Matthew Hopkins – Witchfinder.*
> **MATTHEW HOPKINS** (VINCENT PRICE),
> *WITCHFINDER GENERAL* (1967)

Michael Leith Reeves was a lifelong film buff who had bought his way into movie-making through inherited wealth. His idols were kick-ass American director Don Siegel and Roger Corman. (Corman was the idol of *every* movie-making wannabe in the 1960s.) His rise to prominence was similar to that of Corman's, though on the basis of much less product and considerably less experience.

Reeves' original choice for the lead in *Witchfinder General* was Donald Pleasence, an actor whose physical characteristics closely matched the description of Hopkins in Bassett's novel: "An inch shorter than Stearne, he was also slighter of build, and his short, square-cropped beard showed threads of premature grey. His eyes, slightly bulbous, were a watery blue, and his hair and hands were well-kept. There was little about his appearance, however, to mark him out from the hundreds of others about him, or to stamp him more indelibly upon the memory."

With AIP stumping up half the budget for what was now a co-production, its own star turn Vincent Price, subject to his approval, was allocated the role. After two years as Dr Goldfoot, Price accepted, and in September he headed for the UK and the prospect of working on a new 'Poe' film with a director whom he had been informed was one of the brightest lights on the 'swinging London' scene. If he had known then how he would feel towards both only a few weeks later, he might have had second thoughts about boarding the plane.

Deke Heyward had spun Price a line about the maverick filmmaker which had intrigued the veteran star. "Take me to your goddam boy genius," he said to producer Philip Waddilove on his arrival at London's Heathrow Airport. Thereafter, Price made every attempt to ingratiate himself with his new director as well as his fledgling co-stars, all of whom adopted amenable poses, especially an over-deferential Nicky Henson ("Don't push it, Alice," Price retorted to his flow of compliments). Reeves, however, was churlish and unimpressed with the camp star-turn which he considered AIP had foisted upon him, but, psychologically unable to voice his concerns to the man himself, he left Price to ponder alone on the causes of the growing discord between them. In consequence, Price took the slight personally.

On the first day of filming, Price fell heavily from his horse and was temporarily bedridden. Reeves refused even to pay lip-service to his lead actor's misfortune, which caused Price more hurt to his pride than the horse did to his coccyx. The relationship

WITCHFINDER GENERAL

between the two soured from that point, though the absence of bonhomie paradoxically extracted from Price one of his most assured performances.

That Vincent Price was disgruntled and discomfited throughout the shooting of *Witchfinder General* is unquestioned. He had found himself working with a director in whom he could encourage no rapport; he was his usual hail-fellow-well-met, but Reeves was insular, insecure and antisocial for the most part. With the unit decamped to the wilds of Suffolk in a chill October, the shoot itself was miserable in the extreme. To cap it all, Price had been apprised of the fact that he had not been his director's preferred choice for the role. Thus he was stranded in an alien environment, with a cast and crew who were predominantly young and a director who was treating him as though he were a relic from a bygone age. He felt that he was out of favour and, for much of the time, out of kilter with the production as well.

As far as actors were concerned, Michael Reeves had no 'people skills', a not uncommon trait in those to whom too much money comes too early in life. For Price, therefore, humiliation came on a daily basis as the 'young genius' determined to strip him of all the bits of business which had now become his trademarks. "Don't move your head; don't throw your voice," Reeves reminded him constantly. "Very well," Price would confirm. "Not moving head – not throwing voice." Diane Ogilvy, co-star Ian Ogilvy's wife at the time, recalled an incident that occurred as she was driving from the set after a day's filming. Seeing Price sitting dejectedly nearby, she offered to give him a lift. "Are you going past California?" he enquired in reply.

Being the trouper he was, Vincent Price took all this ignominy with the best grace that he could muster, even when Reeves contrived to have him re-dub his own voice to tone down its inflections. But the shooting of the climax in Orford Castle was the last straw. Whether through inexperience, indiscipline or a pursuit of perfection which hitherto had encouraged him and his cameraman to go repeatedly for multiple 'takes', Reeves had bottlenecked the schedule into the final few days. A 36-hour marathon session in a damp dungeon (which Price leavened with a bottle of wine, to his director's dismay) had Price lying on a cold stone floor for hours on end, while Ogilvy battered him black-and-blue with a hard rubber axe. As a result, Reeves ran out of time, and the film was put in the

can with a patchwork of footage pasting over the gaps in its final frames.

When filming was over, Price flew straight back to the States. He subsequently dispatched his usual round of gifts and 'thank you' notes to cast and crew (the 'application of molasses,' as he referred to this beneficence), including Michael Reeves, and modified his initial opinion of the work after seeing a completed print at the offices of American International. But no amount of post-production diplomacy could mask the insult which the actor felt had come his way in the interim. "Youth is no excuse for incivility," he later told author John Murray.

> *By the way, do you know what they call me now?*
> *– Witchfinder General. There are those who think*
> *I should be appointed such, for all of England...*
> *appointed by Parliament.*
> **MATTHEW HOPKINS** (VINCENT PRICE),
> *WITCHFINDER GENERAL* (1967)

Reeves' quest for realism at all costs may have caused the cast of *Witchfinder General* to be caked continually in mud and blood, as well as exposed to fire, water and farting horses. But it also produced sequences of striking beauty and a film, on the whole, which was more authentic in tone to the period in question than director Ken Hughes' multi-million pound production of *Cromwell*, made three years later.

Taken in isolation, the script of the film is rather banal. Hopkins and Stearne are reduced to mouthing predictable clichés of the sort to be found in Hammer Horror. "The Lord's work – a noble thing" and "The mark of Satan is upon them; they must hang" are the extent to which the depths of the duo's psyche are plumbed by dialogue which relies on imagery to compensate for the motivational void in the storyline. Reeves is at his best when shooting out of doors, where he exhibits flair and style and an instinctive grasp of filmmaking technique, but the blocking of interior scenes required some studio training and a more formal discipline, neither of which he was able to call upon and both of which are noticeable by their absence from the film's more conventional passages.

Witchfinder General is no masterpiece, but Reeves' propitious use of picturesque Suffolk countryside in autumn light, and his employment of extant locations in Hopkins' historical killing-field of

Godfrey James, Hilary Dwyer, Vincent Price and Robert Russell in **Witchfinder General**

Brandeston (though not Lavenham, as depicted) invest it with a breadth of vision which belied its meagre £83,000 budget and echoed clearly of the Western myth – of Delmer Daves, and John Ford and Monument Valley – which Reeves was at pains to evoke. It is elegiac, as well as being ripe with symbolism. Only Sam Peckinpah, in his own fables of the Old West – and with whom Reeves' cinematographer John Coquillon would work in the 1970s – had a similar psychological grasp of an end to things; of the inevitable encroachment of night; of *götterdämmerung*.

> *I intend to instigate a new method of execution. And you, Master Webb – you shall aid me in carrying it out.*
> **Matthew Hopkins** (Vincent Price), *Witchfinder General* (1967)

Unapologetically advertised by Tigon as 'The Most Violent Film of the Year', *Witchfinder General* was thought excessive for its time (though it was soon to be matched and superseded). The height of gratuitousness came in the form of a young woman being lowered onto a flaming pyre from atop a wooden scaffold. There is no precedent in Bassett's novel, or in history itself, for such a torturous form of execution. Hopkins' witches were uniformly hanged, according to the statutes which covered heresy: he might have been capable of inventing their crimes, but he was wholly unable to devise the punishments which went along with them.

Much to Reeves' annoyance – and despite his professed admiration of the young director's work – British film censor John Trevelyan deprived the film of much of its brutality. Trevelyan was a great believer in 'less is more', and any labouring over

Vincent Price and Ian Ogilvy in **WITCHFINDER GENERAL**

scenes of violence was invariably met with a request for the reduction of same to the level where the filmmaker's point was made and no more. *Witchfinder General* suffered particularly in this regard, as many of its sequences had gone well beyond what Trevelyan considered to be necessary.

Reverend Lowes' treatment at the hands of Stearne was shortened to lower the number of 'pricks' which were inflicted upon him in search of the devil's mark. Stearne's vicious beating of a female prisoner was reduced to a brief scene and a single blow. The burning of the witch, shown in full in the director's cut, was shorn of a shot in which her head and body are seen to enter the flames. Hopkins' bloody demise lost the whole of a close shot in which Marshall fells him to the ground under a hail of blows from his axe; the sequence was reduced to a first blow and a last, shown from two different angles. (The excision was doubly injurious for Price, who had been forced to endure the battering in numerous retakes when Reeves chose to vent his

ire on him by proxy.) There were other minor trims, as well.

Deke Heyward had also asked for tavern scenes to be restaged in a 'continental' version – in other words, with added nudity. Accordingly, Price played several scenes to Robert Russell (as John Stearne) twice over, the second time with buxom wenches placed strategically in the foreground, breasts exposed. Reeves commented sarcastically on this crude tactic by awarding Heyward an 'additional dialogue' credit in the film's titles.

In many of these instances, Trevelyan's interventions actually improved the film, as Reeves himself was reluctantly forced to admit. He had over-indulged in the sadism; in toning it down, the censor had allowed the finer qualities of the piece to come to the fore.

The film's notoriety, and therefore its eventual success, forbade Price from condemning it as an amateur work and instead he praised Reeves after the event; not that he was left with much choice. "I told you," the young director ungraciously informed him in a transatlantic phone call before succumbing to neurosis and an untimely demise.

> *You took him from me – you took him from me!*
> **RICHARD MARSHALL** (IAN OGILVY),
> *WITCHFINDER GENERAL* (1967)

Matthew Hopkins is given three separate 'entrances' in *Witchfinder General* – each one building cumulatively to the point when he raps at Lowes' door. The first is merely a series of exchanges between Hopkins and Stearne as they approach the village on horseback, the second is an encounter with Richard Marshall on the road at nightfall (when Hopkins' voice is heard but he remains unseen), and the third and final one is his officious assault on the church door, when he announces his name to priest and audience both. As introductions go, it is pure grandstanding, like Dracula descending the steps in his castle to greet Renfield (though it would have lost little and gained much had the first of these been removed in the final edit). All the more surprising then, that after such a momentous build-up, Hopkins is sidelined by Reeves in favour of the doomed love affair between Richard and Sara for the remainder of the film.

The novel's Hopkins, despite being a lawyer by nature and profession, does not start out as an instrument of calculated greed; he is encouraged to his self-styled calling of Witchfinder by the more opportunistic Stearne through a mixture of his own susceptibility to superstitious fear and delusions of grandeur. When a suitable opening presents itself, Hopkins pursues it with his lawyer's guile, Puritanical zeal and an innate belief in at least some of the tenets which he sets out to uphold. The film ducks this aspect of Hopkins' psychological make-up, choosing instead to characterise him as cynically exploitative from the outset. The novel, however, is the story of Matthew Hopkins, whereas *Witchfinder General* operates from the perspective of the fictional Captain Richard Marshall.

All of this is par for the course when it comes to adapting a novel to the screen and has little bearing on the merit or otherwise of the film itself, but it did bear strikingly on the inclusion of Vincent Price in its cast list.

Michael Reeves had it in mind from the start that Ogilvy was to be his star (as he had been, to all

intents and purposes, when cast opposite Boris Karloff in *The Sorcerers*), with whoever played Hopkins subordinated to that end. When AIP insisted on Vincent Price for the role, this concept appeared in danger of collapse. Reeves' animosity towards Price is more explicable in these circumstances; rather than rework Baker's treatment to accommodate the imposition and status of Price, Reeves stuck to his guns, and Price's actual if not contractual downgrading was the unavoidable result. Consequently, the actor could do little but add flesh to a character who merely comes and goes as the plot demands and is only marginally less wooden than the gibbet from which he lowers his victim into the flames.

Witchfinder General was, and is, Ian Ogilvy's film and Reeves' original plan to cast Donald Pleasence in the role of Hopkins would better have suited the dynamic of the piece. Pleasence was never a star, always a character actor, and his beady eyes, behind which lurked all manner of unspoken vices, were his fame. The part of Hopkins as written is a supporting role and not a central one; the film was not a star-turn for Matthew Hopkins, any more than its story is that of Hopkins himself. On the contrary, it is about the effect that he and those like him have on those whose lives are touched by his particular brand of malice.

Price had featured prominently in every film in which he had so far starred for AIP, as well as those he had made for other companies along the way, and he had been given no reason to believe that *Witchfinder General* would be any different – an attitude on his part which had been encouraged by the sycophantic entreaties of Deke Heyward prior to production. That he found himself idling away his time on set while the cameras rolled on Ogilvy and Dwyer came as more than a surprise, and he had been unprepared for such an eventuality. For the first time in 15 years, the character which he had contracted to play was merely a monster in the wings, a shadow on the wall, as two-dimensionally malevolent as the Frankenstein creature of old and as easily disposable. It had been a humbling experience for Price – but more than that, it was a wake-up call about where his career and his recently renewed contract with AIP seemed intent on taking him.

Witchfinder General had given Vincent Price the first inkling that his time as the Merchant of Menace might be coming to a close. Instead of which, it was Michael Reeves for whom the bell tolled, less than a year after the film went into release. His meteoric rise to critical acclaim was followed by an equally dramatic plunge back down to earth. A manic depressive by nature, Reeves had already attempted to commit suicide before finally being found dead in his Chelsea flat in February 1969, empty bottles of prescription medicines by his side.

> *Out – out are the lights – out all!*
> *And over each quivering form,*
> *The curtain, a funeral pall,*
> *Comes down with the rush of a storm,*
> *And the angels, all pallid and wan,*
> *Uprising, unveiling, affirm*
> *That the play is the tragedy, 'Man,'*
> *And its hero the Conqueror Worm.*
>
> EDGAR ALLAN POE,
> 'THE CONQUEROR WORM' (1843)

The film was retitled for US release as Edgar Allan Poe's *The Conqueror Worm*, though the title on screen read 'Matthew Hopkins Conqueror Worm', which unfortunately called to mind all those early AIP 'giant bug' movies. "Only from the pen of Edgar Allan Poe could come such an horrendous tale of terror – The Conqueror Worm," promised the trailer. "Leave the children at home…" Price was again asked to voice the incongruous opening lines of Poe's poem over a freeze-frame of the titles and the more appropriate last verse over the end credits. The strategy fooled no one, but the success of the film under a Poe header ensured that AIP would continue to employ it whenever possible. "We weren't exactly sure what it meant," Sam Arkoff admitted. "But it was pure Poe and seemed to fit with *The Witchfinder General's* storyline. We felt if we had Vincent recite the poem at the beginning of the film, we could legitimately call the picture a Poe movie."

For Vincent Price, *Witchfinder General* was not the end. Not by a long way. The reception that eventually was accorded Michael Reeves' third and last feature, critically as well as financially, gave a boost to his horror career, while the counter-culture categorised by 'flower power' withered and died as fast as it had sprouted. Edgar Allan Poe was back in business, and the next addition to the never-ending series would at least return to the pen of the master for renewed inspiration.

Having returned to the States, Price took solace after the rigours of working with Michael Reeves by starring opposite Patricia Routledge (best known to British TV viewers for *Keeping Up Appearances*) in a romantic musical comedy by Jule Styne, composer of *Gypsy*, and based on *Buried Alive* and *The Great Adventure* by turn-of-the-century novelist Arnold Bennett. Off-Broadway, the musical was entitled *Married Alive!* but it changed to *Darling of the Day* for its opening on the Great White Way. More than a title change was needed to save it, though, and to a public for whom the only music that now mattered was coming out of England or the West Coast of America, the show closed after only 31 performances to a record-making loss of $ 3/4 million. The failure of *Darling of the Day* represented another blow to Price's self-esteem, and the only other game in town for the summer of 1968 was a cameo in *The Trouble with Girls*, a typical late-career offering from Elvis Presley. The two never met, on screen or off.

By October, time off from AIP for good behaviour had once more run out and Price was headed back to England aboard the good ship Poe, whose next port of call was *The Oblong Box*, a tale of the accursed.

> *My own mistake arose, naturally enough,*
> *through too careless, too inquisitive, and too*
> *impulsive a temperament. But of late, it is a rare*
> *thing that I sleep soundly at night. There is a*
> *countenance which haunts me, turn as I will.*
> *There is a hysterical laugh which will forever ring*
> *within my ears.*
>
> EDGAR ALLAN POE, *THE OBLONG BOX* (1844)

At first, Price thought that he would be working with Michael Reeves again. AIP's newest recruit had now been pencilled in to direct the next Poe and he had taken several stabs already at reworking a draft treatment by industry veteran Lawrence Huntington, who had made *The Vulture* in 1966, a film which ultimately went unreleased in the UK. Huntington had originally been slated to direct as well, but he had fallen ill and died the very month that the film went on the floor.

With his life and career disintegrating around him, Reeves eventually dropped out of the picture, and one-time film journalist Christopher Wicking was hired to knock the extant script into shape. "They were trying to rush something into production to take advantage of Michael's talents and they had

Vincent Price shows Christopher Lee the rudiments of chess during a break in filming THE OBLONG BOX

that one standing by," Wicking explained to author Kim Newman. "But as it got closer and closer to shooting, he got more and more frightened of it, and apparently he had all sorts of problems with doctors. He was on uppers and downers and XYZ and shock treatment, which was all pretty awful." Wicking introduced a whole new subplot about African witchcraft to jolly things along: "I made the theme of imperial exploitation of the natives the subtext, the cause of the curse."

28-year-old American television producer-director Gordon Hessler stepped into the breach on the morning production commenced, and the eighth and last (publicised as the eleventh) AIP Poe adaptation finally got underway. "Because Gordon had directed in America and done other small pictures over here, he just instantly stepped in," Wicking added,

apparently without thought for the adage about fools and angels. He further expanded on the indecent haste which was involved in an interview with Philip Nutman: "I got a call from Gordon on a Monday asking for more scenes for Vincent Price. They also needed scenes with more production value, scenes of extras in taverns. Vincent often felt like Christopher Lee in the Dracula pictures, that he was just being used as a name, and wasn't being given enough to do."

As a result, *The Oblong Box* turned out to be worst of the faux-Poes by a wide margin. The dearth of imagination which afflicted the production was exemplified by the fact that, although the film managed to pull off something of a coup by pairing Vincent Price and Christopher Lee for the first time on screen, no one connected with it could manage to come up with more than a single scene in which the two of them featured together, any more than they were able to glean a suitable quote from Poe with which to embellish the titles. To critics and audiences alike, the impression given was that it had all been a confidence trick for marquee value, and yet the two actors had both worked on the film for several weeks.

> Edward Markham: *You haven't been looking for me, have you, Trench? And we did have a bargain.*
> Trench: *My God... Sir Edward. I thought you'd been –*
> Edward Markham: *– Buried? Yes... Waking up in that horrible oblong box; no air to breathe; trapped, and no escape. The earth raining down on the lid, every shovelful burying you more deeply...*
>
> ALISTER WILLIAMSON AND PETER ARNE,
> THE OBLONG BOX (1968)

The Oblong Box was shot during November and December 1968 at Shepperton Studios in Middlesex. Just as Hammer had begun to utilise standing sets for the features that it made at Elstree or Pinewood, so the

THE OBLONG BOX

same 19th-century street-scene now cropped up in the films of AIP and others who chose to employ the Shepperton facilities for their horrors. More than that, the sets were being populated by the same teams of supporting actors, who alternated between the various companies as need arose. Gordon Hessler, in particular, was fond of using a number of players in an unofficial 'stock' company, whose habitual appearances gave his films the look of an amateur rep at which a camera happened to be present.

The result of this is unmitigated disaster. Hessler's directorial style was the antithesis of the careful control required of the Gothic – all pulsing zooms and zip-pans, and owing more to the hectic pace of his television work on *Alfred Hitchcock Presents* than it did to Edgar Allan Poe. Wicking's absurd conflation of curses and African witchcraft was also anachronistic; the writer had previously worked on the unfilmed screenplay of *The Gold Bug*, an adventure with Aztec overtones, and this may have coloured his thinking with respect to *The Oblong Box*. He was to pursue a fixation with pagan mysticism into *Cry of the Banshee*, whose source of reference was Dr Margaret Murray, author of *The Witch-Cult in Western Europe* (1921) and *The God of the Witches* (1933).

Poe's story needed no such exotic frippery to turn it into a chiller. A minor tale in the canon, it concerns a seafarer who keeps the corpse of his dead wife in his stateroom, and all that required to be added was for the aforesaid corpse to be alive and able to free itself from its confinement at intervals, like Cesare the somnabulist in Robert Wiene's *The Cabinet of Dr Caligari* (1919).

> *The horribly disfigured Edward Markham (Alister Williamson) is kept prisoner in his room after falling victim to a native curse while in Africa. The family's solicitor has come up with a plan to fake Edward's death so that he can whisk him away, supposedly for burial; before he can do so, however, Edward's brother Julian (Price) has the body nailed into a coffin and laid to rest. Edward is disinterred by the only bodysnatchers in history who steal the coffin as well as the corpse and is taken to the mad lab of Dr Neuhartt (Lee). Edward blackmails the latter into letting him stay on and, having found a base for his operations, divides his time between a brothel and the disposal of those who bungled his escape. Unable to differentiate between the two, he cuts the throat of a tart as well.*

Hilary Dwyer and Vincent Price in **The Oblong Box**

He follows this by additionally cutting the throat of his new landlord, thus depriving himself of the very base he just established. He is then forced to return to his former home, where his brother reveals that it was he, Julian, who should have been cursed and promptly shoots Edward dead for having a big hooter; as he expires, he bites Julian on the hand, passing on the facial deformity. Julian retires to Edward's room to wait for his nose to grow. "This is my room," he informs his fiancée as an evil-looking acne heads towards his proboscis.

The pairing of Vincent Price and 23-year-old Hilary Dwyer was less likely this time around than it had been in *Witchfinder General*; the Heyward protégé was meant to be Price's fiancée. The acting honours are stolen instead by Peter Arne as the scheming solicitor, who organises the fatal body-snatching fraud but ends with his throat cut like all the rest. Fifteen years later, Arne himself was to end with his head bashed in on the floor of his London flat, the probable victim of a homosexual lover; his killer was never found.

Wicking's script takes a populist pot-shot at the evils of colonialism to give the story some currency, but the plot is simply a pot-pourri of ideas from *The Premature Burial*, *The Phantom of the Opera* and *The Flesh and the Fiends* (1959), with the gaps filled by funerals, fights and whatever else could be called to mind to spice the mix. "I might find myself buying

RIGHT:
*Michael
Balfour and
Vincent Price,
between takes
on* THE
OBLONG BOX

BELOW:
*Sally Geeson
and Vincent
Price in a
publicity shot
from* THE
OBLONG BOX

your pretty little body one day for a guinea or two," Neuhartt says to his blackmailing parlour-maid in one of the film's few deliverable lines. Hessler started a new trend in stock-footage to make up for the absence of Corman's castles: his films were to become peppered with incongruous shots of extras cavorting about at times when cover was needed for a shortage of plot. A weary-looking Price is accorded the line: "My God, Trench, do you know what that means? – It means that my brother was buried alive!" At this point in time, he was mumbling such retorts in his sleep.

As the villain of the piece, Alister Williamson is a tailor's dummy in a suit of period clothes and crimson hood, his London accent having to be dubbed over throughout. His supposedly 'hideous' make-up is atrocious, being little more than a large, pock-marked nose which Hessler unwisely chose to emphasise with a fish-eye lens. Dwyer was already destined by Heyward for bigger things, but Price finishes up the victim of the creeping acromegaly which was becoming his fate at the hands of AIP.

Downbeat endings in horror films had become the norm; deadbeat execution of same was a newer phenomenon. The most attractive element of the whole production was the design of the elaborately studded leather coffin which featured as the 'Oblong Box.'

Laid against its co-feature in the UK (*The Dunwich Horror*, with its epic Les Baxter score and lush Richard Glouner camerawork), *The Oblong Box* was stale and staid, a poor substitute for craft and creative thinking. American International's Poe series had gone from glory to merely gory in the space of three films and it had now reached the end of its long road. "I wanted so much to break away from the Poe nonsense: that day was over," Deke Heyward confessed after the debacle. "Horror had gotten too old-fashioned, and so had we."

Blood-bedewed *female* corpses lying in state were the stuff of Poe, in both a psychological and a literary sense; voodoo and big-nosed zombies were the stuff of Monogram Pictures. The fact that *The Oblong Box* looked as though it had been produced by a war-time studio from out of 'poverty-row', such as Monogram or PRC, said all that needed to be said about where AIP's Poe series was now going. Effectively, this was the finish, though Arkoff was routinely to tack the poet's name onto one more episode in the saga.

The Oblong Box opened in the US in June 1969, but due to the distribution backlog created by the developing crisis within the industry, as well as changes in the corporate structure of ABC-EMI (which had now absorbed Anglo Amalgamated), it did not go on general release in the UK until July 1970 – four months after Price's next for AIP, *Scream and Scream Again*. Six months later, its follow-up, *Cry of the Banshee*, hit theatres – which meant that after an absence from British screens of more than 18 months, Vincent Price starred in three films in the same year over a nine-month period.

Hammer, in the meantime, had released *Taste the Blood of Dracula* in July, followed by *The Vampire Lovers* in October and *Scars of Dracula* in December – two out of the three featuring Christopher Lee. Many more were lined up to follow. In the short space of a year, the market became saturated with horror product. It was not only AIP which was wilfully mishandling the careers of Price and others who had made their names in the genre; it was Hammer as well, and the whole crumbling edifice of the British film industry in its present form.

With the horror market in decline, it was time for the major players in the field to pool their resources. Price had already appeared in one AIP co-production

with rivals Tigon; next, it was to be Amicus' turn. (For no good reason, Hammer missed out on the opportunity to construct a vehicle for Price and their home-grown star turns of Cushing and Lee, despite the fact that the company was about to co-produce *The Vampire Lovers* with American International.) Had it not been for the internal squabbling infecting Hammer at the time and which consequently affected AIP's judgment about dealing with the company, Price's next British horror might have been a Hammer film, rather than an Amicus one.

> "What the devil is that?" asked the driver.
> The noise continued. It was an unusual sound, unfamiliar and yet at the same time oddly familiar.
> Suddenly Sergeant Peter Jenkins knew what it was. Horror filled him, like a knife piercing his vitals. Scarcely realising what he was doing he wrenched open the door of the police car and tumbled out into the road.
> "You bloody fools!" he screamed. "For Christ's sake, stop him! Don't you understand what he's doing to her?"
>
> PETER SAXON,
> *THE DISORIENTATED MAN* (1966)

Amicus Productions had been Hammer's main rival on the British horror scene since the release of *Dr Terror's House of Horrors* in 1965. Amicus – 'friend' in latin – was a set-up similar to that of AIP but owned and run by two New Yorkers, one of whom was based in the UK: Milton Subotsky was the creative side of the team, while Max J (Joseph) Rosenberg looked after the company's finances from an office on Madison Avenue. Subotsky was an avid reader of horror fiction, from which he derived most of his ideas for films, and Amicus had enjoyed a long-running association with American pulpmeister Robert Bloch, author of *Psycho*, who had supplied the company with numerous scripts in the way that Richard Matheson had for AIP.

The company had also dabbled in science fiction, though less successfully and in a more juvenile vein. In 1969, Subotsky read a sci-fi novel that he thought would afford a perfect opportunity for a first-time teaming of the three 'titans of terror' – Price, Cushing and Lee. The scale of it required a co-producer, however, and, armed with his own script, Subotsky turned to Deke Heyward.

Heyward promptly ditched Subotsky's draft and entrusted its replacement to Chris Wicking. "The book gave me goose-bumps," Wicking told Philip Nutman. "Then I read Milton's script, which was totally flat; it was like watching a soufflé dying, it just caved in after a while. Gordon [Hessler] and I discussed it at length ... The one radical thing we did ... was take out the blobs from space. Blobs from space are great, but we didn't want it to be that kind of picture. We wanted to do a Don Siegel-style horror film – *Coogan's Bluff* meets *Invasion of the Body Snatchers* – and we needed something stronger than lumps from another planet."

Vincent Price was cast on the strength of the new script, which Wicking entitled *Scream and Scream Again*, and the film which resulted went on to turn a healthy profit both for Amicus and AIP – though Subotsky was to maintain that he could never understand the reason for its eventual success: "I don't know why, it wasn't all that good."

> Keene scowled. *"You are seriously suggesting that our killer drinks human blood?"*
>
> David Pine shrugged his shoulders. *"It's one explanation of the facts – in fact, it seems the only explanation. Each victim has been drained of blood – and each has a wound on the wrist."*
>
> **PETER SAXON**,
> THE DISORIENTATED MAN (1966)

Scream and Scream Again was adapted from a 1966 pulp novel by Peter Saxon called *The Disorientated Man*. Originally a pseudonym of W Howard Baker, 'Peter Saxon' came to be used, individually or collectively, by a number of other authors working the same circuit, including Martin Thomas and Stephen Frances. The plot is one of alien invasion along the lines of Nigel Kneale's BBC television serial (and later Hammer film) of 1955, *Quatermass II*. Bastard it may have been, but as an example of pulp sci-fi *The Disorientated Man* is really rather good:

> An alien craft materialises in a suburb of London... A sinister apparatchik in East German security named Konratz begins an inexorable rise to power by disposing of his superiors... An Olympic athlete awakes in a hospital bed to find that his leg has been amputated without his knowledge... Southern England is swept by a wave

> of 'vampire' murders, committed by someone who appears to be possessed of superhuman strength...
>
> As each of these strands develop, their trails lead increasingly to the country retreat of a Dr Malcolm Sanders, surgeon. Under Inspector Keene, the police eventually capture the vampire killer by means of a 'honey trap', but he escapes from their clutches and throws himself into an acid vat in the grounds of Sanders' home. Sanders has now entrapped the investigative David Pine, to whom he reveals the truth: he is one of an advance party of aliens intent on conquering Earth by planting synthetic humans in positions of authority around the world; the bionic robots are built from prize specimens of humanity (like the athlete) and artificially enhanced.
>
> As Pine realises that he has himself been nominated as a donor, Konratz arrives. He is also one of the aliens and he demands that Sanders call a halt to his operations, which have aroused too much suspicion. The two engage in a titanic struggle for supremacy, during which both are killed. Pine resolves to join Keene in the ongoing hunt, while another alien vessel materialises in the suburbs...

Wicking's adaptation stuck unfailingly to its source. The hackneyed theme of invaders from space was ditched and the mysterious events laid at the door of a political conspiracy instead of an alien one; this apart, the film was as the book. As in *Quatermass II*, the aforementioned 'blobs' are metaphorical in any event, and their removal from the plot could be contrived with as clean an incision as 'Dr Sanders' was to make on the Olympic athlete – the 'disorientated man' of the title.

The tale is constructed of several interweaving strands: the machinations of Konratz, the hunt for the mysterious murderer, and the plight of the disorientated man. In novel form, the construct was perfect for a collaborative effort (if such was indeed the case), as each thread could be penned by a different writer and all of them combined after the fact. Its wholesale deployment in *Scream and Scream Again* was more confusing, however, but it nevertheless appeared vital and inventive at a time when the horror genre – as director Jacques Tourneur had predicted – was at last beginning its downward spiral towards endless revivals of Count Dracula and co.

In the film, Malcolm Sanders became Dr Browning (Price), David Pine was turned into David Sorel

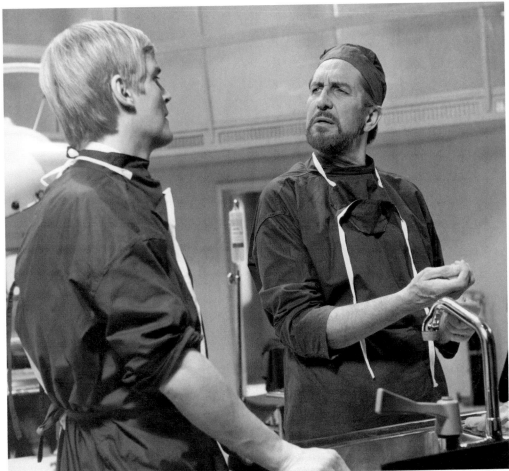

LEFT:
Christopher
Matthews and
Vincent Price in
SCREAM AND
SCREAM AGAIN

BELOW:
Vincent Price,
Alfred Marks
and Clifford Earl
in SCREAM AND
SCREAM AGAIN

(Christopher Matthews), the vampire killer was named Keith instead of Kenny, and Lee and Cushing took on minor roles as functionaries of state governments, British and Eastern European respectively. Wicking retained the idea of 'composites' – synthetic humanoids of superior strength and abilities who have been built to inherit the earth – but in removing the alien intelligence that had masterminded the scheme in the novel, he extended the concept to include the scientist himself. Thus Browning and Konratz (who is oddly addressed as Konrad in the film) are themselves composites, which begs the question of who created *them*? Wicking pastes over the anomaly by the convenient interventions of the inscrutable Fremont (Lee), a secret service bureaucrat who is merely a red herring in the novel. It is sleight-of-hand – in the final analysis, *Scream and Scream Again* makes no more sense than the riddle of the chicken and the egg.

The true horror of the novel and source of 'goose-bumps' for screenwriter Wicking lay in the plight of the titular 'disorientated man', Olympic athlete Ken Sparten, whose fate could not easily be captured by any adaptation. Deprived by stages of his limbs and then his senses, he ends up unable to see, hear, taste, feel or smell, his condition depicted in the wonderfully Lovecraftian phrase "His mind gibbered within his skull." No director could have done justice to such a concept in visual terms, and Hessler shunts the poor chap to the sidelines prior to a last-minute view of his disembodied head.

Unusually, *Scream and Scream Again* was shot almost entirely on location, what money there was available going on a star cast, cars full of constabulary, and a cut-price recreation of a Soviet bloc street scene. The influence of *Bullitt* (1968) can be felt in the frenzied pace of the high-speed car chase which brings about the capture of Keith, though both films suffered from the discontinuity of having their stars' cars pass the same vehicles in the background time and again. The film's makers fought shy of locating Konratz in East Germany and opted instead for the paraphernalia of a fictitious Soviet bloc state, which tended to point up the comic-book origins of the story and make parts of *Scream and Scream Again* look more like an episode of *Thunderbirds*.

Subotsky's former excursions into the pop-star world of musical featurettes like *It's Trad, Dad!* ensured a contribution from chart-toppers Andy Fairweather Low and his band, Amen Corner, who make the most of the film's frenetic title song during a couple of disco scenes – a slice of pop history whose soundtrack has since been wiped from video prints, along with David Whitaker's original score.

The low budget is evident in every frame, but it also produced the benefit of some eccentric casting. The part of the 'vampire' killer, for instance, was only the fourth big screen appearance for the psychotic-looking Michael Gothard, who would be best remembered for his role as fanatical exorcist Father Barré in Ken Russell's *The Devils* two years later; Gothard committed suicide in 1993, aged 54. A neat in-joke has Gothard reply "Not today, lady" to an undercover policewoman who has tried to guess his name and suggested "Michael".

Hessler expends much effort on the police investigation, with long takes emphasising the hustle-bustle of activity in an attempt to capture the pseudo-documentary approach of crime thrillers like Val Guest's *Hell is a City* (1960) or *Jigsaw* (1962). In consequence, the film is stolen from its three stars by one-time stand-up comic-turned-straight actor Alfred Marks as the brusque and world-weary superintendent, who turns in such a sympathetic performance as Bellaver (despite his character's preference for peppering his every sentence with expletives) that his *Psycho*-like demise towards the end is genuinely upsetting.

Strange as it might seem, *Scream and Scream Again* would have been a better and more frightening film had it not featured Price, Cushing and Lee but had instead been populated by a cast of relative unknowns. Without the 'titans of terror', on the other hand, it would not have been made at all.

As a doctor, I think you'll be fascinated with what I'm trying to do. I don't have much of a chance to show off... Well, I couldn't resist telling you anyway. But once you fully understand, your life will have to wind down a very different road.

DR BROWNING (VINCENT PRICE),
SCREAM AND SCREAM AGAIN (1969)

Price is all at sea in this paranoid fantasy of political machination, his implicitly soulless and superhuman scientist being altogether too benign and idealistic for the insidious plot of which he is an integral part. Lee's cold reserve suits the flavour of the piece far better, while Cushing – in the briefest of cameos – is icy efficiency itself. New scenes and extra dialogue were shoehorned into the script to mask the fact that the pair had been hired to complement Price and nothing more, a ploy which may have given Lee and Cushing something to do but helped none of them comprehend what they had got themselves into. "I don't think Vincent Price really liked the films I made," Hessler commented. "He didn't understand *Scream and Scream Again*. He didn't know what he was doing in the picture; he thought it was all weird and strange. Nobody understood it." It was a sentiment echoed by Lee. "We were all aliens, if I remember rightly," he mistakenly recalled, before adding pointedly: "I couldn't work it out at all."

Much had changed in horror films since 1968, during which year *Films and Filming* had devoted a whole issue to the ongoing debate about the perceived increase in screen violence generally. The full-frontal nudity which the director of *House of a Thousand Dolls* had thought to furnish clandestinely when his stars' backs were turned was now an integral feature of the films of the new generation of horror-meisters, of which Hessler was typical. In *Scream and Scream Again*, Price had been required to deliver his 'mad scientist' soliloquy over the inert form of a naked girl, while anatomical details like "vaginal contusions", which hitherto had been the preserve of forensic surgeons, had been allowed to filter into the screenplay of an otherwise conventional sci-fi thriller. The 'vampire' murders were both savage and sadistic, in keeping with a recent easing of censorship restrictions and the self-serving practices of exploitation filmmakers as a whole. And a single star name was no longer sufficient to draw the crowds; now it had to be two, three, even four or more to guarantee a realistic return.

Some of the blame for all this could be laid at the door of George Romero's *Night of the Living Dead*, a stark and explicit 1968 retread of Price's *The Last Man on Earth*, but more of it had to do with a world which had at last awakened from the euphoria of the pot-smoking 1960s into the cold light of the same old pre-existent reality.

It had not gone unnoticed by Vincent Price that he was now being used exclusively for name value and that his week's work on *Scream and Scream Again* had barely been worth the trip from Los Angeles to enact. Coupled with the fact that a similar scenario had begun to apply to his association with Sears, it seemed as though his career had taken a severe turn for the worse on two fronts at the same time.

> *Thy soul shall find itself alone*
> *'Mid dark thoughts of the grey tombstone –*
> *Not one of all the crowd, to pry*
> *Into thine hour of secrecy.*
>
> **OPENING NARRATION** (VINCENT PRICE),
> *SPIRITS OF THE DEAD* (1969)

After *Scream and Scream Again*, AIP had asked Price to recite some lines from another Poe poem – *Spirits of the Dead* – for use on the soundtrack of *Histoires extraordinaires*, a 1967 film to which it had now acquired US distribution rights and which it naturally retitled *Spirits of the Dead*. (It was released in the UK as *Tales of Mystery*.) Constructed like *Tales of Terror* but featuring adaptations of Poe's *Metzengerstein*, *William Wilson*, and *Never Bet the Devil Your Head* (under the less revealing title of *Toby Dammit*, the protagonist in the tale), the film was art-house in nature and boasted a stellar cast – Brigitte Bardot, Alain Delon, Jane Fonda and Terence Stamp – as well as a trio of luminaries behind the separate lenses: Roger Vadim, Louis Malle and Federico Fellini. Given the scale of the project and the less commercially disciplined approach to storytelling of its three *auteurs*, *Spirits of the Dead* played a fraction under two hours. Price's contribution, on the other hand, lasted a little under half-a-minute.

All that AIP could now find for Price to do was what he had always done: play the lead role in a period horror film – though this time round, it would be one which was put into production merely to keep him employed and to help finance bigger (though not better) things in which he was to have no part. Heyward had been sent a script entitled 'Cry of the Banshees' (subsequently reduced to one such) by Tim Kelly, a staff writer on TV Western series *The High Chaparral* who would go on to pen *Sugar Hill* (1974) for AIP. Heyward promptly called for the dynamic duo behind *Scream and Scream Again*; director Gordon Hessler and screenwriter Chris Wicking had both been in the right place at the right time, and their eagerness to work quickly and cheaply had pushed them to the

forefront of AIP's ailing British operation. "The script was awful and Gordon and Chris wanted to do a complete rewrite," Heyward recalled. Their enthusiasm could sometimes run away with them, however, and in the case of *Cry of the Banshee*, it took them all the way to Scotland to research witchcraft. When Sam Arkoff was made aware that AIP was funding a doctorate on Celtic mythology, he rang Heyward: "They've got ten days to finish the script and get on with it," he declared. Hessler and Wicking were duly informed and took the news on the chin: "I think he'd had some testy consultations with Arkoff," Hessler opined of the edict from Heyward, "who could be a difficult customer."

The single saving grace of *Cry of the Banshee* was that in no way did it originate in the writings of Edgar Allan Poe, although Arkoff and Heyward would tag the poet's name onto the finished item for promotional purposes regardless.

> *In the startled ear of night*
> *How they screamed out their affright!*
> *Too much horrified to speak,*
> *They can only shriek, shriek,*
> *(Out of tune)*
>
> EDGAR ALLAN POE, *THE BELLS* (1849)

Having failed to find a suitable quote for *The Oblong Box*, AIP opened the non-Poe *Cry of the Banshee* with some incongruous lines – nonsensical in context – from a poem entitled *The Bells*, which Poe had penned in a delirium in 1848. After some equally incongruous, *Jabberwocky*-style title-cards by Monty Python's Terry Gilliam (whose talents Heyward had wanted to utilise on *Scream and Scream Again* before being overruled by James Nicholson), a new screen caption outlines the premise of the film: "England in the Sixteenth Century – a dark and violent time. Witchcraft and the ghosts of the old religion still hold sway in the minds of the people, preoccupying both the Law and the Church, for who can be sure that this is just superstition and childish fear?"

In 1944, Columbia made a film called *Cry of the Werewolf*, starring Nina Foch. Had that not been the case, such might very well have served as the title of Kelly's screenplay. *Cry of the Banshee*, for all its allusions to Irish folk-myths and witchcraft, is a werewolf tale:

> *Village magistrate Edward Whitman (Price)*
> *decides to persecute a coven of witches led by Oona*
> *(Elisabeth Bergner). In revenge for the deaths of her*

Essy Persson and Vincent Price in CRY OF THE BANSHEE

followers, Oona summons a young stud-groom named Roderick (Patrick Mower) from the Whitman household; he is possessed by a demonic spirit and, one by one, he savagely murders the Whitman clan until Edward's daughter shoots him to save her father's life. But demons cannot die, and after killing Edward's remaining son and daughter, Roderick spirits the magistrate away in his own coach. "He has no soul; he doesn't exist; he's a sidhe," Oona had warned.

The 'old religion' as Wicking has it, or paganism, or Wicca, had nothing whatever to do with devil worship or Satanism (a Christian concept, in any event); it was an admixture of outlawed Druidical practices and nature-worship, and the conflation of the two was brought about by vested interest and the established Church. A pagan bacchanal in a wooded glade is one thing, but Oona's entreaties to "Lord Satan" are some-thing else, and all the research in the world goes for nought if it is perverted to the cause of sensational-ism. In this respect, *Cry of the Banshee* is tabloid anthropology and its air of historical realism a fake.

The 'sidhe' was a novel concept, if only to ring the changes on the more traditional beast. The name, however, refers to a race of faerie people in Celtic mythology (Wicking originally had wanted to locate the story in Scotland), and not a rampaging demon with claws and teeth. Whatever may have been intend-ed in the Kelly draft is not what ended up on screen: Roderick is a 'foundling', raised in the woods, and when he is placed under an enchantment spell, he changes into a hairy, hook-nosed monster – faerie by name, but furry fiend by nature. It could, of course, have been the case that no one told make-up artist Jimmy Evans, who, in consequence, went for the obvi-ous (botched job that it was). Then again, that tends to leave aside the ripping to shreds.

CRY OF THE BANSHEE

I conjure you, Lord Satan, send me an avenger!
OONA (ELISABETH BERGNER),
CRY OF THE BANSHEE (1969)

Cry of the Banshee was the first time in his film career that Price found it impossible to inject any semblance of humanity into a two-dimensional, contradictory and unsympathetic role. Lord Edward Whitman is a village magistrate who holds progressive views about the pagan practices of the peasants over whom he wields power, but utilises primitive methods to try to re-educate them. Price was never convincing when his characters were required to kill people for no reason or issue illogical commands – "To protect you, I must destroy her; to find her, I will kill as many of you as I need to" – and the scene in which he assassinates "the son and daughter of some sorceress" after making sport of them for the amusement of his invited guests is a case in point. The banquet of cruelty during which this incident takes place is a direct lift of the one in Hammer's *The Curse of the Werewolf* (1960), down to the drink-sodden assembly and darkly disapproving wife, and the similarity between the two is compounded by the off-camera howling of a supposed 'banshee' halfway through.

Nudity in these films was now commonplace, and Hessler's camera gloats over the rape of Whitman's wife by his venal son, as it did over Keith's murder of a girl in *Scream and Scream Again*. One tavern wench is stripped and humiliated while a second selling "heathen charms" is threatened with a nipple-slicing. All of it was indicative of how low things could go when desperation was driving them, and Price was dismayed at the result. *Witchfinder*'s cinematographer John Coquillon tries to inject some lyricism into the autumnal forests, but the effect was similar to that of hiring William Goldman to write *Debbie Does Dallas*.

The actual climax was rewritten the night before shooting when it was realised, as Price put it, that "we didn't have an ending." Wicking's script had closed on Whitman alone in the house, awaiting his appointment with death. Hessler thought this anti-climactic and an alternative was devised on the last morning of production. Thus the ending was literally contrived: Whitman is spirited away to his doom by the regenerated Roderick when he could as easily have been slain alongside his son and daughter.

Price at first refused to attend the costumed wrap party for *Cry of the Banshee*, erroneously promoted as his 100th feature by AIP, on the grounds that Sam Arkoff also planned to be present. "We had a special cake made and a nude girl was going to jump out," Gordon Hessler told Christopher Koetting in *Filmfax*. "We had music, dancing – the whole works ... That afternoon, Vincent called and said, 'Look, I'm not coming.' He was stone drunk and said, 'If Arkoff's there, I'm not coming.'"

Hessler dissuaded Price from absenting himself. "He finally did arrive that evening but he was sloshed and in a bad mood. I'd asked Arkoff to make a speech and then cut the cake but Vincent said, 'If Arkoff makes a speech, I'll disappear.' There was obviously serious animosity between them, so I told Arkoff not to make the speech and to just cut the cake instead." A knife was called for, but Price acidly informed Hessler that they could use the one which was to be found protruding from his back.

Heyward had also observed the deterioration in relations between Arkoff and Price: "There was some kind of bad blood between he and Sam. I think Vincent resented the fact that he was taking Sam's money for doing things he disliked. Sam tried to make believe that he was a friend of Vincent's, but Vincent didn't reciprocate. I think sending Vincent to England was probably the line of least resistance for Sam, plus the fact that Vincent enjoyed having a *per diem*, which he would use to buy works of art."

In March 1970, Price wrote to his agent bemoaning the declining quality of the AIP product and asking to be released from his contract: "I'm sure when you made the original contract you never thought of the very serious consequences that all-exclusivity clause could cause. I hope you can make Arkoff see how it keeps me from doing anything for the next three years in that line. It certainly can't hurt to be in a good film – it might even carry me over the next lousy one AIP might make me do." Milton Subotsky had offered Price a role in his upcoming *The House That Dripped Blood*; Price had liked the script and desired to do it, but there was no AIP involvement so his contract precluded his appearing in it.

> Mary Jane: *Now, what you have to do is find someone to give you an honest opinion. You should get in touch with an art expert... like Vincent Price.*
> Lucy: *Vincent Price! Good, I'll call him right now...*
> **MARY JANE CROFT AND LUCILLE BALL,**
> *HERE'S LUCY: LUCY CUTS VINCENT'S PRICE*
> (1970)

Without the likes of Michael Reeves to restrain him, Price was soon back to his old trick of camping up his image like crazy in an episode of the popular CBS sitcom *Here's Lucy*, despite the irrepressible Miss Ball introducing him as "one of our more erudite intellectuals."

With many more television than film appearances behind him, the one-time supporting actor at Universal was almost as famous as a caricature of himself as he was for any specific role he had played on screen. It was a part that Price professed himself happy with, though it inhibited him from being cast in anything that was not designed to take advantage of the fact. He was as well known as a cook and art expert as he was as an actor, thanks in large measure to the wide exposure that his expertise had received through the bottomless public relations purse of Sears, Roebuck & Company.

All good things must come to an end, however, and even Sears was no longer interested in Price the academician – only Price the *name*. Instead of fostering sales of art with the high-minded purpose of bringing culture to the masses, Price was now relegated to selling anything to which the weight of his fame might usefully be attached. His contract was revised and he was paraded around the group's retail outlets, pushing everything from perfume to washing machines.

The lure of lucre was still strong, and Price did all that was asked of him without demur. If movie stars are the closest thing to Royalty for the average American, then Vincent Price had certainly earned his ermine robes. But something had started to eat away at the hitherto placid and ever-affable personality of the King of Horror. Instead of presiding majestically over his court, Price had begun to realise that he was in danger of becoming jester to it.

A sensitive performer beneath his casual exterior, his low-key playing in *The Oblong Box* and inability to pluck any humanity from his character in *Cry of the Banshee* only served to emphasise the feeling that somehow he had lost his way. He looked drawn in both films, heavier and less comfortable with what should have been, for him, straightforward roles – especially as he had been teamed in both with Hilary Dwyer, with whom he had starred in *Witchfinder General*.

In the meantime, fate had conspired in other areas to confirm the presence of an ill wind: his 20-year marriage to Mary Grant was on the rocks and his hometown of Los Angeles was beginning to lose its lustre in the wake of increasing social disorder and industry in-fighting. On top of all this, the projects which might have made his association with AIP bearable – *When the Sleeper Wakes*, *The Gold Bug* – had now been shelved indefinitely in favour of titillating and hurriedly contrived exercises in exploitation like *The Oblong Box* and *Scream and Scream Again*. Even the esteemed *Witchfinder General*, already high on the gross-out scale in its depiction of scenes of violence, had been the recipient of nude shots inserted into it by Deke Heyward. The horror-star image had worked its magic too well for the good of his professional career. Vincent Price had become a commodity, to be used and abused by those whom he had trusted.

Perhaps significantly, in his next film for AIP Vincent Price would mask his famous features beneath mortician's wax for the first time in 18 years. Yet, by a quirk of fate, the end result was to give both Price and its production company some of the best reviews either of them had received since *House of Usher*.

ACT 6

ENTRANCES AND EXITS

Nine killed you, and nine shall die and be returned your loss. Nine times nine. Nine killed you, and nine shall die. Nine eternities in doom...

DR ANTON PHIBES (VINCENT PRICE),
THE ABOMINABLE DR PHIBES (1970)

A t the turn of 1970, Vincent Price had entered his fifth decade as a movie star and his third as a star of almost exclusively horror movies. Since his return to the genre in *Witchfinder General*, he increasingly had become an indigenous part of the British production scene, but it was a scene which was now in danger of dying on its feet. The industry was in trouble, audiences were in decline and fresh thinking was in short supply.

Even before *The Oblong Box*, AIP had once again come to rely on the double-billing of product from its own stable as a means of compensating for lower returns. *The Oblong Box* consequently had played in theatres with *The Dunwich Horror*, another Lovecraft adaptation and the better film of the two. *Cry of the Banshee* had been paired with a picture AIP had picked up for release called *Count Yorga, Vampire*, which was also superior to its A-feature running-mate. But slicker filmmaking and a timely twist on an old tale were not the only aspects of the Yorga film which were destined to disturb the equilibrium of Vincent Price.

Price's position as the king of screen terror – as well as AIP's biggest box-office draw – was now to come under threat from a relative unknown named Robert Quarry, the 47-year-old star of *Banshee*'s co-feature, which had started life as a home movie dreamed up round the pool by its director and originally intended for the porno circuit. That such was the source of the most serious competition Price had to face in his decade-long dominance of the horror film was indicative of the unpredictable state both of the business and of his own career in 1970.

Not only was American International in disarray. The company had disengaged itself from further co-productions with Hammer Films after the two had teamed up in January 1970 on *The Vampire Lovers*, with Deke Heyward citing indecision on Hammer's part as the key factor in his discontinuing their

short-lived partnership. Tigon and Amicus were also struggling – a lack of ideas in both cases leading to diversification into property acquisition for the former and an over-reliance on its staple diet of portmanteau movies for the latter. As AIP had moved into Britain, so American funds in general had started to move out; no longer were the money-men prepared to risk their ill-gotten gains on anything other other than sure-fire bets. In essence, that meant sex and horror. Heyward may have poured scorn on Hammer, but AIP was in danger of becoming just as out of touch with its core audience as everyone else.

Hearken! and observe how healthily – how calmly I can tell you the whole story.

NARRATOR (VINCENT PRICE),
AN EVENING OF EDGAR ALLAN POE:
THE TELL-TALE HEART (1970)

In the meanwhile, it had been assumed that Price would again join director Gordon Hessler and writer Christopher Wicking on another Poe – *Murders in the Rue Morgue* – which Hessler had been slated to direct early in 1970 at the Victorine Studios in Nice. That deal turned out to be unworkable, however, and while an alternative studio was sought, AIP arranged for Price to appear in a television special in which he could perform four tales from the pen of none other than Edgar Allan Poe – all in monologue. *The Pit and the Pendulum* was chosen to climax the quartet and Price, rather than *Tales of Terror*'s Peter Lorre, adopted the persona of Montresor for the third story, *The Cask of Amontillado*, but his repertoire was augmented by two tales which AIP had so far seen fit to exclude from its canon: *The Tell-Tale Heart* and *The Sphinx*.

The 53-minute videotaped production was titled *An Evening of Edgar Allan Poe*, and Price was outfitted in an interesting array of costumes by his designer wife, Mary Grant. Alone on a single set for all four tales,

AN EVENING OF EDGAR ALLAN POE ('The Pit and the Pendulum')

Price was required to recite virtually the whole of each in unbroken takes; to do so was an achievement in itself, but his readings suffer from a lack of variety and a too fast and often too pat delivery of the lines. It was a bravura performance, reminiscent of his 1968 appearance in ITV's adaptation of Henry James' *The Heiress*, but it lacked the subtle shadings he had brought to spoken verse only a few years before.

The Sphinx was a ludicrous tale to adapt in any event, and its visualisation merely showed up the literary conceit of a death's-head moth in close proximity to a narrator's eye being mistaken for a dragon on the distant horizon. *The Tell-Tale Heart* and *The Cask of Amontillado* are briskly conveyed, if unexceptional in impact, and the best of the four is *The Pit and the Pendulum*, with which Price clearly felt more affinity. Alone in his inquisitorial cell, he expertly conjures up the horror of a man confined in a world of his own thoughts and fears, and subject to the whims of invisible and omnipotent authority. It is also the one episode which is served by some ancillary camera-tricks – though none, alas, which try to intimate the presence of either pit or pendulum. Kenneth Johnson's direction is functional, but *An Evening of Edgar Allan Poe* required a more imaginative touch behind the lens to balance out what becomes, in the end, rather a repetitive rant on the part of Price himself.

As Hammer had begun to move downmarket, so AIP had thought to move up. A disastrous production of *De Sade* (1969) had not dissuaded it from venturing further into the classics, and while United Artists was preparing to parade Susannah York and George C Scott around Charlotte Brönte country for *Jane Eyre* (1970), an economical remake of sister

Emily's *Wuthering Heights*, inveigled out of Sam Arkoff under threat of resignation by Heyward, would avail itself of a royal premiere on completion. In the warm glow of monarchic approval, others of the same were announced to follow, including *Camille*, the obligatory *Return to Wuthering Heights*, *A Tale of Two Cities* and *The House of the Seven Gables*. In the more sober light of proletarian day, none of them were to make it.

The last was provisionally earmarked for the director who had brought *Wuthering Heights* to the screen, 43-year-old Robert Fuest. Fuest started out as a set designer, but he had come to the notice of AIP after directing episodes for the final season of popular television series *The Avengers*, as well as the ABC-EMI quickie *And Soon the Darkness* (1969). Working for AIP, however, meant that any new director would inevitably be handed the script of a film that was proposed for Vincent Price. Fuest was no exception, and no sooner had he finished editing *Wuthering Heights* than he was asked to read 'The Curses of Dr Phibes.'

The script had come to AIP courtesy of novice screenwriters James Whiton and William Goldstein; it told of a hideously disfigured madman who lived in a Gothic mansion and sought to enact an elaborate vendetta against the surgical team whom he held to be responsible for the death of his wife. This he does by contriving their deaths to accord with the 'curses' inflicted on Pharaoh by Moses in the Biblical book of Exodus. Whiton and Goldstein's script was twice the usual length for a screenplay, contained no stage direc-tions, was played straight, set in no specific time-period and climaxed at Wembley Stadium, where Phibes escaped the clutches of pursuing police by fleeing the scene of his murderous rampage in a hot-air balloon.

Fuest was unimpressed with the unsolicited story's ponderous flights into Hebrew mysticism and archaic vernacular, but he found himself enamoured of its central premise – that of Biblical 'curses' as a mechanism of murder. With Heyward's tacit agreement, he redrafted the original as a parody of the genre in the self-mocking style of *The Avengers*, setting it in the 1920s, turning Phibes into a mad musician – an Abominable Showman – and retitling it simply as 'Dr Phibes'. 'The Abominable' was prefixed during the shoot to ram the satirical message home, like the horn of the brass unicorn which pins Dr Whitcombe (Maurice Kaufmann) to the wall of his club in the film itself.

With *Murders in the Rue Morgue* still in pre-production due to problems over its proposed

European locations, Price was forced to skip ahead to the next in line. By the time the last Poe was finally in a position to go before the cameras in October, and in Madrid instead of Nice, he had been scheduled to present himself at Elstree instead, for *The Abominable Dr Phibes*.

My love – sweet queen and noble wife... I, alone, remain to bring delivery of your pain. Severed, my darling, too quickly from this life of fires drawn and of memories met. I shall hold our two hearts again, in single time...
DR ANTON PHIBES (VINCENT PRICE),
THE ABOMINABLE DR PHIBES (1970)

Music had replaced the movies as the number one entertainment medium of the young (who comprised the majority of the audience for films), and while Rank and EMI dithered fatally over when – or even whether – to 'twin' or 'triple' existing theatres in order to increase the number of screens currently available, the average 2,000-seat Odeon or ABC had now found

itself plying its wares to mere handfuls of uninterested patrons. Desperate times required desperate measures, and the industry as a whole had fallen back on its old staples of sex and horror. The specialists in the latter – Hammer, Tigon, Amicus – had already upped the ante by turning out an increasing number of films on almost a conveyor-belt basis, adding nudity and graphic gore to the mix. But other companies had since joined the fray to eat into an already-saturated market, where the only rule which now applied with any certainty was that rules no longer applied.

In July 1970, a new system of film classification had come into force in the UK, which had raised the age-limit of the existing 'X' certificate from 16 to 18 years, and thus enabled filmmakers to go much further than before in their depiction of sex and violence. Films like *The Abominable Dr Phibes* were free to exploit the more liberal censorship regime, and its scenes of violent death were more explicit as a result. But the driving force behind what was again to be promoted in the press as Vincent Price's 100th film was not a new-found ability to indulge in horror

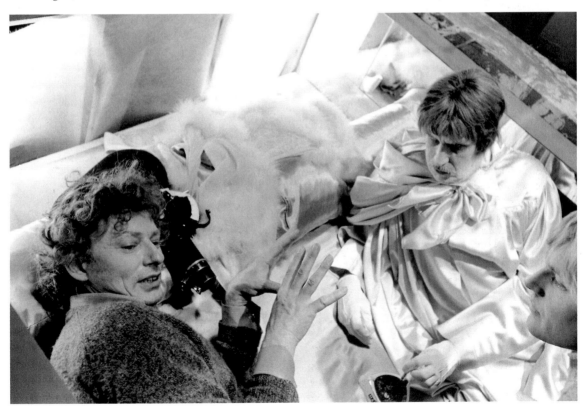

Director Robert Fuest and Vincent Price on the Elstree Studios set of THE ABOMINABLE DR PHIBES

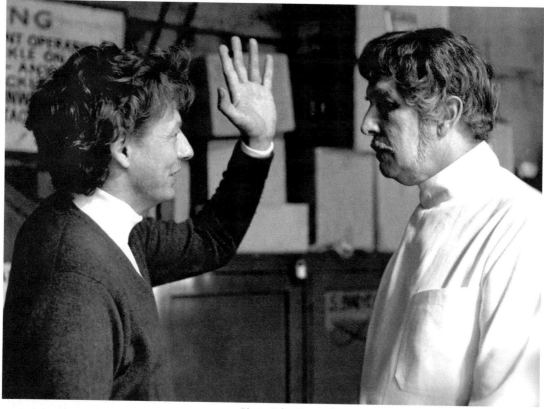

Director Robert Fuest and Vincent Price at work on THE ABOMINABLE DR PHIBES

for horror's sake but Robert Fuest's irreverent approach to his material.

The Abominable Dr Phibes was a return to the kind of horror film epitomised by *House of Wax* – an unpretentious exercise in Grand Guignol revolving around the murderous activities of a mutilated Monster. The tale reunited Price with Joseph Cotten, fresh from *Tora! Tora! Tora!* (1969) and another veteran of Orson Welles' Mercury Theatre, whom he had partnered in *The Shoemaker's Holiday* back in 1938. It also deployed the comedic talents of Terry-Thomas and John Cater (as victim and investigating officer respectively), as well as a number of other actors whose quirky readings of their roles gave the piece a decidedly surrealist edge.

Phibes was not a Poe – or even Byronic – hero, haunted and doomed by some vague sense of past injustice; he was a man of his time, wily, witty and deliciously wicked, bent on a moral crusade where right is might, and which ultimately had its audiences cheering in the aisles each time another of his

metaphorical thunderbolts was unleashed. In its bravura treatment of the elaborately contrived murders of an authoritarian collective of supercilious surgeons, the film chimed with a prevailing mood among the disenchanted youth of the day, who had waved farewell to the hippie dream at Woodstock only 12 months before and to whom Dr Phibes was seen as a champion of a lost ideal, making a last stand against the impersonal cruelties of capitalism in general practice.

The story takes place in 1929. Dr Anton Phibes (Price) is a millionaire eccentric and former music-hall organist who once had an act called 'Dr Phibes' Clockwork Wizards.' He resides in a Georgian mansion filled with art deco furnishings and is accompanied at work and play by an aide-de-camp named Vulnavia (Virginia North), with whom he dances the occasional slow fox-trot before pouring champagne down the back of his neck – his features and vocal chords having been destroyed in a car-accident. He keeps his dear departed wife embalmed in the cellar and plots vengeance against the surgical team whom he holds to be responsible for her demise, exacting his revenge by means of the Biblical 'curses' that were sent against the Egyptians at the time of Exodus: boils, bats, frogs, blood, locusts and so on.

The police pay a visit to a rabbi (Hugh Griffith) and establish a connection between the murders which leads them to Dr Vesalius (Cotten), who headed the team that operated on Victoria Phibes (Caroline Munro). In the meantime, Phibes has kidnapped Vesalius' son and chained him to an operating table over which is positioned a vat of acid. The key to unlock the table has been surgically implanted near the boy's heart, and Vesalius has six minutes to extract it before the acid is released. He makes it in time, and Vulnavia is killed by the acid instead. Phibes retreats to his underground lair, embalms himself, and rests in peace beside his wife.

Nominal producer Ronald S Dunas was part of the baggage that had come with the Whiton and Goldstein screenplay, and he was removed from the film in short order. "Dunas gave us so many problems that I requested he leave the set and he went back home," Heyward said of the screenwriting duo's tennis-playing camp-follower. As a result, *The Abominable Dr Phibes* (and its sequel) were actually produced by an uncredited Albert Fennell, who had made *Night of the Eagle* for AIP release ten years before.

In Robert Fuest's hands, Dr Phibes became the ultimate *Avengers* villain. Later episodes of the series were often set in train with elaborate 'puzzle' sequences which led to bizarre murders contrived by eccentric villains. Fuest utilised the same principle in *The Abominable Dr Phibes*, and having established its organ-playing protagonist in his opulent art deco lair, the film begins with Dr Dunwoody (Edward Burnham) retiring for the night in another part of London. As the doctor tries to sleep, a bat lands on his pillow and another crawls up the coverlet towards his face. In an instant, a whole swarm of the creatures cuts off his screams. "Don't take him out like that; at least cover his face up – what's left of it," Inspector Trout (Peter Jeffrey) instructs his officers as they remove the body, and Phibes puts a blowtorch to a wax bust of Dunwoody that sits alongside eight others in the ballroom of his mansion.

The remaining murders follow a similar pattern, but to ever more contrived effect: the first, that of

bees and boils, has taken place before the film begins, but the next finds psychiatrist Dr Hargreaves (Alex Scott), a self-confessed "head-shrinker", at a costume-ball in Phibes' palatial residence where his head is crushed inside a mechanised frog-mask to the syncopating rhythms of 'The Dark Town Strutter's Ball.' Dr Longstreet (Terry-Thomas) has his blood drained out of him into eight pint bottles while Vulnavia performs a violin solo of 'Close Your Eyes', and Dr Hedgepath (David Hutcheson) is blasted to death by a snow-machine in the back seat of his own chauffeur-driven car, as the Clockwork Wizards play him out to the melancholy refrain of 'One For My Baby (and One More *For the Road*).' "Medical men die every day," Trout is advised by the commissioner. "They're composed of the same flesh and blood as you and I." "I'm aware of that," Trout replies. "I happen to have seen rather a lot of their flesh and blood in the past few days."

Exactly why Dr Phibes, who is portrayed as a Gentile, should choose to inflict Hebrew curses is a question that can be answered only by the original writing team of Whiton and Goldstein. "It never occurred to me," said director Fuest. "Then, or since."

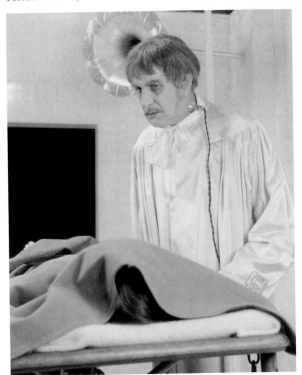

THE ABOMINABLE DR PHIBES

THE ABOMINABLE DR PHIBES

The rigidity of the scriptured formula leaves little room for interpretation, so the mechanics of mayhem become increasingly intricate as the film progresses. By the time it comes to Nurse Allen (Susan Travers), Phibes has gone to the ludicrous extreme of boiling the chlorophyl from a basin-full of sprouts in order to pour the extract over her sleeping form through a hole drilled in the ceiling above her head, so that the requisite plague of locusts can feast on her flesh along with the juice. One is moved to wonder at this juncture why he could not simply have shot her. Elaborate murder is Phibes' raison d'être, however, and Price makes the do-it-yourself deaths a wonder to behold, despite the fact that he is required to perform his routines in uncharacteristic silence. "The great thing Vincent had was his voice," said Fuest, "so what did we do? – make a film where he doesn't use it!"

Price was denied not only the use of his voice (except for a few lines imparted by means of a Victrola) but his range of expression as well: Dr Phibes is a 'self-made man', as the ads wryly described him, which in plot terms means that he hides his hideous visage behind a composite mask of ears, nose and other bits of synthetic flesh, which recreate his pre-crash self but render his features immobile in the process (unlike the supposed 'wax' face of Professor Jarrod). Price had therefore to rely on flamboyant gesture and balletic mime, though he makes the most of his climactic confrontation with Vesalius, using a portable Victrola as a weapon of containment to ward off the latter's menacing advances. "You, I will kill," Vesalius threatens. "But you can't, doctor. I'm already dead," Phibes rejoins.

"That still leaves the final curse," a bemused Superintendent Waverley (John Cater) says at the close of the film in relation to the 'darkness' which seems to have been omitted from the list but which Phibes has reserved for himself. "He'll be working on it, wherever he is," Trout notes portentously, as Phibes goes to his self-preserved rest accompanied by the anachronistic strains of 'Somewhere Over the Rainbow.' By the time *The Abominable Dr Phibes* opened, many more people than he were working on his next 'curse.'

Now it seems to me that, with immaculate precision, you've been arriving on the scene just after the victim's death and this time – due, no doubt, to some organisational oversight – you arrived there before the crime. But, as I've come to expect from you two, that made little difference: it was still committed! A brass unicorn has been catapulted across a London street and impaled an eminent surgeon... Words fail me, gentlemen.

SUPERINTENDENT WAVERLEY (JOHN CATER),
THE ABOMINABLE DR PHIBES (1970)

"Robert Fuest is the best young director I've ever worked with," Price said pointedly, and the film bears witness to the fact that he had found himself on a happy set in the company of old friends and new. "The only problem we had on *Phibes* was that we couldn't stop laughing," Fuest concurred. The air of levity shows in Price's performance: camp and melodramatic it may be, recalling the days of *House of Wax*, but it was what he knew and what he did best, as Fuest conceded: "Vincent loved all that preening around, playing the organ, conducting the clockwork band."

Set designer Brian Eatwell gave Price his most opulently dressed film since the Poe-scapes of Daniel Haller, and one which perfectly encapsulated the twenties' look of coldly impersonal mirrored walls, tubular-steel furniture and frosted lighting. The pastel tones enhance the poetic quality of Fuest's visual feast, as well as affording it an appearance of expense which was far in excess of its modest budget of some £300,000. (The box-office take was more than $3 million.) The canvas-and-paint nature of the illusion is

Vincent Price and Virginia North in a publicity shot from **THE ABOMINABLE DR PHIBES**

only exposed when Vulnavia rather feebly wields an axe against the ballroom at the climax. Production values at Elstree were becoming cheaper by the day; it is to Fuest's credit that he manages to reveal so little of the lowering standards in the film as a whole.

The direction bristles with originality and deep-focus set-ups derived from television: Price swinging a telescope into camera after the commission of yet another diabolical murder; Joseph Cotten expounding a case history by the visual means of a series of diminishing stacks of files, all of them simultaneously in shot. Many of the compositions are even strikingly beautiful, like Vulnavia's entrance through a door which opens of its own volition, as though she were Venus emerging from a sea of light.

Only in its last reel does *The Abominable Dr Phibes* make concessions to convention when Phibes has Vesalius' son strapped to an operating table which is locked into the path of an acid 'sprinkler' – the key to which has been surgically implanted next to the boy's heart. The climax then becomes a race against time as Vesalius is forced to operate on his own son while Phibes makes good his escape. Clever as this ending might appear, it is discordant with what has gone before in that untypical cruelty replaces unnatural justice in Phibes' demented scheme of things. Fuest had himself failed to come up with an appropriate finale for the film and Albert Fennell's writing partner Brian Clemens obliged. Clemens had scripted Fuest's *And Soon the Darkness* and he was a known whizz with formula-thriller plots, most of which found their way onto the small screen in a number of indifferent series. Cotten's sympathetic playing of Vesalius removes the centre of empathy from Phibes in the contradiction of these closing moments, and a similar misjudgment about the doctor's ultimate motivation was to afflict the sequel, as well.

Despite that, *The Abominable Dr Phibes* remained splendidly baroque and suitably radical. It tapped into a vein of cynicism which had descended with the end of the 'swinging' sixties, but in a soft-focus way that was respectful of the iconography which it utilised. While Hammer persisted in trying to convince its dwindling audience that vampires were 'real', or at least dramatically viable, the more politicised Dr Phibes of American International railed against the reinvigoration of clinical materialism and revenged himself on a society which had deprived him of his dreams. Love still supplied the motivational force, but guerilla warfare and urban terrorism were now the methods.

The appeal to a jaded youth was self-evident: betrayal was the theme, but it had been dressed in the florid robes of fantasy, the favoured genre of the 18-30s. Fuest's film struck a frayed nerve in its target audience; how much was intentional can only be surmised, but it was a tale for its times and it endeared Vincent Price even more to the hearts of the faithful, whether he realised it or not.

The Abominable Dr Phibes was accorded a gala premiere at the Pacific Pantages theatre on Hollywood Boulevard when it opened in May 1971, followed by a midnight press screening at the Rialto, Lower Regent Street, prior to its London opening. The former was attended by stars and cars, while the latter played to publicity by having guests turn up in monster costume. The initial ad campaign for the film even sent up the saccharine (and inexplicable) sentiment in the tag-line to the Oscar-winning hit *Love Story* – Middle America's clarion-call for a return to the values of the Eisenhower era – 'Love means never having to say you're sorry.' That for *Dr Phibes* altered the last word to 'ugly', but it gave way to more traditional copy when the show went on the road.

The novel concept of eight or nine murders in a single storyline – one per reel – was later to become integral to the formula of the 'slasher' movie, but within 18 months the structure of *The Abominable Dr Phibes* was to be lifted into another film designed with Price in mind, in addition to the now-inevitable sequel. *Theatre of Blood* would make an actor out of an organist and unashamedly turn nine surgeons into nine critics, but far from stealing the nouveau clothes of its illustrious forerunner, it would rework the template with such verve as to become one of the high watermarks of Vincent Price's entire career in horror.

> *When the acid reaches him, he will have a face like mine!*
>
> Dr ANTON PHIBES (VINCENT PRICE),
> *THE ABOMINABLE DR PHIBES* (1970)

As filming on *The Abominable Dr Phibes* drew to a close at Christmas, the undercurrents in Price's personal life came to the surface. Fuest had arranged for the crew to work an extra hour on the last day before the break to shoot the unmasking scene, in order to save the actor having to return for pick-ups the following week. Price did the scene in a single take and walked off the set without waving his usual

The Abominable Dr Phibes

goodbyes. "He left without saying anything," Fuest recalled. "I was quite hurt, because I'd done it for his sake. Then somebody said: 'He's not looking forward to Christmas'." Price was a Christmas buff (his father had been a candy manufacturer!), but almost for the first time since his divorce from his first wife and consequent 'loss' of son Barrett, he could find no solace in the season of goodwill.

A few months before, his $90,000-a-year contract with Sears, Roebuck had come to an end. "I'll never forget them saying, 'We really don't need you any more, because we can make just as much money selling schlock,' as they call it. Or shit, as I call it," Price confided to his daughter. "So, it ended up very unhappily." Another horror film had come and gone, with the next one in line still subject to the whims of Sam Arkoff. To top it all, the Prices were about to move out of their 9,000-square-foot house in North Beverly Glen into a much smaller Spanish-style property above Goldwater Canyon, with the consequent loss of many long-term staff. The Beverly Glen house was eventually sold in 1974 for $1/4 million; ten years later, it went onto the market again for $6 million.

For Vincent Price, Christmas 1970 held out a very gloomy prospect indeed.

I had been out of work for several months, and my savings were perilously near the vanishing point. Therefore I was naturally elated when I received from John Carnby a favourable answer inviting me to present my qualifications in person.
CLARK ASHTON SMITH,
THE RETURN OF THE SORCERER (1931)

While AIP waited on the results from the openings of both *Wuthering Heights* and *The Abominable Dr Phibes*, Vincent Price guested in the first of two 1971 segments of Rod Serling's *Night Gallery* (a follow-up to the Emmy-award winning writer's long-running *Twilight Zone*), which had gone on air the previous year.

The format of *Night Gallery* was short films in a macabre vein, which Serling introduced by means of the paintings hung in the titular gallery. In a second-season episode entitled *The Class of '99* and written by Serling himself, Price was cast as a university tutor whose brief is to instil prejudice and bigotry into a 'class' of androids created to help repopulate the planet, in order that they will blend seamlessly with the rest of humanity. Price shared billing with a robotic Brandon De Wilde, who as a child star had been seen cooing over Alan Ladd's heroic gunfighter in *Shane* (1953) but who, on this showing, appeared to have preferred Jack Palance's cold-blooded killer, after all.

Price's return performance in the show was a typically comedic and less satisfactory take on a grossly overwritten Clark Ashton Smith story penned in Lovecraft mode called *The Return of the Sorcerer*, in which *The Incredible Hulk*'s Bill Bixby is called in by Price to decipher a passage in the Necronomicon which will confirm to him that his murdered twin has mastered the ability to return from the grave and wreak an unwanted revenge. Neither film was stand-out, but Serling's diatribes against the ethical failings of the society in which he operated were always worthy of note, and *The Class of '99* was no exception.

'Down-sizing', to use American vernacular, was the order of the day in 1971. AIP followed the example which had been set by Price and vacated its elegant office-suite in Upper Grosvenor Street for a smaller and more economical outpost in Berkeley Square. Its European production budget was subjected to similar strictures, and the days of quick-and-easy exploitation returned with a vengeance with the acquisition of Euro-trash like *Helga and Michael* and *Dagmar's Hot Pants*. The trumpeted follow-ups to *Wuthering Heights* (which included *Camille*, *The Gingerbread House* and Hawthorne's *The House of the Seven Gables*) were drastically revised or given the thumbs-down in the process, and Deke Heyward had started to get restless. But all was not well between Arkoff and Nicholson either.

"It was not a happy marriage," Robert Fuest observed of the pair, after seeing them at close quarters during the making of *Phibes* and having subsequently been approached by Nicholson, independently of Arkoff, to direct *The Legend of Hell House* (which he declined): "AIP was a very fragile empire." Nevertheless, Arkoff busied himself in organising an immediate sequel to the company's biggest hit for years and commissioned Whiton and Goldstein to come up with a treatment for the return of Dr Phibes.

This time out, though, the doctor was not to have things all his own way. The novelty value of the original could not be repeated, so formula required that he be pitted against an adversary of similar cunning and equally sinister intent. Ever ready to hedge his bets, Arkoff had the very man to play the role lined up and ready to go.

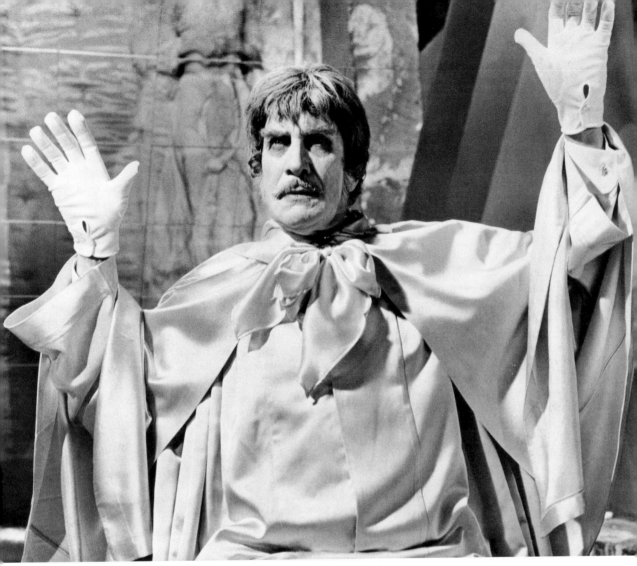

DR PHIBES RISES AGAIN

Robert Quarry was a low-level figure on the Hollywood circuit. His first claim to fame was as a child actor in Alfred Hitchcock's *Shadow of a Doubt* (1943), though his fondest memory was playing opposite the *derrière* of Jeanette MacDonald when the popular 1940s songstress had been required to sit alongside him while he lay in a hospital bed. But Quarry's later career had never really caught fire. In 1970, director Bob Kelljan suggested that the token role of a vampire in a skin-flick he proposed to make might suit the actor's fey style and faintly camp manner. Quarry consented and began to turn in such a show-stopping performance as 'Count Yorga' that the film was rewritten to accommodate more vampire and less skin.

It was eventually sold to AIP with the remnants of its salacious scenes intact, and traces of its original intent can be seen in the version which was cut for theatrical release, notably when Yorga presides over a lesbian interlude between two of the conspicuously female vampire tribe in his dungeon habitat. Nevertheless, the film went on to 'sleeper' success in the US as *Count Yorga, Vampire* and prompted AIP to request a sequel – *The Return of Count Yorga* – but not before it saw fit to install Quarry into its other sequel already set for production.

When it came to the much-anticipated return of Dr Phibes, Vincent Price found that he was no longer alone, and that his opponent in the new film was also to become his main competitor for pole position within American International Pictures.

Robert Fuest, in the meantime, had already asked Deke Heyward if *he* could write the script for the sequel to Phibes; as he had done as much on the first film (though without taking screen credit), Heyward agreed. Aware that the British Museum were planning a large-scale exhibition of artefacts from the tomb of Tutankhamun the following summer, Fuest thought it might be a timely idea to incorporate an Egyptian theme into the new storyline, and he set out to craft a tale in which Phibes awakens from his less-than-eternal sleep to seek out the 'River of Life,' whose waters will restore to him his beloved Victoria. When word trickled through to AIP that an 'untested' writer was plotting the sequel to its latest horror hit, it was decided that the situation required some security.

Arkoff sent Robert Blees to London, to ride shotgun for AIP over the fact that Heyward appeared to be losing his grip. Blees was a script doctor and industry veteran from the days of *Magnificent Obsession*, a classic tear-jerker he had written for Jane Wyman in 1954. As per his brief, he pulled *Camille* out of the fire and salvaged *The Gingerbread House* as *Whoever Slew Auntie Roo?*. Now, it was the turn of Dr Phibes.

"The boys who'd written the first one [Whiton and Goldstein] turned in something that just didn't work," Blees explained. "AIP had a commitment with Vincent for $75,000 to do the sequel and, to Sam,

that was an awful lot of money ... The instruction was basically 'Give us eight reels, and every reel has a guest star and a horror/comedic payoff'." Blees did as he was told, but he found that his ideas were at odds with those of director Fuest.

Blees wrote his pages in the Hilton hotel, while Fuest wrote his at home; Blees turned in a formula horror in which competing archaeologists race against time to reach the 'River of Life' before it is once more swallowed up in the sands of the desert, while Fuest built on the ingredients which he felt had worked best in the original, namely oddball humour, eccentric characters and a mission for Phibes in which he will not be thwarted. The two writers rarely met, and when Blees returned to America, Fuest assembled their separate efforts as *Dr Phibes Rises Again*. The result was "schizophrenic," the director admitted in hindsight.

> *The incredible legends of the Abominable Dr Phibes began a few short years ago. All of them are unfortunately true. It was here in London's fashionable Maldene Square whence Phibes ventured out to work his diabolical revenge against those responsible for the death of his beloved wife, Victoria, making it necessary to talk through an ingenious mechanism in his neck...*
>
> **OPENING NARRATION** (GARY OWENS),
> *DR PHIBES RISES AGAIN* (1971)

The trailer said it all: "He Lives! From the depths of his unholy tomb, the Avenger rises... The Abominable Dr Phibes – the most deadly mastermind of all crime. Specialist in the fine art of bizarre murder – each more different; each more devilish than the last..." That was the theory, at any rate.

"Three years later..." states a screen caption, and after a montage of scenes from the original, like the serials of old, Phibes is back in business by the rudimentary means of a literal reversal of the embalming process. He immediately rides his organ aloft to find that his house has been demolished. Phibes is supposed to reside in "one of London's most fashionable squares," yet his house has been reduced to a rubble which is left untouched to devalue neighbouring properties; Blees might have been thinking of a Los Angeles ghetto when he penned the scene, rather than the 'listed' buildings which predominate in Central London. But more than an unsightly attack of urban redevelopment has occurred in the interim.

Valli Kemp and Vincent Price in DR PHIBES RISES AGAIN

Valli Kemp and Vincent Price in **Dr Phibes Rises Again**

The changes in the character of Dr Phibes are multifarious: his features are more mobile; he pronounces 'Vulnavia' differently ('Voolnāvia' in the original); he can now talk on the move; his white gloves have been embellished with black lines on the back of them, like those of Mickey Mouse – though the real 'Mickey Mouse' aspect of the film is a goofy script which turns its most important asset from a millionaire organist with a knowledge of acoustics into a mystic philosopher who engages in a battle of wits with an archaeologist who has discovered an elixir of youth. No longer is Phibes outlandishly engaging; here, he is simply preposterous.

Phibes ships out to Egypt, saintly sarcophagus in tow, to seek out the River of Life. But the papyrus which maps its location has been stolen from him by Darius Biederbeck (Quarry), an archaeologist with his own reason for beating Phibes to their mutual goal – the elixir of youth which maintains his mortality has run dry and must be replenished in its waters. The body-count mounts as Phibes decorously depletes Biederbeck's expedition, until the two of them are face-to-skull on the banks of the elusive River. Phibes pulls his trick of entrapping Biederbeck's fiancée (Fiona Lewis) in a race-against-time contraption and Biederbeck must choose between his life or hers; he rescues the girl, and reverts to his real age as he watches Phibes sail into the Stygian sunset. "It's not the end of the world," his fiancée assures him as the credits roll.

The whole thrust of the piece was to make a series character out of Dr Phibes. The story contrives to

Keith Buckley and Vincent Price in **DR PHIBES RISES AGAIN**

engineer his 'return' but not that of his hand-maiden Vulnavia, who is now represented as some kind of ethereal spirit to be invoked at will (in an early draft, she was a different woman as well as a different actress), while the requisite murders have become so bizarre as to stretch credulity to breaking point. During the voyage to Egypt, Hugh Griffith is thrown overboard inside a seven-foot gin bottle with a label attached which states "not wanted on voyage". *The Abominable Dr Phibes* might have come up with a device for achieving this end, but *Dr Phibes Rises Again* merely pastes over the implausibility with some extraneous footage and a shot of Phibes, arms upraised, tossing an (unseen) object into the sea. The other murders are equally trite but more laboriously delineated, and one which involves a sandblasting machine in the Almerian desert must have seemed funnier at the script conference than it does on the screen.

Dr Phibes Rises Again had sought to capitalise on what were perceived to be the successful elements of its forerunner – Phibes' cartoonish cavortings, Terry-

Thomas, John Cater's pompous Superintendent, exotic murder machines – without sufficient thought having been given to the plot. And while more money was clearly expended, most of it went to poorer effect. The delicate sensibility and elegant art deco interiors of the original are replaced by corny pastiche, such as a coffin for Victoria which is constructed from the radiator-grilles of Rolls-Royce motor cars. In-jokes still proliferate, although they are writ somewhat larger: the Clockwork Wizards are renamed The Alexandrian Quartet (after the Lawrence Durrell novels) and a member of Biederbeck's team who ends up concertina'd inside a bed goes to sleep having read Henry James' *The Turn of the Screw*.

The sequel has some better jokes than its parent – "I don't think, I know," Waverley says; "I don't think you know either, sir," Trout concurs, adding at another juncture, "Every time we've built a better mousetrap, Phibes has built a better mouse" – but much of the subtle by-play that made *The Abominable Dr Phibes* such a character-driven delight (Trout being referred to by a variety of fish-names throughout) is sacrificed on the altar of a silly story and a confused sense of purpose.

Price brings little continuity to the role of Phibes – which was hardly surprising, given what was going on around him: no sooner had filming wrapped on *Dr Phibes Rises Again* than open warfare broke out between Arkoff and Nicholson. Both demanded to see the negative, and both cut the film according to their ailing dispositions. The result was predictable: "They dumbed it down," Fuest said. Additional scenes which Fuest had shot with Terry-Thomas and Beryl Reid were edited out as being too whimsical, while Price himself was recalled to re-record lines and patch up the glaring holes left in the plot.

As a result, the potential attractions of the piece were swamped by the crass dynamic which was re-imposed upon it: obsessing over a sacred relic (or River of Life) was the derivative stuff of Universal Mummy movies, not of the sophisticated Dr Phibes, and the Biederbeck character is never fully developed. "[Fuest] made changes to my script and took out a lot of the subtleties of the Noël Coward-Gertie Lawrence repartee between Quarry and Fiona Lewis," Robert Blees complained. "While Fuest was a competent director, he wasn't a very good writer."

Quarry was on something of a high due to his new-found star status after almost 30 years in the business, with nothing but a handful of minor roles to show for them until his sleeper success with the Count Yorga franchise. He and Price could sense that AIP was grooming him to be a younger replacement for its ageing horror star and Quarry was no shrinking violet when it came to capitalising on the situation. According to Fuest, he would wander around drawing attention to himself by trilling Gershwin tunes until one day he was observed by Price. "Didn't know I could sing, did you, Vincent?" he enquired of his co-star. "Well, I knew you weren't a fucking actor," Price retorted.

The film was an apprenticeship scheme for Quarry, who plays his unrewarding role with commendable seriousness but who is consequently at odds with the overall tone of the sequel: Biederbeck becomes more sympathetic as the tale progresses, as though someone realised that Phibes was meant to be the villain of the piece only halfway through. The climax is a repeat of that in *The Abominable Dr Phibes* and involves a key, a tethered victim and a potentially lethal contraption – except that the time-limit is halved, though it takes twice as long to play out on screen.

Phibes punts his wife's ornate coffin down the River of Life, like Charon crossing the Styx; the scene is reminiscent of the closing moments of *Confessions of an Opium Eater* and the film as a whole reflects the same high-concept, low-execution mentality. ("If they could have made money making hubcaps, they would have made hubcaps," director Robert Fuest observed of the Philistinism which clouded the judgment of AIP's executives.) "Maybe he won't come back," Waverley suggests, after the River has swallowed up Phibes' golden gondola. "It's Phibes, all right," Trout reminds him. "And he always comes back."

Not after *Dr Phibes Rises Again*. AIP had robbed the theme of its charm; neither Blees nor Arkoff had been able to comprehend what the original film had been about and what had made it such a success. Blees, in particular, had turned a highly operatic and surreal concept into the formulaic B-movie dross in which he had earned his Hollywood living.

Dr Phibes Rises Again was not as commercially successful as its predecessor, but it was successful enough to warrant another bite of Phibes' cherry. No sooner had its director been approached, however, than he heard the sound of distant thunder.

Why? I don't understand... Whose mind could conceive of such a bizarre way to kill... ?
DARIUS BEIDERBECK (ROBERT QUARRY),
DR PHIBES RISES AGAIN (1971)

After years of increasing dissatisfaction with the way things were going at AIP, James H Nicholson

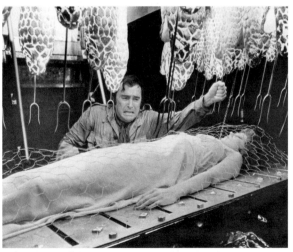

Robert Quarry and Fiona Lewis in DR PHIBES RISES AGAIN

finally left the company in January 1972 to become an independent producer. His first (and last) production was *The Legend of Hell House*, based on the novel *Hell House* by Richard Matheson; by the summer of 1973, Nicholson was dead of a brain haemorrhage. Eight months after Nicholson resigned from the board, Louis 'Deke' Heyward was to depart in the same direction, having by that time had one disagreement too many with Sam Arkoff. "Things fell apart after Jim left," he said. "I told [Sam], I don't want to do any more horror films; I don't want to do any more sex movies." That appeared to restrict Heyward's options somewhat, and with Arkoff content to let him go, the second *Phibes* sequel – often referred to but never confirmed as 'The Bride of Phibes' – left AIP with him.

With the departure of Heyward, the UK arm of AIP became less able than ever to mount a production without rewrites, changes of director, re-cuts, retitles and stirrings of the soup by all and sundry. Box-office results were conversely proportionate to the number of hands involved in each and every mess. Gordon Hessler's swan-song for the company had been *Murders in the Rue Morgue*; Robert Fuest's was now to be *Dr Phibes Rises Again*. With no other projects on the table and the business in a temporary state of disarray, Arkoff agreed to loan Vincent Price out to a United Artists production to plug the gap.

Price was dismayed; he had been offered the summer season at the Rep Theatre in his home state of Missouri, with roles in Eugene O'Neill's *Long Day's Journey into Night* and T S Eliot's *Murder in the Cathedral* (as Becket). But the run conflicted with the start date of the new film and he had reluctantly to decline. Again, he wrote to his agent: "The question before me is not money but peace of mind – some family life – and dignity in my profession. I have *survived* all the crap of AIP, of Sears' destruction of my art image, but the wear and tear has me down at long last." He had just turned 61, and Robert Quarry's presence in *Dr Phibes Rises Again* had hinted of the future which now awaited him. At such a low ebb in his personal and professional life, Vincent Price was a prime candidate for the kind of life-enhancing experience which could only come as a bolt from the blue.

Come it did, and it struck during the shooting of *Theatre of Blood*.

Theatre of Blood was filmed under the more genteel (and apt) title of 'Much Ado About Murder' and its story was that of a demented Shakespearean actor

who, with the help of his daughter Edwina, sets about avenging himself on the self-serving members of a 'Critics Circle' who have denied him the recognition which he believes to be his by right. The appeal of such a role at such a time for Vincent Price hardly warrants explanation.

On the face of it, *Theatre of Blood* owed its inspiration to *The Abominable Dr Phibes*. Both stories involved an elaborate revenge plot set in motion by a perceived injustice and enacted to the edicts of arcane ritual; by rights, *Theatre of Blood* should have been *Phibes'* artistic inferior, betraying all the signs of a cheap copy, made to cash in on a phenomenal success. That was how their respective scripts appeared, and that undoubtedly was why the latter was mounted in the first place. Under the aegis of director Douglas Hickox, however, things worked out rather differently.

Hickox was a dapper, denim-suited, now 44-year-old media professional who, like many of his contemporaries (including Fuest), honed his craft on television commercials when not employed in the making of feature films. He had served as a 'sit-in' director to Eugene Lourié on *Behemoth the Sea Monster* (1959) and had assisted on two other genre offerings: Robert Day's *Grip of the Strangler* and Arthur Crabtree's *Fiend Without a Face* (both 1957) before making his directorial debut in the 1960s. He had lately put Edward Woodward and Oliver Reed through the frenetic pacing of a violent crime thriller called *Sitting Target* (1971), but between these more public engagements, he was co-director of his own commercials outfit, Illustra Films, which was situated in Bateman Street in London's Soho.

Hickox had also directed *Entertaining Mr Sloane*, a black comedy based on the play of the same name by wayward talent Joe Orton. The hard-edged realism of *Sitting Target* combined with the acid humour of Orton's wicked satire made him the perfect choice to blend an unusual admixture of outrageous parody and graphic gore.

By 1972, the more traditional monster movie was dead and horror was seeking out new avenues to explore. *The Abominable Dr Phibes* had started the fad for self-mockery, while at the same time giving hardcore fans what they had now come to expect from an X-certificate or an R-rating. *Theatre of Blood* was to consolidate that trend and raise it to its zenith. The fact that Vincent Price attached himself to the project made it even more apposite: here was the old-time 'monster', barnstorming around in his self-delusional

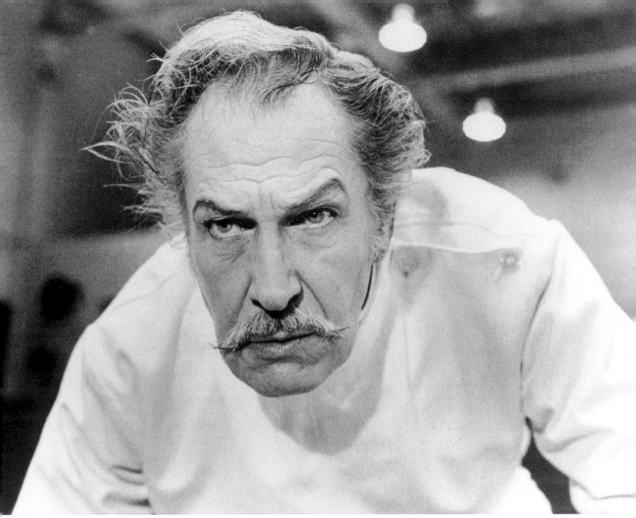

madness, despatching all who irked him via the most violent means which were currently permissible on screen. Not only was the outcome of this alchemical amalgam a triumph for Price and his director, but it also turned out to be one of the best horror films ever made – albeit one with its tongue stuck firmly into a bloody hole in its cheek.

This... my just reward. The whole world knows that it is mine by right. You deliberately withheld it from me. You deliberately humiliated me before the press, my public and my peers. It was the culmination of your determined denial of my genius. For 30 years, the public has acknowledged that I was the master and that this year, my season of Shakespeare was the shining jewel in the crown of the immortal Bard. But you – with your overweening malice – give the award to a twitch-ing, mumbling boy who can barely grunt his way through an incomprehensible performance. No. No... It is mine!
EDWARD LIONHEART (VINCENT PRICE),
THEATRE OF BLOOD (1972)

Price plays Edward Kendall Sheridan Lionheart (his middle names drawn from those of actor-manager William Hunter Kendall and dramatist Richard Brinsley Sheridan), an ageing thespian who notionally has committed suicide after being refused the Critics Circle Award for Best Actor in 1970. Three years on, and the cosy coterie of critics who collectively had denied him the honour start to meet with gruesome deaths, each of them inspired by a scene from a Shakespeare play. Lionheart is not dead but sleepeth, and in the abandoned Burbage Theatre he has been plotting his colourful revenge, ably assisted by a loyal

Diana Rigg and Vincent Price in a publicity shot from THEATRE OF BLOOD

daughter (Diana Rigg) and a community of derelicts.

Supporting Price in the endeavour were Ian Hendry, Harry Andrews, Dennis Price, Milo O'Shea, Robert Morley, Robert Coote, Michael Hordern, Arthur Lowe, Jack Hawkins, Eric Sykes, Diana Dors, Renée Asherson and Coral Browne. "When I first heard the big names that they had assembled for this picture, I just couldn't believe it," Price remarked. Such 'big names' had been assembled, though in less abundance, for *The Abominable Dr Phibes*, and the practice was becoming more commonplace as stars scrambled to be included in whatever work was on offer as the domestic industry went ever deeper into decline; several of those on call had already turned tricks for Hammer or Amicus. Nevertheless, it was an impressive ensemble, made more so by the classy presence of Rigg, Browne and Andrews. "The cast was so good," Douglas Hickox enthused, "that all I had to do as the director was open the dressing room doors and let the camera roll!"

A tense opening sees George Maxwell (Hordern), the first of the nine critics to be called to account,

requested by the police to help evict some squatters from a property in which he has an interest. His wife urges him not to go by reason of a bad dream and the portentous date: 15 March, the 'Ides of March' in Shakespeare's *Julius Caesar*. Laughing off her concerns, he drives across Chelsea Bridge as a storm breaks overhead and arrives at the warehouse to the ominous rhythm of his car's windscreen-wipers, in a neat nod to *Psycho*. There, he finds himself confronted by a rag-bag of 'meths' drinkers, who promptly lay into him with the proverbial canteen of cutlery while two policemen stand idly by. As he bleeds his last on the floor, the taller of the two leans over him and removes a false moustache. "But you're dead," Maxwell says, as he recognises Lionheart. "No," the actor gloats. "Another critical miscalculation on your part, dear boy. I am well. It is *you* who are dead..."

As a curtain-raiser for what is to come, this sequence is brilliantly staged, and not since the days of Corman's Poes had Price been given such a show-stopping entrance. "At last, a headline instead of a by-line," sneers Hector Snipe (Dennis Price) at the news of Maxwell's demise, before being conveyed to the Burbage where his own murder is conducted to the strains of *Troilus and Cressida*. Lionheart's Achilles spears him to death and sends his corpse to pay its respects at the funeral of his colleague, trailing behind a runaway horse. *Cymbeline* next inspires Lionheart to amputate Arthur Lowe's head while his screen wife lies sleeping beside him and to deposit it stickily onto a bottle of Ian Hendry's morning milk. And so it goes on, each more creative than the last and embellished by appropriate quotes from the Bard. "Dive, thoughts, down to my soul: here Clarence comes," Richard III whispers conspiratorially to camera as he prepares to drown Larding (Coote) in a barrel of Chambertine '69.

A light directorial touch and lush orchestration anaesthetises the horror of these scenes, as does the self-parodying antics of Price and Rigg. "Basin – basin!" Lionheart demands, as Horace Sprout's severed jugular fountains up in front of his face. "Two ounces over," he announces impatiently of Trevor Dickman's amputated heart, before slicing off the offending surplus to bring it in line with Shylock's required 'pound of flesh.'

In what is constructed as a two-act play, the explanatory flashback comes at the start of the second. Lionheart had launched himself into the blue after berating the Circle over their omission, but had awoken to find himself in the realm of the senses – mad, mud-caked and ministered to by a motley of human flotsam and jetsam: "Oh, brave new world," he intones, paraphrasing *The Tempest*, "that has such lovely creatures in it." Three years are meant to have elapsed since he was nursed back to health and a hunger for vengeance, but not much is made of this in Hickox' handling of the storyline, so keen is he to move swiftly on to Price's next set-piece Shakespearean death scene. Browne is fried to a frazzle in the manner of Joan of Arc in *Henry VI part I*, Hawkins is set up to murder his wife as did *Othello*, and Morley is fed his own 'children' (his pet poodles) in a pie, as was Tamora in *Titus Andronicus*. Only Hendry remains to have his eyes put out, like Gloucester in *King Lear*.

Lionheart is about to round off his revisionist repertoire with a re-staging of the awards ceremony when the police gatecrash the proceedings. He torches

THEATRE OF BLOOD (*Mark Anthony in 'Julius Caesar'*)

THEATRE OF BLOOD (*'Richard III'*)

the theatre and takes to the roof but falls back into the burning building; unlike Dr Phibes, his last bow puts paid to any notion of a repeat performance.

> *Edwina, you will present me with the award. It will be the last thing that Mr Devlin will ever see...*
> **EDWARD LIONHEART** (VINCENT PRICE),
> *THEATRE OF BLOOD* (1972)

Despite the superficial similarity of their respective plots, the two films were very different in tone. Fuest's *The Abominable Dr Phibes* was an extension of the never-never land which the director had helped to create for television's *The Avengers*, but *Theatre of Blood* was endowed with the pseudo-realism of the conventional thriller. The film is high-camp hilarity for the most part but its murder scenes are gruesome in the extreme, causing some American critics to perplex over the clash of styles. *Theatre of Blood* was the product of a culture in which the high watermark of humour was currently the anarchic antics of *Monty*

Coral Browne and Vincent Price

Python's Flying Circus, and little seemed amiss to critics in its country of origin. In a typical example of Pythonesque bad taste, the film's funniest moment has British comedy institution Eric Sykes (playing a bumbling copper) secreted inside the boot of a police car which Lionheart's daughter contrives to straddle a railway line. "I can hear a train whistle," Sykes informs his superior via walkie-talkie, just as the sound of the inevitable crash removes him from the investigation permanently.

Hickox makes much use of overlapping dialogue and clever transitions to give the piece elegance and fluidity; as a result, *Theatre of Blood* becomes a sublimely cohesive whole, instead of the sum of its murderous parts. Nor are Lionheart's victims picked at random for their singular exits, but chosen according to their own proclivities: thus Dennis Price meets his end through pomposity and an egotistical desire to snatch a scoop from his compatriots, Andrews because of his venality, Hawkins by his jealousy, Coote through being a lush and Morley for being an old 'queen.' Their names are equally fitting: Snipe, Dickman, Psaltery, Larding and Merridew. Shakespearean motifs crop up in abundance throughout the film: a removals van has 'Shakespeare's' sign-written on the side, the wine-cellar where Larding is dunked is called 'Clarence's', an outside broadcast unit is supplied by 'Avon' Television, and Lionheart's Burbage Theatre is itself named after Richard Burbage, the leading player in the Lord Chamberlain's men.

The studios and their restrictive practices were now being abandoned wholesale, and the film glories in the summer sun of a number of well-chosen locations all over the London of 1972, from Brompton Road (with Harrods prominent in the background) to the back streets of Battersea, and from imposing Alembic House on the banks of the Thames to the deserted and soon-to-be demolished Putney Hippodrome. All the gallivanting among the sights and sounds of the city in bloom had an unexpected side-effect: love also blossomed between Price and his co-star, Coral Browne.

Diana Rigg was the one who found herself cast as Cupid after Browne had confided her feelings for Price. "Here was an absolutely adorable man who seemed quite lonely. So, I think they must have eyed each other," Rigg recalled, and as it was Browne's birthday, she suggested to Price that he ask her out to dinner – unaware that he was still married to Mary

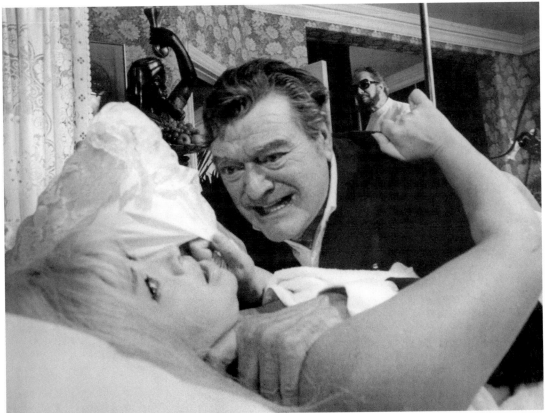

Diana Dors, Jack Hawkins and Vincent Price in **Theatre of Blood**

Grant. "From then on, they never looked back. I think they fell into bed and I think it was a wildly sexual relationship," she said. "And that was the start of it all."

Coral Browne had a vividly chequered past, both in the theatre and out of it, but she had been appended to the cast of *Theatre of Blood* to invest it with a touch of class; in the event, she did more than that – she changed the love life of its star, and his performance in the film benefited enormously from the surprise injection of testosterone.

Theatre of Blood has class stamped all over it, in fact, from its poignant Michael J Lewis score and opening montage of Shakespeare on the silent screen (including Emil Jannings in *Othello*, 1922) to its grand finale when Price, flaming torch in either hand, declaims from the stage, "Come, fire... Consume this petty world and, in its ashes, let my memory lie!" – then turns towards the auditorium and flings a firebrand straight into an adjacent 'box' in a single unbroken take.

One of the 'reviews' which incite Lionheart to enact another exotic revenge is quoted as speaking of "the ageing matinée idol's ranting and posturing," which in other circumstances might have been a hostage to critical fortune for real. Not here. Only Vincent Price had the wherewithal to pull off a role so magnificently over-the-top as that of Edward Lionheart. He does it with talent to spare, rarely putting a foot wrong (a Scottish accent for one 'character' is somewhat misplaced) and makes *Theatre of Blood* a joy to behold – literate, suspenseful, intelligent, intriguing and uproariously funny. It is without doubt one of the genre greats.

The only participant not to have had a rollicking time was actor Ian Hendry, who played nominal hero Peregrine Devlin. Hendry was going through an acrimonious divorce from his actress-wife Janet Munro, who died suddenly at age 38 less than four months after filming was complete; both had a history of alcohol abuse. By the time *Theatre of Blood* went into release in April 1973, Hendry himself had just managed to survive crashing his Jensen Interceptor over the Chiswick flyover.

Vincent Price and Robert Morley in **THEATRE OF BLOOD**

Price, Browne and Hendry all had things on their minds during the filming of *Theatre of Blood*, but for the first two, it was love in bloom. Hendry was merely distracted, but his weariness with life proved useful when he was called upon to deliver the script's pay-off line, after Lionheart has plummeted in fiery farewell from the roof of the theatre. "He was madly overacting as usual," he critiques for Inspector Boot (O'Shea). "But you must admit, he did know how to make an exit."

Ladies and gentlemen, it is always a nostalgic moment when we come to the end of a season – especially one that has been as successful as this one. Will you join me in a toast to the immortal Bard: William Shakespeare!

EDWARD LIONHEART (VINCENT PRICE), *THEATRE OF BLOOD* (1972)

For an actor like Price, who had suffered as much as anyone under the slings and arrows of critics who disparaged his work in the genre as unworthy of serious comment, the role of Edward Lionheart was a once-in-a-lifetime opportunity to give them the finger. Because of the clever construct of the script, which allowed Price to declaim Shakespeare's verse while wallowing in the voluminous blood of his victims, he was able to take that revenge literally as well as figuratively.

Theatre of Blood was thoroughly disarming in its concept; any critic who decried it implicitly allied themselves with the shallow, self-serving, publicity-seeking hacks in the story, who place their own dubious talents above those on whom they comment. In consequence, the film received universally good reviews – some of the best of Price's entire career. The critics were enticed into enjoying the joke, lest they be perceived for the pompous prigs they often were. Had its script been written by Joseph Heller, *Theatre of Blood* could not have contrived a more efficient trap for those who might traditionally have set their faces against it. The fact that it was also populated by the cream of the British acting profession, partaking of the forensic fun for all they were worth, made it doubly a dish to savour.

There had been double the enjoyment for Vincent Price also. "He was very happy, because he was surrounded by first-class actors who gave him the respect he deserved," Hickox said of Price at the time. "That was the best feeling of achievement and satisfaction that I ever got from a film," the actor reciprocated. "A splendid cast. I fell in love with one of them, Coral Browne, married her, and lived happily ever after."

Not quite yet, however.

When Vincent Price returned to Los Angeles in September 1972, after completing *Theatre of Blood*, he was made the subject of the ABC TV show *This Is Your Life*, in which host Ralph Edwards and actor Hans Conreid surprised Price with the Big Red Book at the Pickwick bookstore in Hollywood, where he was autographing copies of *A Treasury of American Art*. Among the guests assembled in the studio to greet him were his wife Mary (behind whose back he was now conducting his long-distance affair with Coral Browne), their children Barrett and Victoria, Helen Hayes, Sam Arkoff and Vincent Graham, vice-president of Sears, Roebuck & Company. Arkoff related his oft-told tale of Price's *per diem* going towards the purchase of art treasures and Hayes reminisced about the far-off days of his debut in *Victoria Regina*.

Price smiled valiantly throughout, but he could be seen to be struggling with mixed emotions. "We're very proud to be Vincent Price's family," Mary said after a moment's hesitation. Not for much longer: the 23-year marriage of Vincent and Eleanor Mary Grant DuPont Price was already on the rocks and, in another month, it would be over for good when Mary filed for divorce.

Price said nothing to Mary about his affair with Coral Browne either before, during or after the divorce; according to daughter Victoria, he had desired to give the impression that no one else had been involved, lest those who knew him thought badly of him. (The news was eventually broken to all by the *National Enquirer*: "Vincent Price admits he's fallen in love," was its 14 October headline.) Price feared less for his public image than for his standing among his friends and associates. "He was always extremely concerned with what people thought of him – a trait he had learned from his mother," Victoria wrote in 1999. "To the outside world, he wished never to seem anything other than content and grateful for his life, but in truth, he frequently struggled with feelings of inadequacy, failure, guilt, and terrible, terrible worry."

If Price was looking for a way out of his present predicament, one road was always open to him. Commenting on Poe's tendency to take solace in drink, he had once said, "He drank a great deal, and there is the terrible thing that the alcoholic has which is a kind of sinking into the ground at moments when you aren't exhilarated. You literally sink. I think that many times the alcoholic feels that if somebody had a spade handy, that they would throw the dirt on him, and he couldn't get out. Poe certainly knew the elements of fear that are in all of us, and they are in everyone I am sure, even the bravest man."

Price was talking from experience. "Vincent could be a mean drunk," his daughter confirmed. "Mary sometimes dreaded coming home after a party where her husband had had a lot to drink" – a view shared by long-time family friend Hank Milam: "At some point, I don't know at what point, it became a problem; but I know that Mary was never very happy about Vincent's drinking ... I only saw evidences of nastiness a couple of times, but he could be nasty."

His taste for Shakespeare reawakened by *Theatre of Blood*, Price was moved to consider an offer to play Pandarus in an adaptation of *Troilus and Cressida*. AIP had other ideas, however, and allocated him to play opposite Robert Quarry again in another horror similar in principle to his last three and provisionally called *The Revenge of Dr Death*, which was now pencilled in to start in England in the late spring of 1973.

The film offered Price the chance to flee the rigours of impending divorce and spend some time with the new love of his life, so he put up little resistance. On arrival at Heathrow Airport, however, he was phoned by a reporter working on the 'Jack Bentley Show Page' of the *Sunday Mirror* and notionally asked about his latest trip to the UK. The resultant article did not make for pleasant reading.

Under the banner headline "Horror! Vincent Price is going straight," the star was depicted as guileless, compulsive and broke. "I have no money," Price was reported as saying. "I live from picture to picture and on fees from TV quiz shows and the like. Without these I'd have trouble supporting my family and keeping up with alimony. As it is I live very simply and except for an art collection that's far from Sotheby's standard, have few possessions." The piece continued in the same confessional tone: "Whenever I make a picture, I blow any spare money on a work of art that may or may not be valuable one day. Then, of course, I subscribe to various charities, including the tax-man."

The usually affable Price was incensed, and he barred AIP's Dennison Thornton from assisting the press in any more 'scoops' for the remainder of his stay.

> Lambert: Finally, in just two seconds, could you tell us what your... mission to England is?
> Toombs: You mean my reason for being here?
> Lambert: Briefly, in just one second.
> Toombs: (smiling broadly): Why, I've come to play the devil!
>
> **ANGUS HALL**, *DEVILDAY* (1969)

Early in 1969, during its regular sweep of galley-proofs, AIP had taken out an option on Angus Hall's novel, *Devilday*. The reason for its decision was not difficult to understand on a superficial level. The plot of *Devilday* revolves around an ageing horror film actor named Paul Harvard Toombs, whose Hollywood career was wrecked by scandal when his wife was found murdered and who subsequently is brought over to England to star in a TV revival of his cinematic alter ego, "the dark and dreaded" Dr Dis. The appeal of this story as a vehicle for AIP's own horror star-in-residence went without saying, and AIP announced in 1970 that it planned to film *Devilday*. No sooner had an announcement been made than the house 'readers' at AIP reported that more than structural deficiencies required to be overcome when it came to any suggestion of adapting this novel for the screen.

The premise itself was straightforward enough: Toombs enjoys success anew in 'The New Adventures of Dr Dis', but his company minder (and nominal hero of the tale), Barry Lambert, becomes increasingly agitated about his star's eccentric behaviour and beliefs – chief among which is that of serial reincarnation. Toombs surrounds himself with female acolytes and establishes a base of operations in an old abbey. Fact and fiction collide when a ritual murder similar to the one which halted Toombs' career in America rocks the community. Lambert thinks that Toombs is responsible but Scotland Yard investigators can find no evidence to connect him with the crime. Feelings begin to run high and a group of vigilantes led by an ex-army major traces Toombs to his lair. Grenades are lobbed into the building and Toombs is killed in the ensuing explosions. Some months later, Lambert is strolling down a London street when he spots a passing Rolls-Royce: the rear-seat passenger is Paul Toombs.

Devilday was pulp fiction with pretensions, as exemplified by the name of its villain: Dr Dis, a grammatical prefix meaning 'separate' or 'apart.' Toombs and Dis are effectively one and the same, an Americanised Aleister Crowley figure who is depicted as a cross between 1930s barnstormer Tod Slaughter and saturnine supporting actor (and ex-Hammer habitué) Francis De Wolff. Toombs suffers from satyriasis and engages in black magic, but the other characters in the novel are equally unsympathetic. Barry Lambert, as narrator and eventual nemesis, is ambitious, amoral and self-seeking, while everyone in between the two is either manipulative or murdered in due course.

But if anyone at AIP had thought the role of Paul Harvard Toombs (spelled Toombes in the film) ideal casting for Vincent Price, they would have changed their minds by the end of chapter one, when Lambert comes upon the actor in the stateroom of his transatlantic liner, a bruised and sexually abused minor lying at his feet, to be greeted by the admonition: "What the fuck do *you* want?"

The novel as a whole is a curious mix, as shallow as the TV types who people its pages and steeped in the hippie fixation with transcendental philosophy. There is little in the way of narrative drive and suspense is non-existent. If that were not enough to have caused all who read it to abandon hope of a potential feature, the climax is fatuous and contrived, with evil emerging typically triumphant.

Accordingly, AIP changed its corporate mind and opted to defer production of *Devilday* until a suitable treatment became available. The film was announced again 18 months later, on the strength of a script by Murray Smith, but it failed to reach a sound-stage in that form either. A further 18 months elapsed and a new screenplay by one-time publicist Greg Morrison, based on an earlier draft by Ken Levison, was finally given the green light to roll at Twickenham Studios in May 1973. *Devilday* was now retitled *The Revenge of Dr Death* and its producers were to be Arkoff, Rosenberg and Subotsky (of Amicus Films), due to the fact that AIP's own James Nicholson had passed away during the rewrites.

> *His old movies show all the time on television. There's a whole new cult today for Dr Death, and I've got him; I've got Dr Death...*
>
> **OLIVER QUAYLE** (ROBERT QUARRY), *MADHOUSE* (1973)

Publicity shot from MADHOUSE

With the cost of space at the major studios becoming more prohibitive by the day, Amicus had now set up shop at the small suburban enclave of Twickenham Studios, whose low-rent stages were used primarily for television production and occasional second features. For its own second feature with new co-production partner AIP, the company had therefore nominated Twickenham as its studio of choice. The reason was economic, but there would be a price to pay in other ways: poor sound quality and perfunctory lighting, while the real corridors and offices of the complex stood in for many of the required sets.

The most striking aspect of what was eventually released as *Madhouse* is therefore how cheap it looks. Some reviewers drew a parallel with Billy Wilder's *Sunset Boulevard*, while Price's co-star Robert Quarry advanced it as a horror version of *All About Eve* (both 1950). Both of these were wildly optimistic. The film turned out to be a poor man's Agatha Christie, the

Between takes on MADHOUSE

diametric opposite of *Theatre of Blood* in production values and *The Abominable Dr Phibes* in originality. Morrison's shooting script had ditched *Devilday* altogether in favour of a retread of *Grip of the Strangler*, in which Boris Karloff had played a writer who set out to investigate a 20-year-old series of murders, only to find them recurring as he dug deeper into the case. In *Grip of the Strangler*, Karloff was himself the killer – his alter ego enacting both sets of crimes. In *Madhouse*, Price only *thinks* that the killer may be he in 'Dr Death' guise; in their essentials, however, the two are the same.

> *Actor Paul Toombes (Price) arrives in England to star in a new film featuring 'Dr Death', the character for which he was most renowned before the murder of his fiancée brought an impromptu end to his Hollywood career. As shooting gets underway, a series of murders occurs and suspicion again falls on Toombes. Fearful for his sanity and concerned that 'Dr Death' may somehow be responsible for the crimes, Toombes fakes his own death to discover the real culprit: it is Herbert Flay (Cushing), scriptwriter of the film, who has harboured a jealous grudge against him from way back. They struggle and Flay is killed. Toombes assumes the personality of his nemesis and lives happily ever after with Flay's wife, who had always loved him from afar in any event.*

Robert Quarry's arrival in England had again passed unnoticed in the press, much to his own chagrin but to the surprise of few others, given that whatever fame he may have thought he had rested solely on the success in America of two low-budget horrors (both of which had gone out as the lower half of double-bills in the UK) and a co-starring role in *Dr Phibes Rises Again*. Price, on the other hand, was always of interest, or was fashioned to be so by AIP's ever-active publicity agent Dennison Thornton. Not this time; the Bentley piece had put paid to that and, for a while, press visits to the set of *The Revenge of Dr Death* as well, except when it came to promoting the cameo that the film occasioned from current chat-show king Michael Parkinson.

Robert Quarry now also wanted to break his contract with AIP, considering Sam Arkoff a "sonofabitch" who planned to put him into a never-ending stream of increasingly dire films, such as the upcoming *Sugar Hill*. Quarry was adamant during filming that he was not about to star in this voodoo-

*Vincent Price
and Julie
Crosthwait in
MADHOUSE*

orientated blaxploitation thriller, though he relented when he returned to Hollywood. "It was Vincent's last movie with AIP," Quarry told *Cinefantastique*. "His contract was up. We never got a script until Sunday morning, and we were to start shooting the next day. That gave us no time to bitch and scream ... They were very smart there."

All of this made for a tense production, not helped by the fact that Quarry felt himself deprived of the role played by Cushing or that Price's marriage of 24 years was all but over. The two Americans consequently spent most of the film bitching at each other or avoiding one another as much as possible. Quarry whiled away his off-duty hours schmoozing with David Hemmings and his then-wife Gayle Hunnicutt, while Price concentrated on his transatlantic love affair with Coral Browne. As to his relationship with AIP and its films – "I hoped it would be my last," Price confided about *The Revenge of Dr Death*. It was.

But you're not bringing me back to life; you're bringing Dr Death back to life – and he terrifies

me! I'm terrified of what he's done. And I'm terrified of what he still may do.

PAUL TOOMBES (VINCENT PRICE),
MADHOUSE (1973)

Devilday opens with a quote from Poe's *Marginalia* – a muse about men who "soared above the plane of their race." *Madhouse* opens with a quote from Robert Quarry: "That's Hollywood for you." If only it were; the closest this film comes to the level of creative expertise which the name Hollywood is commonly held to imply are the extracts which represent the cinematic oeuvre of Paul Toombes, which it was obliged to sample from the glory days of Price under the direction of Roger Corman.

Quarry has gone on record as saying that he was originally cast as scriptwriter Herbert Flay, the part which ultimately went to Peter Cushing; there is some credence to this, as Quarry's role of Oliver Quayle is an Englishman in the novel and, unlike Cushing, he was of similar build to Price and could thus have passed more easily for him when disguised as 'Dr

Death.' The climax of *Madhouse*, in which Toombes makes himself up to look like Flay and then to all intents and purposes 'becomes' him, might have seemed too close to the truth if Quarry, rather than Cushing, had in fact essayed the part; it is uncomfortable enough in the circumstances to watch Price play a made-up monster under the dismissive eyes of Quarry's self-seeking and overbearing producer.

The real-life situation between Price and Quarry is reflected both in dialogue and in the story itself: Toombes is shown mooning over his old movies, while Quayle plots quietly on the sidelines to deprive him of his career. The clips themselves (from *The Haunted Palace, The Raven, Tales of Terror, The Masque of the Red Death, House of Usher* and *Pit and the Pendulum*) are ill chosen, not only because of the difference in quality (the Poes are better) but in relation to the amount of screen time they occupy. Corman should by rights have received co-credit as the film's director; if his contribution had been removed, *Madhouse* would have lost an entire reel.

With Nicholson's departure (and subsequent death), this was Price's first film for AIP to be nominated exclusively as A Samuel Z Arkoff Production, and the line which the company had always drawn between its 'A' features and its exploitation offerings was finally blurred out of existence. The character of Dr Death is accorded a garish but rather effective make-up by George Blackler (who performed a similar service for Price on *Theatre of Blood*), but then he did have the precedent of Phibes to contend with. In the essentially undemanding role of Paul Toombes, Price is unusually introspective and for the most part understated; he comes closer to playing himself in this film than in any previous one.

Considering the possibilities that were inherent in the concept both to pastiche the genre in the manner of *Theatre of Blood* and to turn in something new and inventive, *Madhouse* is merely replete with the clichés of the cheap horror thriller: an old cottage which has enough electricity to operate a 16mm projector appears not to possess sufficient to power up any room lights, so its occupants wander around in semi-darkness clutching candles. Adrienne Corri's demented 'American' actress sports an incongruous collection of spiders in the basement of Flay's country retreat and sends things toppling into bathos, while the crushing of the mock film's director under a prop four-poster bed, whose canopy descends on hydraulic lifts, tips them back into farce. The blackmailing parents of a murdered girl prance around the grounds of Pyrford Manor like Tweedledum and Tweedledee, but without the light sardonic touch of a Robert Fuest (who was at one time pencilled in to direct), the effect is leaden. The film is at its best when it concentrates on the acid exchanges between the stars – given extra bite by their relationship to the *realpolitik* of the production – rather than the unnecessarily prolonged stalking sequences which precede each Dr Death murder.

> *After that, he turned into some kind of weirdo. Couldn't tell where he stopped and Dr Death began. Police used to find him walking up and down Sunset Boulevard in his Dr Death costume... Well, they finally dragged him off to the funny farm but by the time he was cured, there was no career left for him.*
> OLIVER QUAYLE (ROBERT QUARRY),
> *MADHOUSE* (1973)

Director Jim Clark, who was John Schlesinger's editor-of-choice and had previously shot only a brace of forgettable comedies, laid the blame fairly and squarely on the shoulders of producer Milton Subotsky, no longer constrained by the bluff Deke Heyward as he had been on *Scream and Scream Again*. Subotsky, he claimed in a letter to Price, had "bulldozed his way into the cutting room and is at this moment cutting a swathe through the film. They are retaining all the action, of course – but every time anyone opens their mouth, Milton tries to cut the line – for no other reason than 'it bores me' or 'we don't need it.' It is pure butchery." Clark went on to agonise, "It is your name that will sell the film, and mine that will receive the blame for making a poor picture." In the event, the Price name failed to sell the film but Jim Clark did return to editing on Schlesinger's *The Day of the Locust* (1975).

In other hands, *Madhouse* might have acquitted itself as an efficient little thriller were it to have been graced with better production values, a larger budget and a tauter script. It had none of these. Thinking himself to be possessed by his screen persona of Dr Death, Toombes inquires of the police – "Is it *me*? I don't know. Do you?" It was not him in either case; it was simply the agitated slapdash of an industry on which the darkness of night was now descending and which could find no more eloquent exit-line for the actor than the mind-numbingly inept, "There is always room for more in the coffin of time."

Vincent Price and Adrienne Corri in MADHOUSE

Over the end credits (though not, for AIP's usual copyright reasons, in the video release), Price gives a plaintive rendition of a 1926 ballad by Robert Katscher and B G DeSylva called 'When Day is Done', whose melancholy lament serves to underline what a good film *Madhouse* could have been, and what a bad film it actually is.

Madhouse had been one horror too many for Vincent Price. Yet, in a way, some of it was a fitting finale to an illustrious career in fear. Again and again, the story returns to him staring at clips from his own films (disguised as those of Toombes and Dr Death), and with the footage having been supplied by Corman's Poes, Price must at times have felt like a dying man, watching his life pass before his eyes.

The horror cycle which had begun in the mid-fifties was almost over. In the vacuum created in him by his wife's death in 1971, Peter Cushing would gamely carry on flying the flag until it fell in

tatters from his hands, but by 1976, Christopher Lee was to have upped sticks and settled in Los Angeles in search of new roles. As the film's closing scenes seemed to imply, *Madhouse* was little more than Price after the event, alone in a dressing room and waxing nostalgic for times gone by. His loyal audience could well have done without sight of that. It was a poignant curtain-call for one of the greatest icons of screen horror, and only when Vincent Price turned his back on acting in films was the last triumph of his long career finally bestowed upon him.

When Price was finished with *Madhouse*, he felt himself to have supped enough at horror's table. "After that, I began to receive overly violent scripts," he told *Halls of Horror*'s Anthony Tate in 1984. "I didn't see anything that I wanted or needed." He had supped enough with AIP as well; there was to be no renewal of contract this time around – not that one was offered him; Heyward replacement Steve Previn (elder brother of André) did not share Arkoff's taste for lowest-common-denominator product. He settled his affairs with the company by putting in a brief appearance in *Percy's Progress* (a flaccid sequel to Anglo-EMI's 1970 sex-comedy *Percy*), which went unreleased in the US until 1978, when it popped its head out in retitled form as *It's Not the Size That Counts*.

AIP was also to give up on horror with the departure of Vincent Price and the bad reviews which *Madhouse* was duly accorded. Since 1971, it had concentrated effort on a witless slew of 'blaxploitation' thrillers, the latest of which – *Sugar Hill* – had just been foisted onto a reluctant Robert Quarry, whose career collapsed shortly afterwards. Sam Arkoff had taken his company onto the stock market in 1969 and, by 1974, he was predicting in the *Hollywood Reporter* that "American International is upon the threshold of the highest level of motion picture production and distribution in its history." Five years later, Arkoff sold out to Filmways and resigned from the board, pocketing a cool $4.3 million from his shares.

Tigon had already departed the field and Hammer was about to embark on its final, fateful horror film, *To the Devil a Daughter*, from a script by Chris Wicking. While *Madhouse* was still in production at Twickenham, Milton Subotsky added a new name to that of Robert Bloch on his roster of horror-writers in residence: Ronald Chetwynd-Hayes. But *From Beyond the Grave* ended up playing to empty theatres – as did *The Beast Must Die*, with which it was shot back-to-back. In June 1975, Subotsky resigned from the board of Amicus Productions, pocketing only a writ against former partner Max J Rosenberg.

Madhouse notwithstanding, Price had gone out on a high. *The Abominable Dr Phibes* and *Theatre of Blood* were not only two of the finest horror films in the Price canon, they were also among the best of the entire genre. *Phibes* was a darkly humorous hymn to Paradise lost, but in *Theatre of Blood*, both Edward Lionheart and Vincent Price himself had taken revenge on their critics, saved their best performances till last and exited the stage in a blaze of glory.

Price's divorce from Mary Grant, his costume-designer wife of 24 years, was declared final in August 1973. His divorce from AIP had come a few months earlier. Vincent Price had found a soul-mate in Coral Browne; they shared a healthy belligerence

(she disporting it, he admiring it), a zest for living, and the knowing cynicism of two like-minded professionals who had been there, seen it, done it all. Just as Price's artistic intensity had been reflected in his first wife and his cosmopolitanism in his second, so self-mockery and the enthusiasm for the day which were to mark his autumn years were reflected in his partnership with Browne. She externalised what he felt inside and what he was too polite and deferential as a typical Mid-westerner from a good home to exhibit publicly. She was brash, brazen, conspicuously theatrical, supremely talented as a performer and unashamedly bisexual.

Despite two wives and a great many girlfriends ("Since I had dedicated myself to the world of art, I could hardly do better than to study seriously art's greatest source of inspiration – the female form," he wrote at age 17 of his European conquests), Price had erotic encounters of a different kind during his time in London in 1933-4 and rumours of affairs with male co-stars persisted throughout his career. According to his daughter, the 22-year-old Price had shared a Baker Street flat with two Oxbridge graduates who counted among their circle of friends a number of prominent homosexuals and who introduced him to John Gielgud, who later gifted Price with a volume of Konstantin Stanislavsky's *An Actor Prepares*.

Perhaps surprisingly, Price and Browne did not appear to make that strange a pair once the initial shock of their union had worn off. On the contrary, they seemed somehow made for each other, and they were to remain steadfastly together to the end – Browne's, in the first instance, from breast cancer in 1991.

To consummate their relationship in theatrical terms, as well as to rid Price of his horror image now that his contract with AIP had finally come to an end, Browne was first to arrange for the two of them to appear opposite Charles Gray in a West End production of Jean Anouilh's black comedy, *Ardèle*. The play, at the Queen's Theatre, would be a resounding flop. Long years of perfecting a 'Vincent Price' act had robbed Price of his former ability to immerse himself in character to the degree required of a rigorous stage performance, and he proved to be one-dimensional in the role of the Count. It was a set-back, but it was not the end of the world as Price now knew it.

By the end of 1974, Vincent Price had himself both a new wife and a new sense of freedom as a performer. If he had thought to exercise the latter in the UK through cameo roles in films like *Percy's Progress*, stage appearances in plays like *Ardèle*, or television slots along the lines of his ITV series *Cooking Price-Wise*, he was soon disenfranchised of the idea by the punitive rates of income tax which Labour Chancellor Dennis Healey had seen fit to impose. Where American studios had once seen filming in Britain as an economic necessity, they now considered it to be financial suicide. Between union strife and runaway inflation, the country was going rapidly to the dogs and the Prices were inevitably forced to join the exodus of star names who were all fleeing to more amenable climes.

> *Hello, I'm Vincent Price. For many years now, mankind – and his offspring – has been searching for an alternative to peanut butter and jelly...*
> **VINCENT PRICE COMMERCIAL**,
> THE PETER PAUL CANDY COMPANY (1975)

Price returned to Los Angeles and set up home in the West Hollywood hills. With Browne's circle of theatrical friends appended to his own, they took to socialising a great deal and Price fell back on his old mainstay of the small screen, shooting commercials for such as the IRS, Chevrolet, Sun Giant raisins and, ironically, a fly-spray, among others. His frugality with his finances (while working on *The Abominable Dr Phibes*, he was known to the crew as Vincent 'half-Price') enabled him to exchange such endorsements for hotel accommodation and exotic trips on cruise liners for himself and his wife. But in film terms, he was part of a cultural fad which was fast fading from view and the offers began to dry up as a result. By 1975, the horror scene in which Vincent Price had reigned supreme was well and truly over.

> Gwendoline Snoop Nicholson: *It's the Michael Bastion horror festival.*
> Barney: The *Michael Bastion? That actor that does all those spooky pictures?*
> Gwendoline Snoop Nicholson: *Hardly just 'that actor,' Barney. Michael Bastion's a famous star.*
> Barney: *He hasn't done anything in a long time.*
> Gwendoline Snoop Nicholson: *That's precisely the point. And now someone's had a perfectly marvellous idea: they're going to revive all the*

films that made Michael Bastion what he is today.
> Barney: *An out of work actor.*
> **MILDRED NATWICK** AND **LOU ANTONIO**,
> THE SNOOP SISTERS: A BLACK DAY
> FOR BLUEBEARD (1974)

Price had guested in *Columbo* ('Lovely but Lethal') and *The Bionic Woman* ('Black Magic'), donned vampire make-up as an ageing horror film actor named Michael Bastion for *The Snoop Sisters* combo of Helen Hayes and Mildred Natwick ('A Bad Day for Blackbeard'), appeared with Johnny Carson and habitually on *The Carol Burnett Show*, but all of these were time-fillers at best and he had rapidly become dissatisfied with his lot. Against that, Browne was funny and feisty, her waspish wit and acid tongue admirably suiting the Price who, in his mid-sixties, now felt that he had given his all to his chosen career but had got little out of it in return. "Where do I fit in, in a profession I can see so clearly at fault in so many ways?" he confided to his diary. As luck would have it, Browne had her own ideas about that.

In 1975, the actor whom *Variety* had christened "the rock generation's Boris Karloff" erased the dividing line between music and movies by narrating an intermezzo for the latest album by high priest of shock-rock, Alice Cooper. Vincent Price's contribution to *Welcome to My Nightmare* took the form of a soliloquy about spiders, and so successful was it that Cooper (who had been born Vincent Furnier) incorporated it into a television special made to publicise the album, as well as asking Price to join him at selected spots on his nationwide promotional tour. "I've always been a buff of old horror films," Cooper commented. "I think there's a serious side to horror and a fun side. He has that same attitude," he said of the man who played 'the Curator.'

The fun side of Vincent Price was coming to a close, however; the more serious side was about to begin.

> *And the wild regrets, and the bloody sweats,*
> *None knew so well as I:*
> *For he who lives more lives than one*
> *More deaths than one must die.*
> **OSCAR WILDE**,
> THE BALLAD OF READING GAOL (1898)

In the summer of 1977, four months after Price's first wife, Edith Barrett, had died alone in

Albuquerque, New Mexico, his third persuaded him to accept an offer by director Joseph Hardy to play the lead in a one-man show about the life of Oscar Fingal O'Flahertie Wills Wilde, the disgraced Dublin-born playwright and author of *The Picture of Dorian Gray* (1891). Price had needed persuading; not only did he have to carry the entire show on his own with nought but a few props to aid him, but Oscar Wilde had long since been embraced as a cause célèbre by the gay community to whom he represented the championing of gay rights in the face of sexual bigotry. Wilde had himself been bisexual, fathering two sons by his wife Constance before his predilection for the 'rough trade' of grooms and rent-boys eventually got the better of him and brought him two years' hard labour in Reading Gaol, followed by exile and an early death in Paris at the turn of the century. After some heart-searching, Price accepted the role and John Gay's *Diversions and Delights* opened in San Francisco on 11 July to superlative reviews.

Price toured in the show until December 1978, having failed only to set Broadway similarly alight with his electric performance during an abortive two-week run there. But he revived the role of Wilde on a less regular basis thereafter and, over a period of five years in total, he appeared in *Diversions and Delights* on 800 occasions in more than 300 cities (including many around the world), laying the ghost of *Ardèle* in the process.

Through playing Oscar Wilde, Vincent Price had rediscovered the art of the possible – fear was no longer part of the equation. He had been made to see that the best way to combat fright was to grab hold of it by the scruff of its adulterous neck, like Nicholas

Diversions and Delights

Medina in *Pit and the Pendulum*, and shake the life out of it. It had taken a good deal of encouragement for him to do so, but the iconoclastic and adventurous Coral Browne had been on hand to persuade him to face down his haunted and often mediocre past. The courageousness of Wilde the man had been an inspiration in itself – and that of the veteran actor who portrayed him won out in the end.

In 1980, Vincent Price returned to horror films after a six-year absence, much of which time had been spent touring in *Diversions and Delights*. By then, nothing of the film world which he had known remained. Big-budget science fiction followed by big-budget horror had both made a return to the screen in the second half of the 1970s, but their revival in the wake of films like *Jaws* (1975) and *Star Wars* (1977) had come too late for those companies which had made their names in the field during the preceding decade.

American International had managed to scrape through until 1979 by continuing to produce and distribute exploitation quickies in all colours of the rainbow, but it had rejoined the horror bandwagon in 1977 with a number of B-movies (such as *Empire of the Ants*, from old stalwart Bert I Gordon) which harked back to its formative days, before making a more significant entry in 1978 with *The Incredible Melting Man*, on which Amicus money-man Max Rosenberg acted as executive producer. Its last two films prior to its acquisition by Filmways in 1979 were *The Amityville Horror*, based on Jay Anson's best-seller and another story where the 'house' was the monster, and Brian de Palma's *Dressed to Kill*.

Amicus was no more, but its former co-owner Milton Subotsky had survived the upheavals in the domestic industry by retaining his status as an independent producer. His idea of horror, however, remained steadfastly attached to pulp fiction and a predictable format. After *From Beyond the Grave*, he had commissioned a script based on Chetwynd-Hayes' 1975 novel *The Monster Club*, a juvenile parody of traditional elements served with a twist of humour and a cloying overdose of surrealism.

The Monster Club is a compendium of five tales loosely held together by a linking narrative in which a vampire repays a passing stranger for allowing it to partake of his jugular by inviting him to the club in question, wherein co-habitates every species of monster. Their conversation over dinner leads swiftly

Vincent Price and John Carradine in **THE MONSTER CLUB**

to stories about several of the club's incumbents, and the reader is soon regaled by 'The Werewolf and the Vampire', 'The Mock', 'The Humgoo', 'The Shadmock' and 'The Fly-By-Night.' Unlikely as it might seem, Chetwynd-Hayes was a good writer, but the arrant nonsense in which he takes unquestionable delight in *The Monster Club* is very much an acquired taste. Aside from the first two, his motley of monsters are entirely of his own making and are composited by the strictly non-Darwinian mechanics of mating unmatched pairs, thus a werewolf who breeds with a vampire produces a were-vamp and so on, ad nauseam.

The attraction of this book for Milton Subotsky was its inclusion of a 'vampire film producer' called Lintom Busotsky (a lesson for all writers hoping to see their work on screen) and, as a result, he had chosen for his next project a source-novel which was largely unadaptable except as a piece of inane juvenilia. 'The Mock' and 'The Fly-By-Night' were jettisoned, and the three remaining stories with their accompanying

wraparound of the vampire, the victim and the curious club in Swallow Street were handed over to scenarists Edward and Valerie Abraham. They proceeded to further denude the original, so that only the club, 'The Shadmock' and 'The Humgoo' (which became the final tale of the three in the film) were now recognisable as Chetwynd-Hayes' work.

Subotsky was finally given the green light to produce *The Monster Club* by Sir Lew Grade's ITC Productions, and the film was rolled out at Elstree Studios in April 1980, with Price cast in the role of the vampire Eramus and John Carradine as his guest, Chetwynd-Hayes himself (in place of the novel's less inventive 'Donald McCloud' and presumably to make up for all the adaptive changes along the way). Price and Carradine filmed their segment over a single week in May, two months after Sam Arkoff finally took his leave of Filmways with a cheque in his pocket and ideas of forming Arkoff International Pictures spinning around in his head.

RIGHT:
*John Carradine
and Vincent
Price in* THE
MONSTER
CLUB

BELOW:
*Publicity shot
from* THE
MONSTER
CLUB

*Folks... I give you the most stu-pen-dous, the most
outstanding, the gift-ed, the most dia-bolical, the
bloodiest, the most murderous, the great-est
monster of us all. MAN.*

R CHETWYND-HAYES,
THE MONSTER CLUB (1975)

The Monster Club was a puerile slice of hokum,
more akin to the children's series *The Hilarious
House of Frightenstein* (which Price had fronted for
Canadian television in 1975) than it was to any of
Amicus' previous efforts in the field. A feeble
wrap-around in which neither participant emits a
double entendre above the level of a party-cracker
one-liner encases three stories of uniformly dire
quality. The first involves a 'shadmock' and is a
variation on the French fairytale 'Beauty and the
Beast', the second is a woefully unfunny parody
about a squad of vampire-hunters called the Bleeney
(a pun on 'Sweeney', for Sweeney Todd – Flying
Squad), while the third concerns a horror film
director who finds himself trapped in a village
populated entirely by ghouls.

Hammered out by director Roy Ward Baker at a prodigious pace which precluded the creation of atmosphere, *The Monster Club* was a sad and sorry 'welcome home' party for Vincent Price after six years at sea. "Vampires who sup; Ghouls who tear; Mocks who blow; Shadmocks who whistle," teased the sleeve-blurb on the original novel. When it was redesigned to tie in with the release of the film, it neglected to add "Adaptations that suck."

Embroiled in the travesty were Donald Pleasence, Richard Johnson, Stuart Whitman, Britt Ekland and Patrick Magee, all of them appearing acutely embarrassed and none, bar Johnson, able to muster so much as a modicum of enthusiasm for the impoverished proceedings in hand, let alone a performance. The film was miscalculated on all fronts and initially received an 'AA' certificate in the UK. This restricted its potential audience of children under four to teenagers of 14 and over, but a protest from the distributor resulted in minor trims and the granting of an 'A' for Advisory, which reacquainted it with the audience Subotsky originally had in mind.

Price is called upon only to wax expansive about the menagerie of monsters while Carradine looks uncomprehendingly on, and one-time British matinée idol Anthony Steel turns in a cameo as "vampire film producer Lintom Busotsky" that is strictly from hunger. This was the Amicus formula of old, but with the episodes interspersed by pop songs. Among the artistes were B A Robertson (whose rendition of 'I'm Just a Sucker [for your Love]' is the highlight of the movie) and sixties' chart-toppers The Pretty Things, who warble their way through '(Welcome to) The Monster Club' over the end credits as Price and a fat lady dance. The proverbial 'fat lady' had actually sung, but Vincent Price had not yet heard her.

Can we truly call this a Monster Club, if we do not boast amongst our membership a single member of the human race?
ERAMUS (VINCENT PRICE),
THE MONSTER CLUB (1980)

"Scary, but not frightening," was Price's judgment on *The Monster Club* until he saw the masks that had been prepared for its inmates, which clearly were neither. "Subotsky found a milkman who had a hobby of making masks," he opined more candidly after the event. "They were terrible, just terrible... like amateur night."

Grade's company collapsed soon after the film was completed, and consequently the film failed to find a distributor in the all-important US market. Subotsky had produced his last horror and he returned to suing his erstwhile partner in the New York Supreme Court for his share of the profits on a number of their previous features together, in answer to which Rosenberg took out a counterclaim for libel in the London law courts. Subotsky had no such problems over the profits from *The Monster Club*, however, given that there would be none to dispute.

After *The Monster Club*, Price continued to tour in a scaled-down version of his hit one-man show *Diversions and Delights*, and the following year he took over from Gene Shalit as host of the PBS (Public Broadcasting Service) series *Mystery!*, which served as a showcase for British genre offerings and came graced with credit titles and set designs by Edward Gorey, the writer and illustrator who had been responsible for the decor of Frank Langella's Broadway stage success as *Dracula* in 1977. Coral Browne, in the meantime, prepared to play herself in Alan Bennett's *An Englishman Abroad*, a BBC telefilm to be directed by John Schlesinger and recounting her 1958 meeting in Moscow with Cold War spy Guy Burgess.

Price's stint on *Mystery!* was eventually to run for eight years and provided the actor with one of the happiest and most easy-going working environments of his last decade. "It's a wonderful way to end your career, with something really top-notch," he would subsequently say of the show. "All the great mystery writers are English. I think the English do it better than we do – ours are full of car chases."

He had no sooner started work on the series when a young Disney artist named Tim Burton asked him if he would consider narrating a six-minute stop-motion 'short' which he proposed to direct about the inner life of a little boy obsessed with the grim iconography of Edgar Allan Poe as depicted in the films of Vincent Price. Its title was *Vincent*, and it was designed as an homage to the man himself.

Vincent Malloy is seven years old.
He's always polite and does what he's told.
For a boy his age, he's considerate and nice,
But he wants to be just like Vincent Price.
OPENING NARRATION (VINCENT PRICE),
VINCENT (1982)

Price readily agreed to Burton's proposal, and *Vincent* was shot off-lot at a cost of $60,000, with Rick Heinrichs producing. Price recorded his narration in December 1981, before the animation was begun, and remarked that he found it "flattering to be the subject of a Disney film." Burton's experimental short was made before the radical changes in the company that came about during the reign of Michael Eisner and, as a result, *Vincent* received little exposure. But it helped pave the way for Price to voice Professor Ratigan in *The Great Mouse Detective*, a feature-length cartoon which Disney made five years later.

If *Vincent* has a failing, it is its lack of an appropriate resolution, a persistent flaw which would continue to afflict Burton's work when he progressed to bigger things. But the film is stylish and witty and, above all, stylistically original, and again Price had been singled out as the inspiration of a new generation of young creative artists.

Price followed his gracious stint on *Vincent* with *House of the Long Shadows*, ostensibly to play alongside Christopher Lee, Peter Cushing and John Carradine (again). There was no good reason for him to appear in a film which proposed to make over a 1913 stage play by George M Cohan, which had itself been adapted from a novel entitled *Seven Keys to Baldpate* and written that same year by Earl Derr Biggers, the creator of Charlie Chan. But Price came up with one: "I decided to do it because it was a return to the old style of horror ... I've been in this business for almost 50 years and a project has to be right for me now. Fun, interesting, and scary!"

The play had previously been filmed a total of five times and revolves around a writer named William Magee, who has 24 hours in which to complete a novel. He secretes himself in a resort hotel that is closed for the winter, assured that he has the only key, but is mortified to find the place plagued by a series of unwelcome guests, all of whom have their own 'key' to Baldpate Inn and their own reason for having used it. In Biggers' typically tongue-in-cheek style, all is ultimately revealed to be a hoax, and so appealing was this highly theatrical twist-in-the-tale that the play was hugely successful and made Biggers and Cohan small fortunes. Succeeding film versions altered the setting to that of the more melodramatic 'old dark house', but the essentials of the story remained unchanged.

Be that as it may, *Seven Keys to Baldpate* was an old warhorse whose effects depended on stagecraft and sleight-of-hand, and whose success had been predicated on the willingness of its audiences to suspend disbelief in a less sophisticated age. None of this could bode well for a 'new' version of Cohan's play, and the cast of participants assembled behind the scenes in the *House of the Long Shadows* were every bit as inauspicious.

The film was shot by open-top Bentley-driving independent producer-director Pete Walker, a latecomer on the genre scene who had carved a niche for himself in the early seventies with a series of exploitational horrors whose chief attributes were cheapness of production and accent on gratuitous scenes of sex and sadism – *House of Whipcord*, *Frightmare* (both 1974), *House of Mortal Sin* (aka *The Confessional*; 1975) – all of them scripted by David McGillivray, and most of them featuring a matriarch from Hell in the corseted form of Sheila Keith. Walker had inveigled fading crooner Jack Jones into starring in *The Comeback* (1977) and, at something of a hiatus in all their careers, he finally pulled off the casting coup that neither AIP, Amicus nor anyone else had managed to achieve, which was to have Price, Cushing and Lee (accompanied by Carradine) act *together* in the same film.

Walker had been inactive on the exploitation front since the less-than-successful Jones vehicle of 1977, but a bad penny is said always to turn up. His regular writer did not, however, and McGillivray was replaced for the occasion by Michael Armstrong, a one-time contributor to *Films and Filming* and author of an article entitled 'Some Like it Chilled!' which had disparaged the genre. Putting his talent where his mouth had been, he later contributed his own low-brow additions to it: *The Haunted House of Horror* for Tigon/AIP (1969) and the banned *Witchfinder General* clone, *Mark of the Devil* (1970).

House of the Long Shadows was produced by the Cannon Films team of Golan-Globus – the Golan half of which had once been a Corman alumnus, cutting his cinematic teeth on *The Young Racers* (1963). The Israeli cousins also specialised in downmarket fare, from the teen sex-comedy *Lemon Popsicle* (1977) to the violent vigilante thrillers which put new spring into the ageing steps of Charles Bronson after *Death Wish* (1974; Cannon made three sequels to the Paramount-produced original). Cannon's love for low budgets matched that of Walker's so, once the cast had been given their pay cheques, there was little money left for anything else and the film was shot entirely on location at Rotherfield Park, at East Tisted in Hampshire.

John Carradine, Sheila Keith, Peter Cushing and Vincent Price in a publicity shot for HOUSE OF THE LONG SHADOWS

The plot of *House of the Long Shadows* was as creaky as most of those hired to act it out. Its value as exploitation lay in the teaming of its arthritic leads but, as *The Monster Club* had shown, that in itself could no longer guarantee box-office success. *The Monster Club* had effectively brought an end to Milton Subotsky's filmmaking career, and *House of the Long Shadows* was to perform a similar service to those of Pete Walker, Peter Cushing and Vincent Price. Only Lee and Carradine survived the affair to scare another day. Cushing retired to his cottage in Whitstable, and Price to his voice-overs and the stability of a long-term contract as the elegant host of *Mystery!*

> *I have returned.*
>
> LIONEL GRISBANE (VINCENT PRICE),
> *HOUSE OF THE LONG SHADOWS* (1982)

In addition to its cast of Gothic grandees, Price found himself teamed in *House of the Long Shadows* with Desi Arnaz Jr, whom he had last encountered when he guested on his mother Lucille Ball's long-running sitcom in 1970. Arnaz plays Magee, who bets his publisher that he can write a novel in 24 hours if

he is given the peace and solitude so to do. Off he trots to the allocated Baldpate Manor in Wales and, within the space of a couple of reels, finds it busier than Euston Station at rush hour. The uninvited guests (Price, Cushing, Carradine and Keith) all turn out to be members of the Grisbane family, the former owners of the manor, who have convened to free the fifth of their number – a murderous madman named Roderick – from 40 years of enforced confinement in the attic. Christopher Lee is the odd one out, telling the assembly that he dropped by because he thought that he saw a light on (a likely story).

In a timely revision to the plot of James Whale's *The Old Dark House* (1932), which *House of the Long Shadows* shamelessly pilfers, the madman does not escape – he already *has*. And it is, of course, Lee, who then disposes of the rest of his family with a variety of ligatures, but takes an axe to Price before becoming impaled on it himself. Or is he? – No sooner has the last drop of blood dried than all are up and about again, announcing themselves as actors and the whole set-up as an emotional rollercoaster designed not to prevent Magee from winning the bet but to convince him to put more feeling into his books. (This from a publisher who runs a Bentley on his cut of them!) Magee takes the moral to heart and polishes off a brilliant prose-poem in the few hours that remain to him.

The plot of the film is preposterous from the outset. Even Charles Hamilton (who as Frank Richards created 'Billy Bunter'), the most prolific popular author in English letters, 'only' wrote at a speed of 5,000 words a day, which is barely enough to complete a contemporary novel in a matter of weeks, let alone have the prescribed 24 hours interrupted by a bevy of bozos intent on resurrecting a family feud in between the lines. Writer Michael Armstrong makes his own disdain for art (and audience) all too plain. "Anyone can write one of those things," he has Magee say of Brönte's *Wuthering Heights* before proceeding to show how things should be done: "It's a cursed place," Norman Rossington's stationmaster says inventively of Baldpate Manor.

Viewers who had apprised themselves of the cast list before entering the theatre would not surprisingly have expected each of the four leads to make an entrance; they do so individually, and throughout much of the first half of the film, so no suspense is generated and the ponderous events remain singularly inexplicable until the plot starts eventually to unfold. Some of the staging in the last reel is luridly effective and the stars essay their respective roles with gusto, but none of this is compensation for the fact that the story is a con trick which held considerable appeal for audiences in 1913 but was felt to be arcane and annoying by the more sophisticated filmgoers of 1983. One of the 'cast' comments at the close that her make-up has taken "nearly an hour to get off," yet it apparently took only a matter of seconds to apply when she was seen to enact her death scene earlier in the film.

The moral of the tale within a tale is that the whole charade has been staged in order that its benighted author might learn to adopt a more empathetic approach to his work, rather than just churning out words for the money. Even in its rudimentary depiction of the publishing industry, *House of the Long Shadows* was well wide of the mark.

> *There is no escape. Our fate was decided long ago. The old order is gone forever, and now we too must crumble into dust.*
> **Lionel Grisbane** (**Vincent Price**), *House of the Long Shadows* (1982)

House of the Long Shadows did, however, signify one milestone in the history of the horror film. Alone among his contemporaries, Price had now played opposite all of the great names in the genre since the 1930s, with the exception of Lugosi: Karloff, Carradine, Lorre, Steele, Rathbone, Lee and Cushing. He had played opposite a number of lesser ones along the way, but if one name straddled horror cinema in its post-war incarnation, and for more than 30 years, it was that of Vincent Price. He had done it all, and it had now done for him. The character of Lionel Grisbane in *House of the Long Shadows* was Price's last starring role in a horror film. It was hardly a fitting tribute, but he had at least been in good company.

> Sinister Man: *The Master returns tonight.*
> Blind Man: *How shall we recognise him?*
> Sinister Man: *You'll know him when you see him, stupid.*
> **Vincent Price** and **Graham Stark**, *Bloodbath at the House of Death* (1983)

The following year, Price made another 'House' call. *Bloodbath at the House of Death* was the big-screen debut of Liverpudlian deejay-turned-surrealist comedian Kenny Everett. Everett's long-running TV shows, whether for Thames Television or, later, the BBC, were hugely popular, often hilarious and groundbreaking in many ways – not least for their comic creations of Sid Snot and Cupid Stunt and erotic dance interludes by 'Hot Gossip.'

Bloodbath at the House of Death was a predictable lampoon of the genre. Directed by Ray Cameron and written by himself and Barry Cryer, the creative team behind the TV shows, the film is funny and inventive, if somewhat ponderous in execution. The mass murder of 18 people at Headstone Manor becomes the subject of a research trip by a motley crew of psychic investigators led by Lucas Manderville (Everett). Cue a series of extended sketches of variable quality, held together by the premise of a spooky old mansion and a nearby village occupied by devil worshippers intent on repeating the previous murder-spree on the new tenants.

Price's contribution came down to three (lengthy) scenes. As the 700-year-old Sinister Man, leader of the Satanic coven, he is basically required to do his Vincent Price act – all grandiose gestures and verbal eloquence, with the appendix that his oratorical

BLOODBATH
AT THE HOUSE
OF DEATH

flourishes invariably end in four-letter outbursts. Two out of the three are in the style of the TV shows and the best of them is a straight lift from *Monty Python's Life of Brian* (1979), in which Price chants a liturgy while his followers repeat each line. "Oh, shit – my hand," he blurts out, as candle-wax runs down his arm. "Oh, shit – my hand," his disciples echo in unison.

The cast list is populated by a host of well-known comic faces, all ruthlessly engaging with as many sacred cows as the screenwriters can herd together (not many). Pamela Stephenson, as Manderville's assistant, appears in her *Not the Nine O'Clock News* guise and Cleo Rocos is imported direct from Everett's TV show to repeat her role as busty foil for his leering asides. When she asks to be passed a knife, the alternative utensil is offered: "I suppose a fork's out of the question?" her companion enquires. "Not necessarily, but let's have dinner first," she replies.

Among the targets for some over-obvious satire are *Carrie*, *The Legend of Hell House* (after Stephenson is groped by an invisible presence, they share a post-coital cigarette) and *Alien*, but Everett himself

is strait-jacketed by a script which allots him only one character on which to indulge his comic creativity. Price gives his all to the proceedings, but he is plainly out of place among the sea of intrinsically British faces, and the (mild) expletives sit uncomfortably on his lips, at least as far as his public persona was concerned.

Sending up the horror film always seems to be easier than it turns out, and *Bloodbath at the House of Death* was no exception. Its nods to well-known movies are laboured, and its last reel almost lays the comedy aside to pursue what its makers had clearly wanted to do to begin with, which was turn out a real horror film. Nevertheless, it remains a cut above the average vehicle designed to transfer a household name from the small screen to the large.

Everett died from an AIDS-related illness in 1995 at the age of 50, thus depriving the world of comedy of one of its most inventive talents. Vincent Price's stately demeanour in the face of artistic adversity extricated him intact from *Bloodbath at the House of Death*, but only just. His next appearance in the genre would not now come for another three years.

DARKNESS FALLS

One is never too old for nightmares...
JULIAN WHITE (VINCENT PRICE),
THE OFFSPRING (1986)

In 1984, Vincent Price was asked to provide a 'rap' for the title track of a record album that its creator confidently expected would become the biggest seller in pop music history. Michael Jackson, formerly of The Jackson Five, had recently leapt to super-stardom when a bravura performance of his chart-hit 'Billie Jean' during a 25th Anniversary Special for Motown Records introduced 'moon-walking' to the world, and he now intended to consolidate his new-found position as King of Pop with a record-breaking album.

The familiar Price delivery was required for a monologue which was to feature over a long instrumental break in 'Thriller', his contribution carrying over into the accompanying video as well – a 14-minute monster-filled epic, directed by John Landis of *The Blues Brothers* (1980) and, pertinent to the task in hand, *An American Werewolf in London* (1981). Price was paid his usual fee for the job, with no offer of profit-participation. The album went on to sell as its maker had privately predicted, in excess of 50 million copies worldwide.

Price was typically philosophical about this outcome, and a deputation of Jackson's siblings duly presented him with a gold album. But if financial security had long been his goal, then he had just missed out on the best opportunity he ever had to secure it. When the singer later made an extraordinary out-of-court settlement to the family of a young boy with whom he was alleged to have had sexual relations, Price wryly remarked to daughter Victoria: "*I was fucked by Michael Jackson – and I didn't even get paid for it.*"

Price *was* paid for his contribution to the horror anthology *From a Whisper to a Scream*, the linking narrative for which he shot over two days in April 1986, though the graphic gore of the late 1980s was not to his liking. "I'm frankly worried. I'm afraid they might have gone too far," he confided to a columnist after the event.

Price had based his assessment on the second of a quartet of pre-completed tales, which the film's director, 23-year-old Jeff Burr, had screened for him to encourage his participation in the project. This second story was the mildest of the four, so Burr had shown shrewd judgment in choosing it. A small-time hood named Jesse Hardwick (Terry Kiser) finds himself holed up in a Louisiana backwater with a practitioner of voodoo who has discovered the secret of eternal life. He drowns his host in an attempt to prise the secret from him, but the man cannot be killed and returns from the swamp to take his revenge. Hardwick is granted the immortality he seeks, but only after being chopped to pieces with an axe; he is then forced to live out the rest of his days as a limbless torso. The tale was moody, suspenseful and well-made – sufficiently so for Price to agree to carry the can for all four.

Lovecraft and Poe... Well, I'll drink to those two masters of horror. You know, their monsters and demons existed only in their brains until they were able to get them out on paper. Here, they walk in the parks by day and in the streets by night.
JULIAN WHITE (VINCENT PRICE),
THE OFFSPRING (1986)

The film was ultimately released as *The Offspring* – the title being derived from the opening segment of the compendium, which involved the demonic progeny of necrophilic rape, with an excellent Clu Gulager as the psychopathic clerk who fantasises about a female co-worker. The second and third instalments were both tales of voodoo, the latter borrowing from Tod Browning's *Freaks* in its story of a carnival 'glass-eater' whose body is made to forcibly disgorge its non-digestible contents on the vindictive whim of the *obea* priestess who owns the show. The last episode was a Civil War tale featuring Cameron Mitchell, looking not a day older than he did when he was riding the range of *The High Chaparral* 20 years before, in which a community of orphaned children band together to rid themselves of the 'big people' who were instrumental in bringing about their plight in the first place.

The connecting link in this collection of tales was the fictitious town of Oldfield, Tennessee, and Price featured in the wrap-around story as librarian Julian White, who regales an inquisitive journalist with the foregoing examples of the foul deeds which have been generated by the town over the years. "It's as though the very foundation of this place was human suffering," he opines to the sceptical Beth Chandler (Susan Tyrrell). True to form, the situation is reversed at the climax and the fraudulent reporter also has murder in mind. With a flick-knife suddenly embedded in his throat but his tongue in his cheek, White expires with the words, "Welcome to Oldfield."

All the stories which made up *The Offspring* are gore-stained though admirably restrained in their telling, and the other excesses of low-budget film-making – nudity and bad language – are employed sparingly and with discretion. Even so, Price was more than usually concerned about the quality of the product in which he had agreed to appear.

Having gained the actor's consent, Burr and his two co-writers had redrafted their original to enlarge upon Price's role, thinking that they could turn their debut feature into something more substantial with the Price name attached to it. The attempt was greeted with hostility, however, and they were forced to revert the script to the previously agreed draft. "I figure after all these years, I have earned the right to throw my weight around," Price telegraphed his agent. "I know why people want me. I have the name and the reputation, so I figure I should have a say in the way my parts are written."

It is a pity, in many ways, that Price had waited so long to exercise his *droit de seigneur*, then chose to misdirect it onto a team of young filmmakers who were clearly up to speed with what was happening around them, showed more talent and invention than many of those with whom Price had worked in former years and had merely felt that the presence of the great man would be an honour both for them and their film. But age and infirmity were catching up with Vincent Price, and with them a retreat into rigid precepts and the bitterness which comes from yearning for another time and another place.

THE OFFSPRING

Filming **THE OFFSPRING**

While locked in combat with the director over the script of *The Offspring*, Price was himself confronted by an inquisitive journalist who asked for his views about horror films. "I've made a very successful career out of doing them," he replied. "I'm bored talking about it. I'm too old. And they aren't horror films. Edgar Allan Poe is the major short story writer of America. He did not write horror stories; he wrote psychological Gothic tales. Do you ask Al Pacino how he likes doing gangster roles? I'm bored talking about it."

If Price had contemplated more of these cameos in his declining years and had played up to a public image which was now irrevocable, as Boris Karloff did uncomplainingly to the end, he could only have enlarged upon the affection that his legions of fans already felt for him. He thought too late to fight the inevitable, and thus his final appearances in the kinds of roles for which he was already revered were few and far between.

Vincent Price did little to be ashamed of by appearing in *The Offspring*. Any contrition that he may have felt would have been better exercised at an earlier stage, over his affiliations with the likes of Albert Zugsmith, Robert Lippert or Harry Alan Towers.

The Offspring went straight to video, but this fate is not a true indicator of its merits. Price, while frail, gives a commanding performance as White, reading from a good script which gives him a number of lines to savour. His inhibitions about the film seem to come across in a harder edge to his character, but it suits the sombre mood of the piece. On the other

hand, his demeanour in relation to the project might have had more to do with the fact that his marriage to Coral Browne was going through a 'bad patch', his wife having discovered that Price had been having an affair – though whether with a woman or a man went unascertained. Either way, it was soon terminated and relations between the couple returned to normal in due course.

Price's decision to turn his back on the cinema brought about a transformation of his image that was worthy of Edgar Allan Poe himself. In screen terms, Price aged quickly. The thick-set and imposing Vincent Price of the latterday AIP films was still in evidence in what amounted to little more than a cameo in *The Monster Club*, but by the time he reappeared in the appositely titled *House of the Long Shadows* he had become visibly gaunt. Further abdications from the medium only increased the impression of frailty and decline whenever he opted to put his head above the parapet, and when he essayed the role of a Russian count in *The Whales of August* (1987), along with Bette Davis and Lillian Gish, it looked as though all three had been contemporaries of one another, whereas, in reality, Gish and Davis both belonged on an earlier page of Hollywood's book than Price himself. Nevertheless, he received rave reviews for his relatively minor contribution from critics who had forgotten that there had been another Vincent Price before *House of Wax* and that, in truth, he had always been able to act the pants off his co-stars when he had *wanted* to.

Towards the end of 1987, Price shot a three-day cameo for a 'zombie' gore-fest called *Dead Heat*, starring Treat Williams and Joe Piscopo, in which he played the billionaire financier of a process to revivify the dead. His appearances were confined to the first reel and the last, when his character is revealed to be a beneficiary of his own miraculous medical breakthrough. After a short cruise on completion of the film, Price was himself in receipt of medical breakthroughs, though with less beneficial effects: he was required to undergo thyroid treatment, and he had a pacemaker installed to regulate a weakening heart. In addition, he was increasingly afflicted by the arthritis which had crippled his father – and Boris Karloff – before him. "I see him 'leaving' me day by day," Browne wrote at the time. "He fell apart so suddenly."

By 1990, Tim Burton had advanced from animator for Disney to fully fledged film director, with *Pee*

Johnny Depp
and Vincent
Price in
EDWARD
SCISSORHANDS

Wee's Big Adventure (1985), *Beetlejuice* (1988) and the megabucks comic-strip caper of *Batman* (1989) among his credits. After gallivanting in Gotham City, Burton had decided on a return to the homespun whimsy of *Beetlejuice* with another suburban fantasy entitled *Edward Scissorhands*, in which existed the small role of a Gepetto-like inventor of mechanical marvels. Given Burton's self-confessed adoration of Price, there had been no debate about whom he had wanted to play the part: "His cameo had a real emotional content," Burton explained of his decision. "He was in the first film I ever made and was so supportive of it and me. He's an amazing guy, and I got through my childhood watching his movies."

> *I know it's a little early for Christmas, Edward, but... I have a present for you.*
> LAST WORDS OF **THE INVENTOR** (VINCENT
> PRICE), *EDWARD SCISSORHANDS* (1989)

Vincent Price's last film role was a poignant affair, with his name well down the cast list as 'The Inventor' of a bio-mechanical man with scissors for hands. The aged inventor drops dead before he has time to replace the temporary appendages with something more appropriate; thus Burton's Gothic

fable is set in motion, and Edward finds himself thrust into the big wide world as an innocent at large, with a particularly unusual affliction.

Edward Scissorhands owes its central image of a man with scissors for hands to the wicked Tailor in Heinrich Hoffman's *Struwwelpeter* (1845), a bogeyman who threatened to snip off the thumbs of little boys who insisted on sucking them. Hoffman's tale was intended to be a parody of the political correctness of the children's fables of his day, though his creations soon joined the ranks of the very bogeys he had sought to satirise when the ironies in them were lost on a readership less sophisticated than he. A similar lack of irony afflicts Burton's film, which is an uneasy mix of hometown whimsy and dark fantasy, as emphasised by the contrast between the real-life Florida location of Edward's adventures in Smalltown USA and the Gothic castle on a hill by which it is supposedly overlooked.

That failing apart, *Edward Scissorhands* is a highly personal statement on the plight of the 'outsider' or nonconformist, who initially is greeted with indulgence by the community before ultimately being cast out, his eccentricity and otherness having become too extreme to be tolerated by a populace whose sense of communal well-being is marked by passive acceptance and consensual mundanity.

Director Tim Burton, Vincent Price and Johnny Depp on the set of EDWARD SCISSORHANDS

The film makes a mawkish plea for tolerance, but its young director's sympathies clearly lie within the brooding atmosphere of the keep, as he literally paints the sterile suburban scenery below it with a bland brush and more jaded point-of-view, allowing Edward alone to carry the creative impulse for artists everywhere. Burton's flair for imaginative imagery is typical of one who spent his formative years in Hollywood at the Disney studios in Burbank, but it allows the narrative pace of *Edward Scissorhands* to slacken dramatically and its dialogue to be thrown to the four winds. It is never explained why Edward's Inventor should have chosen to provide him with scissors for hands in the first place (other than as the means by which to ingratiate himself with the local matriarchs by first manicuring their hedges and then their hair), nor how he managed to contrive the transition from pastry-making to the manufacture of proxy humans – but this is Grimm territory, so these matter little in context.

Burton, like his contemporary David Lynch, is an original filmmaker of inventiveness and vision, but he is also Jekyll to Lynch's Hyde. *Edward Scissorhands* is saccharine-sweet, a point underlined by Danny Elfman's over-romanticised score. The downbeat ending of the film is depressing and unsatisfactory, a trait which would afflict other entries in Burton's oeuvre in years to come, but even that is not enough to waft away the overpowering odour of flowers in bloom that pervades the drama from beginning to end.

Vincent Price, now in the grip of the Parkinson's disease which would contribute to his final exit three years on, has but few scenes, all of them portrayed in flashback. He is tragically frail, walking with the aid of a stick, and the famous voice has finally lost its timbre. Still, he manages to put a twinkle in his pained eyes as he gazes in awe upon his Pinnocchio-like creation. When he eventually expires in a huge close-up, as though bidding silent farewell both to his proxy son and to his audience at large, Edward leans over and caresses his pallid face with bladed fingers, which leave a trail of blood across the old man's cheek. It is an unsettling metaphor, because its juxtaposition serves to remind one of just how bloodless Price's own horror films had been and how, through all his years as the king of screen terror, he had managed to induce his delightful frights without having to resort to the cheap trick of gore galore. By 1990, however, blood was already thought of as sufficient in itself to horrify an audience, where skill and imagination had once served instead.

Boris Karloff had always been considered the grand old man of horror, but with his death in 1969, the mantle Karloff had worn so gracefully and for so long passed to Vincent Price.

Unlike his predecessor, however, Price had not induced Fright in his films by attempting to evoke it, rather he had done so by the *exhibition* of it. Dominated throughout his life by strong women (beginning with his mother), prone to the company of like-minded men, he had always been non-confrontational to a fault. His particular brand of bemused terror was as reflective of the actor as it was of the characters whom he came to play on screen. Also like Karloff, Price was a gentle man as well as a gentleman, though a more cosseted home life as a child and the early success of his Broadway years deprived him of the steely reserves that Karloff could bring to bear to get his own way.

Vincent Price's mastery of his craft can be evidenced throughout the Poe series. On the face of it, and by critical consent, he effectively played the same character in all the Corman films, and there is more than a touch of Roderick Usher in *The Tomb of Ligeia*'s Verden Fell, just as an echo of Nicholas Medina surfaces in the character of Locke in the *Morella* episode of *Tales of Terror*. But the others – Fortunato, Erasmus Craven, Prince Prospero, M. Valdemar, Charles Dexter Ward, Joseph Curwen – are each distinctive in their own way.

On screen and off, Price was at his best reacting to events, rather than initiating them; he played few real monsters in truth – Professor Jarrod in *House of Wax*; Sebastian Medina in *Pit and the Pendulum* – preferring to confine himself to the psychological arena with which he felt most comfortable, as the victim of circumstance, plagued by doubt and finding refuge in times past. He was often referred to as a Renaissance man; he could as easily have been considered a man out of time.

Price remains to this day well thought-of by those who knew him – no mean achievement in itself. He was that rare commodity in Hollywood: a man of infinite talents. In many ways, that was the mark of him; his horror films were but a single strand. As Oscar Wilde once said of himself, so might Vincent Price had he not lacked the playwright's consummate immodesty – "I put my talent into my work, but my genius into my life."

Prior to the making of *Dragonwyck* in 1945, Price had not fully understood the character of Nicholas Van Ryn as written and found himself unable to empathise with the man's overriding instinct for self-preservation at all costs. Only when he rooted the cause of Van Ryn's actions in *fear* did he manage to find an interpretation of the patroon which he felt he could carry off with a degree of success; only in Van Ryn's terror at the prospect of losing all he had gained could he comprehend the reasons for him behaving as he did. Later in life, Price came to appreciate the contradictions in play in Nicholas Van Ryn only too well.

Refuge from the ravages of existence took many forms for Price, from his obsessive love of art and habitual escapes to foreign climes, through his workaholism, drinking bouts and sexual uncertainty, to the outwardly effervescent persona which cloaked a more private and thoughtful individual beneath. His chosen career was often derailed by character traits which encouraged him to make decisions that were at odds with his best interests as a performer but which inured him financially against the slings and arrows of artistic fortune. He ultimately regretted the fact that he had often opted for expediency in the face of an unpredictable profession. "I'm Welsh," he once remarked, "and the Celtic twilight sometimes descends at odd moments." (Price was of Welsh descent on his father's side, and his wife Mary had also been born in the valleys.)

Price had earned his reputation through sheer hard work and prolific public appearances in his 50-year career, not through shrewd negotiation or the ability to capitalise on a star name; on the contrary, he had allowed his name and his hard-earned fame to be attached to too many projects which benefited others beside himself. For every Tim Burton with a genuine love and affection for what the Price name stood for, there had been a half-dozen Sam Arkoffs ready to pimp off his talents for a fast buck. If ever he felt that he had sold his soul to the Devil by signing that oath of loyalty back in 1954, then he undoubtedly had paid the price.

Vincent Price was an icon – the pre-eminent star in the Horror Hall of Fame. Whenever he was asked what were his personal favourites among his many film appearances, however, he would invariably hark back to *Laura*, or *Champagne for Caesar*, or *The Baron of Arizona*. A kind word might occasionally be advanced for *Master of the World* or even *Theatre of Blood*, but the rest were anecdotes, oft-told and endlessly re-heated. His legacy endures in the hearts of his fans, but the success that he had sought in the theatrical mainstream eluded him after *House of Wax*. The anxieties that he had felt over money and his prospects of employment within the industry had encouraged him to accept parts that no actor of his stature should reasonably have contemplated; their cumulative effect was to instil a public image that he professed to enjoy but which left him professionally unfulfilled. "How do I make a living in it when it dies in my arms at each embrace," he had said of the vagaries of his profession. Price put a brave face on what amounted to failure by his own standards, channelling his energies instead into a diverse array of alternative pursuits in the hope of recognition on another front.

The gulf between public affability and private angst was one of the inherent contradictions in a man who preferred shepherd's pie or the wares of hot-dog wagons and barbecue stands to the "tostado with tortillas, beans and avocado" which he had advertised for Sun Giant, and who was as likely to finish off a meal with bread-and-butter pudding than a "raisin party dessert with ladyfingers".

Vincent Price was often all things to all men; at least, he tried to be. But behind the urbane image and carefully cultivated veneer of self-possession was another man that few saw, who better exemplified the Price of fame. "He was so frightened. He seemed to me to be a man out of control of his life," his son observed. "He was constantly complaining that he was being forced to do things, that things that looked like opportunities were not really opportunities, and although he really tried to doctor it up and laugh it off, it used to seem to me that he never was doing what he ought to be doing. But I don't think he *knew* what he ought to be doing." For Vincent Price, 'the art of fear' was not so easy to master in life as it always appeared to be on the screen.

Coral Browne died of cancer in May 1991, barely a year after film director and friend John Schlesinger had shot a documentary about her life called *Caviar to the General*. Price himself died on 25 October 1993, from lung cancer and complications brought on by the

Parkinson's disease which had struck him in the late 1980s; he was 82 years old. A documentary on *his* life, called *A Visit with Vincent* and shot by Tim Burton, is as yet uncompleted.

Vincent Price had been diarist, playwright, author, lecturer, broadcaster, connoisseur, cook, collector, traveller, authority, advocate, ambassador and actor. He had lived many lives. Many of those lives live after him, in books, on audio and videotapes, and day and night on television stations throughout the world. He has been immortalised by his own talent. He lives still – and through him, so do we.

ENCORE

In 1999, producers Robert Zemeckis and Joel Silver formed Dark Castle Entertainment. The new company's inaugural project was a remake of William Castle's *House on Haunted Hill*, on which his 41-year-old daughter Terry acted as a co-producer. The film retained the premise of the original, upping the ante to $1 million, but it switched the setting to a real haunted house of spectacular proportions and abandoned Robb White's plot in favour of a roller-coaster ride into the extremes of graphic gore.

The Frederick Loren character in this high-octane spook-fest was renamed Stephen Price and was

played with pencil-thin moustache by Oscar-winner Geoffrey Rush. Part of the climax to *House on Haunted Hill* was an homage to the famous scene in *Pit and the Pendulum* where a spent Nicholas Medina finds himself at the mercy of his taunting wife, only this time it is Rush who grabs Famke Janssen around the throat before announcing, "I'm going to murder you, Evelyn – with the greatest of pleasure."

For all the changes which were applied to the storyline of *House on Haunted Hill* in keeping with modern tastes, as well as the changes to the style and substance of horror cinema which had taken place since the days of Vincent Price, it was nevertheless an indication of how iconic the original films – and their star – had become in the intervening years.

The end credits of *House on Haunted Hill* were accompanied by a creepy rendition of Annie Lennox and Dave Stewart's 'Sweet Dreams (are Made of This),' performed by Marilyn Manson. All things considered, it seemed entirely fitting.

Geoffrey Rush in the remake of HOUSE ON HAUNTED HILL

This is not only one man – this is the father of those who shall be fathers in their turns;
In him the start of populous states and rich republics;
Of him countless immortal lives, with countless embodiments and enjoyments.

WALT WHITMAN,
I SING THE BODY ELECTRIC
(VINCENT PRICE'S FAVOURITE POEM)

AFTERWORD

British advertisement for THE FALL OF THE HOUSE OF USHER

Although Vincent Price's career encompassed a wide range of roles which, taken as a whole, show his mastery of both tragedy and comedy, he is perhaps most popularly known as an icon of the horror film.

As a young producer-director, I had the good fortune to work with him on a number of the Edgar Allan Poe-based movies that I made between 1960 and 1964, and I experienced at first hand the unique qualities Vincent Price brought to his roles in horror movies.

When I set out to make *The Fall of the House of Usher*, I knew that I very much wanted Vincent Price to play the leading role. He was a first-rate actor and handsome leading man with a distinguished career, and I believed he would bring intelligence, intensity and cultural refinement to the role of Roderick Usher. I wanted the audience to fear him – but not on the conscious, physical level that they fear a monster. Vincent Price gave me exactly what I wanted and what Richard Matheson's well-crafted, literate script suggested: a man with a brilliant but tormented mind that works on a register beyond that of ordinary men and thus inspires a deeper fear. A big part of Vincent Price's genius was his ability to portray a man trying to keep his inner demons in check.

Vincent knew and admired Poe's tales and poems, and understood my approach to making the movies based on them – which was that Poe's world was, to a large extent, the world of the unconscious. In addition, as an art aficionado, Vincent took a great interest in helping to select a painter to create the expressionistic portraits of the Usher ancestors.

Vincent Price was the consummate professional: he had been classically trained, and he was also well able to work with colleagues committed to 'the Method.' There wouldn't be much discussion on the set, because he and I discussed the role before shooting and worked out the major characteristics. During shooting, Vincent would prepare, but it seemed to me to be more of an internal process. Characteristically, he would sit quietly and think about it, and be ready.

Perhaps his most striking characteristic was his deep, emotional, mellifluous voice. This, together with the fact that he was highly intelligent and well-read, gave him the rare ability to deliver dialogue of a more literary, ornate style without it seeming laughable. In *The Fall of the House of Usher*, *Pit and the Pendulum*, *The Masque of the Red Death* and *The Tomb of Ligeia*, Vincent Price's voice and haunted demeanour convey the spirit of Poe.

Vincent was also a very witty man. I had convinced Samuel Arkoff and Jim Nicholson to let me make *The Fall of the House of Usher*, a departure from my previous horror films which always featured a monster, by persuading them that in this movie the house itself would become the monster. In one scene, Vincent had to utter the line, "The house lives, the house breathes." "What does that mean?" he asked, quite reasonably. "That's the line that allowed us to make this movie." "Well, fine," he said, "I suppose I can breathe some life into it then."

ROGER CORMAN
LOS ANGELES, CALIFORNIA
FEBRUARY 2003

APPENDIX

CAST AND CREDITS

The films of Vincent Price which are listed in detail in this Appendix are those that fall into the wide-ranging categories of mystery and horror. In one or two, like Universal's 1940 adaptation of Nathaniel Hawthorne's *The House of the Seven Gables*, the supernatural element is absent in the screen version but it was nevertheless present in the novel on which the film was based and therefore warrants inclusion. *Master of the World* and *The City Under the Sea* were both stories of fantasy and science fiction, while *House of a Thousand Dolls* is, by any critical criterion, a (sub) standard crime yarn – but even these were sold on the back of the Price image when it was widely perceived to stand for only one thing: horror. Consequently, they are included here also.

Films where the vocal talents of Vincent Price were appended as an afterthought (like *Spirits of the Dead*) have been excluded, the guiding principle being that any contribution was integral to original intent. Television series episodes with no bearing on the genre beyond the employment of the actor for the value of his name, or to provide a comedy cameo, have also been excluded.

Film titles given are those under which the film in question was produced, with its overseas alternative in brackets where relevant (whether it be UK or US). In all cases, credits are as they appear on the title-cards of the films themselves, with the addition of data from other sources to make them as complete as possible.

1939

TOWER OF LONDON

· CAST

Richard, Duke of Gloucester..........*Basil Rathbone*
Mord..................................*Boris Karloff*
Queen Elyzabeth............*Barbara O'Neil*
King Edward IV....................*Ian Hunter*
Duke of Clarence..............*Vincent Price*
Lady Alice Barton.....................*Nan Grey*
Tom Clink........................*Ernest Cossart*
John Wyatt..........................*John Sutton*
Lord Hastings....................*Leo G Carroll*
King Henry VI..................*Miles Mander*
Beacon............................*Lionel Belmore*
Anne Neville......................*Rose Hobart*
Boy King Edward............*Ronald Sinclair*
Young Prince Richard....................*John Herbert-Bond*
Henry Tudor.......................*Ralph Forbes*
Duchess Isobel............*Frances Robinson*
Wales.............................*G P Huntley*
Lord DeVere........................*John Rodion*
Chimney Sweep.................*Walter Tetley*
Baby Prince.................*Donnie Dunagan*
Thirsty prisoner.................*Ernie Adams*
Page boy..........................*Charles Peck*

Sexton...................................*Russ Powell*
Priests......*Francis Powers /Edgar Sherrod*
Beggar woman....................*Evelyn Selbie*
Princesses...........*Venetia Severn/Yvonne Severn/Ann Todd*
Majordomo...............*C Montague Shaw*
Anne's protector.............*Ivan F Simpson*
Forrest...............................*Jack C Smith*
Page...........................*Schuyler Standish*
Soldiers......*Arthur Stenning/Guy York Jr*
Torturer Bunch.................*Donald Stuart*
Prisoner............................*Cyril Thornton*
Civilian woman..............*Claire Whitney*
2nd gate guard..............*Richard Alexander*
Councilmen........*Holmes Herbert/Harry A Bailey/Murdock MacQuarrie/Claude Payton/Charles F Miller/Arthur Mulliner*
Sheriff..........................*Reginald Barlow*
Beggars....*Jim Mason/Merrill McCormick/Denis Tankard/David Thursby/Ted Billings/Edward Brady/Fred Farrell/Patrick J Kelly*
First gate guard..............*Stanley Blystone*
Lady in waiting...................*Louise Brien*
Cardinal.........................*Howard Brooks*
Dowager...........................*Georgia Caine*
Lady Mowbray.....................*Joan Carroll*
Woman............................*Carolyn Cooke*
Lead murderer.................*Harry Cording*

Archbishop....................*Nigel De Brulier*
Dighton.............................*Martin Faust*
Lady in waiting..................*Jean Fenwick*
Cleric.....................................*Al Ferguson*
Spy.......................................*John George*
Friar...................................*Robert Greig*
Soldier.............................*Frank Hagney*
Woman.................................*Sibyl Harris*
Haberdeer.......................*Ivo Henderson*
Soldier..................................*Colin Kenny*
Moat guard.........................*George Lloyd*
Henry VI's servant...........*Michael Mark*

· CREDITS

Directed and Produced by.........*Rowland V Lee*
Original Screenplay by........*Robert N Lee*
Music Composed by....*Ralph Freed/Hans J Salter/Frank Skinner*
Music Associate....................*Lou Forbes*
Music Arranger.................*Hans J Salter*
Musical Director...............*Charles Previn*
Orchestrations...................*Frank Skinner*
Director of Photography..............*George Robinson*
Camera Operator............*Edward Colman*
Process Photographer....*George J Teague*
Art Director.......................*Jack Otterson*
Associate.....................*Richard H Riedel*
Set Decorations.........*Russell A Gausman*

Film Editor........................*Edward Curtiss*
Sound Supervisor.........*Bernard B Brown*
Technician....................*William Hedgcock*
Asst Director............................*Fred Frank*
2nd Unit Director....................*Ford Beebe*
Make-up.....*Sam Kaufman/Otto Lederer/*
Jack P Pierce
Gowns..*Vera West*
Technical Advisors..............*Major G O T*
Bagley/Sir Gerald Grove
Fencing Master....................*Fred Cravens*
Special Effects by.............*Jack Cosgrove/*
Russell Lawson
UNIVERSAL 92 MINUTES
BLACK-AND-WHITE

THE INVISIBLE MAN RETURNS

· **CAST**

Richard Cobb.........*Sir Cedric Hardwicke*
Geoffrey Radcliffe..............*Vincent Price*
Helen Manson..........................*Nan Grey*
Doctor Frank Griffin...........*John Sutton*
Inspector Sampson..........*Cecil Kellaway*
Willie Spears........................*Alan Napier*
Ben Jenkins...................*Forrester Harvey*
Plainclothesmen.............*Jimmy Aubrey/*
Colin Kenny
Jim...*Billy Bevan*
Woman...................................*Clara Blore*
Policemen.................*Matthew Boulton/*
Edward Brady/Frank Hill
Griffin's secretary.................*Louise Brien*
Miners......*Harry Cording/George Hyde/*
Ellis Irving/George Kirby/George Lloyd/
Edmund MacDonald/Denis Tankard
Detective............................*Paul England*
Constable Briggs...................*Rex Evans*
Passerby..................................*Mary Field*
Prison governor............*Edward Fielding*
Cookie...............................*Mary Gordon*
Bill....................................*Frank Hagney*
Chauffeur......................*Leyland Hodgson*
Secretary...........................*Hugh Huntley*
Chaplain.............................*Bruce Lester*
Constable.....................*Frank O'Connor*
Clinic nurse................*Frances Robinson*
Mr Cotton......................*Ivan F Simpson*
Constable Tewsbury..........*Harry Stubbs*
Policeman......................*Cyril Thornton*
Bob....................................*David Thursby*
Fingerprint expert................*Eric Wilton*
with *Ernie Adams/Stanley Blystone/*
Charles Brokaw/Jean Brooks/Frank
Coletti/Sidney Grayler/Barry Hays/Boyd
Irwin/William Newell/Crane Whitley
· **CREDITS**
Directed by...............................*Joe May*
Associate Producer..........*Ken Goldsmith*
Screenplay by...*Lester Cole/Kurt Siodmak*
Story by................*Joe May/Kurt Siodmak*
[A Sequel to *The Invisible Man* by
H G Wells]

Musical Director...............*Charles Previn*
Musical Score..........*Hans J Salter/Frank*
Skinner
Director of Photography...*Milton Krasner*
Art Director........................*Jack Otterson*
Associate........................*Martin Obzina*
Set Decorations.........*Russell A Gausman*
Film Editor............................*Frank Gross*
Sound Supervisor.........*Bernard B Brown*
Technician....................*William Hedgcock*
Asst Director........................*Phil Karlstein*
Gowns..*Vera West*
Special Photographic Effects.............*John*
P Fulton/David S Horsley
UNIVERSAL 82 MINUTES
BLACK-AND-WHITE

1940

THE HOUSE OF THE SEVEN GABLES

· **CAST**

Jaffrey Pyncheon.............*George Sanders*
Hepzibah Pyncheon....*Margaret Lindsay*
Clifford Pyncheon..............*Vincent Price*
Matthew Holgrave.................*Dick Foran*
Phoebe Pyncheon....................*Nan Grey*
Philip Barton...................*Cecil Kellaway*
Fuller.......................................*Alan Napier*
Gerald Pyncheon...............*Gilbert Emery*
Deacon Foster....................*Miles Mander*
Judge........................*Charles Trowbridge*
Driver......................................*Hal Budlong*
Town Gossips.......*Caroline Cooke/Martin*
Faust/Margaret Fealy/Jane Loofbourrow/
Murdock MacQuarrie
Blacksmith Hawkins.......*Harry Cording*
Man with blacksmith.......*Edward Brady*
Workman........................*Kernan Cripps*
Abigail.............................*Leigh De Lacey*
Jury foreman......................*Robert Dudley*
Mrs Foster.............................*Sibyl Harris*
Man drinking from cup.........*Ellis Irving*
Man with rake............................*P J Kelly*
Foreman.................................*Colin Kenny*
Man reading Tribune........*Michael Mark*
Coroner........................*Nelson McDowell*
Mrs Reynolds..................*Mira McKinney*
Phineas Weed....................*Edgar Norton*
Grocer/Juror.......................*Russ Powell*
Prison guard.......................*Jack C Smith*
Reverend Garrison Smith...*Hugh Sothern*
Printer..................................*Harry Stubbs*
Witness............................*Claire Whitney*
Mr Wainwright....................*Harry Woods*
· **CREDITS**
Directed by...............................*Joe May*
Associate Producer...................*Burt Kelly*
Screenplay...............................*Lester Cole*
Adaptation.......................*Harold Greene*

Based on the novel by *Nathaniel*
Hawthorne
Musical Score.....................*Frank Skinner*
Musical Director...............*Charles Previn*
Song: '*The Color of Your Eyes*'
Music by.............................*Frank Skinner*
Lyrics by..................................*Ralph Freed*
Director of Photography...*Milton Krasner*
Art Director........................*Jack Otterson*
Associate........................*Richard R Riedel*
Set Decorations................*R A Gausman*
Film Editor............................*Frank Gross*
Sound Supervisor.........*Bernard B Brown*
Technician....................*William Hedgcock*
Asst Director........................*Phil Karlson*
Gowns..*Vera West*
Dialogue Director.................*Lester Cole*
UNIVERSAL 88 MINUTES
BLACK-AND-WHITE

1945

DRAGONWYCK

· **CAST**

Miranda Wells.................*Gene Tierney*
Ephraim Wells.................*Walter Huston*
Nicholas Van Ryn..............*Vincent Price*
Dr Jeff Turner...................*Glenn Langan*
Abigail Wells........................*Anne Revere*
Magda..........................*Spring Byington*
Katrine Van Ryn...........*Connie Marshall*
Klaus Bleecker.................*Henry Morgan*
Johanna Van Ryn.........*Vivienne Osborne*
Peggy O'Malley...................*Jessica Tandy*
Elizabeth Van Borden....*Trudy Marshall*
Nurse............................*Gertrude Astor*
Farmers...........*Arthur Aylesworth/Trevor*
Bardette/Robert Baldwin/Walter
Baldwin/Clancy Cooper
Boy dancers....*Shelby Bacon/Edwin Davis*
Men......*Bill Carter/Nestor Eristoff/George*
Ford/Ted Jordan/Alexander Sascha
Dowagers...*Ruth Cherrington/Elizabeth*
Williams
French Count......................*John Chollot*
Seth Wells...........................*Jamie Dana*
Servants.........*Wally Dean/Tom Martin/*
Larry Steers/Art Thompson/Al Winters
Tom Wells...........................*Scott Elliott*
Otto Gebhardt......................*Tom Fadden*
Mrs McNab......................*Betty Fairfax*
Cornelia Van Borden..............*Ruth Ford*
Zack Wilson...............*Michael Garrison*
Messenger boy........*Robert 'Buzz' Henry*
Mr McNabb....................*Keith Hitchcock*
Farmers............*Harry Humphrey/Robert*
Malcolm/Charles Waldron
Tompkins.............................*Boyd Irwin*
Helena Vanderhyde...........*Virginia Lee*
Tabitha Wells........................*Jane Nigh*
Vendor on boat......................*Steve Olsen*

Dr Brown..........................Francis Pierlot
Head farmer.................Addison Richards
Nathaniel Wells..................Mickey Roth
Count De Grenier......Reinhold Schünzel
Astor House clerk.............Grady Sutton
Obadiah............................David Vallard
French Countess..............Nanette Vallon
Countess De Grenier....Maya Van Horn
Mayor Curtis.....................Douglas Wood

· CREDITS

Directed by.............Joseph L Mankiewicz
Produced by...........Ernst Lubitsch/Darryl
    F Zanuck
Screenplay by..........Joseph L Mankiewicz
Based on the novel by Anya Seton
Music..............................Alfred Newman
Orchestral Arrangements............Edward
    B Powell
Director of Photography......Arthur Miller
Art Direction............Lyle Wheeler/Russell
    Spencer
Set Decorations...Thomas Little/Paul S Fox
Film Editor.....................Dorothy Spencer
Sound...............W D Flick/Roger Heman
Asst Director..........F E 'Johnny' Johnston
Make-up Artist...........................Ben Nye
Costumes.............................René Hubert
Dances Staged by................Arthur Appel
Special Photographic Effects....Fred Sersen
TWENTIETH CENTURY-FOX 103 MINUTES
BLACK-AND-WHITE

1946

SHOCK

· CAST

Dr Richard Cross................Vincent Price
Elaine Jordan..........................Lynn Bari
Lt Paul Stewart...............Frank Latimore
Janet Stewart.....................Anabel Shaw
Stevens...........................Stephen Dunne
O'Neill.............................Reed Hadley
Mrs Hatfield......................Renee Carson
Dr Harvey.................Charles Trowbridge
Mr Edwards.....................John Davidson
Dr Blair...........................Selmer Jackson
Hotel Manager...................Pierre Watkin
Miss Penny.........................Mary Young
Patient.................................Cecil Weston
Hotel clerk....................Charles Tannen
Male nurse..............................Bob Adler
Nurses...Margaret Brayton/Claire Richards
Cab driver........................George E Stone
with Michael Dunne

· CREDITS

Directed by.........................Alfred Werker
Produced by...................Aubrey Schenck
Screenplay by......................Eugene Ling
Based on a story by Albert De Mond
Additional Dialogue by....Martin Berkeley
Music..............................David Buttolph

Musical Direction.............Emil Newman
Orchestral Arrangements...Arthur Morton
Directors of Photography.................Glen
    MacWilliams/Joe MacDonald
Art Direction.....Lyle Wheeler/Boris Leven
Set Decoration...................Thomas Little
Associate...............O Clement Halverson
Film Editor.......................Harmon Jones
Sound....Alfred Bruzlin/Harry M Leonard
Asst Director............................Eli Dunn
Make-up Artist...........................Ben Nye
Costumes..............................Kay Nelson
Special Photographic Effects...Fred Sersen
TWENTIETH CENTURY-FOX 70 MINUTES
BLACK-AND-WHITE

1953

HOUSE OF WAX

· CAST

Professor Henry Jarrod......Vincent Price
Lieutenant Tom Brennan...Frank Lovejoy
Sue Allen...............................Phyllis Kirk
Cathy Gray.........................Carolyn Jones
Scott Andrews.....................Paul Picerni
Matthew Burke....................Roy Roberts
Mrs Andrews..................Angela Clarke
Sidney Wallace................Paul Cavanagh
Sergeant Jim Shane.............Dabbs Greer
Igor............................Charles Buchinsky
Leon Averill.....................Nedrick Young
The Barker.........................Reggie Rymal
Pompous man...................Oliver Blake
Girlfriend.........................Joanne Brown
Portly man...........................Leo Curley
Medical examiner...........Frank Ferguson

From a story by *Charles Belden*
Music by..........................*David Buttolph*
Orchestrations...........*Maurice de Packh*
Directors of Photography.................*Bert Glennon/Peverell Marley*
Art Director....................*Stanley Fleischer*
Set Decorator................*Lyle B Reifsnider*
Film Editor...............................*Rudi Fehr*
Sound by............................*Charles Lang*
Asst Director..............*Jimmy McMahon*
Make-up Artists...*George Bau/Gordon Bau*
Wardrobe by....................*Howard Shoup*
Property Master.....................*Eric Stacey*
Props..*Red Turner*
Natural Vision Supervision...............*M L Gunzburg*
Visual Consultant.........*Julian Gunzburg*
Natural Vision Consultant.........*Lothrop Worth*
WARNER BROS 88 MINUTES
WARNERCOLOR

THE MAD MAGICIAN

· CAST

Don Gallico 'the Great'......*Vincent Price*
Karen Lee.........................*Mary Murphy*
Claire Ormond.......................*Eva Gabor*
Rinaldi...................................*John Emery*
Ross Ormond.............*Donald Randolph*
Alice Prentiss.......................*Lenita Lane*
Lt Alan Bruce....................*Patrick O'Neal*
Frank Prentiss.....................*Jay Novello*
Program hawker....................*Lyle Talbot*
with *Conrad Brooks/Roy Engel*
· CREDITS

Directed by...........................*John Brahm*
Produced by...........................*Bryan Foy*
Story and Screenplay by......*Crane Wilbur*
Music.........*Emil Newman/Arthur Lange*
Director of Photography.....*Bert Glennon*
Art Director............................*Frank Sylos*
Set Decorations..............*Howard Bristol*
Film Editor.....................*Grant Whytock*
Asst Director........................*Hal Herman*
Sound......................................*John Kean*
Make-up created by..........*Gustaf Norin/ George Bau*
Wardrobe.........................*Robert Martien*
Special Effects....................*David Koehler*
Magical Effects.....................*Bob Haskell*
Musician: theremin...*Dr Samuel Hoffman*
COLUMBIA 73 MINUTES
BLACK-AND-WHITE

Lodgers...*Darwin Greenfield/Jack Kenney*
Millie......................*Mary Lou Holloway*
Waiter......................................*Lyle Latell*
Detectives...*Richard Lightner/Jack Mower*
Morgue attendant................*Eddie Parks*
Surgeon.........................*Grandon Rhodes*
Ma Flanagan.........................*Riza Royce*
Bruce Allison......................*Philip Tonge*

Ticket taker....................*Merry Townsend*
Scrubwoman.....................*Ruth Warren*
with *Terry Mitchell/Grace Lee Whitney/ Trude Wyler*
· CREDITS

Directed by.........................*André de Toth*
Produced by............................*Bryan Foy*
Screenplay by.....................*Crane Wilbur*

1957

ALFRED HITCHCOCK PRESENTS
THE PERFECT CRIME
· CAST

Charles Courtney...............*Vincent Price*
John Gregory...................*James Gregory*

Harrington...........................*Mark Dana*
Ernest West......................*Gavin Gordon*
Alice West...................*Marianne Stewart*
West's housekeeper.............*Therese Lyon*
Photographer...................*John Zaremba*
with *Charles Webster/Nick Nicholson*

· **CREDITS**

Directed by....................*Alfred Hitchcock*
Produced by.....................*Joan Harrison*
Teleplay by....................*Stirling Silliphant*
Based on a story by *Ben Ray Redman*
Music Supervisor.............*Stanley Wilson*
Director of Photography....*John L Russell*
Art Director.......................*John Lloyd*
Set Decorator....................*James S Redd*
Editorial Supervisor........*Richard G Wray*
Film Editor................*Edward W Williams*
Sound...............................*William Lynch*
Asst Director.......................*Hilton Green*
Make-up...........................*Bob Dawn*
Hairstylist...........................*Florence Bush*
Costume Supervisor............*Vincent Dee*
SHAMLEY/REVUE 26 MINUTES
BLACK-AND-WHITE

1958

THE FLY

· **CAST**

André Delambre....................*Al Hedison*
Helene Delambre............*Patricia Owens*
François Delambre.............*Vincent Price*
Inspector Charras........*Herbert Marshall*
Emma.........................*Kathleen Freeman*
Nurse Anderson...........*Betty Lou Gerson*
Philippe Delambre.........*Charles Herbert*
Dr Ejoute.........................*Eugene Borden*
Orderly...............................*Harry Carter*
French waiter.....................*Arthur Dulac*
Gaston...........................*Torben Meyer*
Police doctor.......................*Franz Roehn*
Doctor............................*Charles Tannen*

· **CREDITS**

Directed and Produced by...............*Kurt Neumann*
Screenplay...........................*James Clavell*
Based on a story by *George Langelaan*
Music...............................*Paul Sawtell*
Director of Photography.........*Karl Struss*
Art Direction...................*Lyle R Wheeler/ Theobold Holsopple*
Set Decorations..............*Walter M Scott/ Eli Benneche*
Film Editor.......................*Merrill G White*
Sound...............*Eugene Grossman/Harry M Leonard*
Asst Director....................*Jack Gertsman*
Make-up by................................*Ben Nye*
Hairstyles by.......................*Helen Turpin*
Executive Wardrobe Designer......*Charles Le Maire*

Costumes Designed by.......*Adele Balkan*
Colour Consultant..............*Leonard Doss*
Special Photographic Effects...*L B Abbott/ James B Gordon*
TWENTIETH CENTURY-FOX 94 MINUTES
DE LUXE COLOUR

HOUSE ON HAUNTED HILL

· **CAST**

Frederick Loren..................*Vincent Price*
Annabelle Loren...............*Carol Ohmart*
Lance Schroeder.................*Richard Long*
Dr David Trent..................*Alan Marshal*
Nora Manning...................*Carolyn Craig*
Watson Pritchard..............*Elisha Cook Jr*
Ruth Bridgers...................*Julie Mitchum*
Mrs Slydes......................*Leona Anderson*
Jonas Slydes................*Howard Hoffman*

· **CREDITS**

Directed/Produced by.......*William Castle*
Associate Producer...............*Robb White*
Written by...............................*Robb White*
Music Composed/Conducted by......*Von Dexter*
Theme: 'House on Haunted Hill' by *Richard Kayne* and *Richard Loring*
Music Editor.............................*Jerry Irvin*
Director of Photography....*Carl E Guthrie*
Art Director........................*David Milton*
Set Decorator.................*Morris Hoffman*
Film Editor.........................*Roy Livingston*
Sound Editor.................*Charles Schelling*
Recording Engineer.............*Ralph Butler*
Production Manager......*Edward Morey Jr*
Asst Director.......................*Jack R Berne*
Make-up Artist......................*Jack Dusick*

Hairstylist.........................*Gale McGarry*
Men's Wardrobe...........*Roger J Weinberg*
Ladies Wardrobe...............*Norah Sharpe*
Property.........................*Teddy Mossman*
Set Continuity..............*Virginia Mazzuca*
Construction Supervisor.......*James West*
Special Effects.............*Herman Townsley*
ALLIED ARTISTS 75 MINUTES
BLACK-AND-WHITE

1959

RETURN OF THE FLY

· CAST

François Delambre.............*Vincent Price*
Philippe Delambre..............*Brett Halsey*
Inspector Beecham..............*John Sutton*
Alan Hinds...................*David Frankham*
Max Berthold.....................*Dan Seymour*
Cecile Bonnard...........*Danielle De Metz*
Granville.................................*Jack Daly*
Mme Bonnard.................*Janine Grandel*
Gaston..............................*Michael Mark*
Sgt Dubois........................*Richard Flato*
Lt MacLish.......................*Barry Bernard*
Inspector Evans....................*Pat O'Hara*
Priest.......................*Francisco Villalobas*
Nurse.................................*Joan Cotton*
Nun................................*Florence Strom*
Philippe as The Fly..................*Ed Wolff*
with *Gregg Martell*

· CREDITS

Directed by.....................*Edward L Bernds*
Produced by....................*Bernard Glasser*
Screenplay by................*Edward L Bernds*
Based upon *George Langelaan*'s short
  story '*The Fly*'

Music by.........*Paul Sawtell/ Bert Shefter*
Director of Photography.....*Brydon Baker*
Art Direction............*Lyle R Wheeler/John Mansbridge*
Set Decorations....*Walter M Scott/Joseph Kish*
Film Editor.....................*Richard C Meyer*
Asst Director.....................*Byron Roberts*
Make-up.................................*Hal Lierley*
Chief Set Electrician.....*Robert A Petzoldt*
TWENTIETH CENTURY-FOX 80 MINUTES
BLACK-AND-WHITE

THE BAT

· CAST

Dr Malcolm Wells..............*Vincent Price*
Cornelia van Gorder...*Agnes Moorehead*
Lt Andy Anderson............*Gavin Gordon*
Warner................................*John Sutton*
Lizzie Allen..........................*Lenita Lane*
Dale Bailey.....................*Elaine Edwards*
Judy Hollander....................*Darla Hood*
Mark Fleming.....................*John Bryant*
John Fleming...............*Harvey Stephens*
Jane Patterson........................*Riza Royce*
Detective Davenport...*Robert B Williams*
with *Mike Steele*

· CREDITS

Directed by.........................*Crane Wilbur*
Produced by...........................*C J Tevlin*
Screen Story and Screenplay by.....*Crane Wilbur*
Based on the Wagenhals-Kemper play
  by *Mary Roberts Rinehart* and *Avery Hopwood*
Musical Score......................*Louis Forbes*
'The Bat' theme played by.......*Alvino Rey*
Music Editor.................*Neil Brunnenkant*

Director of Photography.......*Joseph Biroc*
Art Director.........................*David Milton*
Set Decorator.........................*Rudy Butler*
Film Editor........................*William Austin*
Recording Engineer..............*Ralph Butler*
Sound Editor.................*Charles Schelling*
Production Manager......*Edward Morey Jr*
Asst Director.................*Clifford Broughton*
Make-up Artist...................*Kiva Hoffman*
Wardrobe...*Roger Weinberg/Norah Sharpe*
Set Continuity..............*Virginia Mazzuca*
Property Master..................*Ted Mossman*
Construction Supervisor........*James West*
ALLIED ARTISTS 80 MINUTES
BLACK-AND-WHITE

THE TINGLER

· CAST

Dr Warren Chapin.............*Vincent Price*
Martha Higgins.................*Judith Evelyn*
David Morris.................*Darryl Hickman*
Isabel Chapin....................*Patricia Cutts*
Lucy Stevens..................*Pamela Lincoln*
Oliver Higgins................*Philip Coolidge*
Screaming convict..........*Bob Gunderson*
Projectionist....................*Dal McKennon*

· CREDITS

Directed and Produced by...*William Castle*
Associate to the Producer...*Dona Holloway*
Written by.............................*Robb White*
Music.....................................*Von Dexter*
Director of Photography....*Wilfred M Cline*
Art Director..........................*Phil Bennett*
Set Decorator..................*Milton Stumph*
Film Editor................*Chester W Schaeffer*
Recording Supervisor.........*John Livadary*
Sound....................................*Harry Mills*
Asst Director..................*Herb Wallerstein*
COLUMBIA 81 MINUTES
BLACK-AND-WHITE

1960

HOUSE OF USHER

· CAST

Roderick Usher..................*Vincent Price*
Philip Winthrop...............*Mark Damon*
Madeline Usher.................*Myrna Fahey*
Bristol.................................*Harry Ellerbe*
Ghosts..........*David Andar/Bill Borzage/
  Mike Jordor/Eleanor LeFaber/Nadajan/
  Ruth Oklander/George Paul/Géraldine
  Paulette/Phil Sulvestre/John Zimeas*
· CREDITS
Directed and Produced by.............*Roger Corman*
Screenplay by..............*Richard Matheson*
Based on *Edgar Allan Poe*'s 'The Fall of
  The House of Usher'
Music by..................................*Les Baxter*
Musical Editor.....................*Eve Newman*

Director of Photography......*Floyd Crosby*
Production Design by.........*Daniel Haller*
Paintings by...................*Burt Schoenberg*
Film Editor......................*Anthony Carras*
Sound Editor.....................*Al Bird*
Sound..........................*Philip Mitchell*
Asst Director.........................*Jack Bohrer*
Make-up..........................*Fred Phillips*
Wardrobe.......................*Marjorie Corso*
Properties............................*Dick Ruben*
Special Effects.........................*Pat Dinga*
Photographic Effects.............*Ray Mercer*
Process Photography Directed by..........
....*Larry Butler*
Stills Photographer..............*Frank Tanner*
Executive Producers.....................*James H Nicholson/ Samuel Z Arkoff*
AMERICAN INTERNATIONAL
79 MINUTES EASTMANCOLOR

MASTER OF THE WORLD

· CAST
Robur...............................*Vincent Price*
John Strock...................*Charles Bronson*
Prudent................................*Henry Hull*
Dorothy Prudent..............*Mary Webster*
Phillip Evans...............*David Frankham*
Alistair..........................*Richard Harrison*
Topage...............................*Vitto Scotti*
Turner..............................*Wally Campo*
Wilson..............................*Peter Besbas*
Weaver..............................*Steve Masino*
Talkative townsman..........*Gordon Jones*
Shanks.................................*Ken Terrell*

· CREDITS
Directed by.....................*William Witney*
Produced by.............*James H Nicholson*
Associate Producers......*Bartlett A Carré/ Daniel Haller*
Co-Producer....................*Anthony Carras*
Screenplay by.........*Richard Matheson*
Based on two novels by *Jules Verne*, 'Master of the World' and 'Robur, the Conqueror'
Music Composed and Conducted by......
....*Les Baxter*
Music Co-Ordinator...................*Al Sims*
Song: 'Master of the World' Music by *Les Baxter*/Lyrics by *Lenny Addelson*/ Sung by *Darryl Stevens*
Orchestration......................*Albert Harris*
Music Editor.......................*Eve Newman*
Director of Photography....*Gil Warrenton*
Production Design and Art Direction.....
....*Daniel Haller*
Set Decorator..........................*Harry Reif*
Film Editor......................*Anthony Carras*
Sound...*Karl Zint*
Sound Editor.......................*Alfred R Bird*
Sound Engineers...........*Jerry Alexander/ Vinnie Vernon/William A Wilmarth*
Production Manager.......*Bartlett A Carré*

Asst Director.....................*Robert Agnew*
Production Asst........................*Jack Cash*
Make-up..............................*Fred Phillips*
Wardrobe.........................*Marjorie Corso*
Property Master......................*Dick Ruben*
Special Props and Effects........*Pat Dinga*
Special Effects.....*Tim Barr/Wah Chang/ Gene Warren*
Miniature Maker.................*Jim Danforth*
Photographic Effects...........*Ray Mercer*
Aerial Photography...............*Kay Norton*
Additional Grip.........................*Bob Rose*
Executive Producers.....................*James H Nicholson/Samuel Z Arkoff*
AMERICAN INTERNATIONAL
98 MINUTES PATHECOLOR

1961

PIT AND THE PENDULUM

· CAST
Nicholas Medina/Sebastian Medina......
....*Vincent Price*
Francis Barnard......................*John Kerr*
Elizabeth Medina............*Barbara Steele*
Catherine Medina.............*Luana Anders*
Doctor Charles Leon.....*Antony Carbone*
Maximillian.................*Patrick Westwood*
Maria..................................*Lynne Bernay*
Nicholas as a child..............*Larry Turner*
Isabella.............................*Mary Menzies*
Bartolome.........................*Charles Victor*

· CREDITS
Directed and Produced by......................
....*Roger Corman*
Screenplay by...............*Richard Matheson*
Based on *Edgar Allan Poe*'s 'The Pit and the Pendulum'
Script Supervisor.................*Betty Crosby*
Music by...............................*Les Baxter*
Musical Co-Ordinator...............*Al Simms*
Music Editor.......................*Eve Newman*
Director of Photography......*Floyd Crosby*
Production Design and Art Direction.....
....*Daniel Haller*
Set Decorator..........................*Harry Reif*
Film Editor......................*Anthony Carras*
Sound Recording..............*Roy Meadows*
Sound Editor............................*Kay Rose*
Production Manager.......*Bartlett A Carré*
Asst Director........*Jack Bohrer/Lou Place*
Production Asst........................*Jack Cash*
Unit Manager....................*Robert Agnew*
Make-up..............................*Ted Coodley*
Wardrobe.........................*Marjorie Corso*
Properties....................*Richard M Rubin*
Construction Co-Ordinator.....*Ross Hahn*
Special Effects...........................*Pat Dinga*
Scenic Effects................*Tom Matsumoto*
Photographic Effects.............*Ray Mercer*
Stills Photographer..............*Frank Tanner*

Do you have the guts to sit in this chair?

PERCEPTO! newest and most startling gimmick on the screen!...

Can you take it when The Tingler breaks loose?

COLUMBIA PICTURES presents

The Tingler

starring **VINCENT PRICE**

with **JUDITH EVELYN**

DARRYL HICKMAN · PATRICIA CUTTS

Written by ROBB WHITE

Produced and Directed by WILLIAM CASTLE

A WILLIAM CASTLE PRODUCTION

GUARANTEED

Executive Producers.....................*James H Nicholson/Samuel Z Arkoff*
AMERICAN INTERNATIONAL
80 MINUTES TECHNICOLOR

CONFESSIONS OF AN OPIUM EATER

· CAST
Gilbert De Quincey............*Vincent Price*
Ruby Lo..................................*Linda Ho*
George Wah..........................*Richard Loo*
Lotus...*June Kim*
Chin Foon.............................*Philip Ahn*
Child..................................*Yvonne Moray*
Lo Tsen.............................*Caroline Kido*
Scrawny man..............*Terence De Marney*
Fat Chinese..........................*Gerald Jann*
Catatonic girl...............*Vivianne Manku*

Look Gow...............................*Miel Saan*
1st dancing girl....................*Joanne Miya*
2nd dancing girl.......................*Geri Hoo*
3rd dancing girl..............................*Keiko*
Auctioneer...............................*John Mamo*
Wing Young...................*Victor Sen Yung*
Wah Chan.................................*Ralph Ahn*
Kwai Tong............................*Arthur Wong*
Ping Toy.......................................*Alicia Li*
Slave girl............................*Carol Russell*
Captain..............................*Vincent Barbi*
Opium eater........................*David Chow*
Boat crewman...........................*Roy Jenson*
with *Richard Fong/Charles Horvath*

· **CREDITS**
Directed and Produced by.............*Albert Zugsmith*
Associate Producer.................*Robert Hill*
Written by................................*Robert Hill*
Based on *'Confessions of an English Opium Eater'* by Thomas De Quincey
Music by............................*Albert Glasser*
Music Editor..........................*Victor Lewis*
Director of Photography......*Joseph Biroc*
Art Director.....................*Eugène Lourié*
Set Decorator..............................*Joe Kish*
Film Editors...........*Roy Livingston/Robert Eisen*
Sound...................................*Ralph Butler*
Sound Editor................*Charles Schelling*
Production Manager..........*Lonnie D'orsa*
Asst Director.....................*Lin Parsons Jr*
Make-up.................................*Bill Turner*
Hairdresser...........................*Alice Monte*
Wardrobe.....................*Roger J Weinberg/ Norah Sharpe*

FANTASY OR FACT...DREAM-WORLD OR REALITY? Dare you enter the nightmare zone of the incredible?

THOMAS DE QUINCEY'S CLASSIC
Confessions OF AN **Opium Eater**
STARRING VINCENT PRICE

Property Master.................*Ted Mossman*
Set Continuity.......................*Eylla Jacobs*
Stunts.........*Paul Stader/Marvin Willens/ Gil Perkins*
ALLIED ARTISTS/PHOTOPLAY
79 MINUTES BLACK-AND-WHITE

TALES OF TERROR

· **CAST**
MORELLA
Locke.................................*Vincent Price*
Lenora...............................*Maggie Pierce*
Morella................................*Leona Gage*
THE BLACK CAT
Fortunato Lucresi...............*Vincent Price*
Montresor Herringbone........*Peter Lorre*
Annabel Herringbone...................*Joyce Jameson*
THE CASE OF M. VALDEMAR
Valdemar.............................*Vincent Price*
Carmichael......................*Basil Rathbone*
Helene Valdemar.................*Debra Paget*
Dr Elliot James............*David Frankham*
also
Driver.......................................*Ed Cobb*
Policemen...............*John Hackett/Lennie Weinrib*
Barman Wilkins.................*Wally Campo*
Chairman of Wine Society....*Alan Dewit*
with *Scott Brown*

· **CREDITS**
Directed and Produced by...*Roger Corman*
Screenplay by.............*Richard Matheson*
Based on three *Edgar Allan Poe* stories
Music by.................................*Les Baxter*
Music Co-Ordinator.................*Al Simms*
Music Editor......................*Eve Newman*
Director of Photography.....*Floyd Crosby*
Production Design and Art Direction....
....*Daniel Haller*
Set Decorator.........................*Harry Reif*
Title Backgrounds............*Murray Laden*
Film Editor.....................*Anthony Carras*
Sound.......................................*John Bury*
Sound Editor................*Charles C Woods*
Production Manager......*Bartlett A Carré*
Asst Director.........................*Jack Bohrer*
Production Asst......................*Jack Cash*
Unit Manager...................*Robert Agnew*
Make-up..............................*Lou La Cava*
Hairdressing........................*Ray Forman*
Wardrobe..........................*Marjorie Corso*
Property Master.....................*Dick Rubin*
Construction Co-Ordinator....*Ross Hahn*
Special Effects.........................*Pat Dinga*
Optical Effects......................*Ray Mercer*
Technical Advisor for wine tasting sequence in *'The Black Cat'* segment: Harry H Waugh
Technical Advisor for hypnotism scenes in *'The Case of M. Valdemar'* segment: William J Bryan Jr

Executive Producers......................*James H Nicholson/ Samuel Z Arkoff*
AMERICAN INTERNATIONAL
88 MINUTES PATHECOLOR

1962

TOWER OF LONDON

· **CAST**
Richard of Gloucester........*Vincent Price*
Sir Ratcliffe.........................*Michael Pate*
Lady Margaret.....................*Joan Freeman*
Sir Justin............................*Robert Brown*
Earl of Buckingham..........*Bruce Gordon*
Anne...................................*Joan Camden*
Tyrus......................................*Richard Hale*
Mistress Shore.................*Sandra Knight*
Clarence......................*Charles Macaulay*
Edward IV..........................*Justice Watson*
Queen.....................................*Sarah Selby*
Prince Richard....................*Donald Losby*
Richard's mother......................*Sara Taft*
Edward V..........................*Eugene Martin*
Archbishop....................*Morris Ankrum*

· **CREDITS**
Directed by.......................*Roger Corman*
Produced by.....................*Gene Corman*
Screenplay by..........*Leo V Gordon/Amos Powell/James B Gordon*
Story by *Leo V Gordon* and *Amos Powell*
Musical Director..........*Michael Andersen*
Director of Photography....*Arch R Dalzell*
Key Grip.....................*Charles Hanawalt*
Art Director........................*Daniel Haller*
Set Decorator.........................*Ray Boltz*
Supervising Editor............*Ronald Sinclair*
Sound..................................*Phil Mitchell*
Production Manager..........*Joseph Small*
Asst Director..........................*Jack Bohrer*
Make-up Artist......................*Ted Coodley*
Hair Stylist...........................*Ray Forman*
Costumes..........................*Marjorie Corso*
Properties.....................*Richard M Rubin*
Chief Set Electrician............*Lloyd Garnell*
Dialogue Director....*Frances Ford Coppola*
ADMIRAL/UNITED ARTISTS
80 MINUTES BLACK-AND-WHITE

DIARY OF A MADMAN

· **CAST**
Simon Cordier....................*Vincent Price*
Odette Mallotte DuClasse............*Nancy Kovack*
Paul DuClasse.................*Chris Warfield*
Jeanne D'Arville.................*Elaine Devry*
Pierre......................................*Ian Wolfe*
Captain Robert Rennedon.........*Stephen Roberts*
Father Raymonde...............*Lewis Martin*
Louise...................................*Mary Adams*
Andre D'Arville............*Edward Colmans*

Dr Borman.....................*Nelson Olmsted*
Louis Girot....................*Harvey Stephens*
Martin..................................*Dick Wilson*
Buggy driver....................*George Sawaya*
'The Horla'........................*Joseph Ruskin*
with *Wayne Collier/Gloria Clark/Don Brodie/Joseph Del Nostro Jr*

· CREDITS

Directed by.....................*Reginald Le Borg*
Produced and Written by....*Robert E Kent*
Based on stories by *Guy De Maupassant*
Script Supervisor...................*Jane Ficker*
Music by.........................*Richard La Salle*
Music Editor........................*Edna Bullock*
Director of Photography.....*Ellis W Carter*
Art Director.........................*Daniel Haller*
Set Decorator..................*Victor Gangelin*
Sculptor...............................*Lowell Grant*
Supervising Editor............*Grant Whytock*
Sound.................................*Ralph Butler*
Production Manager..........*Joseph Small*
Asst Director............................*Al Westen*
Make-up Artist.....................*Ted Coodley*
Hair Stylist.........................*Carmen Dirigo*
Costumes..........................*Marjorie Corso*
Property Master...................*Irving Sindler*
Special Effects.............*Norman Breedlove*
Effects Editor................................*Al Bird*
Executive Producer............*Edward Small*
ADMIRAL/UNITED ARTISTS
97 MINUTES TECHNICOLOR

TWICE TOLD TALES

· CAST

Alex Medbourne/Giacomo Rappaccini/
 Gerald Pyncheon.............*Vincent Price*
Dr Carl Heidegger.........*Sebastian Cabot*
Giovanni Guasconti.............*Brett Halsey*
Alice Pyncheon/Nora Holbrook............. ....*Beverly Garland*
Jonathan Maulle..........*Richard Denning*
Sylvia Ward....................*Mari Blanchard*
Prof Pietro Baglioni......*Abraham Sofaer*
Hannah Pyncheon......*Jacqueline de Wit*
Beatrice Rappaccini.............*Joyce Taylor*
Lisabetta..........................*Edith Evanson*
Ghost of Mathew Maulle...............*Floyd Simmons*
Cabman...................................*Gene Roth*

· CREDITS

Directed by........................*Sidney Salkow*
Produced and Written by....*Robert E Kent*
Based on the famous *Hawthorne* stories
Script Supervisor..............*Jean Downing*
Music by.........................*Richard LaSalle*
Music Editor........................*Edna Bullock*
Director of Photography.....*Ellis W Carter*
Art Director.....................*Franz Bachelin*
Set Decorator.............*Charles Thompson*
Supervising Editor............*Grant Whytock*
Sound.................................*Lambert Day*

THE TERROR BEGAN AT MIDNIGHT!

American International presents EDGAR ALLAN POE'S **THE RAVEN**
FILMED IN PANAVISION AND PATHECOLOR
STARRING VINCENT PRICE · PETER LORRE · BORIS KARLOFF
HAZEL COURT · OLIVE STURGESS · JACK NICHOLSON

Production Manager..........*Joseph Small*
Asst Director............................*Al Westen*
Make-up Artist.....................*Gene Hibbs*
Hair Stylist.........................*Jane Shugrue*
Costumes..........................*Marjorie Corso*
Property Master...................*Irving Sindler*
Special Effects....................*Milton Olsen*
Effects Editor................................*Al Bird*
ADMIRAL/UNITED ARTISTS
119 MINUTES TECHNICOLOR

THE RAVEN

· CAST

Dr Erasmus Craven...........*Vincent Price*
Dr Adolphus Bedlo...............*Peter Lorre*
Dr Scarabus.........................*Boris Karloff*
Lenore.................................*Hazel Court*
Estelle Craven....................*Olive Sturgess*
Rexford Bedlo...................*Jack Nicholson*
Maid...............................*Connie Wallace*
Grimes...........................*William Baskin*
Gort.....................................*Aaron Saxon*

· CREDITS

Directed and Produced by.............*Roger Corman*
Screenplay by.............*Richard Matheson*
Based on a story by *Edgar Allan Poe*
Music by.................................*Les Baxter*
Music Co-Ordinator.................*Al Simms*
Music Editor......................*Eve Newman*
Orchestrator.......................*Albert Harris*
Director of Photography......*Floyd Crosby*
Production Design and Art Direction..... ....*Daniel Haller*
Set Decorator...........................*Harry Reif*
Film Editor.......................*Ronald Sinclair*
Sound.....................................*John Bury*

Sound Editor.........................*Gene Corso*
Production Supervisor....*Bartlett A Carré*
Asst Director.........................*Jack Bohrer*
Unit Manager.....................*Robert Agnew*
Production Asst.......................*Jack Cash*
Make-up...............................*Ted Coodley*
Hairdresser.........................*Betty Pedretti*
Costume Supervisor.........*Marjorie Corso*
Properties...........................*Karl Brainard*
Construction Co-Ordinator.....*Ross Hahn*
Special Effects.........................*Pat Dinga*
Raven Trained by...................*Moe Disesso*
Executive Producers.......................*James H Nicholson/ Samuel Z Arkoff*
AMERICAN INTERNATIONAL
86 MINUTES PATHECOLOR

1963

THE LAST MAN ON EARTH

· CAST

Robert Morgan...................*Vincent Price*
Ruth Collins....................*Franca Bettoia*
Virginia Morgan..............*Emma Danieli*
Ben Cortman........*Giacomo Rossi-Stuart*
Kathy Morgan..............*Christi Courtland*
with *Umberto Rau/Tony Corevi/Hector Ribotta/Giuseppe Mattei*

· CREDITS

Directed by........................*Sidney Salkow*
Produced by...................*Robert L Lippert*
Associate Producer...........*Harold E Knox*
Screenplay by...................*Logan Swanson (Richard Matheson)/William F Leicester*
From the novel '*I Am Legend*' by *Richard Matheson*

THE HAUNTED PALACE

· CAST

Charles Dexter Ward/Joseph Curwen...*Vincent Price*
Ann Ward.............................*Debra Paget*
Simon Orne.......................*Lon Chaney Jr*
Ian Willet/Dr Willet........*Frank Maxwell*
Edgar Weeden/Ezra Weeden...*Leo Gordon*
Gideon Smith/Micah Smith.........*Elisha Cook Jr*
Benjamin West/Mr West...*John Dierkies*
Jabez Hutchinson...........*Milton Parsons*
Hester Tillinghast.........*Cathie Merchant*
Gideon Leach/Mr Leach...*Guy Wilkerson*
Carmody..........................*Stanford Jolley*
Minister.............................*Harry Ellerbe*
Mrs Weeden..................*Barboura Morris*
Victim................................*Darlene Lucht*
Bruno................................*Bruno Ve Sota*

· CREDITS

Directed and Produced by..............*Roger Corman*
Associate Producer..........*Ronald Sinclair*
Screenplay by.............*Charles Beaumont*
From the poem by *Edgar Allan Poe* and a story by *H P Lovecraft*
Music by...............................*Ronald Stein*
Director of Photography......*Floyd Crosby*
Art Director.........................*Daniel Haller*
Set Decorator...........................*Harry Reif*
Film Editor.......................*Ronald Sinclair*
Sound.....................................*John Bury*
Sound Editor..........................*Gene Corso*
Production Manager.............*Jack Bohrer*
Asst Director...........................*Paul Rapp*
Make-up...............................*Ted Coodley*
Hairdressing................*Lorraine Roberson*

Costumes..........................*Marjorie Corso*
Property Master.................*Richard Rubin*
Titles Designed by..........*Armand Acosta*
Lighting..............................*Harry Sundby*
Dialogue Director.....*Francis Ford Coppola*
Executive Producers....................*Samuel Z Arkoff/James H Nicholson*
AMERICAN INTERNATIONAL
87 MINUTES PATHECOLOR

THE COMEDY OF TERRORS

· CAST

Waldo Trumbull.................*Vincent Price*
Felix Gillie..............................*Peter Lorre*
Amos Hinchley....................*Boris Karloff*
Amaryllis Trumbull.........*Joyce Jameson*
Cemetery keeper.................*Joe E Brown*
Mrs Phipps.........................*Beverly Hills*
John F Black.......................*Basil Rathbone*
Black's servant....................*Alan De Witt*
Mr Phipps.........................*Buddy Mason*
Doctor.........................*Douglas Williams*
Phipps' maid......................*Linda Rogers*
Girl....................................*Luree Holmes*
Riggs...............................*Paul Barselou*
Cleopatra.................................*Rhubarb*

· CREDITS

Directed by...................*Jacques Tourneur*
Co-Produced by...............*Anthony Carras*
Produced by....................................*James H Nicholson/Samuel Z Arkoff*
Associate Producer.....*Richard Matheson*
Written by.................*Richard Matheson*
Music by...................................*Les Baxter*
Music Co-Ordinator.................*Al Simms*
Music Editors....................*Eve Newman/Milton Lustig*
Director of Photography......*Floyd Crosby*

Music Composed by..........*Paul Sawtell/Bert Shefter*
Music Editor...............*Norman Schwartz*
Orchestration by...........*Alfonso D'artega*
Director of Photography..............*Franco Delli Colli*
Art Director.................*Giorgio Giovannini*
Film Editor.......................*Gene Ruggiero*
Production Manager...........*Vico Vaccaro*
Asst Production Manager..........*Lionello Melicci*
Asst Director..................*Carlo Grandone*
Make-up...........................*Piero Mecacci*
Executive Producer........*Samuel Z Arkoff*
ASSOCIATED PRODUCERS/PRODUZIONI
LA REGINA 86 MINUTES
BLACK-AND-WHITE

Lighting Co-Ordinator........Harry Sundby
Production Design and Art Direction.....
....Daniel Haller
Set Decorator..........................Harry Reif
Film Editor.......................Anthony Carras
Asst Film Editor................Harold Hazen
Sound.......................................Don Rush
Sound Editors.........Kathleen Rose/James
  Nelson
Production Manager........Joseph Wonder
Asst Director....................Robert Agnew
Production Asst........................Jack Cash
Make-up..............................Carlie Taylor
Hairdresser.........................Betty Pedretti
Costumes by....................Marjorie Corso
Properties...........................Karl Brainard
Special Effects..........................Pat Dinga
Stunts....................................Jesse Wayne
Executive Producers......................James
  H Nicholson/ Samuel Z Arkoff
AMERICAN INTERNATIONAL
81 MINUTES Pathecolor

THE MASQUE OF THE RED DEATH
· Cast

Prince Prospero.................Vincent Price
Juliana...................................Hazel Court
Francesca...............................Jane Asher
Gino....................................David Weston
Ludovico...............................Nigel Green
Alfredo.............................Patrick Magee
Scarlatti....................Paul Whitsun-Jones
Guards............Robert Brown/John Stone
Señor Veronese.................Julian Burton
Hop-Toad...........................Skip Martin
Señora Escobar....................Gaye Brown
Esmeralda....................Verina Greenlaw
Anna-Marie.....................Doreen Dawne
Lampredi...........................Brian Hewlett
Old woman....................Gladys Dawson
Clistor...............................Harvey Hall
Scarlatti's wife.......................Jean Lodge
Man in Red...................John Westbrook
Male dancers.............David Allen/Gerry
  Atkins/Julian Bolt/Ricky Clarke/
  Ronald Curran/Alan Dalton/Robert de
  Warren/Gale Law/ Tony Manning/Bill
  Owen/Fred Peters/Roy Staite/Stanley
  Tiller/David Wishart
Female dancers........Dorothy Anelay/Jill
  Bathurst/Norris Boyd/Jane Evans/
  Dorothy Fraser/Edith Gey/Sally
  Gilpin/Janet Hall/ Janet Kedge/
  Brigitte Kelly-Espinoza/Joanna
  Kubik/Seraphina Lansdown/Delia
  Linden/Joan Palethorpe/Maureen
  Sims/Angela Symonds/Caroline
  Symonds/Jenny Till/Selina Wylie
Special dancers.........Terry Gilbert/Bertie
  Green/ Len Martin/Norman McDowell
  with David Davies/Sarah Brackett/
  Rosemarie Dunham/Hugh Morton

· CREDITS
Directed by.......................Roger Corman
Produced by.....George Willoughby/Roger
  Corman
Screenplay by............Charles Beaumont/
  R Wright Campbell
From a story by Edgar Allan Poe
Music by.................................David Lee
Photographed by................Nicolas Roeg

Camera Operator...............Alex Thomson
Production Designer..........Daniel Haller
Art Direction........................Robert Jones
Set Dresser....................Colin Southcott
Titles Designed by..................Jim Baker
Film Editor....................Ann Chegwidden
Sound...............Richard Bird/Len Abbott
Asst Director.........................Peter Price
Make-up.......................George Partleton

LOOK INTO THIS FACE

SHUDDER...
at the blood-
stained dance
of the Red Death!

TREMBLE...to the
hideous tortures of
the catacombs of Kali!

GASP...at the sacrifice
of the innocent virgin
to the vengeance
of Baal!

AMERICAN INTERNATIONAL presents
VINCENT PRICE STARRING IN
EDGAR ALLAN POE'S IMMORTAL MASTERPIECE OF THE MACABRE
THE MASQUE OF THE RED DEATH
in PATHÉCOLOR

Also Starring HAZEL COURT·JANE ASHER Screenplay by CHARLES BEAUMONT and R. WRIGHT CAMPBELL · From a Story by EDGAR ALLAN POE · Produced and Directed by ROGER CORMAN

Hairdresser..............................Elsie Alder
Costume Designer......Laura Nightingale
Special Effects..............George Blackwell
Choreography by...................Jack Carter
Executive Producers............Nat Cohen/
  Stuart Levy
Dubbing Editor................Allan Morrison
Continuity...............................Joan Davis
Construction Manager........Richard Frift
Casting Director....................G B Walker
AMERICAN INTERNATIONAL
90 MINUTES EASTMANCOLOR

1964

THE TOMB OF LIGEIA
· CAST
Verden Fell.........................Vincent Price
Lady Rowena Trevanion..........Elizabeth
  Shepherd
Christopher Gough........John Westbrook
Lord Trevanion.................Derek Francis
Kenrick...........................Oliver Johnston
Dr Vivian.......................Richard Vernon
Peperel...........................Frank Thornton
Minister............................Ronald Adam
Livery boy........................Denis Gilmore
Rowena's maidservant........Penelope Lee
· CREDITS
Directed and Produced by.............Roger
  Corman/Samuel Z Arkoff
Associate Producer.................Pat Green
Screenplay by.....................Robert Towne
From the story by Edgar Allan Poe
Music Composed and Conducted by......
  ....Kenneth V Jones
Played by Sinfonia of London
Photographed by.................Arthur Grant
Camera Operator.................Moray Grant
Art Director...Colin Southcott/Daniel Haller
Titles Designed by.............Peter Howitt/
  Francis Rodker
Editor...Alfred Cox
Sound Recordists.....Bert Ross/John Aldred
Sound Editors...............Les Wiggins/Don
  Ranasinghe
Asst Director..................David Tringham
Asst to the Producer......Paul Mayersberg
Make-up Artist...............George Blackler
Hairdresser............................Pearl Orton
Wardrobe Mistress.............Mary Gibson
Cat Trained by.....................John Holmes
Special Effects..................Ted Samuels
AMERICAN INTERNATIONAL
81 MINUTES EASTMANCOLOR

THE CITY UNDER THE SEA
· CAST
The Captain, Sir Hugh Tregathion........
  ....Vincent Price
Harold Tuffnel-Jones....David Tomlinson

Ben Harris...........................Tab Hunter
Jill Tregillis...........................Susan Hart
Ives..............................John Le Mesurier
Mumford............................Harry Oscar
Dan.................................Derek Newark
Simon....................................Roy Patrick
George...................................Tony Selby
Bill........................Michael Heyland
Ted................................Steven Brooke
Tom.......................William Hurndell
Jack................................Jim Spearman
Harry..................................Dennis Blake
Fisherman........................Arthur Hewlett
1st male guest....................Bart Allison
2nd male guest...............George Ricarde
Woman guest.....Hilda Campbell-Russell
Herbert the Chicken...................himself
· CREDITS
Directed by...................Jacques Tourneur
Produced by.............George Willoughby/
  Daniel Haller
Screenplay by................Charles Bennett/
  Louis M Heyward
Based on Edgar Allan Poe's 'City in
  the Sea'
Additional Dialogue.......David Whittaker
Music by...............................Stanley Black
Photographed by...............Stephen Dade
Camera Operator...............Ronnie Maasz
Under Water Photography by..........John
  Lamb/Neil Ginger Gemmell
Art Direction.........................Frank White
Set Dresser....................Colin Southcott
Scenic Artist...........................Peter Wood
Film Editor.........................Gordon Hales
Sound..........Ken Rawkins/C Le Messurier
Dubbing Editor.................Allan Morrison
Production Manager................Pat Green
Asst Director..................David Tringham
Make-up.......Bill Partleton/Geoff Rodway
Hairdresser............................Elsie Adler
Wardrobe Supervisor.............Ernie Farrer
Continuity..................................Tilly Day
Construction Manager..........Leon Davis
Special Effects....Frank George/Les Bowie
Executive Producers....Nat Cohen/Stuart
  Levy/Samuel Z Arkoff/George Willoughby
AMERICAN INTERNATIONAL
84 MINUTES EASTMANCOLOR

1967

HOUSE OF A THOUSAND DOLLS
· CAST
Felix Manderville................Vincent Price
Rebecca...............................Martha Hyer
Stephen Armstrong..........George Nader
Inspector Emil.............Wolfgang Kieling
Marie Armstrong...............Ann Smyrner
Diane...................................Maria Rohm
Abdu.....................................Herbert Fux

Fernando........................Sancho Gracia
Madame Viera.............Yelena Samarina
Ahmed.....................................Jose Jaspe
Liza.......................................Diane Bond
Paul.....................................Louis Rivera
Salim................................Juan Olaguivel
Dolls........Andrea Lascelles/Ursula Janis/
  Caroline Coon/Karin Skarreso/Loli
  Munoz/ Marisol Anon/Jill Echols/
  Monique Aime/ Sandra Petrelli/Kitty
  Swan/Lara Lenti/Francoise Fontages
  with Irene Caba Alba/Fernando Cebrian/
  Milo Quesada/Nieves Salcedo
· CREDITS
Directed by....................Jeremy Summers
Produced by................Harry Alan Towers
Screenplay by..........Peter Welbeck (Harry
  Alan Towers)/María del Carmen/
  Martínez Roman
Music Composed and Conducted by.....
  ....Charles Camilleri/Johann von Storr
Song: 'House of a Thousand Dolls' words
  by Don Black/Music by Mark London/
  Sung by Cliff Bennett and the Rebel
  Rousers
Director of Photography...Manuel Merino
Art Director.................Santiago Ontanon
Editor.......Allan Morrison/Hermann Storr
Production Manager....Francisco Romero
Production Supervisor...........Tibor Reves
1st Asst Director................Juan Estelrich
Executive Producer.......Louis M Heyward
CONSTANTIN-FILM/HISPAMER FILM
98 MINUTES COLOUR

WITCHFINDER GENERAL
· CAST
Matthew Hopkins..............Vincent Price
Richard Marshall....................Ian Ogilvy
John Stearne.....................Robert Russell
Swallow....................................Nicky Henson
Sara......................................Hilary Dwyer
Salter.......................................Tony Selby
Captain Gordon................Michael Beint
Fisherman...........................Bernard Kay
Priest..................................Beaufoy Milton
Harcourt.........................John Treneman
Gifford................................Bill Maxwell
Farrier..................................Peter Thomas
Elizabeth.....................Maggie Kimberly
Villagers....Dennis Thorne/Michael Segal
Old woman...........................Ann Tirard
Hanged woman..................Hira Talfrey
Brandeston innkeeper............Jack Lynn
Jailer.......................................David Webb
Girls at inn...Maggie Nolan/Sally Douglas
Shepherd........................Edward Palmer
Sergeant....................................Lee Peters
Lavenham magistrate..........Peter Haigh
Webb................................Godfrey James
Old man..............................Toby Lennon
Paul..Morris Jar

Footsoldier............................David Lyell
Sentry.....................................Alf Joint
Hoxne innkeeper..............Martin Terry
John Lowes.......................Rupert Davies
Paul Clark............................Paul Ferris
with Gillian Aldham/Philip Waddilove/
  Derek Ware/John Kidd/Susi Field
with Special Guest Stars
Oliver Cromwell...........Patrick Wymark
Master Loach................Wilfrid Brambell

· CREDITS

Directed by.......................Michael Reeves
Produced by...............Louis M Heyward/
  Philip Waddilove/Arnold Miller
Screenplay by...Tom Baker/Michael Reeves
From the novel by Ronald Bassett
Additional Scenes by....Louis M Heyward
Music Composed and Conducted by......
  ....Paul Ferris
Photographed by..............John Coquillon
Camera Operators........Brian Elvin/Gerry
  Anstice
Camera Assts...Tony Breeze/Chris Reynolds
Grip..................................Freddie Williams
Art Director.........................Jim Morahan
Asst Art Director.................Peter Sheilds
Set Dresser....Jimmy James/Andrew Low
Construction Manager....Dennis Cantrell
Film Editor.....................Howard Lanning
Asst Editor.......................Marion Curran
Sound Recordist.................Paul Le Mare
Sound Mixer........................Hugh Strain
Dubbing Editor...............Dennis Lanning
Production Manager...........Ricky Coward
Production Secretary......Pat O'Donnell
Asst Directors...Ian Goddard/Iain Lawrence
Location Manager.............Euan Pearson
Make-up..........................Dore Hamilton
Hairdresser...................Henry Montsash
Wardrobe..........................Jill Thomson
Continuity............................Lorna Selwyn
Props...............Sid Davies/Fred Harrison
Gaffer...................................Laurie Shane
Stills.......................................Jack Dooley
Casting Director...................Freddie Vale
Special Effects...................Roger Dicken
Executive Producer...............Tony Tenser
TIGON BRITISH/AMERICAN
INTERNATIONAL 83 MINUTES
EASTMANCOLOR

1968

THE OBLONG BOX

· CAST

Sir Julian Markham..........Vincent Price
Dr Newhartt...................Christopher Lee
Joshua Kemp...................Rupert Davies
Heidi...Uta Levka
Sally Baxter........................Sally Geeson
Samuel Trench........................Peter Arne

Sir Edward Markham....................Alister
  Williamson
Elizabeth............................Hilary Dwyer
Tom Hackett.....................Maxwell Shaw
Mark Norton...........................Carl Rigg
N'Galo...............................Harry Baird
Holt.......................................James Mellor
Hawthorne.............................Ivor Dean
Witchdoctor...................Danny Daniels
Franklin...............................John Barrie
Weller...............................Godfrey James
Ruddock........................Michael Balfour
Martha.................................Hira Talfrey
Parson...........................John Wentworth
Mrs Hopkins.......................Betty Woolfe
Sailor....................................Martin Terry
Prostitutes.......Anne Clune/Jan Rossini/
  Jackie Noble/Ann Barrass
Trench's girl....................Zeph Gladstone
Gypsy dancer...................Tara Fernando
Man in tavern.................Tony Thawnton
Talbot.............................Anthony Bailey
Groom............................Richard Cornish
Doctor................................Colin Jeavons
Baron.....................Andreas Malandrinos
Major...........................Hedger Wallace
Constable.......................Martin Wyldeck
Tavern ruffian............Sean Barry-Weske
Africans.................Oh: Ogunde Dancers

· CREDITS

Directed and Produced by...........Gordon
  Hessler
Associate Producer.................Pat Green
Screenplay.............Lawrence Huntington
Based on a story by Edgar Allan Poe
Additional Dialogue.............Christopher
  Wicking
Music Composed by......Harry Robertson

Music Conducted by...........Philip Martell
Director of Photography...John Coquillon
Camera Operator....................Les Young
Production Designer..........George Provis
Asst Art Director.................George Lack
Set Dresser....................Terence Morgan
Scenic Artist...........W Simpson-Robinson
Editor...................................Max Benedict
Asst Editor.....................Oliver Waterlow
Sound Recordist........................Bob Peck
Sound Mixer........................Bob Jones
Sound Editor.............Michael Redbourne
Boom Operator..............Rowland Fowles
Asst Director.................Derek Whitehurst
Production Manager...........Bryan Coates
Make-up..............................Jimmy Evans
Hairdresser........................Bobbie Smith
Wardrobe..........................Kay Gilbert
Continuity....................Barbara Rowland
Titles.....................................Peter Howitt
Executive Producer.......Louis M Heyward
AMERICAN INTERNATIONAL
96 MINUTES EASTMANCOLOR

1969

SCREAM AND SCREAM AGAIN

· CAST

Dr Browning......................Vincent Price
Fremont...........................Christopher Lee
Benedek............................Peter Cushing
Det Supt. Bellaver...............Alfred Marks
David Sorel..........Christopher Matthews
Sylvia....................................Judy Huxtable
Erika...........................Yutte Stensgaard
Ludwig.....................Anthony Newlands
Griffin............................Julian Holloway

Prof Kingsmill................Kenneth Benda
Helen Bradford.....................Judi Bloom
Konratz.............................Marshall Jones
Schweitz..................................Peter Sallis
Jane..Uta Levka
Det Sgt Jimmy Joyce...........Clifford Earl
Ken Sparten......................Nigel Lambert
Keith.................................Michael Gothard
Det Insp Strickland.............David Lodge
Nurse......................................Kay Adrian
Rogers...........................Edgar D Davies
Valerie.............................Rosalind Elliot
Tramp.......................................Leslie Ewin
Matron.....................................Lee Hudson
Fryer...............................Stephen Preston
Wrestler..............................Lincoln Webb
with *The Amen Corner*

· CREDITS

Directed by.....................Gordon Hessler
Produced by...................Max Rosenberg/
  Milton Subotsky
Screenplay by...........Christopher Wicking
From Press Editorial Services novel
'The Disorientated Man' by Peter Saxon
Music composed and conducted by.......
..................................David Whitaker
Musical Director....................Shel Talmy
Director of Photography...John Coquillon
Camera Operator.....................Les Young
Lighting Cameraman.......John Coquillon
Production Designer.........Bill Constable
Art Director.........................Don Mingaye
Set Dresser..........................Scott Slimon
Editor......................................Peter Elliott
Sound...Bert Ross
Sound Mixer.............................Bert Ross
Dubbing Mixer..................Hugh Strain
Dubbing Editor...........Michael Redbourn
Production Manager........Teresa Bolland
Asst Director...............................Ariel Levy
Make-up................................Jimmie Evans
Hairdresser.........................Betty Sherriff
Wardrobe..............................Evelyn Gibbs
Construction Manager........Bill Waldron
Continuity..............................Eileen Head
Police Car Chase Arranged & Executed
  by..Joe Wadham
Executive Producer.......Louis M Heyward
AMICUS/AMERICAN INTERNATIONAL 94
MINUTES EASTMANCOLOR

CRY OF THE BANSHEE

· CAST

Lord Edward Whitman......Vincent Price
Lady Patricia Whitman........Essy Persson
Mickey...............................Hugh Griffith
Roderick..............................Patrick Mower
Maureen Whitman...........Hilary Dwyer
Harry Whitman.......................Carl Rigg
Sean Whitman................Stephen Chase
Father Tom.......................Marshall Jones
Bully Boy.....................Andrew McCulloch

Burke...............................Michael Elphick
Margaret Donald........Pamela Farbrother
Maggie..............................Quinn O'Hara
Bess...Jan Rossini
Sarah..................................Sally Geeson
Head villager.....................Godfrey James
Tavern keeper.................Gertan Kaluber
Brander................................Peter Benson
Party guests..............Joyce Mandre/Guy
  Deghy/Robert Hutton
Timothy............................Richard Everett
Apprentice..........................Louis Selwyn
Rider.....................................Mickey Baker
Naked girl...............................Jane Deady
Girl.....................................Carol Desmond
Maid..........................Pamela Moiseiwitsch
Oona.............................Elisabeth Bergner
Villagers................Ann Barrass/Maurice
  Colbourne/Neil Johnston/Nancy
  Meckler/Guy Pierce/Hugh Portnow/
  Stephen Rea/Maya Roth/Ron Sahewk/
  Tony Sibbald/Dinah Stabb/Tim
  Thomas/Rowan Wylie/Philly Howell

· CREDITS

Directed by.....................Gordon Hessler
Produced by.................Louis M Heyward
Associate Producer..........Clifford Parkes
Screenplay by........Tim Kelly/Christopher
  Wicking
Story by Tim Kelly
Music Composed by........Wilfred Josephs
Conducted by.....................Philip Martell
Director of Photography...John Coquillon
Camera Operator.....................Les Young
Lighting Cameraman.......John Coquillon
Art Director.........................George Provis
Set Dresser..........................Scott Slimon
Titles....................................Terry Gilliam
Editor.....................Oswald Hafenrichter
Asst Editor................................Ean Wood
Sound Mixer.....................Kevin Sutton
Dubbing Mixer...................Peter Lodge
Dubbing Editor...........Michael Redbourn
Asst Director...............................Ariel Levy
Make-up..........Tom Smith/Betty Blattner
Hairdressing....................Ivy Emmerton
Wardrobe..............................Dora Lloyd
Continuity.............................Zelda Barron
Electrician..............................Peter Bloor
Construction Manager.............Bill Miller
Executive Producers.......Gordon Hessler/
  Samuel Z Arkoff/James H Nicholson
AMERICAN INTERNATIONAL
91 MINUTES EASTMANCOLOR

1970

THE ABOMINABLE DR PHIBES

· CAST

Dr Anton Phibes................Vincent Price
Dr Vesalius........................Joseph Cotten

Vulnavia............................Virginia North
Rabbi.................................Hugh Griffith
Dr Longstreet...................Terry-Thomas
Inspector Harry Trout.......Peter Jeffrey
Commissioner Crow.......Derek Godfrey
Sgt Tom Schenley.............Norman Jones
Superintendent Waverley.......John Cater
Goldsmith..........................Aubrey Woods
Darrow...................................John Laurie
Dr Whitcombe........Maurice Kaufmann
Mrs Frawley................Barbara Keogh
Lem Vesalius.........................Sean Bury
Chauffeur........................Charles Farrell
Nurse Allen.....................Susan Travers
Dr Hedgepath.............David Hutcheson
Dr Dunwoody.............Edward Burnham
Dr Hargreaves........................Alex Scott
Dr Kitaj............................Peter Gilmore
1st police official.................Alan Zipson
2nd police official.............Dallas Adams
Sergeant.............................James Grout
1st policeman............Alister Williamson
2nd policeman...........Thomas Heathcote
3rd policeman........................Ian Marter
4th policeman.......................Julian Grant
Graveyard attendant.........John Franklyn
Butler..........................Walter Horsbrugh
Victoria Regina Phibes....Caroline Munro

· CREDITS

Directed by..........................Robert Fuest
Produced by.............Albert Fennell/Ronald
  S Dunas/Louis M Heyward
Written by............James Whiton/William
  Goldstein/Robert Fuest
Original Music Composed and Arranged
  by...................................Basil Kirchin
In Association with.............Jack Nathan
Vocal renditions by..................Paul Frees
Director of Photography............Norman
  Warwick
Camera Operator..............Godfrey Godar
Camera Asst......................Steve Clayton
Art Director....................Bernard Reeves
Asst Art Director.........Christopher Burke
Sets Designed by...............Brian Eatwell
Editor.................................Tristam Cones
Recording Director..............A W Lumkin
Sound Recordist............Dennis Whitlock
Sound Asst............Ken Nightingale
Dubbing Editor.................Peter Lennard
Production Manager........Richard Dalton
Asst Director.........................Frank Ernst
Make-up.....................Trevor Crole-Rees
Hairdresser.............Bernadette Ibbetson
Wardrobe..............................Elsa Fennell
Properties..............................Rex Hobbs
Continuity...................Gladys Goldsmith
Casting Director................Sally Nicholl
Construction Manager...George Gunning
Supervising Electrician.........Steve Birtles
Special Effects..............George Blackwell
Stills...John Jay

Executive Producers.....Samuel Z Arkoff/
James H Nicholson
AMERICAN INTERNATIONAL
94 MINUTES DE LUXE COLOUR

AN EVENING OF EDGAR ALLAN POE
· NARRATORS
*The Tell-Tale Heart/The Sphinx/The
Cask of Amontillado/The Pit and the
Pendulum...........................Vincent Price*
· CREDITS
Produced and Directed by....*Ken Johnson*
Associate Director.............*Dick Harwood*
Associate Producer...............*Dan Kibbie*
Television Adaptation by................*David
Welch/Ken Johnson*
Music composed and conducted by.......
....*Les Baxter*
Cameramen.........*Jim Angel/Jim Balden/
Bob Kemp*
Art Director........................*Henry C Lickel*
Video Tape Editor.................*Jerry Greene*
Audio..*Bill Smay*
Sound Effects.................*Norm Schwartz*
Unit Manager........................*Tim Steele*
Stage Manager...........*James Woodworth*
Production Assistant..............*Jane Elliot*
Assistant to the Producer........*Judi Jones*
Make-up.......................*Joseph Dibella*
Costumes Designed by........*Mary Grant*
Lighting Director.................*Jack Denton*
Senior Video...........................*Jim Smith*
Engineering Supervision...................*Mel
Morehouse/Jack Neitlich*
Technical Director............*Gene Lukowski*
Production Executive.................*William
J Immerman*
Executive Producers.....*Samuel Z Arkoff/
James H Nicholson*
AIP/KEN JOHNSON PRODUCTIONS
53 MINUTES COLOUR

1971

NIGHT GALLERY
· CAST
THE CLASS OF '99
The Professor.....................*Vincent Price*
Johnson.....................*Brandon de Wilde*
Elkins.....................*Randolph Mantooth*
Clinton...........................*Frank Hotchkiss*
Barnes.....................................*Hilly Hicks*
Miss Fields.................*Suzanne Cohane*
Miss Peterson............*Barbara Shannon*
Bruce.................................*Richard Doyle*
Templeton.................*Hunter von Leer*
McWhirter............................*John Davey*
Miss Wheeton.................*Lenore Kasdorf*
RETURN OF THE SORCERER
John Carnby........................*Vincent Price*
Noel Evans...............................*Bill Bixby*

Love means never having to say you're ugly.

JAMES H. NICHOLSON and SAMUEL Z. ARKOFF present

VINCENT PRICE
JOSEPH COTTEN

the abominable
dr. phibes

also starring
HUGH GRIFFITH and **TERRY-THOMAS** presenting **VIRGINIA NORTH** as Vulnavia
WRITTEN BY JAMES WHITON and WILLIAM GOLDSTEIN · PRODUCED BY LOUIS M. HEYWARD and RONALD S. DUNAS
EXECUTIVE PRODUCERS SAMUEL Z. ARKOFF and JAMES H. NICHOLSON · ORIGINAL MUSIC COMPOSED BY BASIL KIRCHIN · DIRECTED BY ROBERT FUEST
GP ALL AGES ADMITTED Parental Guidance Suggested · **COLOR** BY MOVIELAB An AMERICAN INTERNATIONAL Picture

Fern................................*Patricia Sterling*
· CREDITS
Executive Story Consultant..........*Gerald
Sanford*
Theme.......................................*Gil Mellé*
Art Director.......................*Joseph Alves Jr*
Gallery Paintings...................*Tom Wright*
Gallery sculptures..............*Logan Elston/
Phil Bandierle*
Editorial supervision......*Richard Belding*
Costumes....................................*Bill Jobe*
Main Title Design.........*Wayne Fitzgerald*
THE CLASS OF '99
Directed by.....................*Jeannot Szwarc*
Produced by............................*Jack Laird*
Written by...............................*Rod Serling*

Director of Photography.....*Lionel Linden*
Set Decorations.............*Chester R Bayhi*
Film Editor.........................*David Rawlins*
Sound........................*James R Alexander*
Unit Manager...........................*Burt Astor*
Asst Director.........................*Lester Berke*
Asst to Producer..........*Anthony Redman*
RETURN OF THE SORCERER
Directed by.....................*Jeannot Szwarc*
Produced by...........................*Burt Astor*
Associate Producers...................*Anthony
Redman/Herbert Wright*
Screenplay by....................*Halsted Welles*
Based on the story by *Clark Ashton Smith*
Music by...............................*Eddie Sauter*
Musical Supervisor..............*Hal Mooney*

The Sting's in the tale! Another horrendous story from the Merchant of Menace.

DR. PHIBES RISES AGAIN

JAMES H. NICHOLSON and SAMUEL Z. ARKOFF PRESENT

Dr. PHIBES RISES AGAIN x
Starring VINCENT PRICE, ROBERT QUARRY
Guest Stars PETER CUSHING, BERYL REID, TERRY THOMAS

Director of Photography...............Gerald Perry-Finnerman
Set Decorations...............Sal Blyenburgh
Film Editor...........................Larry Lester
Sound.......................Melvin M Metcalfe
Asst Director..................Brad H Aronson
JACK LAIRD/UNIVERSAL
52 MINUTES TECHNICOLOR

DR PHIBES RISES AGAIN

· CAST

Dr Anton Phibes...............Vincent Price
Darius Biederbeck...........Robert Quarry
Vulnavia...............................Valli Kemp
Trout.....................................Peter Jeffrey
Diana.....................................Fiona Lewis
Harry Ambrose..................Hugh Griffith
Waverley................................John Cater
Hackett.................................Gerald Sim
Baker..................................Lewis Fiander
Shavers..................................John Thaw
Captain...............................Peter Cushing
Miss Ambrose.......................Beryl Reid
Lombardo.........................Terry-Thomas
Stewart..............................Keith Buckley
Manservant.........................Milton Reid
Victoria Regina Phibes...Caroline Munro
Narrator...............................Gary Owens

· CREDITS

Directed by..........................Robert Fuest
Produced by............Albert Fennell/Louis M Heyward/Samuel Z Arkoff
Written by........Robert Fuest/Robert Blees
Based on characters created by James Whiton & William Goldstein
Original Music Composed by..John Gale
Director of Photography....Alex Thomson

Camera Operator...................Colin Corby
Focus Puller.........................John Golding
Asst Art Director................Peter Withers
Sets Designed by.................Brian Eatwell
Editor...................................Tristam Cones
Recording Director..............A W Lumkin
Sound Recordists........Leslie Hammond/ Dennis Whitlock
Sound Asst...........................Fred Tomlin
Dubbing Editor.................Peter Lennard
Production Manager........Richard Dalton
Asst Director.........................Jake Wright
Make-up.......................Trevor Crole-Rees
Hairdresser..............Bernadette Ibbetson
Vulnavia's Costumes designed by...........
....Brian Cox
Costume Supervisor.........Ivy Baker Jones
Properties.................................Rex Hobbs
Construction Manager........Harry Phipps
Supervising Electrician............Roy Bond
Continuity................................Jane Buck
Casting Director..................Sally Nicholl
Executive Producers.....Samuel Z Arkoff/ James H Nicholson
AMERICAN INTERNATIONAL
89 MINUTES DE LUXE COLOUR

1972

THEATRE OF BLOOD

· CAST

Edward Lionheart...............Vincent Price
Edwina Lionheart..................Diana Rigg
Peregrine Devlin...................Ian Hendry
Trevor Dickman...............Harry Andrews
Chloe Moon.......................Coral Browne

Oliver Larding.....................Robert Coote
Solomon Psaltery.............Jack Hawkins
George Maxwell..........Michael Hordern
Horace Sprout.....................Arthur Lowe
Meredith Merridew..........Robert Morley
Hector Snipe.......................Dennis Price
Maisie Psaltery......................Diana Dors
Rosemary........................Madeline Smith
Mrs Sprout.........................Joan Hickson
Mrs Maxwell.....................Renée Asherson
Inspector Boot....................Milo O'Shea
Sergeant Dogge.......................Eric Sykes
Policemen....Bunny Reed/Peter Thornton
Vicar............................Charles Sinnickson
Maid...........................Brigid Erin Bates
Meths drinkers...Tutte Lemkow/Stanley Bates/Eric Francis/Sally Gilmore/John Gilpin/Joyce Graeme/Jack Maguire/ Declan Mulholland
Police photographer.............Tony Calvin

· CREDITS

Directed by.....................Douglas Hickox
Produced by.....John Kohn/Stanley Mann
Screenplay by.........Anthony Greville-Bell
Based on an idea by Stanley Mann/ John Kohn
Music Composed and Conducted by......
...................................Michael J Lewis
Director of Photography..........Wolfgang Suschitzky
Camera Operator...............Ronnie Taylor
Production Designer....Michael Seymour
Set Decorator.........................Ann Mollo
Editor................................Malcolm Cooke
Asst Editor.............................Chris Kelly
Sound Editor.........................Les Wiggins
Sound Mixer.........................Simon Kaye
Dubbing Mixer................Douglas Turner
Production Manager.......David Anderson
Asst Director..................Dominic Fulford
Asst to the Producers..........Sara Romilly
Make-up.........................George Blackler
Hairdresser..........................Pearl Tipaldi
Costume Designer........Michael Baldwin
Wardrobe Asst......................Terry Smith
Construction Manager........Peter Verrard
Continuity............................Angela Allen
Choreographer of Meths Drinkers..........
...................................Tutte Lemkow
Special Effects by..................John Stears
Stunts Arranged by...................Terry York
Executive Producers........Gustave Berne/ Sam Jaffe
CINEMAN/UNITED ARTISTS
102 MINUTES DE LUXE COLOUR

1973

MADHOUSE

· CAST

Paul Toombes.....................Vincent Price

Herbert Flay......................Peter Cushing
Oliver Quayle....................Robert Quarry
Faye............................Adrienne Corri
Julia...............................Natasha Pyne
Elizabeth Peters...............Linda Hayden
Blount............................Barry Dennen
Alfred.................................Ellis Dale
Louise.......................Catherine Willmer
Harper................................John Garrie
Bradshaw.....................Ian Thompson
Carol..........................Jenny Lee Wright
Ellen.........................Julie Crosthwait
TV interviewer..........Michael Parkinson
Psychiatrist......................Peter Halliday
Make-up artist...........George Blackler
CID Inspector...............Robert Cawdron
Boy..................................Earl Rhodes
Reporter................Christopher Sandford
'with special participation by Boris
   Karloff and Basil Rathbone'
· CREDITS
Directed by.............................Jim Clark
Produced by.................Max J Rosenberg/
   Milton Subotsky
Associate Producer.................John Dark
Screenplay by...Greg Morrison/Ken Levison
Based on the novel 'Devilday' by
   Angus Hall
Original Music Composed and Conducted
   by.........................Douglas Gamley
Song Written and Performed by.............
   ....Gordon Clyde
Director of Photography.......Ray Parslow
Camera Operator.....................Ken Coles
Art Director............................Tony Curtis
Asst Art Director.................John Siddall
Set Dresser.........................Keith Wilson
Editor.....................................Clive Smith
Sound Recordists.............Danny Daniel/
   Gerry Humphreys
Sound Editor..................Peter Horrocks
Production Manager...............Pat Green
Asst Director.......................Allan James
Chief Make-up.................George Blackler
Chief Hairdresser...............Helen Lennox
Wardrobe Mistress.......Dulcie Midwinter
Continuity...........................Lorna Selwyn
Casting Director...........Rose Tobias Shaw
Construction Manager...........Bill Waldron
Special Effects.................Kerss & Spencer
Executive Producer.........Samuel Z Arkoff
AMERICAN INTERNATIONAL/AMICUS 90
MINUTES EASTMANCOLOR

1980

THE MONSTER CLUB

· CAST
Eramus..............................Vincent Price
R Chetwynd-Hayes.........John Carradine
Sam................................Stuart Whitman
Busotsky's father...........Richard Johnson
Angela.....................Barbara Kellermann
Busotsky's mother..............Britt Ekland
George..............................Simon Ward
Mooney.....................Anthony Valentine
Innkeeper..........................Patrick Magee
Lintom Busotsky...............Anthony Steel
Buxom beauty..............Fran Fullenwider
Entertainers..........B A Robertson/Night/
   The Pretty Things/The Viewers
Club secretary....................Roger Sloman
Stripper............................Suzanna Willis
Raven............................James Laurenson
Psychiatrist.................Geoffrey Bayldon
Pickering.....................Donald Pleasence
Lintom as a child...............Warren Saire
Watson.............................Neil McCarthy
Luna................................Lesley Dunlop
Ghoul.........................Sean Barry-Weske
Policeman.....................Prentis Hancock
Villager......................................Liz Smith
· CREDITS
Directed by....................Roy Ward Baker
Produced by...................Milton Subotsky
Associate Producer......................Ron Fry
Screenplay by................Edward & Valerie
   Abraham
From the novel by R Chetwynd-Hayes
Music Co-Ordinator........Graham Walker
Director of Photography........Peter Jessop
Camera Operator................Peter Sinclair
Focus Puller.......................Chris Howard
Clapper/Loader................Howard Baker
Camera Grip..........................Ted Whitby
Production Designer..............Tony Curtis
Asst Art Director..............Richard Rooker
Set Decorator.......................Lionel Couch
Animation.................................Reg Lodge
Concept Artist.......................John Bolton
Editor......................................Peter Tanner
Sound Editor............................Russ Hill
Sound Mixer.................Norman Bolland
Boom Operator.....................John Salter
Sound Asst..........................Bill Barringer
1st Asst Director............Dominic Fulford
2nd Asst Director..............Mick Daubeny
3rd Asst Director.....................Nick Laws
Production Asst.........Pauline Stevenson
Production Accountant.....Jeffrey Broom
Make-up Artists..........Roy Ashton/Ernest
   Gasser
Supervising Hairdresser...Joan Carpenter
Hairdresser.......................Ronnie Cogan
Wardrobe Supervisor........Eileen Sullivan
Monster Masks.........................Vic Door
Production Buyer..........Dennis Maddison
Construction Manager.........Bill Waldron
Chief Electrician...............Micky Thomas
Continuity............................June Randall
Unit Publicist.........................Lily Poyser
Stills Photography.......................John Jay
Casting Director...........Simone Reynolds
Executive Producer...Bernard J Kingham/
   Jack Gill
CHIPS/SWORD & SORCERY
97 MINUTES COLOUR

1982

VINCENT

narrated by........................Vincent Price
· CREDITS
Written Designed & Directed by.......Tim
   Burton
Produced by.....................Rick Heinrichs

Director of Photography....*Victor Abdalov*
Music.......................................*Ken Hilton*
Technical Director..........*Stephen Chiodo*
Sculpture and Additional Design.....*Rick Heinrichs*
Animation......................*Stephen Chiodo*
DISNEY/BUENA VISTA
6 MINUTES BLACK-AND-WHITE

HOUSE OF THE LONG SHADOWS

· CAST

Lionel Grisbane.................*Vincent Price*
Corrigan/Roderick Grisbane.................
.....................................*Christopher Lee*
Sebastian Grisbane..........*Peter Cushing*
Kenneth Magee.................*Desi Arnaz Jr*
Lord Grisbane.................*John Carradine*
Victoria................................*Sheila Keith*
Mary Norton.....................*Julie Peasgood*
Sam Allyson.......................*Richard Todd*
Diana...............................*Louise English*
Andrew...........................*Richard Hunter*
Stationmaster..........*Norman Rossington*

· CREDITS

Directed by...........................*Pete Walker*
Produced by................*Menahem Golan/ Yoram Globus*
Associate Producer..............*Jenny Craven*
Screenplay by............*Michael Armstrong*
Based on the novel '*Seven Keys to Baldpate*' by *Earl Derr Biggers* and the play by *George M Cohan*

THE CANNON GROUP INC PRESENTS
Vincent Price Christopher Lee Peter Cushing
in a GOLAN-GLOBUS Production of a PETE WALKER film
House of the Long Shadows

Music Composed by........*Richard Harvey*
Director of Photography....*Norman Langley*
Camera Operator...........*John Simmonds*
Follow Focus.....................*Mike Metcalfe*
Boom Operator...........*Tony Gould-Davis*
Camera Loader.................*Fraser Taggart*
Camera Grip.....................*Malcolm Smith*
Stills Photographer..............*Sarah Quile*
Art Director......................*Mike Pickwood*
Editor.............................*Robert Dearberg*
Asst Editors....*Sarah Vickers/Brian Trenerry*
Sound Recordist..............*Peter O'Connor*
Sound Asst.....................*John Thurston*
Dubbing Mixer....................*Richard King*
Dubbing Editor...................*Mike Crowley*
Production Manager..........*Jeanne Firbir*
Asst Directors.......*Brian Lawrence/Glynn Purcell/Paul Carnie/Nick Godden*
Make-up........................*George Partleton*
Wardrobe.......*Polly Hamilton/Alan Flyng*
Ladies' fashion by.................*Brenda Jane*
Property Master.................*Bert Gadsden*
Gaffer...*Ted Davis*
Chief Electrician....................*Ray Snooks*
CANNON/GOLAN-GLOBUS
101 MINUTES COLOUR

1983

BLOODBATH AT THE HOUSE OF DEATH

· CAST

Dr Lucas Mandeville..........*Kenny Everett*
Dr Barbara Coyle......*Pamela Stephenson*
Sinister Man.....................*Vincent Price*
Elliot Broome.....................*Gareth Hunt*
Stephen Wilson.............*Don Warrington*
John Harrison.....................*John Fortune*
Sheila Finch......................*Sheila Steafel*
Henry Noland.............*John Stephen Hill*
Deborah Redding.................*Cleo Rocos*
Blind man........................*Graham Stark*
Barmaid................................*Pat Ashton*
Inspector Goule...................*David Lodge*
Sheila's Mother.................*Davilia David*
Attractive girl...................*Debbie Linden*
Doctors...........*Tim Barrett/Oscar Quitak*
Patient.....................................*Ellis Dale*
Police Inspector..................*Barry Cryer*
Nurse...............................*Anna Dawson*
Man at bar.....................*Gordon Rollings*
Old man..........................*Jack Le White*
Policeman........................*Ray Cameron*
Dog..............................*Sandy Donaldson*

· CREDITS

Directed and Produced by...*Ray Cameron*
Co-Produced by.................*John Downes*
Written by........*Ray Cameron/Barry Cryer*
Music by........*Mike Moran/Mark London*
Photographed by...*Brian West/Dusty Miller*

Camera Operator................*John Maskell*
Art Director...................*John Sunderland*
Animation....................*Graham Carside*
Film Editor.............................*Brian Tagg*
Sound Recordist.................*Chris Munro*
Asst Director..........................*Ken Baker*
Make-up Artist...................*Eric Allwright*
Hairdresser...............*Elaine Bowerbank*
Wardrobe...........................*Paul Vachon*
Property Master.................*Dennis Fruin*
Continuity.............................*Cheryl Leigh*
Casting Director...........*Susn Whatmough*
Executive Producers......*Laurence Myers/ Stuart D Donaldson*
WILDWOOD 92 MINUTES COLOUR

1986

THE OFFSPRING

· CAST

Julian White.....................*Vincent Price*
Stanley Burnside.................*Clu Gulager*
Jesse Hardwick.....................*Terry Kiser*
Felder Evans....................*Harry Caesar*
Snakewoman...................*Rosalind Cash*
Sergeant Gallen..........*Cameron Mitchell*
Beth Chandler....................*Susan Tyrrell*
Steven Arden.........................*Ron Brooks*
Eileen Burnside....*Miriam Byrd-Nethery*
Amarrillis..............................*Didi Lanier*
Andrew...........................*Tommy Nowell*
Amanda................................*Ashli Bare*
Burt.....................................*Terry Knox*
Grace Scott................*Megan McFarland*
Tinker................................*Angelo Rossitto*
Leonard.......................*Gordon Paddison*
Pike..*C J Cox*
McBride............................*Leon Edwards*
Warden.........................*Lawrence Tierney*
Bullock................................*Tim Wingard*
Katherine White...........*Martine Beswick*
Ambrose.............................*Sergio Aguire*
Priest...................*Nicos Argentiogorgis*
Jake...................................*Jajary Bennett*
Lester McCoy.................*Tommy Burcher*
No Face.........................*Barney Burman*
Our Gang..........*Christopher Cobb/David Ford/Justin Nowell/David Styncromb/ Chastity Waters*
Doctor......................................*Rick Cox*
Confederates..........*George Davies/Mark Hannah/Tony Wright*
Physician.............................*Whit Davies*
Witness at execution......*David Del Valle*
Harry Essex.........................*Bob Hannah*
Mary Hardwick............*Katherine Kaden*
Truck loaders..........*Frank Shaheen/Paul Barberi*
Nurse............................*Nancy Shaheen*
Execution reporter...............*Alan White*
Jack McCoy........................*Gene Witham*

· CREDITS

Directed by....................................Jeff Burr
Produced by.....Darin Scott/William Burr
Associate Producers....Ron Arnold/Craig Greene/Mark Hannah/Mike Malone/Allan Posten
Written by............Darin Scott/C Courtney Joyner/Jeff Burr
Music by..................................Jim Manzie
Director of Photography......Craig Greene
Production Designers................Cynthia K Charette/C Allen Posten
Set Dressers....Whit Davies/Terese Mitchell
Editor...W O Garrett
Sound Mixer............................Jerry Wolfe
Production Manager.............John Dalve
Asst Director.....................Mark Hannah
Make-up Artist.......................Lisa Taylor
Special Make-up Effects Designed and Created by..........Rob Burman
Wardrobe Supervisor.............Cathy Sims
Costume Designer............Cindy Charette
Property Master....................Tony Wright
Stunts...Kelly Ott
Special Effects.................Anthony Showe
Executive Producer......Bubba Truckadaro
CONQUEST/WHISPER-SCREAM
101 MINUTES COLOUR

1987

DEAD HEAT

· CAST

Roger Mortis....................Treat Williams
Doug Bigelow......................Joe Piscopo
Randi James.......................Lindsay Frost
Doctor Ernest McNab.................Darren McGavin
Arthur P Loudermilk.........Vincent Price
Rebecca Smythers.......Clare Kirkconnell
Mr Thule....................................Keye Luke
Lieutenant Herzog...........Robert Picardo
Captain Mayberry................Mel Stewart
Butcher................Professor Toru Tanaka
Newscaster.....................Martha Quinn
Bob...................................Ben Mittleman
Smitty..Peter Kent
Saleswoman..........................Cate Caplin
Mrs Von Heisenberg........Monica Lewis
Jewelry Store Manager......Peggy O'Brien
Wilcox..Chip Heller
The Thing.................Steven R Bannister
Whitfield.............................Lew Hopson
Jonas......................................Tom Nolan
Freman.....................................Steve Itkin
Patrolman..........................Shane Black
Guard #1...............................Mike Saad
Guard #2...............................Monty Cox
Walter......................................Monty Ash
Cop..................................H Ray Huff
Pool zombies....Pons Maar/Dawan Scott

End zombie...........................Ivan E Roth
Shoot out zombie...................Ron Taylor
Gertrude Bellman............Yvonne Peattie
Harry Latham..................Clarence Brown
Lab technicians............Pamela Vansant/Beth Toussaint
Officer Liptak.................Stephen Jacques
Cemetery security guard.......Dick Miller
Zombie go-go girl...........Linnea Quigley

· CREDITS

Directed by......................Mark Goldblatt
Produced by....................David Helpern/Michael T Meltzer
Screenplay by..........................Terry Black
Music Composed by............Ernest Troost
Director of Photography...............Robert D Yeoman
Production Designer...........Craig Stearns
Set Decorator.................Greta Grigorian
Editor..........................Harvey Rosenstock
Supervising Sound Editor....Mike Le Mare
Asst Director...................Mike Topoozian
Make-up.............................Steve Johnson
Costume Designer.................Lisa Jensen
Special Effects........Patrick Read Johnson
HELPERN/MELTZER 83 MINUTES COLOUR

1989

EDWARD SCISSORHANDS

· CAST

Edward Scissorhands.........Johnny Depp
Kim Boggs.......................Winona Ryder
Peg Boggs...........................Dianne Wiest
Jim.......................Anthony Michael Hall
Joyce Monroe......................Kathy Baker
Kevin Boggs.....................Robert Oliveri
Helen...........................Conchata Ferrell
Marge..............................Caroline Aaron
Officer Allen.......Dick Anthony Williams
Esmeralda..........................O-Lan Jones
The Inventor.....................Vincent Price
Bill Boggs..............................Alan Arkin
Tinka........................Susan J Blommaert
Cissy.....................................Linda Perry
Host-TV.........................John Davidson
George Monroe.....................Biff Yeager
Suzanne........................Marti Greenberg
Max....................................Bryan Larkin
Denny............................John McMahon
TV newswoman................Victoria Price
Retired man...................Stuart Lancaster
Granddaughter...............Gina Gallagher
Psychologist........................Aaron Lustig
Loan officer..........................Alan Fudge
Dishwasher man...................Steven Brill
Editor...................................Peter Palmer
Reporters.........Marc Macaulay/Carmen J Alexander/Brett Rice
Beefy man..........................Andrew Clark
Pink girl.................................Kelli Crofton

Older woman/TV...........Linda Jean Hess
Young woman/TV.......Rosalyn Thomson
Red-haired woman/TV..............Lee Ralls
Teenage girl/TV.................Eileen Meurer
Rich widow/TV....................Bea Albano
Blonde/TV........................Donna Pieroni
Policemen..............Ken DeVaul/Michael Gaughan
Teenage girls....Tricia Lloyd/Kathy Dombo
Police Sergeant...........................Rex Fox
Max's mother.................Sherry Ferguson
Little girl on bike................Tabetha Thomas
Neighborhood extras......Tammy Boalo/Jackie Carson/Carol Crumrine/Suzanne Chrosniak/Ellin Dennis/Kathy Fleming/Jalaine Gallion/Miriam Goodspeed/Dianne L Green/Mary Jane Heath/Carol D Klasek/Laura Nader/Doyle Anderson/Harvey Bellman/Michael Brown/Gary Clark/Roland Douville/Russell E Green/Cecil Hawkins/Jack W Kapfhamer/Bill Klein/Phil Olson/Joe Sheldon/James Spicer
Kid on slip 'n' slide................Nick Carter
Girl in diner........................L A Rothman

· CREDITS

Directed by............................Tim Burton
Produced by..............Tim Burton/Denise Di Novi
Screenplay by...........Caroline Thompson
From a story by Tim Burton/Caroline Thompson
Music Composed by.........Danny Elfman
Director of Photography...............Stefan Czapsky
Camera Operator..................Frank Miller
Production Designer.................Bo Welch
Art Director.........................Tom Duffield
Set Decorator....................Cheryl Carasik
Film Editors.........Colleen Halsey/Richard Halsey
Sound Editors...........James Christopher/Warren Hamilton Jr/ Michael J Benavente
Production Manager...............Bill P Scott
Asst Director.............................Jerry Fleck
Make-up..............Ve Neill/Fern Buchner/Selena Miller/Matthew W Mungle/Rick Stratton/Brad Wilder/Stan Winston
Hairdressing.............Yolanda Toussieng/Irene Aparicio/Bridget Cook/Rick Provenzano/Kim Santantonio/Susan Schuler-Page/Werner Sherer/Liz Spang/Lynda Kyle Walker
Wardrobe.......................Kathryn 'Bird'
Costume Designer..........Colleen Atwood
Special Effects by.............Michael Wood/Michael Arbogast/James Reedy/Gary Schaedler/Brian Wood/David Wood
Executive Producer....Richard Hashimoto
20TH CENTURY FOX
105 MINUTES DE LUXE COLOUR

BIBLIOGRAPHY

incent Price has been the subject of few books but a great number of magazine articles; he is now featured prodigiously on websites. To list them all would serve no useful purpose so I have decided instead to confine this appendix to those materials which were instrumental in helping me with the writing of the present volume. My thanks go to their authors and creators.

Christopher Lee: The Authorised Screen History
Jonathan Rigby/*Reynolds and Hearn/London/2001*

Cinefantastique Vol. 19 Nos. 1/2: Vincent Price, Horror's Crown Prince
Steve Biodrowski & David Del Valle/*Cinefantastique/New York/1989*

Complete Films of Vincent Price, The
Lucy Chase Williams/*Citadel/Secaucus, N J/1995*

Extraordinary Mister Poe, The
Wolf Mankowitz/*Weidenfeld & Nicolson/London/1978*

Fast and Furious: The Story of American International Pictures
Mark Thomas McGee/*McFarland/Jefferson/1984*

Films of Roger Corman: Brilliance on a Budget, The
Ed Naha/*Arco/New York/1982*

Films of Vincent Price, The
Iain F McAsh/*BCW/Isle of Wight/1974*

Flying Through Hollywood by the Seat of my Pants
Sam Arkoff & Richard Trubo/*Birch Lane/New York/1992*

Heroes of the Horrors
Calvin Thomas Beck/*Collier Macmillan/New York & London/1975*

Horror Film Handbook, The
Alan Frank/*Batsford/London/1982*

How I Made a Hundred Movies in Hollywood and Never Lost a Dime
Roger Corman & Jim Jerome/*Delta/New York/1990*

Movie World of Roger Corman, The
Ed. J Philip de Franco/*Chelsea House/New York/1979*

Remarkable Michael Reeves, The: His Short and Tragic Life
John B. Murray/*Cinematics/London/2002*

Roger Corman: The Millennic Vision
Ed. David Will & Paul Willemen/*Cinema/Edinburgh/1970*

Scare Tactic: The Life and Films of William Castle
John W Law/*Writers Club/New York/2000*

Step Right Up! I'm Gonna Scare the Pants Off America
William Castle/*Pharos/New York/1992*

Suspense in the Cinema
Gordon Gow/*Zwemmer & Barnes/London & New York/1968*

Tim Burton
Jim Smith & J Clive Matthews/*Virgin Books/London/2002*

Vincent Price: A Daughter's Biography
Victoria Price/*St Martin's/New York/1999*

Last, but not least, for the art of Neil Vokes check out http://groups.msn.com/neilsstudio

INDEX